MFC
Programming

The Advanced Windows Series

The Advanced Windows Series focuses on programming for the 32-bit Windows operating system. The series provides experienced programmers with practical books that are technically sophisticated. Each book covers in detail a specific aspect of Windows programming and contains interesting sample programs that can be used as a springboard for writing other applications. A CD-ROM containing the source code described in the text, pertinent reference material, useful tools, and links to related sites on the Internet accompanies each book.

Additional books in the Advanced Windows Series include:

Win32 Programming
Brent Rector, Joseph Newcomer
0-201-63492-9

Win32 Systems Programming
Johnson Hart
0-201-63465-1

Win32 Telephony Programming: A Developer's Guide to TAPI
Chris Sells
0-201-62492-9

Creating Components with DCOM and C++
Don Box
0-201-63446-5

Windows Sockets Network Programming
Bob Quinn
0-201-63372-8

ActiveX Controls
Brent Rector
0-201-69589-8

For additional information, publication dates, and prices, visit the Advanced Windows Series site: http://www.aw.com/devpress/series/AdvWinSer/advwinser.html

To contact the Consulting Editor for the Advanced Windows Series, send email to advwsed@aw.com.

MFC Programming

Alan R. Feuer

ADDISON-WESLEY DEVELOPERS PRESS
An imprint of Addison Wesley Longman, Inc.

Reading, Massachusetts • Harlow, England • Menlo Park, California
Berkeley, California • Don Mills, Ontario • Sydney
Bonn • Amsterdam • Tokyo • Mexico City

Many of the designations used by manufacturers and sellers to distinguish their products are claimed as trademarks. Where those designations appear in this book, and Addison Wesley Longman, Inc. was aware of a trademark claim, the designations have been printed in initial capital letters or all capital letters.

The author and publisher have taken care in preparation of this book, but make no express or implied warranty of any kind and assume no responsibility for errors or omissions. No liability is assumed for incidental or consequential damages in connection with or arising out of the use of the information or programs contained herein.

Library of Congress Cataloging-in-Publication Data

Feuer, Alan R.
      MFC Programming / Alan R. Feuer.
         p. cm. -- (Advanced Windows series)
      Includes index.
      ISBN 0-201-63358-2
      1. C++ (Computer program language) 2. Microsoft Foundation class
library. 3. Microsoft Windows (Computer file) I. Title. II. Series.
QA76.73.C153F48   1997
005.13'3--dc21   97-7958
                                                CIP

A-W Developers Press is a division of Addison Wesley Longman, Inc.

Printed in the United States of America. Published simultaneously in Canada.

Sponsoring Editor: Ben Ryan
Project Manager: Sarah Weaver
Set in 10-point Bookman by Alan R. Feuer and Octal Publishing, Inc.

1 2 3 4 5 6 7 8 9 -MA- 0100999897
First printing, May 1997

Addison Wesley Longman, Inc., books are available for bulk purchases by corporations, institutions, and other organizations. For more information please contact the Corporate, Government, and Special Sales Department at (800) 238-9682.

Find A-W Developers Press on the World Wide Web at:
http://www.aw.com/devpress/

Contents

Part I: Basic Windows

Gives a brief overview of Win32 programming, MFC, and the coding conventions used in the book.

Presents two introductory programs: the simplest Win32 program and a basic MFC program. Discusses Win32 and MFC program architecture.

Presents the CMenu class to create and manipulate the various types of menus: menu bar, drop-down, cascade, context, and system.

Discusses modal and modeless dialogs. Presents message boxes and the CDialog class.

Presents the CWnd class and its relation to Win32 windows. Discusses window creation and termination.

Presents and illustrates programming of the standard Win32 controls, including the common controls.

Discusses simple and customized usage of the common dialogs. The dialogs are illustrated by controlling a rich-text edit control.

Presents basic drawing implements and functions. Introduces the concept of device context and the CDC class. Responds to mouse and keyboard events.

Part II: The Application Framework

Discusses single and multiple document interface, gives an overview of document/view architecture, and presents new generic programs based on document/view.

Part III: Extended Examples

Detailed Contents

Part I: Basic Windows

Part II: The Application Framework

Part III: Extended Examples

Preface

Programming requires the ability to organize abstract concepts while being mindful of minute details. Details make the difference between success and failure in programming, but in attending to the details the overall structure can be forgotten. The Microsoft Foundation Classes (MFC) help with both the big picture and the small. They organize Windows objects and operations, bringing order to an otherwise chaotic landscape; and they embody much Windows programming protocol, handling the intricate dance that can cause a program to slip.

The Foundation Classes have their cost by adding additional, not always transparent, layers between a program and the operating system. While an MFC programmer does not need the depth of Windows understanding required by a raw API programmer, without some Windows knowledge, MFC comes to mean Much Frustration and Consternation. However, if you survive the initial learning curve and develop the skills required to make effective use of the class library, then MFC will surely help you write More Functional Code.

In teaching MFC, this text presents the whole picture, MFC *and* Windows. Along the way, it develops strategies for answering the myriad questions that arise in any real programming project. Always a source of amazement, you'll find yourself asking of MFC: How did it do that? Mastery of MFC programming requires that you understand the connective web between MFC and Windows to demystify the operation of MFC's application framework.

The form of this text has been heavily influenced by my experience teaching MFC to professional software developers. Although many concepts in MFC are easily grasped, some are complex and quite difficult. Accordingly, you'll find some topics treated lightly (the easy ones for you, I hope), while others are covered in great detail (such as the relationship between documents and views, and the process of serialization).

One thing this text does not try to do is replace the reference manual. I assume that you have easy access to reference material. One of the primary goals of this text is to help you over the conceptual hurdles to using MFC and give you the background information needed to understand the reference manual.

Neither does the text attempt to teach usage of a particular compiler or development environment. All of the examples were created using Microsoft's Visual C++, but you'll find no screen shots of Developer's Studio. The operation of programming environments seems to change with the seasons, unlike the more durable programming concepts.

MFC and Windows are moving targets. As a result, reference material sometimes lags reality, as will this book, in time. From time to time I'll expose the process that I went through to determine why various functions did not work as advertised in the manual. Understanding the overall organization of the class library will help you decipher the details.

What You Should Already Know

Despite the ability of some tools to generate a working Windows program from just a few clicks of the mouse, successful programming using MFC requires expertise in several areas of computing. I assume that you are competent programming in C++ and are at least familiar with Windows as a user. Competency in C++ entails knowing the language syntax, the object-oriented programming paradigm, and fundamental ideas of data structure and control flow. Although the text does not assume Windows programming knowledge, that knowledge certainly helps. Don't be fooled into thinking that you can ignore the Windows API by using MFC.

Organization of this Book

This text presents MFC from the ground up. It has three major parts. The first part looks toward the operating system, concentrating on Windows concepts. It presents the components of nearly every Windows program such as menus, dialogs, text, and graphics. Each chapter in this part has a companion program that illustrates the concepts expressed in the chapter.

The second part looks at the high-level code that drives many MFC applications. MFC's application framework is based on a document and view architecture that resembles Smalltalk's Model/View/Controller framework. In this architecture, the responsibility for a program's data resides with a document object while the responsibility for the user interface is handled by a view. MFC's framework is quite flexible and can be used to create a wide variety of programs. The chapters in this section develop three applications: one textual, one graphical, and one form-based.

The final part of the text consists of a collection of applications that build on the concepts from the first two parts. Topics include dialog-based applications, dynamic link libraries, and Internet clients.

As you'd expect in a programming text, this book is filled with programs. In creating an example program, there is always a tension between pedagogy and realism. Too many details bury the lesson, but attention to details distinguishes a toy from a tool. I've tried to make every example realistic, although I have skimped on error handling. To keep the text readable, only code excerpts are usually shown. The full program text, as well as the ancillary files needed for building the programs, can be found on the accompanying disk. The Appendix describes the disk.

Thank You

Many people have helped me to make this book what it is. The basis for the text was a course I wrote for the Technology Exchange Company. The material has benefited from the comments of programmers at many companies. Instructors of the course have given me invaluable feedback on the programs and the presentation. Ralph Davis, Joe Newcomer, Bob Oberg, Brent Rector, Ron Reeves, Dick Walter, and Al Williams have all influenced the text. I also appreciate the efforts of those reviewers who read and commented on all or part of the manuscript, including Jack Mathews, Joe Newcomer, Hadar Ziv, Chris Sells, and Sergiu Simmel.

The staff at Addison Wesley Longman has worked diligently to see the book become a reality. My thanks to Ben Ryan, Mike Hendrickson, and John Wait for initiating and guiding the process; Sarah Weaver for riding herd to see the book through production; Arlene Richman for improving the quality of the writing; Jason Jones for assisting with the translation of the text into Adobe FrameMaker; and Carol Nelson for getting the book into bookstores. My thanks also to Bob Russell of Octal Publishing for helping me tame FrameMaker.

Finally and especially, I thank my family—Georgia, Daniel, and Jeannette—for their unbending support during the long march to publication.

Alan Feuer
Brookline, MA
April, 1997
arf@Blossom.com

Part I: Basic
          Windows

1 Win32 and MFC

1.1 The Win32 Operating System

To an end user, Windows is a collection of utilities and a style of operation. Most users would probably say that the Windows Explorer, the Clipboard, perhaps WordPad, and maybe even their spreadsheet program are all part of Windows.

As a programmer you understand the distinction between an operating system and an application. If you have programmed a Graphical User Interface (GUI) before, you probably also understand the difference between a window manager and application code. All operating systems provide low-level services, such as file I/O, access to devices, and maybe interprocess communication. GUI systems also provide interface services, allowing the creation of interactive objects such as menus and dialogs. To a programmer, Windows is both an operating system and a GUI. Win32, 32-bit Windows, is particularly rich in both domains.

For this text, I assume that you are a user, as well as programmer, of Win32. A window like that in Figure 1.1 should be familiar to you. Technically, a window is divided into two mutually exclusive regions: the *client area* and the *nonclient area*. The terms are from the viewpoint of Win32 itself; an application is a client of Win32. Typically, Win32 draws the nonclient area based on suggestions from the application. The client area is under application control. In Figure 1.1, the various parts of the nonclient area are labeled with the terms used in the reference manual.

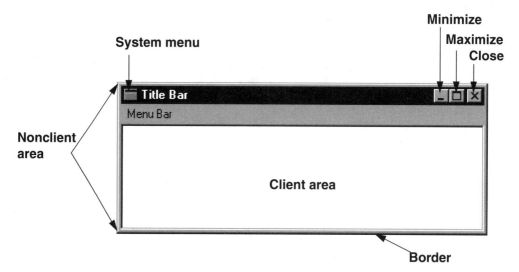

Figure 1.1   A window is divided into two primary pieces, the client and nonclient area.

The internal organization of Win32 differs somewhat among its various implementations. On all systems there are four primary functional partitions that a program communicates with:

- Window Manager, known as User
- Graphical Device Interface, GDI
- System Services, Kernel
- Character-Mode Screen, Console

On Windows 9X, these components are packaged in dynamic link libraries (DLLs) and run within the client-process address space. On NT, Win32 is partitioned into client and server-side functions. Some functions run in DLLs attached to the client process, but others run in the micro-kernel or perhaps in a Win32 server process. For the most part, a program cannot tell where particular functionality is located.

It's probably obvious, but still worth pointing out, that no matter how a Win32 program is generated, it runs the same Win32 components. And there are many ways to create Win32 programs, as illustrated by Figure 1.2. The native interface to Win32 is the C Application Program Interface (API). A C program makes calls into the Win32 library. The library used to be delivered with something called the Software Development Kit (SDK), so programming to the API is often called SDK programming.

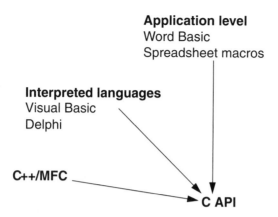

Figure 1.2   There are many ways to create a Windows program.

The Microsoft Foundation Class (MFC) library calls the C API to access Win32. Although not all the functionality of Win32 has been encapsulated by MFC classes, C++ gives access to all of Win32 because all of the C API functions are callable from C++.

The further you climb up Figure 1.2, the easier it is to write certain programs but the narrower the program domain and typically the less efficient the program. Being an expert in C++ shouldn't blind you to the advantages of using higher-level languages and systems.

1.2   The Win32 API

If you have never programmed Windows using the Win32 API, let me briefly fill you in on what you're missing.[1] API programming has a well-deserved reputation for being difficult. This is partly because the API is huge, with more than 2,000 function calls and over 6,000 names when macros are included!

In addition, programs that call the API have an unusual organization. They are event driven. That is, once they initialize themselves, they wait around for events. Here is the top-level algorithm of every Win32 program:

---

[1] For an in-depth look at the Win32 GUI API, see *Win32 Programming*, by Brent Rector and Joe Newcomer, Addison Wesley Longman, 1997. *Win32 Systems Programming*, by Johnson Hart, Addison Wesley Longman, 1997, covers the non-GUI portion of Win32.

```
Initialize
Loop until termination
    Process events
Terminate
```

There are hundreds of events, everything from movement of the mouse to the user changing the fonts on the system. Also, responding to one event may trigger others. As a result, it can be difficult to follow the flow of a program because control is determined not just by the program but also by the order in which events occur.

Besides being event driven, Win32 is also object oriented with regard to its windows. By object oriented, I mean that every window has a class and the class of a window determines its behavior. Since C has neither the concept of object nor class, both concepts are implemented on top of C and are not always apparent.[2]

1.3   The MFC Library

MFC uses C++ to simplify Win32 programming. Two features of C++, in particular, contribute to MFC's utility: encapsulation and inheritance.

1.3.1 Encapsulation

From the earliest versions of the MFC library there have been wrapper classes encapsulating the objects implemented in Windows. Objects like pens, brushes, fonts, and buttons each have a data structure and a set of operations defined in Win32. It can be difficult to find the complete set of operations directly from the API because C lacks higher-order structure. One can only hope that the reference manual is current and accurate. With classes like CPen, CBrush, CFont, and Cbutton, MFC organizes the objects implemented in Win32 and makes it easier to create and manipulate them, even if MFC doesn't add any new functionality.

1.3.2 Inheritance

The SDK came with a minimal Windows program in a file generic.c. Generic.c contained two of the essential pieces of nearly every Windows application, a main routine and a main window procedure. The main routine handled initialization and had the loop that waited for events. The main window procedure

---

[2] Perhaps it should be no surprise that Windows is object oriented because that model fits GUIs particularly well. The earliest GUI, for Xerox PARC's Alto, spawned object-oriented Smalltalk language. The object model of Windows is very close to that of Smalltalk.

handled operations on the application's main window, such as menu commands and showing the window's contents. Many a Windows program began in a text editor as a copy of `generic.c`.

C programs typically use libraries for low-level operations—for example, the string and I/O functions of the ANSI C library. High-level algorithms are rarely retrieved from a library. One example of a high-level algorithm in the ANSI C library is the `qsort` function. `qsort` implements the Quicksort algorithm, while the program supplies the data and the low-level less-than operator. If you have used `qsort`, you know that its program interface is a bit messy and prone to error.

Inheritance, along with virtual functions, makes it much more convenient in C++ than in C to put a high-level algorithm into a library. A library class is created to implement the high-level algorithm. Each replaceable step in the algorithm is implemented as a virtual function. An application-defined class derived from the library class can override those virtual functions to customize the steps. Instead of modifying code like that in `generic.c`, MFC programmers derive new classes from those in the library, inheriting and replacing behavior as appropriate. These high-level classes are known as an *application framework.*

As a result of using application-framework classes to drive a program and wrapper classes to access Win32 objects, programs written using MFC are a bit like a sandwich. The application supplies the lettuce and tomato while MFC supplies the bread (see Figure 1.3).

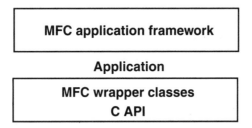

Figure 1.3   An application written using MFC is a lot like a sandwich.

The application framework and the wrapper classes are Win32 specific. The MFC library also includes general classes for manipulation of strings, files, time, and exceptions. In addition, there are collection classes for building arrays and lists of objects.

One last thing. Although programming Win32 using MFC is much easier than programming using the API, it would be misleading to give the impression that C++ and Win32 are a perfect fit. Win32 uses messages to communicate with objects; any object can receive any message. C++ uses a functional model. To communicate with an object a program must call a function defined for the object. You'll see a few odd constructs in MFC with the purpose of bridging the gap between these different points of view.

CHAPTER

2 | Hello, World

On the accompanying disk, the programs in the `Hello` and `Generic\Simple` directories illustrate the concepts discussed in this chapter. The corresponding executables in the `bin` directory are `Hello.exe` and `GenericSimple.exe`. (Please see the Appendix for a description of the disk.)

2.1 Introduction

Ever since Brian Kernighan and Dennis Ritchie wrote in *The C Programming Language*

> The first program to write is the same for all languages: Print the words "Hello, world".

authors have felt obliged to follow their advice. Writing the "Hello, world" program for a new system is just as instructive as it is for a new language. Using the tools of the development environment, the program must be created, compiled, and linked. Using the system, the program must be run.

When run, the Win32 Hello program produces the window shown in Figure 2.1. The code for Hello is nearly as simple as Kernighan and Ritchie's original. It is in the file `main.cpp` of the `Hello` directory:

```
#include <afxwin.h>

int WINAPI
WinMain(HINSTANCE,HINSTANCE,LPSTR,int)
{
    ::MessageBox( NULL,
        _T("Hello, world"),
        _T("MFC Programming"),
        MB_OK);

    return 0;
}
```

Figure 2.1   The output from the Windows version of "Hello, world"

Hello illustrates the basic form of a Win32 program. All Win32 programs
include windows.h, the header of all headers for the C API. This program
includes afxwin.h, which in turn includes windows.h. Windows.h contains prototypes for most of the C API and definitions of many macros. Among the
macros are pseudo data types, such as WINAPI, HINSTANCE, and LPSTR (see Section 2.4.1 for a short list of common Win32 data types). Afxwin.h contains class
declarations for most of MFC.

The "main" function in a Win32 program is called WinMain. It takes four parameters, only three of which are used in Win32:[1]

```
WinMain(HINSTANCE hInstance, HINSTANCE, LPSTR cmdArgs, int cmdShow)
```

where

hInstance	is the instance handle. It is a magic number needed by various API functions.
cmdArgs	is the command line excluding the command name. In a GUI environment command lines are far less important than on command-oriented systems.
cmdShow	is the suggested initial state of the application window, such as minimized or normal.

MessageBox displays a window containing a few lines of text and from one to four
push buttons. The function returns when the message box is dismissed by the
user. In Hello, the message box has a single OK push button. The program terminates when WinMain exits.

---

[1] The second parameter was used in 16-bit Windows to distinguish the first invocation of an
application from other invocations. Because of the scarcity of resources, some programs used this
distinction to share objects between invocations.

In this book, you'll find all string literals wrapped by the macro _T, allowing the programs to work with either 8-bit or wide characters, depending on compile-time flags. All of MFC and the underlying API support wide characters. (See Chapter 4 for more detail.)

The :: prefix is the unary scope resolution operator in C++; ::MessageBox specifies the global function MessageBox, i.e., the MessageBox function from the C API. MFC uses many of the same function names as the API. To avoid confusion, I will always use the :: prefix when referring to an API function.

2.2   MFC's Generic Program

Although the Hello program gets us started, it doesn't take us very far. In this section we'll look at a simple program that uses MFC's application framework to create a main window with a menu bar. Figure 2.2 shows the initial screen of the program.

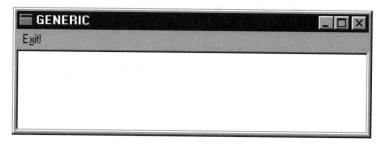

Figure 2.2   Running the simple Generic program displays a main frame window with a menu bar. The menu bar has a single item, labeled Exit.

The source code files for the program could have been created by a program generator such as AppWizard from Visual C++, but I've written them by hand to show just the essentials. The Generic application is built from seven files (in the directory Generic\Simple):[2]

app.h, app.cpp	Declaration and implementation of the application class
mainfrm.h, mainfrm.cpp	Declaration and implementation of the main window class

---

[2] When you look in the directory, you'll also find an eighth source file, stdafx.cpp. It is created just to trigger building of the precompiled header file described in Section 2.2.2.

resource.h, app.rc   Definition of menu resource

stdafx.h   Header file to include all standard header files

At this point, the files are very short. We'll use the same organization in later programs where the files will become more substantial. Figure 2.3 shows how the files are related.

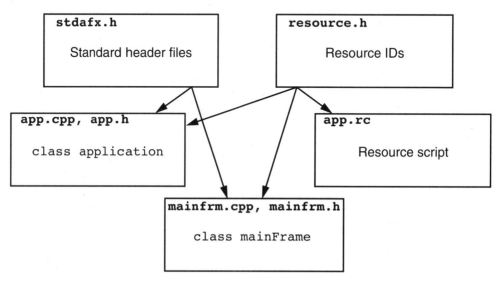

Figure 2.3   The program files for the simple Generic program are in the Generic\Simple directory. The arrows represent the relationship "is included by".

2.2.1 The Resource Script

Before looking at the code, take a look at the build procedure in Figure 2.4. In addition to an assortment of code generators and editors, MFC programming requires three basic tools: a C++ compiler, a resource compiler, and a link editor. The resource compiler creates Win32-readable representations of various program objects, such as menus, dialogs, icons, cursors, and strings. Resource compilation is driven by a *resource script,* a textual description of a program's resources. Resource scripts are usually created in a resource editor, although occasionally you may need to edit one in an ordinary text editor. The resource script for the Generic application describes the menu. It is in the file app.rc:

```
#include <windows.h>
#include "resource.h"

IDR_MainMenu MENU DISCARDABLE
BEGIN
    MENUITEM "Exit",  IDM_Exit
END
```

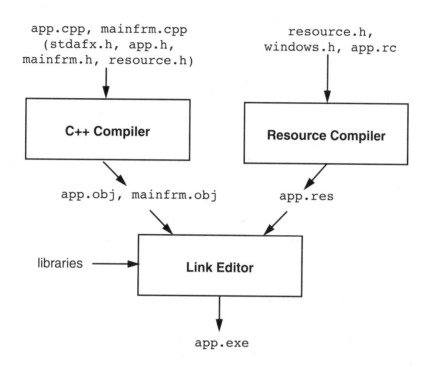

Figure 2.4   The build procedure for a typical Win32 program uses a C++ compiler, resource compiler, and link editor. The arrows represent flow of data.

The menu is named IDR_MainMenu. It consists of a single item, labeled "Exit". The item has an associated ID, IDM_Exit. App.rc includes resource.h, a header file maintained by the resource editor with macros to define IDs. The important definitions in resource.h are

```
#define IDR_MainMenu    103
#define IDM_Exit        40000
```

Resource.h is also included in the code files, so these #define statements will be seen by both the C++ and the resource compilers. The numeric values are chosen by the resource editor and, except for a few rules, are arbitrary. You might be wondering why resource.h has #define statements instead of the manifest constants offered by C++. The resource compiler understands a very simple language with little resemblance to C++. Before resource compiling, the resource script is processed by a simplified version of the C preprocessor. Therefore, #define and #include statements are understood, but not language statements such as const.

2.2.2 Precompiled Headers

Each of the program modules of the Generic program begins by including stdafx.h. In stdafx.h we put standard definitions and file inclusions needed everywhere:

```
#include <afxwin.h>
```

The file afxwin.h includes most class definitions needed by MFC programs and, as you saw earlier, the definitions needed to use the C API. As a result, after pre-processing, even the smallest MFC program is huge—well over 60,000 lines of text! To speed up compilation, most compilers have a facility to precompile statements in header files. Thus to compile a file that uses the standard header, the compiler does not need to reread all of the text but can use the predigested information.

Version control becomes an issue with precompiled headers. If any of the header matter changes, the predigested information must be regenerated. Also, in order for the compiler to use the precompiled information, the file being compiled must begin with exactly the same sequence of #include and #define statements, because changing the order could change the meaning. Putting these initial statements in a single header file, such as stdafx.h, is the simplest way to guarantee that all modules begin with exactly the same sequence.

2.2.3 The Application Object

The primary task in writing the code for an MFC program is to create classes. MFC provides a rich foundation for Win32 programs, so most classes you write will be derived from a library class. Figure 2.5 shows the classes used by the Generic program.

Every MFC program instantiates an application object from a CWinApp-derived class. The application object plays two important roles:

- It holds commonly used global variables, such as the name of the module, the name of the associated help file, the command line, and a process identifier.
- It provides access to the default steps of the top-level Win32 algorithm.

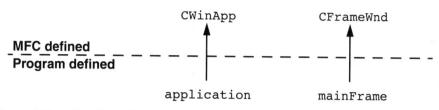

Figure 2.5   The simple Generic program defines two classes. The arrows represent the class relationship "is derived from".

app.h declares the application class derived from CWinApp:

```
class application : public CWinApp {
public:
    BOOL InitInstance();
};
```

app.cpp implements the class and defines the application object:

```
application theApp;
```

Recall that a Win32 program initializes itself and then waits for events to occur. The highest level algorithm can be written as

```
Initialize
Loop until termination
    Process events
Terminate
```

This algorithm is usually implemented in WinMain. But unlike the Hello program described at the beginning of this chapter, a program that uses MFC's application framework does not have its own WinMain; it uses the one stored in the library. MFC's WinMain implements the top-level algorithm by calling member functions of CWinApp:

```
InitApplication
InitInstance
Run
ExitInstance
```

These functions are declared virtual so that a class derived from CWinApp can override the default implementation. And this is usually the case. In the Generic program, the application class overrides InitInstance.[3]

WinMain is a global function, not a member of any class. It makes calls into CWinApp by using a pointer to the application object. Since WinMain is the first function executed, the pointer must be initialized right at the start of the program. The constructor for CWinApp sets the pointer. It is important that the application object be created in static memory (for instance, a global object) so that its constructor will be called before WinMain executes. Figure 2.6 shows how WinMain and CWinApp work together.

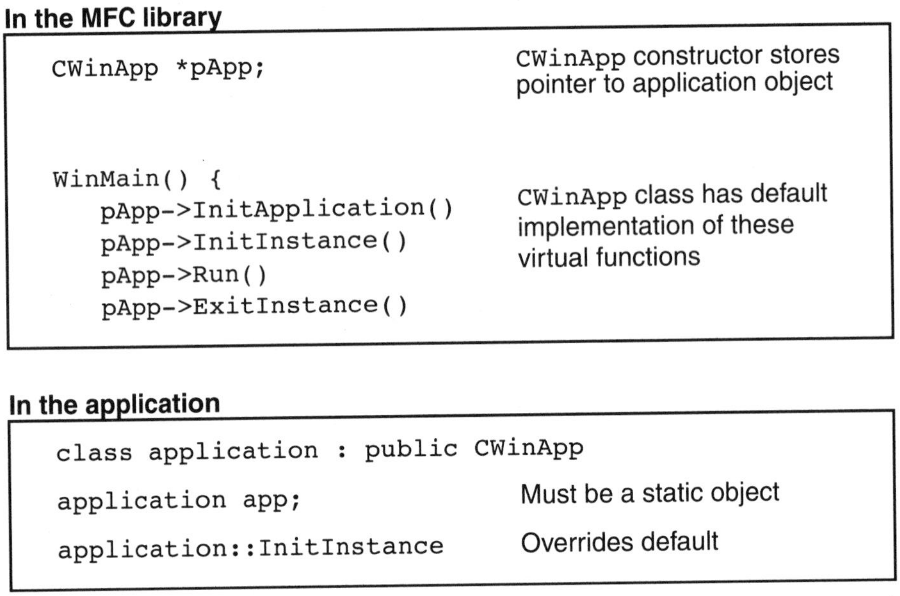

In the MFC library

```
CWinApp *pApp;                          CWinApp constructor stores
                                        pointer to application object


WinMain() {                             CWinApp class has default
    pApp->InitApplication()             implementation of these
    pApp->InitInstance()                virtual functions
    pApp->Run()
    pApp->ExitInstance()
```

In the application

```
class application : public CWinApp

application app;                        Must be a static object

application::InitInstance               Overrides default
```

Figure 2.6 MFC maintains a pointer to the application object. Each step of WinMain is implemented as a virtual function in the CWinApp class. By overriding these functions in the application class, a program can customize the steps in WinMain.

The constructor sets a variable pApp to point to the application object. WinMain uses the pointer to access virtual functions. For virtual functions, the target of a function call depends on the actual type of the pointed-to object. Even though the declared type of pApp is CWinApp *, when WinMain calls pApp->InitInstance, the function application::InitInstance will be executed because the actual type of pApp is application *.

---

3 MFC's WinMain calls on two initialization functions, InitInstance and InitApplication. In 16-bit Windows, InitApplication was called only for the first instance of running a program. The second running instance of a program would sometimes share objects created by the first instance. Under Win32, InitApplication is called for every instance and therefore serves no special purpose.

On initialization, the Generic program creates and displays the window for the application:

```
BOOL application::InitInstance()
{
    m_pMainWnd = new mainFrame;
    return TRUE;
}
```

2.2.4 The Main Window

The application's main window is an instance of the `mainFrame` class. Windows that contain other windows are often called *frames*, thus the main window is the *main* frame. Its primary job is to handle menu commands. It is declared in `mainfrm.h`:

```
class mainFrame : public CFrameWnd {
public:
    mainFrame();
    afx_msg void onExit();
    DECLARE_MESSAGE_MAP()
};
```

Creating a C++ object, such as a `mainFrame`, in itself does not create a window. To create a window, the program must make a call into Win32. In `mainfrm.cpp`, the constructor for `mainFrame` creates a default frame window:

```
mainFrame::mainFrame()
{
    if( !Create(NULL,                          // Window class name
        _T("GENERIC"),                         // Window title
        WS_OVERLAPPEDWINDOW | WS_VISIBLE,// Window style
        rectDefault,                           // Origin and extent
        NULL,                                  // Parent
        MAKEINTRESOURCE(IDR_MainMenu))   // Menu
    )
        AfxAbort();
}
```

The call to `Create` eventually calls the API function `CreateWindow`, which creates and displays a Win32 window object. We'll cover many details of the `Create` call in Chapter 5.

The `mainFrame` class has two other declarations. The member function `onExit` is called when the Exit menu item is selected. The DECLARE_MESSAGE_MAP macro provides part of the chain connecting the menu selection with the `onExit` function.

2.3   Events and Messages

Earlier I mentioned that Win32 programs are driven by events. A program learns about events through *messages*. There is a message for every event, such as resizing, moving, selecting, and closing a window, pressing a keyboard or mouse key, moving the mouse, activating or closing a program, selecting a dialog or menu item. The recipient of a message is always a window.

Recall from Chapter 1 that Win32 is object oriented, meaning that every window belongs to some (Win32) class. Each Win32 class has a function for processing messages, called a *window procedure.* It follows, then, that there is a window procedure associated with each window. Typically, a window procedure contains a `switch` statement, where the cases of the `switch` correspond to the messages that the procedure processes.

Consider the event of selecting a menu item, for example the Exit item in the Generic program. Selecting an item generates a WM_COMMAND message. The ID associated with the menu item, in this case IDM_Exit, is passed with the message as a parameter. A window procedure that processes this message will have a case for WM_COMMAND and a handler for IDM_Exit. Figure 2.7 shows the basic flow of control at the Win32 level.

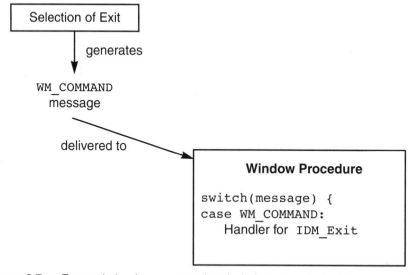

Figure 2.7   Every window has an associated window procedure. The job of a window procedure is to process messages.

2.3.1 Events in MFC

MFC builds a layer on top of Win32 to connect messages to C++ member functions. In an MFC program, most windows use the same window procedure, one supplied by the library. Class structure is built using C++, not Win32. A primary role of the library window procedure is to find the member function that corresponds to the current message. The window procedure uses a look-up table, known as a *message map*, to make the connection. Figure 2.8 shows the flow of control

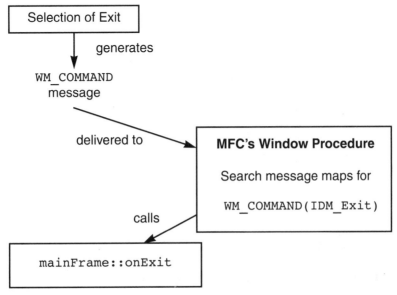

Figure 2.8   In an MFC program, most windows use a standard window procedure in MFC's library. The window procedure searches message maps to find the handler for a message.

2.3.2 Message Maps

A message map is a linked list of tables. Each table contains entries that consist of a message number and a function pointer. Here is the expansion of the DECLARE_MESSAGE_MAP macro from the declaration of class `mainFrame`:

```
private: \
    static const AFX_MSGMAP_ENTRY _messageEntries[]; \
protected: \
    static AFX_DATA const AFX_MSGMAP messageMap; \
    virtual const AFX_MSGMAP* GetMessageMap() const;
```

Each class has its own table in the _messageEntries data member, a pointer to the map for the base class, and a virtual function to retrieve the map. When a message arrives for a window, MFC's window procedure finds the C++ object that corresponds to the window, calls GetMessageMap to get a pointer to the map for the window, and searches for a map entry that corresponds to the current message. If a match is found, the associated function is called. If no match is found, the window procedure follows the base-class pointer and searches the message map for the base class. It continues searching up the class hierarchy to the CCmdTarget class.

The _messageEntries table is declared static, and is thus class data. All instances of a class share the same message map. In C++, class data must be defined in an implementation file. Again, special macros are used for the message map. Here is the map definition for mainFrame in the file mainfrm.cpp:

```
BEGIN_MESSAGE_MAP(mainWindow,CFrameWnd)
    ON_COMMAND(IDM_Exit,onExit)
END_MESSAGE_MAP()
```

Notice that the BEGIN_MESSAGE_MAP macro takes the name of the base class as a parameter. It saves a link to the message map for the base class independent of the C++ class structure. It is important that the base class specified in the BEGIN_MESSAGE_MAP macro and the C++ class declaration agree. Otherwise, inheritance for the class will be inconsistent. Because the compiler cannot guarantee that the macro and class declaration agree, you must.

After establishing the link to the base class, the expansion of the BEGIN_MESSAGE_MAP macro opens an initializer for the message-map table:

```
const AFX_MSGMAP_ENTRY mainWindow::_messageEntries[] =
{
```

The table is initialized by message-map macros specialized for each message. ON_COMMAND, for example, is the message-map macro for the WM_COMMAND message. The ON_COMMAND macro for mainWindow shown above expands to:

```
{ WM_COMMAND, CN_COMMAND, (WORD)IDM_Exit, (WORD)IDM_Exit,
AfxSig_vv, (AFX_PMSG)onExit },
```

It connects a WM_COMMAND message with the ID IDM_Exit to the member function onExit. AfxSig_vv specifies the signature of the member function. In Win32, the actual parameters for a message are packed into two 32-bit variables.[4] The

---

[4] The variables are known as lParam and wParam. Under Win16, wParam is 16 bits.

signature tells MFC how to turn the packed values into parameters suitable for the member function.

There are similar macros for other standard messages, although most don't take parameters. Search the MFC help file for "ON" to see a complete list of the message-map macros. END_MESSAGE_MAP marks the end of the table and closes the table initializer:

```
    {0, 0, 0, 0, AfxSig_end, (AFX_PMSG)0 }
};
```

2.3.2.1 Why Message Maps?

You can see that message maps reimplement the class structure specified in C++, adding complexity and a chance of error. The maps are an implementation optimization, borrowing from both Windows and C++.

In Windows, a message is delivered to a window procedure. Usually a switch statement in the window procedure pulls out some messages while other messages are passed on to the window procedure for the base class in order to inherit behavior. A message handler is found by run-time comparisons of the switch expression with the switch cases. Searching a message map is like searching for a switch case.

The C++ approach to finding a message handler would be to implement the handlers as virtual functions with the default behavior in some base class. Processing a message would not require run-time searching, just indexing into the virtual function table, the *vtable,* associated with the current window.[5] Unfortunately, since there are hundreds of messages, and over one hundred classes, the space occupied by the vtables becomes an issue, particularly for 16-bit Windows. The vtable for each class must include all of the inherited virtual functions plus any it defines. A message map is like a vtable, but instead of accessing a member function by index, MFC searches for the function. Thus unlike a vtable, the message map only contains entries for functions actually defined. Inherited functions are accessed via the base-class link.

---

[5] For an interesting discussion of virtual functions and their implementation, see *The Design and Evolution of C++,* by Bjarne Stroustrup, Addison-Wesley Publishing Co., 1994.

2.3.3 Handling a Message

In summary, adding a message handler to a class takes these three steps:[6]

1. Declare a handler as a member function.
2. Create a message map entry binding the message to the function.
3. Write the function.

The Generic program uses the function onExit to handle the Exit menu item. In onExit, the window tells itself to close by posting a WM_CLOSE message to itself:

```
void mainFrame::onExit()
{
    PostMessage(WM_CLOSE);
}
```

Sometime later, the main window will receive the message WM_CLOSE. You may have noticed that there is no message map entry for WM_CLOSE in the mainFrame class. mainFrame will inherit processing for WM_CLOSE from its base class.

WM_CLOSE itself does not cause a window to close. The message is like the question, "Is it okay to close?" In response to WM_CLOSE, many programs ask for confirmation if data in the window has not been saved. The default behavior for WM_CLOSE is to call the API function DestroyWindow, which causes the window to go away. To ask for confirmation, override WM_CLOSE.

2.4   Naming Conventions

While the rules for naming program objects can be contentious, one thing everyone will agree on is that the Win32 and MFC libraries contain lots of names. In addition to the couple of thousand API function names and the thousands of macro names, MFC adds a couple of hundred classes and countless member functions.

To keep the names straight, there are some naming conventions you should learn.

---

[6] These are exactly the steps that tools like ClassWizard carry out for you (except that they can't write the whole function, but almost). In later programs, I'll rely on the tools to add new message handlers.

2.4.1 Names in the Win32 API

Windows has been around long enough to have evolved a set of conventions and to have generated exceptions to the conventions. Generally,

- Function names are phrases with each word capitalized. You have already seen several examples: `GetMessage`, `MessageBox`, `WinMain`.

- Parameters and variables are named like functions, but they have a prefix in lower case.[7] The prefix identifies the data type of the variable. Here are some common prefixes:[8]

h	A handle
w	A WORD (a 16-bit unsigned integer)
sz	A string terminated with a zero byte
p	A pointer
lp	A long (or far) pointer
lpsz	A long pointer to a zero-terminated string
f	A flag (Boolean)

- Data types are defined either as macros or by using `typedef`. Some common examples are:

HANDLE	A magic cookie for identifying a Win32 object
HWND	A handle for a window
PSTR	A pointer to a string
PCSTR	A pointer to a constant string
PCTSTR	A pointer to a constant string, in which a character may not be the same as a byte
LPSTR	A long pointer to a string

- Macros are used for constants, including message numbers. Macro names are written in uppercase. To keep the numerous macro names from collid-

---

[7] This convention is known as Hungarian notation, reportedly in honor of Charles Simonyi, a Windows pioneer at Microsoft.

[8] The concepts of near and far pointers were part of Win16; they have no meaning in Win32. Nevertheless, the reference manual makes heavy use of "far" data types such as LPSTR.

ing, the names are given a prefix followed by an underscore. Here are some common prefixes:

WM	A window message
WS	A window style
MB	A message-box style
EM	A message you can send to an edit control
EN	A message an edit control can send to you
IDC	An ID for a cursor, also used in dialogs for controls

2.4.2 Names in MFC

- Function names follow the convention used with the API. In fact, many member functions have the same name as the corresponding API functions. There aren't too many global MFC functions. They all have the prefix "Afx" (for **A**pplication **F**rameworks), e.g., AfxMessageBox.

- Classes are named like functions with the addition of a prefix of "C". Thus a pen is represented by a CPen, a window by a CWnd, and a string by a CString.

- Parameter names follow the rules for the API.

- Data members of a class are named similarly to parameters and variables in the API. Instance members are given a prefix of "m_"; class members (*static* data members) do not have a prefix. For example, every CWnd object has a unique m_hWnd member, but there is just one wndTop member for all CWnd objects.

2.4.3 Names in This Text

To help you distinguish the names I've invented from those defined in MFC, I have used slightly different naming rules:

- Function names that I've invented are phrases like those in MFC except that the first letter will be lower-case rather than capitalized. Thus onExit is not a standard name. Overriding a virtual function, of course, requires that the name be spelled as in the base class. So even though I wrote InitInstance, it is capitalized because it is a virtual function defined in CWinApp.

- Parameter and variable names forgo the data-type prefix and are generally like function names. However, there are some names so ingrained that the standard name must be used, such as hWnd for a window handle. Also, for standard member functions like message handlers, the standard names are used.
- Macro names for constants generally follow the API convention of using a special prefix. In contrast to macros defined in the API, names I've invented will use mixed case following the prefix instead of just uppercase, e.g., IDM_Exit.

3 | Menus

The program in the `Menu` directory illustrates the concepts discussed in this chapter. The corresponding executable in the `bin` directory is `Menu.exe`.

3.1 Introduction

Nearly every program has at least one menu. Many programs have multiple menus, some of stunning complexity. Simple menus are easy to understand and work well. Complex menus can be frustrating to use. The problem is primarily one of screen area. Menu names must be kept short to fit on the menu bar, but short names don't always give a good description of what follows on the sub-menu. Also, menus are by nature hierarchical. Not all commands in a program may fit cleanly into a hierarchy. This leads to odd conventions where, for example, Search appears under Edit, and Exit appears under File. As toolbars have become more common, menus have shrunk in size.[1]

From a programmer's perspective, menus are attractive from two standpoints:

- Menus are very easy to create since Win32 does all the work of displaying the menu items.
- Menu commands are very easy to handle. Also, the same code that handles a menu command can be used to respond to an accelerator key, toolbar, or palette selection.

---

[1] For a thorough discussion of menus and other forms of program interface, see *Designing the User Interface*, by Ben Shneiderman, Addison-Wesley Publishing Co., 1992.

3.2   Menu Basics

A Win32 menu is a tree where each leaf of the tree has an associated integer ID. The items on the menu bar represent the first level of nodes in the tree below an invisible root. Clicking on a menu item may execute a command or it may bring up items from the next level of the tree.

Win32 displays two basic types of menus:

Menu bar	A horizontal menu representing the top level of the menu tree attached to a window.
Popup	A vertical menu. A popup menu can appear • Below a menu bar, in which case it represents the second level of the menu tree. Such a menu is also known as a *drop-down* menu.[a] • Next to an item on a popup menu. It represents deeper levels of a menu tree. This kind of menu is also known as a *cascaded* menu. • Floating anywhere on the screen, commonly triggered by a click of the right mouse button. This type of menu is also known as a *context* menu.

[a] On some GUI systems, the user must keep the mouse button pressed to see the next level of menu. Such menus are called *pull-downs*. A Win32 drop-down menu can also be operated as a pull-down.

The menu bar, drop-down, and cascaded menus are drawn automatically by Win32 in response to manipulation of the menu. Context menus are drawn by calling the TrackMenuPopup function. Figures 3.1 and 3.2 illustrate the various menu types.

3.3   Menu Events

Win32 generates a series of messages while a menu is being manipulated. The messages are sent to the window that owns the menu, typically the main frame window.[2] Programs respond to the messages by changing the state of menu

---

[2] Win32 also supports menus on popup windows, such as dialogs. A child window, such as a document window in a word processor, cannot have a menu.

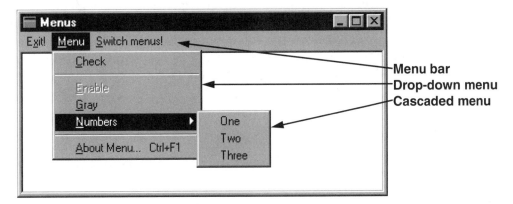

Figure 3.1   Win32 handles the menu bar, drop-down, and cascaded menus automatically.

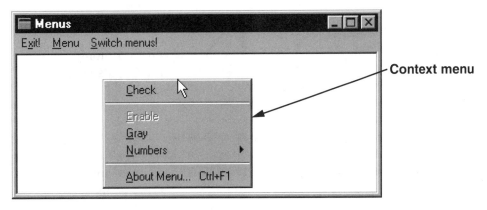

Figure 3.2   Context menus are triggered explicitly by the program, usually in response to a right mouse-click.

items and displaying explanatory text for the current item. Here are the important messages from the sequence:[3]

Click on top-level menu item	WM_INITMENU
	WM_MENUSELECT
	WM_INITMENUPOPUP
	WM_ENTERIDLE
Click on leaf menu item	WM_COMMAND

---

[3] If you examine the message flow during menu traversal, you'll see that some of these messages repeat. In addition, there are a few other messages, such as WM_ENTERMENULOOP and WM_MOUSEMOVE. They are less important for menu handling and will be ignored.

WM_INITMENU tells a window that the user has either clicked on the menu bar or used the keyboard to access the menu. If a menu item is not a leaf of the menu tree, selecting it triggers a drop-down submenu. WM_INITMENUPOPUP is received before the drop-down menu is displayed. Programs respond to WM_INITMENU-POPUP by adjusting the state of the items in the submenu.

Whenever a menu item is highlighted, Win32 sends WM_MENUSELECT along with the ID of the item. In response, some programs display help information about the item, although others post help text during idle time, when Win32 sends WM_ENTERIDLE. MFC's application framework uses idle time to display help text automatically (see Chapter 11).

Finally, if the selected menu item is a leaf of the menu tree, WM_COMMAND is received along with the ID of the item. An MFC program typically has an ON_COMMAND message-map entry that binds each ID to a member function. Here is an excerpt from the message map for the main window of the Menu program:

```
BEGIN_MESSAGE_MAP(mainFrame, CFrameWnd)
    //{{AFX_MSG_MAP(mainFrame)
    ON_COMMAND(IDM_Check, onCheck)
    ON_COMMAND(IDM_Enable, onEnable)
 . . .
    //}}AFX_MSG_MAP
END_MESSAGE_MAP()
```

When the WM_COMMAND message is received, MFC's window procedure calls the specified member function. For example, when IDM_Check is received, the function onCheck is called.

3.4   Creating a Menu

In MFC, Win32 menus are encapsulated by the CMenu class. CMenu has operations for creating and modifying a menu dynamically, but it is far easier to create a menu in a resource editor.

In creating a menu resource, as for other resources like bitmaps and dialogs, you will need to give the menu a name, either a string or an integer ID. At run-time, when Win32 needs to load the menu resource, it will search for the menu name. Most resource editors will suggest an ID, as this is marginally more efficient in space and time. Also, if you misspell the identifier in the source code, the compiler will complain. If you give a string name, Win32 will perform a case-insensitive string comparison instead of a simple integer test. If you misspell the name, the result will usually be that nothing will happen.

Still, there is one advantage to using a string name. Integer IDs are customarily defined using a #define statement in a header file like resource.h. Every time you add a resource, a new #define statement needs to be added. Since resource.h is included by nearly every source file, modifying it could require recompiling lots of source. Naming a resource with a string does not require modifying a header file.[4]

3.4.1 Loading and Attaching a Menu

Like all resources, before a menu can be used it must be loaded. A menu associated with a frame window, such as the main frame, will be loaded automatically when the window is created. The name of the menu is supplied in the Create call that creates the window. A string resource name can be placed directly in the call; an integer ID must be marked as a resource identifier using the MAKEINTRESOURCE macro.

To have more than one menu associated with a window or to retrieve popup menu resources, you'll need to load a menu explicitly. CMenu::LoadMenu takes the name of a menu, just like the Create call.

The Menu program has two menu bars, one given an integer ID and one given a string name. I'll show you their definitions in the resource file, but you'll undoubtedly want to manipulate menu resources in a resource editor:[5]

```
IDR_MainMenu MENU PRELOAD DISCARDABLE
BEGIN
    MENUITEM "E&xit!",                      IDM_Exit
    POPUP "&Menu"
    BEGIN
        MENUITEM "&Check",                  IDM_Check
  . . .
        MENUITEM "&About Menu...\tCtrl+F1", IDM_AboutMenu
    END
    MENUITEM "&Switch menus!",              IDM_SwitchMenus
END
```

---

[4] To avoid recompiling everything when a new resource is added, most environments exclude files like resource.h when deciding what needs to be rebuilt. In Visual C++, if the first line in a file is // {{NO_DEPENDENCIES}}, modifying the file will not trigger rebuilding.

[5] Notice that you can't tell by looking at the resource whether the name is a string or an ID. If the name is an ID, it will be replaced by an integer after preprocessing. To help the reader, you should follow the convention of using a capitalized prefix for IDs, like IDR. The ampersand that appears in the menu-item text specifies a mnemonic for the item. Mnemonics are discussed in Section 3.7.

```
ALTMENU MENU PRELOAD DISCARDABLE
BEGIN
    MENUITEM "E&xit!",                          IDM_Exit
    MENUITEM "&Switch menus!",                  IDM_SwitchMenus
END
```

When the main window is created, IDR_MainMenu will be loaded implicitly. The
second menu, AltMenu, is loaded explicitly:

```
mainFrame::mainFrame()
{
    if( !Create(NULL,                       // Window class name
        _T("Menus"),                        // Window title
        WS_OVERLAPPEDWINDOW | WS_VISIBLE,   // Window style
        rectDefault,                        // Origin and extent
        NULL,                               // Parent
        MAKEINTRESOURCE(IDR_MainMenu))      // Menu
    ) {
        AfxAbort();
        return;
    }

    m_mainMenu.Attach( GetMenu()->m_hMenu );
    m_altMenu.LoadMenu( _T("AltMenu") );
```

Like all Win32 objects, a menu exists in Win32 without regard for whether there
is a C++ object wrapper. Yet a wrapper object is needed to manipulate the menu
using MFC. The mainFrame class has two CMenu objects that correspond to its
two menu bars (see the Switch Menus command described in Section 3.6.1.1).
Here is part of the class declaration in mainfrm.h:

```
class mainFrame : public CFrameWnd
{
. . .
private:
    CMenu m_mainMenu;
    CMenu m_altMenu;
```

Since Win32 loads IDR_MainMenu implicitly, the menu is not automatically connected to the m_mainMenu wrapper. The Attach function call in mainFrame's
constructor binds the Win32 menu to the C++ object. By contrast, LoadMenu
attaches the menu to the wrapper object after it loads the menu resource.

3.5 Menu Items

Each item on a menu has a state reflecting its appearance and whether it can be selected. The state is stored within Win32, so it persists until the menu is destroyed.

This is a subtlety of programming Win32 using C++. Sometimes state is stored in the C++ object and sometimes in the Win32 object. The location of the state information affects its persistence. In this case, since the state is stored in the menu itself, the state of each item would be unchanged if the CMenu wrapper object were to be deleted and then recreated.

3.5.1 Item State

Menu items can be in one of three states:

Enabled	Item is selectable; it is displayed in normal font.
Disabled	Item is not selectable; it is displayed in normal font. Can be used as a title for a group of items.
Grayed	Item is not selectable; it is displayed with gray text

CMenu::EnableMenuItem changes the state of an item:

```
UINT EnableMenuItem( UINT id, UINT state );
```

where

state	is one of MF_ENABLED, MF_DISABLED, or MF_GRAYED, corresponding to the item states.
id	is either the command ID associated with the item or the ordinal position of the item in the menu (with the first position being zero). If ID is the position, add the MF_BYPOSITION flag to state, otherwise add the MF_BYCOMMAND flag.

There is an additional subtlety for MFC-wrapped objects. As already noted, because menu items remember their own state, the CMenu object is not needed for persistence. Its primary purpose is to provide a convenient set of operations on menus. Thus, creating a temporary CMenu object to manipulate a menu often suffices. For example, the Menu program's Enable command enables and grays items on its menu. It uses a temporary CMenu:

```
void mainFrame::onEnable()
{
    CMenu *menu = mainMenu.GetSubMenu(1);
    menu->EnableMenuItem(IDX_DynMenu,MF_BYPOSITION|MF_ENABLED);
    menu->EnableMenuItem(IDM_Enable,MF_BYCOMMAND|MF_GRAYED);
    menu->EnableMenuItem(IDM_Gray,MF_BYCOMMAND|MF_ENABLED);
}
```

In the above code, GetSubMenu retrieves a pointer to a temporary CMenu for the Enable submenu. Temporary objects are deleted by MFC during idle time, so they should only be used during the processing of the message in which they were created.[6]

3.5.2 Item Contents

In addition to state, text menu items have a string and may have an attached bitmap. ModifyMenu changes the string and ID of an item; CheckMenuItem sets and clears a standard checkmark bitmap. Both are illustrated by the Menu program.

Initially the submenu appears as it does in Figure 3.1. The Check command changes the menu to that of Figure 3.3:

```
void mainFrame::onCheck()
{
    m_mainMenu.ModifyMenu(IDM_Check,MF_BYCOMMAND,IDM_Uncheck,
     _T("un&Check"));
    m_mainMenu.CheckMenuItem(IDM_Uncheck,MF_BYCOMMAND|MF_CHECKED);
}
```

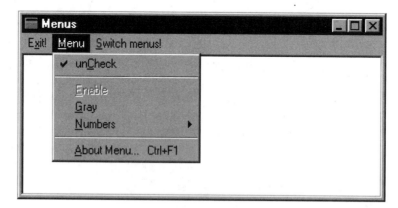

Figure 3.3   The Check command changes the text and bitmap of the first menu item.

---

[6] You might be concerned that deleting the temporary CMenu might delete the underlying menu. Temporary wrapper objects in MFC are detached from the underlying Win32 object before being deleted.

The item that used to be Check is now Uncheck. The Uncheck command restores the menu's original state:

```
void mainFrame::onUncheck()
{
    m_mainMenu.ModifyMenu(IDM_Uncheck,MF_BYCOMMAND,IDM_Check,_T("&Check"));
    m_mainMenu.CheckMenuItem(IDM_Check,MF_BYCOMMAND|MF_UNCHECKED);
}
```

As with `EnableMenuItem`, the item can be referenced either by ID or by position. Referencing by ID is preferable, since the code won't break if menu items are rearranged. Also, when referring to a menu item by ID, it is not necessary to get the submenu that contains the ID, as would be required for `MF_BYPOSITION` (see `onEnable` in the previous section). If you look at Figure 3.3 you'll see that the Check/Uncheck item appears not on the menu bar encapsulated by `m_mainMenu` but on a submenu.

3.6 Dynamic Menus

There are times when a program must create a menu dynamically. The Window menu in many applications is a good example. It grows and shrinks depending on the windows displayed in the application. User-configurable menus are another example, as is modification of the system menu and replacement of the menu bar.

The operations to grow and shrink a menu are just what you'd expect: *Append*, *Insert*, and *Delete*. The Menu program creates a dynamic menu with three items (shown cascaded in Figure 3.1):

```
mainFrame::mainFrame()
{
. . .
    CMenu dynMenu;
    dynMenu.CreatePopupMenu();
    dynMenu.AppendMenu(MF_STRING,IDM_Numbers+1,_T("One"));
    dynMenu.AppendMenu(MF_STRING,IDM_Numbers+2,_T("Two"));
    dynMenu.AppendMenu(MF_STRING,IDM_Numbers+3,_T("Three"));

    CMenu *menu = m_mainMenu.GetSubMenu(1);
    menu->InsertMenu(IDX_DynMenu,MF_POPUP|MF_BYPOSITION,
        (UINT)dynMenu.m_hMenu,_T("&Numbers"));
    dynMenu.Detach();
}
```

CreatePopupMenu creates and attaches a menu to the CMenu object dynMenu. The dynamic menu is then inserted into the menu at position IDX_DynMenu with the text "<u>N</u>umbers". We have no choice but to use MF_BYPOSITION in the call to InsertMenu because submenus do not have associated IDs.

Calling Detach disconnects the C++ object from the underlying menu, preventing the newly created menu from being destroyed when dynMenu is destructed. Unlike the case of deleting a temporary wrapper object, deleting dynMenu *would* delete the attached Win32 menu.

3.6.1 The Menu Bar

Many programs have more than one menu tree. A common case is for a program to have a very simple menu on startup and a more complex menu after the user opens a file.

CWnd::SetMenu changes the menu for a window. The Menu program's Switch Menu command switches between m_mainMenu and m_altMenu:

```
void mainFrame::onSwitchMenus()
{
    if( GetMenu()->m_hMenu == m_mainMenu.m_hMenu )
        // Switch to alternate
        SetMenu(&m_altMenu);
    else
        // Restore main menu
        SetMenu(&m_mainMenu);
}
```

GetMenu returns the menu associated with a window, but notice I don't compare the CWnd * returned from GetMenu with m_mainMenu or m_altMenu. Like GetSub-Menu, GetMenu may return a pointer to a temporary CMenu, not necessarily the pointer used in the call to SetMenu. All that is guaranteed is that the Win32 menu will be the same. The Win32 menu is referenced by its handle, m_hMenu (see Figure 3.4).

3.6.2 The System Menu

The system menu is triggered by clicking on the button in the upper-left corner of a window or by pressing Alt+Space. Most applications share a standard system menu. To use a modified system menu, an application asks for a copy of the standard and then applies the changes. The Menu program appends an

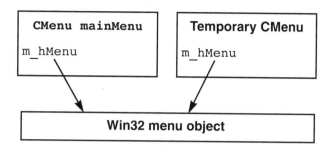

Figure 3.4 . Attaching a Win32 menu to a CMenu object sets the m_hMenu field. Although every menu has a unique handle, two CMenus can refer to the same menu.

About Menu command to the system menu (see Figure 3.5). This code is in the constructor for mainFrame:

```
mainFrame::mainFrame()
{
. . .
    CMenu *sysMenu = GetSystemMenu(FALSE);
    sysMenu->AppendMenu(MF_STRING|MF_ENABLED,IDM_AboutMenu,
        _T("About Menu...\tCtrl+F1"));
```

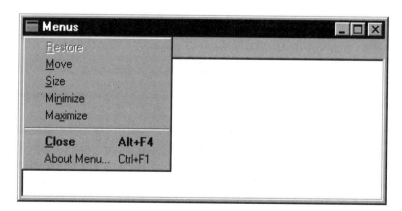

Figure 3.5 The Menu program adds the About Menu command to the system menu.

GetSystemMenu retrieves a copy of the system menu when its parameter is false. When the parameter is true, it restores the standard system menu.

When the user selects an item from the system menu, the application receives the WM_SYSCOMMAND message instead of WM_COMMAND. To pick up a command on the system menu, create an OnSysCommand handler:

```
void mainFrame::OnSysCommand(UINT id, LPARAM lParam)
{
    switch(id) {
    case IDM_AboutMenu:
        onAboutMenu();
        return;
    }
    CFrameWnd::OnSysCommand(id,lParam);
}
```

3.6.3 Context Menus

A common use of the right mouse button is to trigger a context popup menu for operating on the currently selected object. By default, the right mouse button is the rightmost button, but since a user may swap the buttons using the control panel, the "right" button may actually be the leftmost button on the mouse. The context menu usually appears underneath the mouse so that an item can be selected easily.

When the right mouse button is pressed, Win32 generates the WM_CONTEXTMENU message. The Menu program responds to WM_CONTEXTMENU by showing the Menu popup (see Figure 3.2):

```
void mainFrame::OnContextMenu(CPoint point)
{
    CMenu *menu = m_mainMenu.GetSubMenu(1);
    menu->TrackPopupMenu(TPM_CENTERALIGN|TPM_RIGHTBUTTON,
        point.x,point.y,
        this);
}
```

The parameter point indicates the mouse position in screen coordinates when the button was pressed. TrackPopupMenu triggers the floating popup menu. In this example, the context menu is a copy of the Menu drop-down from the main menu. The style TPM_CENTERALIGN specifies that the top-center of the menu is placed directly underneath the mouse cursor. Notice again that I am using a temporary CMenu for convenience.

Pressing Shift+F10, or the "context-menu key" on some keyboards, also triggers WM_CONTEXTMENU. In this case, the X and Y parameters are each set to -1. If the negative coordinates are used directly, as in the OnContextMenu function above, the menu will appear in the upper-left corner of the screen. Since a right-mouse click will never generate negative coordinates, a program can easily determine when WM_CONTEXTMENU is triggered by the keyboard and perhaps move the context menu to someplace within the application.

The message WM_CONTEXTMENU was new in Windows 95. Before Windows 95, programs triggered context menus in response to the WM_RBUTTONDOWN message. For example:

```
void mainFrame::OnRButtonDown(UINT nFlags, CPoint point)
{
    CMenu *menu = mainMenu.GetSubMenu(1);
    ClientToScreen(&point);
    menu->TrackPopupMenu(TPM_CENTERALIGN|TPM_RIGHTBUTTON,
        point.x,point.y,
        this);
}
```

Unlike WM_CONTEXTMENU, WM_RBUTTONDOWN gives the mouse position relative to the origin of the window's client area. Since TrackPopupMenu wants the position relative to the origin of the display screen, a call to ClientToScreen is needed to perform the translation.

3.7   Keyboard Commands

Although most people use a mouse to operate graphical programs, there are times when a mouse is unavailable or inconvenient. All of a program's functionality should be accessible using the keyboard.

Win32 provides three ways that keystrokes trigger commands:

Mnemonic key   Pressing the Alt key in combination with a specified character from a menu item triggers the item. The character is called the item's *mnemonic*. By default, the mnemonic is the first character of the item. When creating a menu, place an ampersand (**&**) in front of any character in the item to make that character the mnemonic and to have the mnemonic character underlined.

Menu key   Pressing the Alt key by itself causes the first item on the menu bar to be highlighted. Keystrokes that follow are then interpreted in the context of the menu. For example, the left and right arrow move the highlight along the menu bar.

Accelerator key   An accelerator key is a program-defined binding of certain keystrokes to a WM_COMMAND message with a specified ID. The keystrokes can be single keys or various shift combinations. If the ID associated with an accelerator is the same as a menu item, then pressing the accelerator behaves like selecting the item.

3.8 Accelerators

An *accelerator* is a combination of keystrokes that are bound to a command. The keystrokes can be any alphanumeric key, either alone or in combination with Shift, Alt, or Ctrl. The function keys and the special keys like Home and End, again in combination with the shift keys, can also be specified as accelerators.

Accelerators are specified statically in a resource file, or dynamically using the API function CreateAcceleratorTable. The steps for creating accelerators statically are:

1. Create the accelerator table resource.
2. Load the accelerator table.
3. Watch for accelerator keystrokes.

The accelerator table can be created inside most resource editors or it can be created easily in a text editor. The table for the Menu program defines a single accelerator, F1+Ctrl, for the About Menu command:

```
IDA_MainFrame ACCELERATORS DISCARDABLE
BEGIN
  VK_F1,  IDM_AboutMenu,  VIRTKEY, CONTROL, NOINVERT
END
```

The table is loaded in the constructor for the main window:

```
LoadAccelTable(MAKEINTRESOURCE(IDA_MainFrame));
```

The API has a function, TranslateAccelerator, that translates accelerator keystrokes into commands given an accelerator table. MFC's standard message loop calls the API with a reference to the accelerator table associated with the current frame window. Besides loading the accelerator resource, CFrameWnd::LoadAccelTable associates the table with the frame window.

When the user presses an accelerator, Win32 generates a WM_COMMAND message, just as when a menu item is selected. As a result, the same code that processes a menu item can process the corresponding accelerator. Of course, just as not all menu items need to have a corresponding accelerator, not all accelerators need to correspond to a menu item. That is, an accelerator can be a keyboard command that does not appear on any menu.

3.9   More on Menus

This chapter presented the basic types of menus and operations on them. In Chapter 10 we'll look at how MFC's application framework helps manage menus. Chapter 11 illustrates how the Framework enhances menus by displaying help text.

CHAPTER

4 | Dialogs

The program in the `Dialog` directory illustrates the concepts discussed in this chapter. The corresponding executable in the `bin` directory is `Dialog.exe`.

4.1   Introduction

A dialog consists of a collection of child windows contained inside a frame window. The child windows are called *controls*, just like the buttons and switches on a control panel. There are two basic types of controls, static and dynamic. Static controls display information but don't directly respond to user input. Examples of static controls are text labels, icons, and gauges. Dynamic controls accept user input and send notification messages to the frame window. Buttons, sliders, list boxes, and edit fields are all dynamic controls. Figure 4.1 shows a simple dialog onscreen; Figure 4.2 shows the parent-child relationships of the dialog's windows.

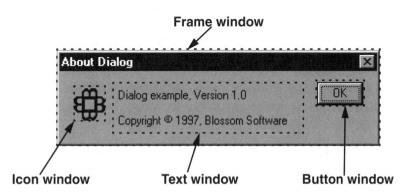

Figure 4.1   A dialog is a collection of child windows, called controls, contained inside a frame window.

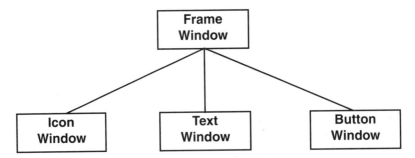

Figure 4.2   The frame window is the parent of the control windows.

Dialogs come in a variety of forms and behave in different ways. The basic divide in behavior is modal versus modeless. *Modal* dialogs query for information, waiting for the user to confirm or abort the query. They are modal in that the program has entered dialog-input mode; only the dialog box and its controls are active. Selections made in the dialog do not take effect until the dialog is confirmed, typically by pressing an OK button. The File Open dialog is an example of a modal dialog.

By contrast, *modeless* dialogs don't inhibit input to other parts of the program. The user can switch between a modeless dialog and other windows in the program without having to confirm or abort the dialog. Selections in a modeless dialog often take effect immediately. Search dialogs are usually modeless.

4.2   Message Boxes

The simplest modal dialog to create is a message box, as in the Hello program in Chapter 2. A message box displays lines of text, an optional icon, and from one to four buttons.[1] The size of the box will adjust to the amount of text. The return value from the message-box function tells the program which button was selected. To create a message box, create a string and then call one of three different message-box functions:

```
int AfxMessageBox( LPCTSTR text, UINT type=MB_OK, UINT helpID=0 );
int AfxMessageBox( UINT textID, UINT type=MB_OK, UINT helpID=-1 );
int CWnd::MessageBox( LPCTSTR text, LPCTSTR caption=NULL,
    UINT type=MB_OK );
```

---

[1] In Win16, message boxes can only have three buttons. Specifying MB_ABORTRETRYIGNORE|MB_HELP for the type parameter generates a four-button message box.

where

text	is the message displayed in the box. The data type LPCTSTR is a pointer to a constant TSTR. A TSTR is a string with either 8- or 16-bit characters; the size is determined by compile time flags (see Section 4.6).
textID	is the ID of a string resource containing the message to be displayed in the box.
type	controls the number of buttons, the labels on the buttons, and the icon to be displayed in the box.
caption	is the title of the box.
helpID	is a context number used in a call to WinHelp if F1 is pressed while the box is active.

Both CWnd::MessageBox and AfxMessageBox call the Win32 MessageBox function. AfxMessageBox puts the application name into the title bar of the dialog and allows a resource ID to be used instead of a string for the message. CWnd::MessageBox gives the program control over the title bar.

The Message Box command in the Dialog program brings up the Yes/No message box shown in Figure 4.3. The code is in mainfrm.cpp:

```
void mainFrame::onMessageBox()
{
    if( AfxMessageBox(IDS_MessageBox,MB_YESNO|MB_ICONQUESTION)==IDYES )
        onSimple();
}
```

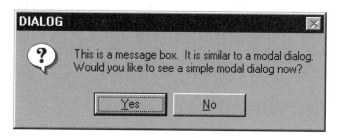

Figure 4.3 The Message Box command in the Dialog program brings up this Yes/No message box.

The message box contains an icon, two push buttons, and a string. The icon and the number of buttons are specified by setting flags in the type parameter. The icon can be one of a fixed set that message boxes can display.

Pressing the Yes button causes AfxMessageBox to return IDYES. In the Dialog program, IDYES triggers the simple modal dialog shown in Figure 4.1.

The string is specified by resource ID. Putting strings in a resource file is good practice. Not only does collecting the strings in one place make it easier to guarantee consistency of wording, it simplifies translation of the strings to other languages.[2] IDS_MessageBox refers to a string in the resource script app.rc:

```
STRINGTABLE DISCARDABLE
BEGIN
  IDS_MessageBox   "This is ... a modal dialog.\nWould you ... now?"
END
```

In specifying the string for the message box, you can let the box wrap the text itself or you can force an explicit line break by inserting a literal \n into the string.

4.3 Simple Modal Dialogs

To get more control over the appearance of a dialog than message boxes provide, create a dialog resource. The resource specifies the layout of the controls inside the dialog frame. A simple dialog consisting of just static controls and one or two push buttons doesn't require much more code than a message box. Follow these steps:

1. Create a dialog resource.
2. Instantiate the CDialog class. Pass the name of the dialog resource as a parameter to the constructor.
3. Call DoModal on the CDialog object.

Figure 4.4 illustrates how the steps relate for a dialog named IDD_About.[3]

---

[2] After having praised the virtues of using string resources, you'll find that the programs in this text usually use string literals. I've chosen to ignore my own advice in order to make the programs more readable.

[3] Prior to MFC 4, DoModal called ::DialogBox, as indicated in the figure. However, ::DialogBox has its own message loop, which would circumvent MFC's ability to alter default message handling via routines such as PreTranslateMessage and PumpMessage.

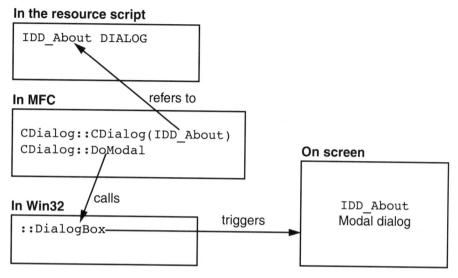

In the resource script

```
IDD_About DIALOG
```

In MFC   refers to

```
CDialog::CDialog(IDD_About)
CDialog::DoModal
```

On screen

In Win32   calls

```
::DialogBox
```
triggers

```
IDD_About
Modal dialog
```

Figure 4.4   CDialog::DoModal triggers a modal dialog based on the associated resource. It simulates a call to the Win32 function DialogBox to run the dialog.

4.3.1 Creating a Dialog Resource

Resource editors make it easy to lay out dialog controls and set their properties. However, you may need to tune the resource script in a text editor, depending on the capability of the resource editor. An important property of each control is its integer ID. The ID is delivered in notification messages from the control to the parent. Static controls generally don't need unique IDs because they don't generate notifications.

Modal dialogs nearly always have confirm and cancel buttons. The confirm button is usually labeled OK or Done, and has the associated ID IDOK. The cancel button is usually named Cancel or perhaps Quit and has the ID IDCANCEL.

Most controls have style flags that affect appearance and behavior, depending upon the type of the control (see Chapter 6 for a rundown of each control type). One thing to remember when working with controls is that they are windows. This simple fact has important ramifications. For example, controls can be moved, resized, disabled, and hidden using member functions from the MFC wrapper class for windows, CWnd. Chapter 5 covers properties of and operations on windows.

The dialog resource needs to be named. As with other resources but unlike controls, the dialog name can either be a string or an integer ID.

4.3.1.1 Meta Keys and Tab Order

Although most people operate dialogs using the mouse, some people use the keyboard. When creating a dialog, keep keyboard usage in mind by setting the tab order and creating mnemonics. The following meta keys are active in a dialog:

Key	Action
Tab (Shift+Tab)	Activates the next (previous) control with the WS_TABSTOP style. Most dynamic controls have WS_TABSTOP set by default.
Arrow	Operates some controls, such as list boxes, edit controls, and sliders. For buttons in a group, an arrow moves the focus to the next button in the direction of the arrow.
Alt+letter	Specifies a mnemonic, as for menus. Use & in the text label for a control to specify the mnemonic. When pressed, the next dynamic control following the label will become active.
Enter	Presses the button if the focus is on a button. Otherwise it presses the default button. One button in a dialog can be given the BS_DEFPUSHBUTTON style. If no button is the default, Enter generates WM_COMMAND with IDOK.
Esc	Generates WM_COMMAND with IDCANCEL.

The choice of the "next" control is determined by the order in which the controls appear in the dialog resource. This order is called the *tab order*, and is setable from the resource editor.[4] Users expect the Tab key to activate controls left-to-right (or, possibly, right-to-left) and top-to-bottom. It is up to you to set the tab order so that activation flows in a natural way.

4.3.2 Instantiating CDialog

CDialog has two constructors: one takes a string, the other an integer ID. The constructor binds a dialog resource to the C++ dialog object. The two constructors correspond to the two ways of naming a resource. A simple dialog doesn't have persistent state and so it can be wrapped with an automatic variable just before use.

---

[4] In Visual C++, look for Tab Order under the Layout menu.

The Dialog Simple command in the Dialog program triggers the simple About dialog shown in Figure 4.1. Here is the code that instantiates CDialog and triggers the dialog:

```
void mainFrame::onSimple()
{
    CDialog dlg(IDD_About);
    dlg.DoModal();
}
```

4.3.3 Calling DoModal

DoModal runs the dialog. Simple dialog boxes run by themselves; the static controls and buttons draw themselves. While DoModal is running, windows outside of the dialog are disabled, so they don't receive keyboard or mouse input.

Responding to a button press is just like responding to a menu selection. The button generates a WM_COMMAND message containing its ID, so the dialog object must have an ON_COMMAND message-map entry for the ID. CDialog has map entries for IDOK and IDCANCEL, binding them to the virtual functions OnOK and OnCancel. The default implementation of these functions terminates the dialog.

4.4   More Complex Modal Dialogs

Dialogs of more complexity, containing other buttons or active controls, require more program support. To extend the behavior of CDialog, derive a new class from it. The derived class typically adds startup behavior and handlers for each of the controls added to the dialog.

In MFC there are two basic ways of overriding a function implemented in a base class:

- If the function is virtual, reimplement the function in a derived class.
- For non-virtual message handlers, create a message-map entry that binds the message to the function.[5]

To create handlers for the OK and Cancel buttons, it is sufficient to create the member functions OnOK and OnCancel, since they are virtual. For other controls, you'll need to create the member functions and the message-map entries that

---

[5] Recall that MFC uses message maps to mimic virtual functions. I suppose such functions could be called "virtual" virtual functions, in contrast to the "real" virtual functions of C++.

correspond to the notification messages sent by the control. Tools like Class-Wizard make this job simpler by letting you choose from a list of all the notifications generated by the standard controls.

The Dialog Modal command in the Dialog program illustrates initializing a dialog and handling of custom commands. It triggers the dialog shown in Figure 4.5.

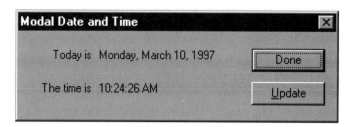

Figure 4.5   The Dialog Modal command brings up this modal dialog box.

On startup, the date and time are set according to the system clock. When the Update button is pressed, the date and time are updated. The dateDialog class, derived from CDialog, wraps the dialog. Here is the start of the class declaration as generated by ClassWizard (it's in the file date.h):

```
class dateDialog : public CDialog
{
// Construction
public:
    dateDialog(CWnd* pParent=NULL,BOOL modal=TRUE);

// Dialog Data
    //{{AFX_DATA(dateDialog)
    enum { IDD = IDD_Date };
    //}}AFX_DATA
```

Interspersed in the declaration are special comments used by ClassWizard to demarcate the blocks of code it maintains. Among other chores, ClassWizard adds and deletes declarations for member functions. However, ClassWizard doesn't parse C++, it just looks for its special commands embedded in comments. The start-of-block comments always begin with {{AFX_ and the end-of-block comments with //}}AFX_. If you want to use ClassWizard on your files, don't delete these comments. Also, ClassWizard will throw away lines in its blocks that it doesn't understand. It's best to add your own entries outside the ClassWizard blocks.

The constructor for `dateDialog` connects the dialog resource to the C++ object via the class constant IDD[6] and then triggers the dialog by calling DoModal:

```
dateDialog::dateDialog(CWnd* pParent /*=NULL*/, BOOL modal)
   : CDialog(dateDialog::IDD, pParent)
{
    m_isModal = modal;
    if(m_isModal)
        DoModal();
    else
        Create(IDD);
}
```

The `modal` flag allows `dateDialog` to be used as a modeless dialog as described in Section 4.5.

4.4.1 OnInitDialog

Before a dialog is displayed, the dialog frame window receives the WM_INITDIALOG message. The corresponding member function, OnInitDialog, is a good place to give controls their initial values and make any dynamic modifications to the dialog, such as moving or resizing it.

In `OnInitDialog`, `dateDialog` sets the dialog title and the initial date and time:

```
BOOL dateDialog::OnInitDialog()
{
    CDialog::OnInitDialog();
    SetWindowText( m_isModal ?
        _T("Modal Date and Time") : _T("Modeless Date and Time"));

    setDateAndTime();

    return TRUE; // return TRUE unless you set the focus to a control
}
```

`SetWindowText` is a member of `CWnd` that, depending on the window style, sets either the title bar or the window contents. It is described in Chapter 5.

`dateDialog::setDateAndTime` retrieves the current time, formats it, and writes it to the date and time controls:

---

[6] C++ doesn't support class-scope constants directly. IDD is defined as an enumeration in the class declaration. Since the enumeration has class scope, the constants in the enumeration have class scope.

```
void dateDialog::setDateAndTime()
{
    CTime t = CTime::GetCurrentTime();
    SetDlgItemText(IDC_Date,
        t.Format(_T("%A, %B %#d, %Y")));
    SetDlgItemText(IDC_Time,
        t.Format(_T("%I:%M:%S %p")));
}
```

SetDlgItemText takes the ID of the control to modify and a string to write. The control will make a copy of the string. This is fortunate, since setDateAndTime uses temporary CString objects to hold the date and time strings. The objects are created by the CTime::Format function. Each CString is coerced to a LPCT-STR because that's how the second argument to SetDlgItemText is declared; then it's passed to SetDlgItemText. Some time after they are used and before the end of setDateAndTime, the temporary CStrings will be deleted.

4.4.2 Responding to Dialog Controls

I mentioned that CDialog has default behavior for buttons that return either IDOK or IDCANCEL. There is no default behavior for other ID values, such as IDC_Update in the date and time dialog of Figure 4.5.

To handle the Update command, a message-map entry and member function must be added to the dateDialog class. The notification BN_CLICKED is sent when the Update button is pressed; the corresponding message-map entry in date.cpp is ON_BN_CLICKED:[7]

```
ON_BN_CLICKED(IDC_Update, onUpdate)
```

IDC_Update is the ID of the Update button and onUpdate is the handler function. Other controls send other notifications. See Chapter 6 for more details.

The onUpdate function calls setDateAndTime to update the dialog:

```
void dateDialog::onUpdate()
{
    setDateAndTime();
}
```

---

[7] MFC treats notifications like messages. The notification BN_CLICKED is delivered as a parameter in a WM_COMMAND message. Hence, a button click could also be picked up with an ON_COMMAND message-map entry.

4.5 Modeless Dialogs

The advent of larger and higher resolution displays has made modeless dialogs more attractive as an alternative to choosing commands from a menu. A single click on a control in a modeless dialog can trigger a command that might take several clicks and mouse moves through a menu.

Modeless dialogs are similar to modal in that their layout is specified by a resource. In fact, the same resource can be used for both a modal and a modeless dialog, as illustrated by the Dialog program. The same code that responds to controls in a modal dialog works for modeless dialog as well. When a button is pressed, for example, it sends the BN_CLICKED notification to the dialog frame window. However, there are some important differences in the way the two types of dialogs are programmed:

Operation	Modal	Modeless
Invocation	DoModal	CDialog::Create
OnOK, OnCancel	Can inherit	Must not inherit
Termination	Inherit from OnOK and OnCancel	CWnd::DestroyWindow
Meta keys	Automatic in Windows	Inherit from CWnd[a]

[a] If you have programmed a modeless dialog using the API, you know that meta keys are handled by the roundabout technique of putting a call to ::IsDialogMessage into the program's message loop. MFC accomplishes this by calling the virtual function PreTranslateMessage in the message loop. CWnd::PreTranslateMessage calls ::IsDialogMessage.

The dateDialog class illustrates these differences since the class can be used both modally and modelessly. The second parameter to the constructor determines which type of dialog is created:

```
dateDialog::dateDialog(CWnd* pParent /*=NULL*/, BOOL modal)
    : CDialog(dateDialog::IDD, pParent)
{
    m_isModal = modal;
    if(m_isModal)
        DoModal();
    else
        Create(IDD);
}
```

For modeless dialogs, the constructor calls Create. CDialog::Create creates the dialog frame and child windows, calls OnInitDialog, then displays the dialog. Unlike DoModal, Create returns immediately after the dialog is created; thus the dialog object is created on the heap rather than the stack:

```
void mainFrame::onModeless()
{
    dateDialog *dlg = new dateDialog(this,FALSE);
}
```

The Update command is the same for both types of dialogs, but OnOK and OnCancel are different. Recall that the default behavior for these functions is to terminate a modal dialog. The modeless dialog must not inherit this behavior. Instead, it terminates the dialog window explicitly by calling CWnd::-DestroyWindow:

```
void dateDialog::OnOK()
{
    if(m_isModal)
        CDialog::OnOK();
    else
        DestroyWindow();
}
```

Even if a modeless dialog does not have buttons with IDs IDOK and IDCANCEL, it must override OnOK and OnCancel. Recall from Section 4.3.1.1 that the Enter key can generate IDOK and Esc can generate IDCANCEL.

Destroying the frame window destroys all the controls as well. Once the windows are destroyed, it is safe to delete the dateDialog wrapper object. The virtual function PostNcDestroy performs this final task:

```
void dateDialog::PostNcDestroy()
{
    if(!isModal) delete this;
}
```

See Chapter 5 for a complete discussion of how to destroy a window.

4.6 Internationalization

The problem of representing the characters of the world's languages has spawned a variety of solutions.[8] All the solutions use characters wider than the C++ default of 8 bits. The C data type wchar_t, the multi-byte library functions, and the concept of *locale*, were invented to assist in the creation of language-neutral programs.

---

[8] For an in-depth reference, see *Developing International Software for Windows 95 and Windows NT*, by Nadine Kano, Microsoft Press, 1995.

Win32 encapsulates the various representations of text with the _T macro and the TCHAR data type. Based on compile-time macros, _T turns string literals into either narrow or wide strings. For instance, if _UNICODE is defined, _T("stuff") becomes L"stuff"; otherwise it becomes simply "stuff". Likewise, the TCHAR data type and its derivatives are sensitive to the same compile-time macros. When _UNICODE is defined, TCHAR is synonymous with wchar_t; otherwise it is the same as char.

The issue extends to the string functions in the standard C and Win32 libraries. For functions that take strings or characters, the prototype will change according to whether _UNICODE is defined. For example, while the prototype for the ANSI C function strcmp will always be pointers to char, the Win32 string comparison function lstrcmp will take pointers to char or wchar_t, depending on the value of _UNICODE.

Although I won't pay attention to most issues of internationalization, the string literals in this book will be wrapped by _T and the char data type by TCHAR. Also, I'll use the locale-sensitive string functions—for example, lstrcmp instead of strcmp—although mostly I'll use CString and resources to avoid the whole issue. CStrings are based on TCHAR so that they automatically adapt at compile time. The resource compiler always generates wide strings, narrowing them only if needed.

4.7 More on Dialogs

This chapter presented just the basics of dialogs. The real work in dialogs goes on in the dialog controls. Chapter 6 covers the standard controls. Built into Win32 are dialogs for common tasks like getting a file name or setting up a printer. Chapter 7 covers these Common Dialogs. Some programs are not much more than a collection of dialogs. Form-based programs are described in Chapter 12 and dialog-based programs in Chapter 14.

CHAPTER

5 | Windows and Messages

The program in the `Window` directory illustrates the concepts discussed in this chapter. The corresponding executable in the `bin` directory is `Window.exe`.

5.1 Introduction

All activity in Win32 revolves around window objects. In Chapter 2 you saw that events trigger messages and that messages always have a target window. In an MFC program, each window has a corresponding C++ object from a CWnd-derived class. When a message arrives for a window, a corresponding member function is found by searching through a series of message maps.

In Win32, each window has an integer ID known as its *handle*. API functions use the handle to identify the window. CWnd has a data member, m_hWnd, that contains the handle and allows CWnd member functions to call the API. Figure 5.1 shows the relationship of a CWnd to a window.

5.2 Win32 Window Classes

Every window in Win32 belongs to some window class. Just as a C++ class implements member functions that determine the behavior of an object, a *window class* implements responses to messages. Associated with each class is a *window procedure* that receives a message number as a parameter and responds appropriately for the class.

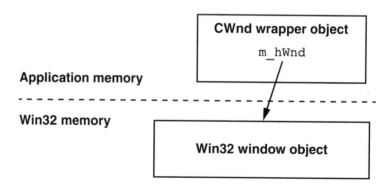

Figure 5.1   The C++ object is attached to the Win32 object via the m_hWnd data member. Member functions in the CWnd class use m_hWnd in calls to the API to affect the underlying window.

Win32 comes with about 30 built-in window classes, most of which are dialog controls. Common examples include:[1]

`Button`	For push-buttons, radio buttons, and check-boxes
`Edit`	For text editors
`Static`	For labels, icons, bitmaps, and rectangles
`msctls_trackbar32`	For sliders
`SysTreeView32`	For trees

5.3 MFC Window Classes

The MFC library has specialized classes for each of the classes built into Win32, as well as classes unique to MFC. For the Win32 classes listed above, the corresponding MFC classes are `CButton`, `CEdit`, `CStatic`, `CSliderCtrl`, and `CTreeCtrl`. Usually, the dividing line between functionality implemented in Win32 and MFC is not important. In fact, as Windows has evolved, classes that first appeared in MFC, such as toolbars and tabbed dialogs, have migrated into Win32.

There are times, however, when you'll need to know whether a class is implemented in Win32 or in the MFC library. Although you should first look in the MFC manual for reference material about a class, occasionally the MFC reference falls

---

[1] The different naming conventions reflect the era in which the classes were added to the API. The Win32 header file `commctrl.h` has macros to hide the naming differences.

short. If you know that the class is implemented in Win32, you can look in the API manual for more details.

A primary challenge in writing a Win32 program is knowing which events need a response and what the response should be. The Spy[2] program lets you watch messages as they are delivered to a window. Since messages trigger member functions, tools like Spy are an important part of the MFC programmer's toolbox.

5.4 The Lifecycle of a Window

Each window receives a sequence of messages as it goes through its lifecycle of creation, existence, and termination. The following sections examine the important messages of each phase.

Just as a window is divided into client and nonclient areas, some messages apply to the nonclient area and thus are usually handled by the window manager. If you want to change the appearance or behavior of a window's title bar or border, your program can process these messages. Nonclient message names begin with the prefix WM_NC. Many nonclient messages have a client-area counterpart. The nonclient messages are not listed below.

5.4.1 Window Creation

A window is created in response to the CreateWindow API call. MFC has many specialized Create functions that call ::CreateWindow. Here are prototypes for a few of them to give you the idea:

```
BOOL CWnd::Create(
    LPCTSTR className,
    LPCTSTR windowName,
    DWORD style,
    const RECT& rect,
    CWnd* ownerWnd,
    UINT id,
    CCreateContext* context = NULL)
```

---

[2] Spy was an early message-watching tool. Many Spy-like programs are available. Visual C++ comes with an enhanced version of Spy called Spy++.

```
BOOL CFrameWnd::Create(
    LPCTSTR className,
    LPCTSTR windowName,
    DWORD style = WS_OVERLAPPEDWINDOW,
    const RECT& rect = rectDefault,
    CWnd* ownerWnd = NULL,
    LPCTSTR menuName = NULL,
    DWORD styleEx = 0,
    CCreateContext* context = NULL )

BOOL CButton::Create(
    LPCTSTR lpszCaption,
    DWORD style,
    const RECT& rect,
    CWnd* ownerWnd,
    UINT id )
```

where

className	is the name of a Win32 window class.
windowName	is the text for the title bar, if the window can have one. Otherwise, it is the text inside the window.
style	is a set of flags that control the behavior and appearance of the window.
rect	specifies the position and size of the window.
ownerWnd	is the owner or parent window. See the distinction between WS_CHILD and WS_POPUP in Section 5.4.1.2.
menuName	is the name of the menu resource for frame windows.
styleEx	contains flags for the extended (newer) styles, such as WS_EX_TOPMOST and WS_EX_ACCEPTFILES.
id	is the ID associated with a control. The ID is delivered with notifications to the parent.
context	is used by MFC's application framework to connect a frame window to the objects it contains.

5.4.1.1 Window Classes

The window class in the Create calls above refers to the *Win32* window class. Often this is NULL, indicating that MFC should use its default window class. You'll need to specify a class if you want to have other than the standard cursor, background color, or icon for a window, since these attributes are specified in the Win32 class.

The easiest way to get a class with the desired attributes is to create one with the global MFC function AfxRegisterWndClass:

```
LPCTSTR AFXAPI AfxRegisterWndClass(
    UINT nClassStyle,
    HCURSOR hCursor = 0,
    HBRUSH hbrBackground = 0,
    HICON hIcon = 0 );
```

AfxRegisterWndClass returns the name of a class with the specified attributes, so it can be used right in a Create call.[3] Other than the changed attributes, the new window class has no effect on the window's behavior. As an example, the Window Explorer program described later in this chapter creates each new child window with a different background color. It uses AfxRegisterWndClass to specify the color:

```
CreateEx(
    AfxRegisterWndClass(CS_HREDRAW|CS_VREDRAW, // Class style
        theApp.LoadStandardCursor(IDC_ARROW),   // Cursor
        (HBRUSH)brush.m_hObject,                 // Background color
        theApp.LoadIcon(IDI_APPLICATION)),       // Icon
.  .  .
)
```

5.4.1.2 Window and Class Styles

A window's style controls its appearance and affects its behavior. There are style flags to control the type of border for a window, the buttons within the title bar, when and how the window is redrawn, and whether the window is active and visible. Some style flags are part of the class definition, such as the CS_HREDRAW and CS_VREDRAW flags, which force redrawing of the window when its size changes. Other flags are specified in the Create call. Look up ::Register-Class in the API manual for the class styles and ::CreateWindow for the window styles.

A primary determinant of window behavior is the choice of the WS_CHILD or WS_POPUP window style. A *child* window is clipped by its parent; that is, it cannot extend beyond the boundaries of its parent window. By contrast, a *popup* window can be moved anywhere on the screen. Document windows in a word processor are WS_CHILD; dialogs are usually WS_POPUP.

---

[3] The class name generated by AfxRegisterWndClass will begin with the prefix Afx. If you use Spy to look at the windows in an application, you can tell if the program was written using MFC by the presence of window classes with the Afx prefix.

The child and popup window styles point out a subtle difference between an owner window and a parent. The ownerWnd parameter to the Create call specifies both. For child windows, the owner is also the parent. The *parent* is the clipping window; child windows are always contained inside their parent. Because popup windows are not clipped they have no parent, but they still may be owned. The *owner* controls window activation, appearance, and destruction. When an owner window is minimized, all its owned windows disappear. When an owner is closed, all its owned windows are closed.

You can get a feel for child versus popup and owned versus unowned in the Window Explorer program (see Section 5.6). Try creating owned and unowned popup windows, then change applications by pressing Alt+Tab. Since child windows always have a parent for clipping, they are never unowned.

5.4.1.3 Position and Size

The initial position and size of a window are specified as a rectangle, either a RECT or a CRect. RECT is the data structure from the API, CRect is the MFC wrapper class. Rectangles have sides parallel to the axes of the display device. They are specified by two coordinates: the upper left and the lower right. For child windows, the coordinates are relative to the origin of the client area of the parent window; for popup windows, the coordinates are relative to the origin of the screen. When creating a frame window, you can specify a default rectangle, CFrameWnd::rectDefault, to let Win32 choose the initial position and size. For more control, you can create a CRect and use CW_USEDEFAULT for just some of the coordinates. The main window in the Window Explorer uses the default size, but it's always located at the top-left corner of the screen:

```
mainFrame::mainFrame()
{
    // Put window at upper left-hand corner of screen
    CRect rect(0,0,CW_USEDEFAULT,CW_USEDEFAULT);

    if( !Create(
. . .
        rect,                          // Origin and extent
. . .
```

The relationship of CRect to RECT is typical of MFC's wrapper classes. A RECT is a simple structure, as shown in Figure 5.2. A CRect consists of the RECT data structure plus member functions that manipulate the structure. A convenient benefit of this wrapper relationship is that a CRect can be used wherever a RECT is required.

```
class CRect {

    struct RECT {
        LONG left;
        LONG top;
        LONG right;
        LONG bottom;
    };

    int Width();
    int Height();
    CPoint& TopLeft();
    CPoint& BottomRight();
    void CopyRect(CRect *);
    BOOL EqualRect(CRect *);
    . . .
```

Figure 5.2   A CRect is a RECT plus member functions to operate on a RECT.

5.4.1.4 Startup Messages

The call to Create triggers a flurry of messages. Here are the ones you're most likely to be interested in:

WM_GETMINMAXINFO	A resizable window responds to this message to set limits on resizing.
WM_CREATE	This message is used in Win32 like a constructor is used in C++. In MFC, the handler for WM_CREATE is used to create child windows such as tool and status bars.
WM_SIZE	This tells the initial size of the window.
WM_MOVE	This tells the initial coordinates of the window.

5.4.2 Window Existence

While a window exists, it receives many messages. Win32 breaks events into micro steps, each step announced with a message. For most messages the default behavior is usually adequate. Here are some messages that you may commonly need to customize:

WM_PAINT	The window should restore part or all of the client area.
WM_SIZE	The window has been resized.
WM_CHAR	A character has been typed on the keyboard.
WM_MOUSEACTIVATE	A mouse button has been pressed in the window.
WM_MOUSEMOVE	The mouse has been moved.
WM_LBUTTONDOWN	The left mouse button has been pressed.
WM_LBUTTONDBLCLK	The left mouse button has been double clicked.

One message that every visible window needs to process is WM_PAINT. A window receives WM_PAINT when some of its pixels need to be restored. To update the information displayed in a window, programs usually tell Win32 that some portion of the window is out of date, rather than just writing directly to the window. You'll see this behavior in Chapters 8 to draw pictures as well as in Chapter 14 to update a form. Sometimes Win32 itself tells the program that pixels in the window need to be redrawn, such as after the window has been uncovered or resized.

The basic operations for manipulating and inspecting a window are implemented in Win32 and made accessible via member functions of the class CWnd. As a result, CWnd is huge with more than 200 members. Programmers new to MFC are often surprised to learn that functions for manipulating the clipboard, timers, and even dialog controls are part of CWnd. One benefit of putting nearly everything in CWnd is that these functions can be applied to *any* window, since every window class in MFC is derived from CWnd.

Here are some of the more common operations along with the corresponding CWnd member functions:

Move and resize	Use MoveWindow or SetWindowPos.
Retitle	Use SetWindowText.
Enable and disable	Use EnableWindow to enable and disable input. Use SetRedraw to enable and disable output.
Redraw	Use InvalidateRect to repaint a portion of a window; Invalidate to repaint the whole window.

Control over focus	Keyboard messages are posted to the window with the focus. Use SetFocus to give a window the focus.
Show state	A window can be in one of several show states controlled by ShowWindow. The show states are maximized or full screen, minimized or iconized, and normal. In addition, a window is either visible or hidden.

5.4.3 Window Termination

Two messages are associated with terminating a window:

WM_CLOSE	Request to close the window.
WM_DESTROY	The window is gone.

The best way to close a window is to send it a WM_CLOSE message. This gives the window an opportunity to shut down gracefully—for example, by asking the user whether changes in the window should be saved. The default behavior for WM_CLOSE is to call ::DestroyWindow, which causes the window to be deleted.

Deleting a window raises the delicate issue of when and how to delete the CWnd wrapper object. Wrapper objects allocated on the stack, such as modal dialogs, take care of themselves. Objects on the heap, like the modeless dialog of Chapter 4 must be deleted explicitly. If the wrapper object is deleted too soon, strange things can happen when it comes time to search the message map for the next message.[4] The right time to delete the wrapper is after all of the termination messages have been received. Win32 guarantees that WM_NCDESTROY will be the last message a window will ever see. After WM_NCDESTROY is processed— that is, *post* WM_NCDESTROY—the CWnd object can be deleted. CWnd has a virtual function, PostNcDestroy, that can be overridden to perform the delete.

Typical behavior for PostNcDestroy is simply to delete the current object:

```
delete this;
```

---

[4] If the wrapper isn't deleted, the program will leak memory or, worse, crash if it tries to operate on the wrapper after it no longer refers to a valid window.

The flow of control during window termination is illustrated in Figure 5.3. You can probably surmise that it would not be a good idea to call DestroyWindow in the destructor for the window.

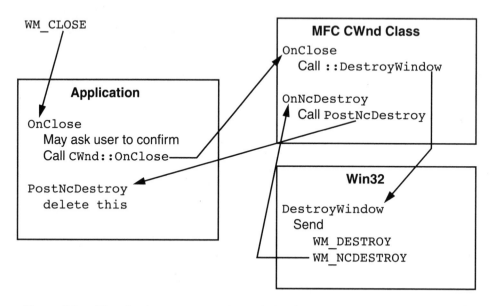

Figure 5.3   The shutdown sequence for a window is triggered by WM_CLOSE. CWnd objects allocated on the heap delete themselves after the last message has been received. The arrows indicate flow of control.

5.5 Message Delivery

Up to this point we've been working with a partial view of how Win32 processes messages, illustrated in Figure 5.4. This picture depicts the event loop in WinMain picking up messages from a queue. Queued messages are *asynchronous* because the originator of the message is decoupled from the receiver. That is, after placing the message on the queue, the originator keeps on executing even though the message hasn't been processed yet. Messages like keyboard and mouse input, window activation, menu commands, and dialog notifications are *posted* to the message queue and picked up in the message loop.

Responding to messages in the message loop serializes the messages for the receiver. There is no concern that processing a keystroke message will be interrupted by a newly arrived mouse message.

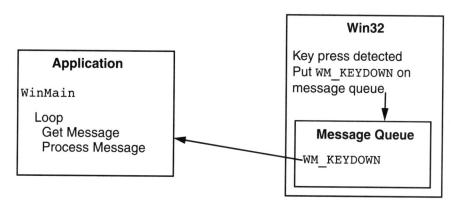

Figure 5.4   Various events, such as key presses, place messages onto an application's message queue. The message loop, typically in an application's `WinMain` function, picks messages off the queue.

Placing messages on the queue also makes a program more responsive by allowing repeat messages to be combined. For example, as the mouse is dragged across a window, mouse-move messages can be generated at the sample rate of the mouse. If a program cannot process the mouse messages fast enough, it would be undesirable to have a queue filled with old mouse-move messages. Win32 combines the messages so that only one message with the latest mouse position is on the queue.

5.5.1 Synchronous Messages

Sometimes this loose arrangement between originator and recipient is not sufficient. Consider the case of window creation. During the call to `::CreateWindow`, the new window receives the sequence of startup messages shown in Figure 5.5. How can these messages be pulled from the queue and processed if the program is waiting for the `::CreateWindow` call to return?

The answer is that the startup messages cannot be posted to the message queue, they must be *sent* directly to the window procedure. A sent, or *synchronous,* message is like a direct call to the window procedure and therefore to a member function in the wrapper class. While the program is waiting in one place for the `Create` call to return, it is executing elsewhere in response to messages sent by Win32.

In general, a program will be more responsive if it posts messages, since that will minimize the amount of time needed to process any particular message. Send a message when the message must be processed immediately or when the

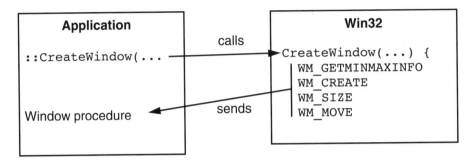

Figure 5.5   `::CreateWindow` sends a sequence of messages to the window procedure for the new window.

return value from the message is important. The return value from a sent message is the value returned by the message handler. The return value from posting a message just tells the poster that the message made it successfully onto the message queue.

5.6   The Window Explorer Program

The sample program for this chapter, in the `Window` directory, lets you create new windows with a wide range of characteristics. Try out different combinations of settings to see how they affect a window's behavior. A modeless dialog, shown in Figure 5.6, controls the parameters for window creation.

The Window Explorer is organized like the programs in the previous chapters, but it is a bit more complex. It uses these classes:

`application`	The usual application class; also contains an instance of a `style`.
`mainFrame`	The usual main window, except that the background is set to black. It has command handlers for creating and deleting windows and terminating the program.
`sample`	Derived from `CWnd`, each window created is an instance of `sample`.
`styleDlg`	Wrapper for the modeless dialog. It has handlers for the dialog controls.
`style`	Encapsulates all the style options.

Figure 5.6 A modeless dialog is used for selecting and viewing window characteristics. Pressing New creates a new window with the specified characteristics.

5.6.1 Initialization

On startup, the application class creates the main window and the modeless dialog:

```
BOOL application::InitInstance()
{
    m_pMainWnd = new mainFrame;
    m_style.Create(IDD_WindowStyle);
    return TRUE;
}
```

The main window is placed in the upper-left corner of the screen to keep it away from the modeless dialog. I've given it a black background to make it easier to see the various window border styles:

```
mainFrame::mainFrame()
{
    // Put window at upper left-hand corner of screen
    CRect rect(0,0,CW_USEDEFAULT,CW_USEDEFAULT);
```

```
        if( !Create(
            AfxRegisterWndClass(
                CS_HREDRAW|CS_VREDRAW,                      // Class style
                theApp.LoadStandardCursor(IDC_ARROW),       // Cursor
                (HBRUSH)::GetStockObject(BLACK_BRUSH),      // Background color
                theApp.LoadIcon(IDI_Blossom)),              // Icon
            "Window",                                       // Window title
            WS_OVERLAPPEDWINDOW | WS_VISIBLE,               // Window style
            rect,                                           // Origin and extent
            NULL,                                           // Parent
            MAKEINTRESOURCE(IDR_MAINMENU))                  // Menu
        ) {
            AfxAbort();
            return;
        }
    }
```

The style dialog is moved to the lower-right corner of the screen during initialization:

```
    BOOL styleDlg::OnInitDialog()
    {
        CDialog::OnInitDialog();

        CRect rect;
        GetWindowRect(&rect);
        MoveWindow(
            ::GetSystemMetrics(SM_CXSCREEN)-rect.Width(),
            ::GetSystemMetrics(SM_CYSCREEN)-rect.Height(),
            rect.Width(), rect.Height());

        return TRUE; // return TRUE unless you set the focus to a control
                     // EXCEPTION: OCX Property Pages should return FALSE
    }
```

The call to GetWindowRect returns the coordinates of the dialog frame. MoveWindow moves the upper-left corner of the window to the specified location. ::GetSystemMetrics returns various values from Win32—in this example, the width and height of the display screen. Figure 5.7 shows how the computation was derived.

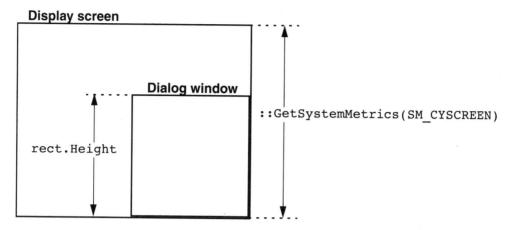

Figure 5.7   The dialog window is moved to the lower-right corner of the display screen by the location for its upper-left corner.

5.6.2 The style Class

All of the style options are represented as members of the style class, declared in the file style.h:

```
class style {
public:
    DWORD      getExtWindowStyle();
    HWND       getWindowOwner();
    DWORD      getWindowStyle();

    BOOL       maximizeButton;
    BOOL       minimizeButton;
    BOOL       helpButton;
    BOOL       systemMenu;
    BOOL       title;
    BOOL       scrollBars;
    BOOL       owned;
    int        border;
    int        edge;
    BOOL       clipSiblings;
    BOOL       transparent;
    BOOL       alwaysOnTop;
    BOOL       acceptFiles;
    BOOL       toolWindow;
    int        windowType;
#define CHILD0
#define POPUP1
};
```

The member functions getWindowStyle and getExtWindowStyle turn the various options into window styles:

```
DWORD style::getWindowStyle()
{
    DWORD flags = borders[border] | type[windowType];

    if(minimizeButton) flags|=WS_MINIMIZEBOX;
    if(maximizeButton) flags|=WS_MAXIMIZEBOX;
    if(systemMenu) flags|=WS_SYSMENU;
    if(title) flags|=WS_CAPTION;
    if(scrollBars) flags|=(WS_HSCROLL|WS_VSCROLL);
    if(clipSiblings) flags|=WS_CLIPSIBLINGS;

    return flags;
}

DWORD style::getExtWindowStyle()
{
    DWORD extStyle = edges[edge];

    if(acceptFiles) extStyle|=WS_EX_ACCEPTFILES;
    if(alwaysOnTop) extStyle|=WS_EX_TOPMOST;
    if(border==DLGFRAME) extStyle|=WS_EX_DLGMODALFRAME;
    if(helpButton) extStyle|=WS_EX_CONTEXTHELP;
    if(toolWindow) extStyle|=WS_EX_TOOLWINDOW;
    if(transparent) extStyle|=WS_EX_TRANSPARENT;
    return extStyle;
}
```

borders, type, and edges are tables that map small integers to window styles:

```
// Style tables
DWORD borders[] = {
    WS_THICKFRAME, // Resizable
    WS_BORDER,     // Thin
    WS_DLGFRAME,   // Thick, non-resizable
#define DLGFRAME 2
    0
};

DWORD edges[] = {
    WS_EX_STATICEDGE,
    WS_EX_CLIENTEDGE,
    WS_EX_WINDOWEDGE,
    0
};

DWORD type[] = {
    WS_CHILD,
    WS_POPUP
};
```

5.6.3 The styleDlg Class

styleDlg, derived from CDialog, reads the dialog controls and sets the style member in application. It also sets the dialog controls based on the currently active window. Because styleDlg and style are closely related, I've put them in the same set of files, style.h and style.cpp.

When the New button in the dialog is pressed, a new window is created using the current style settings:

```
void styleDlg::onNew()
{
    UpdateData();
    AfxGetMainWnd()->PostMessage(WM_COMMAND,IDM_New);
}
```

styleDlg uses MFC's Dialog Data Exchange (DDX) mechanism for moving data between the modeless dialog and the style object. The CWnd function Update-Data triggers the exchange. DDX is described in Chapter 6.

The creation of the new window is carried out by the main window. styleDlg calls on the main window by posting a WM_COMMAND message. mainFrame handles the message just as though it were a menu command:

```
void mainFrame::onNew()
{
    sample *wp = new sample;
    sample::tile();
}
```

5.6.4 The sample Class

Each sample window is instantiated from the sample class. sample is derived from CWnd:

```
class sample : public CWnd
{
. . .
// Attributes
public:
    style m_style;
. . .
```

```
        // Overrides
           // ClassWizard generated virtual function overrides
           //{{AFX_VIRTUAL(sample)
           protected:
           virtual void PostNcDestroy();
           //}}AFX_VIRTUAL
  . . .

           int m_windowNumber;
  . . .

        private:
           static int nextWindowNumber;
           static sample *activeWindow;
           static CPtrList wnd;
           static CFont font;

        };
```

sample maintains class data to keep track of the windows created. It uses the MFC CPtrList class to keep a list of the windows. CPtrList is a collection class. Collection classes are discussed in Chapter 8. When a new window is created, it is numbered and given a background color based on the class data (see Figure 5.8). The style object in application determines the style flags for the window:

```
        sample::sample()
        {
           if( font.m_hObject==0 )   // First time
               font.CreateFont(50,0,0,0,FW_BOLD,0,0,0,0,0,0,0,0,NULL);

           m_style = theApp.m_style.m_s;
           m_windowNumber = nextWindowNumber++;
           CString title;
           title.Format("Window %d",m_windowNumber);
           CBrush brush(RGB(
               m_windowNumber*60%255,   // Red
               m_windowNumber*30%255,   // Green
               m_windowNumber*15%255    // Blue
           ));

           if( CreateEx(
               m_style.getExtWindowStyle(),
               AfxRegisterWndClass(CS_HREDRAW|CS_VREDRAW,  // Class style
                  theApp.LoadStandardCursor(IDC_ARROW),    // Cursor
                  (HBRUSH)brush.m_hObject,                 // Background color
                  theApp.LoadIcon(IDI_APPLICATION)),       // Icon
               title,
               m_style.getWindowStyle(),
               0,0,100,100,                                // Location and extent
               m_style.getWindowOwner(),
               NULL                                        // ID, used in dialogs
           )) {
```

```
        brush.Detach();  // Don't want to delete Windows object
        wnd.AddHead(this);
        activate();
    } else AfxMessageBox("Can't create a window with these attributes");
}
```

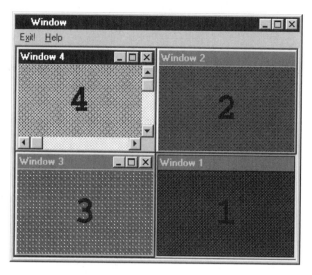

Figure 5.8   Each window is numbered and given a unique background color. The style
dialog shows the attributes of the currently selected window.

Clicking on a window generates the WM_MOUSEACTIVATE message to activate the
window. There is no default behavior in CWnd for showing activation, because an
active button looks quite different than an active scrollbar. On activation, sample uncovers the window and gives it the focus:

```
int sample::OnMouseActivate(CWnd* pDesktopWnd, UINT nHitTest, UINT message)
{
    BringWindowToTop();
    SetFocus();
    return CWnd::OnMouseActivate(pDesktopWnd, nHitTest, message);
}
```

Windows sit on the screen in a three-dimensional space. Besides the obvious X
and Y coordinates, each window has a Z coordinate that specifies its relative
position along an axis perpendicular to the screen. The Z coordinate specifies
an ordering. A window is said to be below another or on top of it. BringWindow-
ToTop puts a window on top of all others. Use SetWindowPos to put one window
underneath another.

CHAPTER

6 | Controls

The program in the `Controls` directory illustrates the concepts discussed in this chapter. The corresponding executable in the `bin` directory is `Controls.exe`.

6.1   Introduction

Win32 controls come from two epochs. Ever since the earliest versions of Windows there have been buttons, lists, scrollbars, and text. Windows 95 introduced the common controls: sliders, spins, trees, animation, gauges, list views, tool tips, headers, and property pages.

The basic programming protocol is the same for all controls. Each type of control is implemented in a Win32 window class. The code for the control lives inside the window procedure for the class. The window procedure understands and emits a set of messages. MFC wraps the Win32 class with a `CWnd`-derived class. The MFC class has member functions that correspond to the control's messages.

Because each control is a window, a program can create a control by calling the `Create` function of the corresponding MFC wrapper class. The `Create` call has a parameter for setting the control ID and flags for setting the control's style. The style flags modify the appearance and behavior of the control. Although controls usually appear inside dialogs, they can be created as children of any window.

Rather than call `Create`, it is easier to create a dialog using a resource editor, which is what I did for nearly all of the dialog examples in the sample programs. A dialog resource specifies the types, placement, and styles of the control windows. Dialog resources can be used to lay out ordinary windows as well as dialogs. See Chapter 12 for a form designed using a resource editor.

All controls accept messages that modify their appearance. Also, since the controls are windows, they respond to the whole range of CWnd functions. In addition, some controls send notifications to their parent when the user manipulates the control. The original Windows controls send the notifications via WM_COMMAND messages. The common controls send notifications via WM_NOTIFY. A few controls use more specialized messages. MFC hides the message by providing a message-map macro for each notification code. For example, to catch a button click, you can use the map entry ON_BN_CLICKED, based on the notification, instead of ON_COMMAND, based on the message.

6.2 Dialog Data Exchange

While a dialog is operating, much of the data in the dialog may be contained as state information in the controls. For example, list boxes know what item is currently selected and check boxes know whether they are checked. At dialog startup, you usually want to initialize the data in the controls, and at various times you will want to read the data. The state of a control can be set and retrieved using wrapper-class member functions that communicate with the control window.

MFC can automate the task of setting and retrieving state information from a control if you use the Dialog Data Exchange (DDX) functions in the dialog class. For each control to be managed:[1]

1. Create a member variable in the dialog class to associate with the control.
2. Override the virtual function DoDataExchange.
3. Put a DDX function call in DoDataExchange to communicate with the control.

DoDataExchange moves data in both directions. It will be called by CDialog::OnInitDialog to set the controls from the associated member variables and by CDialog::OnOK to read the controls before the dialog terminates. A program can force a data exchange at other times by calling CWnd::UpdateData.

The DDX function to call depends on the type of the member variable and the type of the control. There are DDX functions for each of the standard controls. Sometimes there is just one DDX function defined for a control, so the member variable will need to be of a predefined type. For example, the variable for a two-state check box must be an integer with a value of either 0 or 1. For some controls, the DDX function is overloaded. Text edit controls, for example, may have

---

[1] In ClassWizard, use the Member Variables page to carry out these tasks.

an integer, floating point, or string variable associated with them. Depending on the type of the variable, the DDX function carries out the appropriate conversion. You'll see DDX functions used in the examples throughout this chapter.

It is not always appropriate to have a scalar variable represent the state of a control. Simple controls may not have any state information and complex controls may have lots. In these cases, it can be convenient to create a member variable instantiated from the MFC wrapper class for the control. The DDX function for a wrapper-class object doesn't read and write the control, but it does attach the control to the wrapper object so that the program can operate on the control using the object. This is a subtle but important point about embedded wrapper objects. Even though there is no data to be exchanged, the wrapper object still needs a DDX function. The Animation dialog in Section 6.3.3.2 shows an example of this use of DDX.

6.3   A Catalog of Controls

This section describes the various types of controls. The MFC and API reference manuals group the controls based on how they are implemented. In the descriptions that follow, I've grouped the controls based on how they are used. Thus you'll find spin buttons under buttons, list and tree views under lists, and the rich-text edit control under editable text. Also, controls are traditionally divided between *static* and *dynamic*, where static controls are those that don't respond to user input. Since there is also a STATIC window class that implements a subset of the static controls, I'll use the categories output-only and input/output. Here are the output-only controls:

Boxes
    Borders
        Frames
        Group boxes
    Solids
        Rectangles
Labels
    Persistent text
    Popup text
Pictures
    Icons
    Animation
    Gauges

These are the input/output controls:

Buttons
   Push buttons
   Check boxes
   Radio buttons
   Picture buttons
      Icon buttons
      Bitmap buttons
      Owner-draw buttons
   Spin buttons
   Headers
Sliding
   Sliders
   Scroll bars
Text
   Edit
   Rich-text edit
Lists
   List boxes
   Combo boxes
   Trees
   List views

All of the examples that follow are taken from the Control Sampler program in the `Controls` directory. You can use the Control Sampler to experiment with how a control's style affects its appearance and behavior.

6.3.1 Boxes

Boxes are one type of control drawn by the `STATIC` window class. The style flags, accessible from a resource editor, specify the kind of box.[2] Boxes can be outlined, called *frames*, or filled, called *rectangles*. Group boxes, rectangular outlines with an embedded label, appear similar to frames but are actually implemented as a style of button. This is because they typically surround groups of buttons.

Boxes can be used to make nice backgrounds, as shown in Figure 6.1, but overlapping controls are a little tricky to work with. To place one control on top of

---

[2] Look in the reference manual under `::CreateWindow` for a complete list of styles for the `STATIC` class.

another, the background must be drawn before the foreground. Controls are drawn in the order they appear in the resource, therefore the background control should be before the foreground control in the tab order.

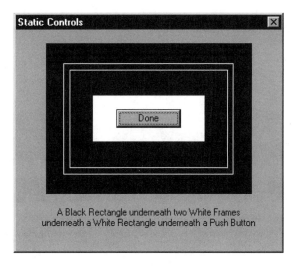

Figure 6.1   A dialog containing rectangles, frames, and text

MFC wraps the STATIC window class with the class CStatic, but there isn't much you can do specifically to a static control. CStatic is derived from CWnd, so all the standard window operations are available, such as resizing, moving, and hiding. To access a static control, either embed a CStatic wrapper object into the dialog object or use the CWnd::GetDlgItem function to get a pointer to the control.

6.3.2 Labels

Most labels are persistent; they remain on the screen throughout the dialog. Persistent labels are known as static text and are implemented in the STATIC class. They can be centered or left- or right-justified inside the control window. Long lines of text will be wrapped and aligned according to the justification style. The descriptive text in Figure 6.1 is a long centered line. Explicit line breaks can be added by inserting the \n escape sequence into the text string. C-style escape sequences can also be used to insert special symbols, such as \251 for the copyright symbol shown in the About box of Figure 6.2. Here is the dialog resource that generates the About box:

```
IDD_ABOUTBOX DIALOG DISCARDABLE  34, 22, 217, 43
STYLE DS_MODALFRAME | WS_POPUP | WS_CAPTION | WS_SYSMENU
CAPTION "About dialog"
FONT 8, "MS Sans Serif"
BEGIN
    ICON            IDI_Blossom,IDC_STATIC,10,10,18,20
    LTEXT           "Control Sampler, Version 1.0",
                    IDC_STATIC,40,10,119,8
    LTEXT           "Copyright \251 1997, Blossom Software",
                    IDC_STATIC,40,25,119,8
    DEFPUSHBUTTON   "OK",IDOK,176,6,32,14,WS_GROUP
END
```

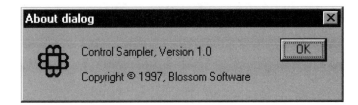

Figure 6.2   An About box showing text that contains the copyright symbol and an icon

Text controls can be manipulated via member functions of CWnd. For example, in a dialog member function, the following code fragment would set the text in the control with the ID IDC_Text:

```
CWnd *ctl = GetDlgItem(IDC_Text);
ctl->SetWindowText("New text");
```

GetDlgItem returns a pointer to a temporary CWnd for the control.

6.3.2.1 Tool Tips

Popup text, known as *tool tips,* is a slick solution to the what's-that problem. They are usually used with toolbars, as described in Chapter 11, but can appear anywhere in a program. Posting a tool tip involves two windows: the window under the mouse, called the *tool,* and the tool-tip window containing the popup text.

A tool-tip window is unusual in that most of the time it is hidden. Also, since only one tool tip is displayed at a time, a tool-tip window can handle more than one tool. As shown in Figure 6.3, the tool-tip window procedure monitors messages from multiple tool windows. When the tool-tip window detects the mouse pausing over a tool, it moves and shows itself.

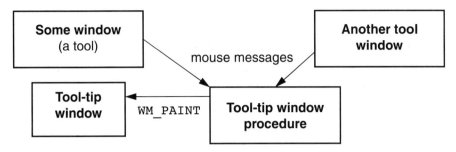

Figure 6.3   The tool-tip window monitors mouse messages for tool windows. When the mouse is stationary over a tool, the tool-tip window displays the tool tip.

To add tool tips to a tool bar or dialog bar, you can forget about all these details and just follow the directions in Chapter 11 for specifying the tool-tip text. To add tool tips in other places, you can almost forget about the details and just call CWnd::EnableToolTips. For example, each of the dialogs in the Control Sampler uses tool tips to show the Win32 class name of each control (see Figure 6-5). The implementation is in a common base class called dialog:

```
class dialog : public CDialog
{
// Construction
public:
    dialog(UINT id, CWnd *pParent);
    afx_msg BOOL onToolTip(UINT id, NMHDR *pHdr, LRESULT *pResult);

. . .
    virtual BOOL OnInitDialog();
. . .
```

OnInitDialog calls EnableToolTips, telling MFC to set up a tool-tip control:[3]

```
BOOL dialog::OnInitDialog()
{
    CDialog::OnInitDialog();
    EnableToolTips();
    return TRUE;
}
```

All that's left to do is specify the text for the tool tip. The tool-tip window queries for the text by sending the notification TTN_NEEDTEXT. The notification is picked up in the message map:

---

[3] The actual code looks a little more complex, as described in the next section.

```
BEGIN_MESSAGE_MAP(dialog, CDialog)
    //{{AFX_MSG_MAP(dialog)
    ON_WM_PAINT()
    //}}AFX_MSG_MAP
    ON_NOTIFY_EX(TTN_NEEDTEXT,0,onToolTip)
END_MESSAGE_MAP()
```

onToolTip grabs the class name of the tool window and copies it to a buffer provided by the tool tip:

```
BOOL dialog::onToolTip(UINT id, NMHDR *pHdr, LRESULT *)
{
    TOOLTIPTEXT *ttt = (TOOLTIPTEXT *)pHdr;
    TCHAR className[32];
    if( ::GetClassName((HWND)ttt->hdr.idFrom,className,
        sizeof(className)) > 0 )
            lstrcpy(ttt->szText,className);

    return TRUE;
}
```

If you compile the Control Sampler with the macro SIMPLE defined,[4] the dialogs will have tool tips enabled just as I've described. When you run the program, what you'll discover is that tool tips almost work. For some controls, such as labels and the animation control, there are no tool tips.

6.3.2.1.1 A Closer Look at Tool Tips[5]

To post a tool tip, the tool-tip window must know the location of the mouse and the positions of the tool windows. Normally, mouse messages are delivered just to the window directly underneath the mouse. Feeding those messages to the tool-tip window procedure is an essential step in getting tool tips to show. There are a few ways to pass the messages on:

• Cooperatively, by having the tool windows relay selective messages to the tool-tip window (see CToolTipCtrl::RelayEvent);
• Via brute force, by relaying all messages to the tool-tip window;
• Via subterfuge, by having the tool-tip window hook into the message stream for each of the tool window procedures.

The tool-tip window maintains a list of tools. In the SIMPLE version of the Control Sampler, EnableToolTips causes MFC to build the list dynamically and use the brute-force method of relaying mouse messages to the tool tip. The tool list

---

[4] In Visual C++, you can set compile-time switches in the Build Settings dialog.

[5] MFC's handling of tool tips is a wild piece of hackery. If you don't have a need to know the details, you may want to skip this section.

is built dynamically to handle expanding windows, such as combo boxes (see Section 6.3.7.1) and customizable tool bars.

The big question is where can the code go to build the list of tools? There is only one place in the program guaranteed to see all mouse messages: the message loop.[6] MFC's message loop calls `CWinApp::PreTranslateMessage`. If the message is a mouse or keyboard message, and if tool tips are enabled, and if the window receiving the message is a child of the window for which tool tips are enabled, then `PreTranslateMessage` adds the child to the list of tools and passes the message on to the tool-tip window.

There are a couple of potential problems with this approach. To avoid popping up tool tips for labels, `PreTranslateMessage` filters out any window with the ID of -1, the value of `IDC_STATIC`. This explains why tool tips fail to show up on the static windows in the SIMPLE version of the Control Sampler.

Some controls are more complex than they appear on the screen because they may be composed from multiple windows, some of which are transparent. For example, a combo box can consist of two, or even three, overlapping windows. A group box is a transparent window, often sitting on top of a group of radio buttons (see Section 6.3.4); an animation control (Section 6.3.3.2) consists of a transparent window surrounding a play-back window. Mouse messages are never sent to transparent windows; they flow through to the window underneath. Since `PreTranslateWindow` will never receive a mouse message for a transparent window, transparent windows will not be added to the list of tools. This explains why tool tips fail on the animation control and some of the list boxes in the SIMPLE version of the Control Sampler.

6.3.2.1.2 Adding a Tool-Tip Control

To enable tool tips for transparent and static windows, I added a second tool-tip control. The program builds an explicit tool list for the control. MFC wraps the Win32 tool-tip control by the class `CToolTipCtrl`. The dialog class contains a tool-tip object:

---

[6] This holds true only if the program has just *one* message loop. As a result, MFC cannot call API functions like `::DialogBox` that have their own message loop.

```
class dialog : public CDialog
{
    . . .
#ifndef SIMPLE
private:
    CToolTipCtrl m_toolTip;
#endif
};
```

In `OnInitDialog`, the tool-tip control is created and attached to the C++ wrapper object:

```
BOOL dialog::OnInitDialog()
{
    CDialog::OnInitDialog();

    EnableToolTips();
```

Then each child window is added to the tool-tip control's list of tools:

```
#ifndef SIMPLE
    // Create tool tip for transparent and static controls
    m_toolTip.Create(this,TTS_ALWAYSTIP);
    m_toolTip.Activate(TRUE);

    CWnd *wnd = GetWindow(GW_CHILD);
    for( ; wnd!=NULL; wnd=wnd->GetWindow(GW_HWNDNEXT) ) {
        if( IsChild(wnd) ) {
            CRect rect;
            wnd->GetWindowRect(&rect);
            ScreenToClient(&rect);
            TOOLINFO ti = {
                sizeof(TOOLINFO),   // Size of structure
                TTF_SUBCLASS,       // Tool style
                m_hWnd,             // Tool owner
                (UINT)wnd->m_hWnd,  // Tool window
                { rect.left,        // Window rectangle
                  rect.top, rect.right, rect.bottom },
                NULL,               // Instance handle, not used
                LPSTR_TEXTCALLBACK  // Tool text, will call parent
            };
            m_toolTip.SendMessage(TTM_ADDTOOL,0,(LPARAM)&ti);
        }
    }
#endif // SIMPLE

    return TRUE;
}
```

To get mouse messages to the tool-tip control, I used the second strategy listed in Section 6.3.2.1.1. When adding a tool to the list of tools, the flag

TTF_SUBCLASS tells the tool-tip window procedure to patch its way into the message stream for the tool. Unfortunately, CToolTipCtrl::AddTool doesn't provide access to the style field, so I sent the TTM_ADDTOOL message to the control directly.

Specifying the tool rectangle is a little tricky. The coordinates are relative to the parent window. GetWindowRect retrieves the coordinates relative to the screen; ScreenToClient performs the translation to client coordinates. Finally, putting LPSTR_TEXTCALLBACK in the text field tells the tool to send the TTN_NEEDTEXT notification, so tools detected by this tool-tip control can be handled by the same routine as for those detected by the Framework.

6.3.3 Pictures

6.3.3.1 Icons and Bitmaps

There are a few ways to put pictures, animated and static, into a dialog. The simplest picture to add is an icon, as in the About box of Figure 6.2. Icons, again drawn by the STATIC class, are fixed-size bitmaps, normally 32 by 32 pixels. They can be created in most resource editors.

An icon is actually represented as two bitmaps, a mask and an image. Although the icon bitmaps are always square, the mask is applied to the image to generate other shapes. The mask divides the icon into opaque and transparent regions. Where the icon is transparent, the background shows. Where it is opaque, the image shows. In a resource editor, when you paint a mask with the "screen color", you set the transparent portion of the mask. Figure 6.4 shows how the mask, image, and backgrounds combine to form the final picture.

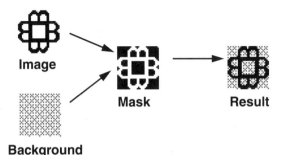

Figure 6.4   An icon is represented as two bitmaps: a mask and an image. In this drawing, the transparent region of the mask is represented as black and the opaque portion as white.

The biggest problem with icons is that they are relatively small. For larger pictures, put a bitmap into a dialog using a static control with the style SS_BITMAP. You can either associate a bitmap with the control in the resource editor or load the bitmap explicitly using CStatic::SetBitmap. The latter technique is illustrated by the Hangman program in Chapter 14.

Icons can be used to achieve a modest form of animation. By using a timer and replacing the icon several times per second, the picture will appear to move. Watch the icon in the Animation dialog of the Control Sampler program when you press the Start/Resume button, for an example. (Figure 6.5 shows a static version of the dialog.)

To replace the icon in a static control, you'll need a handle to the new icon. The CWinApp::LoadIcon function retrieves an icon resource. Alternatively, use the ::ExtractIcon function to read an icon from an executable or library file. Both of these functions return a handle to the icon. With some work, it's also possible to create icons dynamically by creating a matrix of bits.

After you have the icon by its handle, use the CStatic class member function SetIcon to put the icon into the control. You don't have to worry about making the static control window the right size in the dialog resource; only the upper-left coordinates are used. The window will resize itself to accommodate the icon.

6.3.3.2 Animation

Richer animation, derived from a video file, is implemented by the Win32 animation control class, SysAnimate32. The animation control spawns a new thread of execution that plays an Audio-Video Interleaved (AVI) clip.[7] You can pass the control either the name of a file or the name of an AVI resource. I've found that not all resource editors can handle AVI resources. If yours doesn't, add it by hand using the following syntax in your resource script:

```
Resource-name  AVI  File-name
```

For example, the video clip for the Animation dialog in the Control Sampler, pictured in Figure 6.5, is specified in the file app.rc2:

```
IDA_Clock AVI "clock.avi"
```

---

[7] A *thread* is the unit of execution. Every process has at least one thread. Every thread has its own program counter, registers, and stack. For more details, see Chapter 16.

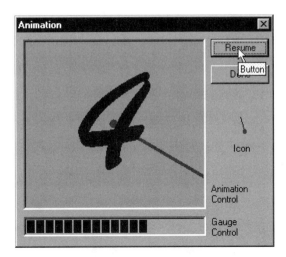

Figure 6.5   The Animation dialog in the Control Sampler program illustrates simple animation using an icon, a gauge, and an animation control. The mouse was placed over the Resume button, causing the tool tip to show.

The CAnimateCtrl class wraps the functionality of the animation control. It presents a simple Play/Stop/Seek interface. To use an animation control:

1. Create the CAnimateCtrl object. If the CAnimateCtrl object is inserted into the dialog object, the animation control will be created automatically when the dialog is created.
2. Insert a call to DDX_Control into the DoDataExchange function. DDX_Control attaches the animation control to the CAnimateCtrl object.[8]
3. During initialization, call CAnimateCtrl::Open to attach the control to a video clip.
4. If the control has the ACS_AUTOPLAY style, it will begin playing after loading. Otherwise, call CAnimateCtrl::Play to start the animation.

The Animation dialog in the Control Sampler implements these steps. The class animationDlg has a CAnimateCtrl member named m_animation, inserted by ClassWizard:

---

[8] ClassWizard will do this for you if you use it to add the CAnimateCtrl member variable.

```
class animationDlg : public dialog
{
. . .
// Dialog Data
    //{{AFX_DATA(animationDlg)
. . .
    CAnimateCtrlm_animation;
    //}}AFX_DATA
```

ClassWizard also inserted a call to DDX_Control in DoDataExchange:

```
void animationDlg::DoDataExchange(CDataExchange* pDX)
{
    dialog::DoDataExchange(pDX);
    //{{AFX_DATA_MAP(animationDlg)
. . .
    DDX_Control(pDX, IDC_Animation, m_animation);
    //}}AFX_DATA_MAP
}
```

In OnInitDialog, I added a call to Open to connect the animation resource to the animation control:

```
BOOL animationDlg::OnInitDialog()
{
    dialog::OnInitDialog();

    m_animation.Open(IDA_Clock);
. . .
    return TRUE; // return TRUE unless you set the focus to a control
                 // EXCEPTION: OCX Property Pages should return FALSE
}
```

Before using m_animation, it is important that CDialog::OnInitDialog be called since it will call DoDataExchange.

The "OK" button in the dialog wears three different labels. Initially, the button is labeled Start. While the animation is playing, it is labeled Stop. If the animation is stopped, the label is changed to Resume. OnOk handles the three states:

```
void animationDlg::OnOK()
    // Start/Stop button
{
    switch(m_buttonState) {
    case Start:
        m_animation.Play(0,(UINT)-1,1);
        setButtonState(Stop, _T("Stop"));
        SetTimer(1,100,NULL);
        break;
```

```
    case Resume:
        m_animation.Play((UINT)-1,(UINT)-1,1);
        setButtonState(Stop, _T("Stop"));
        SetTimer(1,100,NULL);
        break;

    case Stop:
        m_animation.Stop();
        setButtonState(Resume, _T("Resume"));
        break;
    }
}
```

CAnimateCtrl::Play starts the animation. It takes three parameters:

```
    BOOL Play( UINT nFrom, UINT nTo, UINT nRep );
```

where *nFrom* and *nTo* are specified as frame numbers beginning at zero. Thus *nFrom*=0 starts at the beginning. -1 is used as a special value: *nFrom*=-1 resumes playing from the last stop; *nTo*=-1 plays to the end. *nRep* is the number of repetitions. *nRep*=-1 plays until the control is stopped. The control spawns a thread to play the animation, so Play returns quickly, keeping the program interface alive.

OnOk also changes the text on the button and starts a timer, by calling CWnd::SetTimer, to trigger ten times per second. The timer generates a WM_TIMER message. animateDlg responds in OnTimer by changing the icon to implement a clock pendulum:[9]

```
    void animationDlg::OnTimer(UINT nIDEvent)
    {
        nextIcon();  // Replace the icon and update the gauge
    }

    void animationDlg::nextIcon()
    {
    . . .
        m_icon.SetIcon( AfxGetApp()->LoadIcon(IDI_0+id) );

        m_gauge.SetPos(id);  // Gauge will mimic pendulum
    }
```

The animation control sends the notification ACN_STOP to its parent when it stops. animationDlg picks up the notification in onStop:

---

[9] The icons for the successive pendulum positions were given successive IDs beginning at IDI_0.

```
BEGIN_MESSAGE_MAP(animationDlg, dialog)
    //{{AFX_MSG_MAP(animationDlg)
    ON_CONTROL(ACN_STOP, IDC_Animation, onStop)
    ON_WM_TIMER()
    //}}AFX_MSG_MAP
END_MESSAGE_MAP()
```

There is no way to query the animation control as to its current frame position. The program distinguishes between end-of-animation and the user pressing Stop by looking at the state of the "OK" button:

```
void animationDlg::onStop()
{
    // Distinguish end-of-animation from press of Stop button
    if( m_buttonState==Stop )
        setButtonState(Start,"Start");
    KillTimer(1);
}
```

CWnd::KillTimer terminates the timer, stopping the pendulum.

6.3.3.3 Gauges

The Win32 progress-bar class, msctls_progress, implements a specialized type of animation. The control is usually called a *progress bar* because that's how it is often used. But progress bars can go down as well as up, as illustrated by the Animation dialog, so I'll call them gauges.

The MFC class CProgressCtrl wraps the Win32 gauge control. To use a gauge:

1. Create a CProgressCtrl object. It can, of course, be an object embedded in the dialog object.
2. If the CProgressCtrl object is embedded in the dialog object, put a call to DDX_Control for it into the DoDataExchange function.
3. Call SetRange to set the range (the default range is 0 to 100).
4. Change the gauge value. To use a gauge as a progress bar, call StepIt to advance the gauge one increment. Set the increment using SetStep. For more general use, call SetPos to set the gauge to an arbitrary value within the range.

The Animation dialog has a CProgressCtrl member variable m_gauge. The range for the gauge is set during OnInitDialog:

```
BOOL animationDlg::OnInitDialog()
{
    dialog::OnInitDialog();

    m_animation.Open(IDA_Clock);
    m_gauge.SetRange(0,MaxCount-1);
. . .
}
```

The gauge value is changed when the icon is replaced so that the gauge follows the pendulum:

```
void animationDlg::nextIcon()
{
. . .
    m_icon.SetIcon( AfxGetApp()->LoadIcon(IDI_0+id) );

    m_gauge.SetPos(id);   // Gauge will mimic pendulum
}
```

6.3.4 Buttons

Buttons are input/output controls. When clicked, they change state and issue a notification message. Depending on the type of the button, an application may issue a command or change an option. Most buttons are instances of the Win32 BUTTON class. They come in a variety of styles as illustrated by the Control Sampler's Button dialog shown in Figure 6.6. Here are the standard button types:

Push buttons	A button with a text label attached to a command. Pressing the button triggers the command.
Radio buttons	For selecting one from a set of mutually exclusive choices. Usually there is one radio button per choice and the set is surrounded by a group box.
Check boxes	For indicating the state of a two- or three-state choice.
Picture buttons	Used like a push button except that the surface of the button is derived from a specified icon or bitmap.
Owner-draw buttons	Used like a push button except that the appearance of the button is under program control.

The CButton class wraps all of these button types. When pressed, buttons send the BN_CLICKED notification to their parent, which can be attached to a dialog member function using the ON_BN_CLICKED message-map macro.

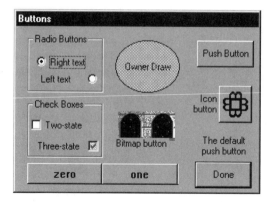

Figure 6.6   The Button dialog in the Control Sampler program illustrates the wide range of button appearance and behavior.

Push buttons are the simplest of the buttons. Typically, they trigger a command when pressed. The button can be disabled using the `EnableWindow` function. Use `CWnd::SetWindowText` to change the label.

Check boxes are also simple. They can have either two or three states which can be completely represented by a single integer variable. `CButton::SetCheck` sets the button state; `SetWindowText` changes the associated label.

Radio buttons are slightly more complex. The buttons themselves have just two states, but they are usually grouped to implement a mutually exclusive choice. The DDX for radio buttons function takes a range of button IDs and the index of the currently selected button. For radio buttons to be a group, they must:

- Have sequential IDs.
- Have the `WS_GROUP` window style on only the first button in the group, where first means the button with the lowest ID. The `WS_GROUP` style begins a new group and thus terminates any current group.

For the buttons to work together automatically, give each button the `BS_AUTORADIOBUTTON` style.

The Button dialog in the Control Sampler has member variables for the check boxes and radio buttons. The declarations were added by ClassWizard:

```
class buttonDlg : public dialog
{
. . .
    //{{AFX_DATA(buttonDlg)
    enum { IDD = IDD_Buttons };
    ownerDrawButtonm_ownerDraw;
    CButtonm_iconButton;
    int m_radioVal;
    int m_threeStateVal;
    BOOLm_twoStateVal;
    //}}AFX_DATA
```

The member variables communicate with the controls via DDX functions in
DoDataExchange. Again, ClassWizard added the code:

```
void buttonDlg::DoDataExchange(CDataExchange* pDX)
{
    dialog::DoDataExchange(pDX);
    //{{AFX_DATA_MAP(buttonDlg)
    DDX_Control(pDX, IDC_OwnerDraw, m_ownerDraw);
    DDX_Control(pDX, IDC_Icon, m_iconButton);
    DDX_Radio(pDX, IDC_RightRadio, m_radioVal);
    DDX_Check(pDX, IDC_ThreeStateCheck, m_threeStateVal);
    DDX_Check(pDX, IDC_TwoStateCheck, m_twoStateVal);
    //}}AFX_DATA_MAP
}
```

6.3.4.1 Picture Buttons

Icons and bitmaps can be placed onto the surface of a button. Icons are simpler,
showing a standard-size image. An icon is attached to a button by

1. Setting the BS_ICON style for the button control.
2. Embedding a CButton object into the dialog (or using CWnd::GetDlgItem).
3. Calling CButton::SetIcon to attach the icon to the button.

SetIcon can be used repeatedly to change the button image. The icon button in
the Button dialog switches images whenever the button is pressed, giving the
effect of an alternate-action switch. The onIcon function is called when the button is pressed:

```
void buttonDlg::onIcon() // Switch icons
{
    HICON hIcon = AfxGetApp()->LoadIcon(IDI_Blossom);

    if( m_iconButton.GetIcon()==hIcon )
        hIcon = AfxGetApp()->LoadIcon(IDI_InvertedBlossom);

    m_iconButton.SetIcon(hIcon);
}
```

Using a bitmap button, you can create buttons of arbitrary size. There are two ways to create bitmap buttons:

- Give the button the style BS_BITMAP, then set the image using the CButton member function SetBitmap, just like using SetIcon for BS_ICON buttons.
- Give the button the style BS_OWNERDRAW and use the CBitmapButton class.

When using the CBitmapButton class, you provide up to four different bitmaps for the various button states. MFC takes care of resizing the button and swapping the bitmap images as the button state changes.

The procedure for specifying the bitmaps shows, to be kind, the resourcefulness of MFC's designers. The text label given to the button is taken as the base name for bitmap resources. The name is modified by appending one of the letters "U", "D", "F", or "X" to indicate the bitmap for the up, down, focused, and disabled button states. You don't have to create a bitmap for every state. Those that exist are loaded by the CBitmapButton::AutoLoad function.

For example, to create the bitmap button in the Button dialog I put the label "Bitmap" on the button and created an embedded CBitmapButton data member called m_bitmapButton. I also created two bitmap resources and gave them the *string* names "BITMAPU" and "BITMAPD". These two bitmaps are loaded during OnInitDialog:

```
BOOL buttonDlg::OnInitDialog()
{
    dialog::OnInitDialog();

    // Connect bitmaps to buttons
    m_bitmapButton.AutoLoad(IDC_Bitmap,this);
    . . .
```

It is very important that the bitmap resources be named with strings.[10] If you use integer IDs, AutoLoad will not find them and no image will appear. Also, make sure that the button control has the style BS_OWNERDRAW.[11]

---

[10] To create a resource with a string name in Visual C++, surround the "ID" in the properties dialog with double quotes. As for all resources named by string, Win32 ignores the case of the letters during lookup.

[11] Don't use the BS_BITMAP style. CBitmapButton relies on the owner-draw messages WM_MEASUREITEM and WM_DRAWITEM.

6.3.4.2 Owner-Draw Buttons

To get complete control over the appearance of a button, use an owner-draw button. Owner-draw buttons have the style BS_OWNERDRAW. The original idea of an owner-draw button was that when the button needed to be drawn, the owner of the button, namely the dialog frame, would draw it. In response to WM_PAINT, the button sends its owner WM_DRAWITEM. Drawing the button in the dialog class makes it difficult to reuse the drawing code. A better way is to put the code for implementing the control in the control class itself. The problem is, the control expects its owner to do the drawing.

6.3.4.2.1 Using Message Reflection

MFC solves this problem with a technique called *message reflection*. Instead of processing WM_DRAWITEM, CWnd::OnDrawItem passes the message back to the control. (Figure 6.7 illustrates the flow of control.) The CButton class turns the message into a call on the virtual function DrawItem, passing the ID of the control and its state inside a DRAWITEMSTRUCT structure. By overriding DrawItem, you can take control of drawing. Follow this procedure to override DrawItem:

1. Derive a class from CButton.
2. Instantiate the class creating the button object. The easiest way to do this is to create the button as a member of the dialog class.[12]
3. Connect the Win32 button window to the button object. DDX_Control will do this for you.
4. Implement DrawItem in your derived class.

The Control Sampler implements an owner-draw button in the class ownerDrawButton:

```
class ownerDrawButton : public CButton
{
    virtual void DrawItem( LPDRAWITEMSTRUCT lpDrawItemStruct );
};
```

An instance of ownerDrawButton is created by adding a data member to buttonDlg:

---

[12] You can create the data member using the ClassWizard Member Variables property page. However, it will only give you the option of creating a CButton. You'll need to edit the class declaration to change the data type to your derived class.

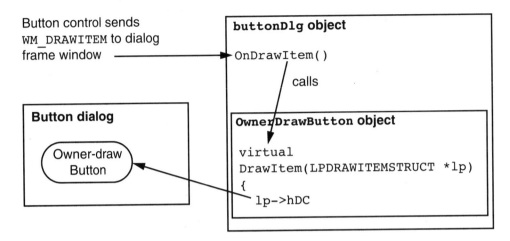

Figure 6.7   The virtual function DrawItem is called in response to WM_DRAWITEM. DrawItem accesses the button through the device context passed via the LPDRAWITEMSTRUCT parameter.

```
class buttonDlg : public dialog
{
. . .
// Dialog Data
    //{{AFX_DATA(buttonDlg)
    enum { IDD = IDD_Buttons };
    ownerDrawButtonm_ownerDraw;
```

DDX_Control connects m_ownerDraw to the appropriate Win32 window:

```
void buttonDlg::DoDataExchange(CDataExchange* pDX)
{
    dialog::DoDataExchange(pDX);
    //{{AFX_DATA_MAP(buttonDlg)
    DDX_Control(pDX, IDC_OwnerDraw, m_ownerDraw);
. . .
```

The DrawItem function looks at the itemState member of DRAWITEMSTRUCT to determine the button's state. The state ODS_FOCUS means that the button is the currently active window. The state ODS_SELECTED means that the button has been pressed.

```
void ownerDrawButton::DrawItem(LPDRAWITEMSTRUCT lpDrawItemStruct)
{
    register int state = lpDrawItemStruct->itemState;
    CString text = T("");
    CBrush brush;

    if( state&ODS_SELECTED ) {
        brush.CreateSolidBrush(RGB(255,0,0));
        text = _T("Selected");
    } else if( state&ODS_FOCUS ) {
        brush.CreateSolidBrush(RGB(0,255,0));
        text = _T("Has focus");
    } else {
        brush.CreateSolidBrush(RGB(191,191,191));
        text = _T("Owner Draw");
    }

    CRect rect;
    GetClientRect(&rect);
    CDC *dc = CDC::FromHandle(lpDrawItemStruct->hDC);
    dc->SelectObject(&brush);
    dc->Ellipse(&rect);
    dc->SetBkMode(TRANSPARENT);
    CSize textLen = dc->GetTextExtent(text,text.GetLength());
    dc->TextOut((rect.right-textLen.cx)/2,
        (rect.bottom-textLen.cy)/2,text);
}
```

After setting the background color and text based on the button state, `DrawItem` centers the text inside an elliptical button. All drawing in Win32 requires a device context. The `DRAWITEMSTRUCT` contains a handle to a device context. `CDC::FromHandle` wraps a CDC object around the handle. We'll cover drawing and the CDC class in Chapter 8.

6.3.4.3 Spin Buttons

The MFC class `CSpinButtonCtl` wraps the Win32 class `msctls_updown32`. Spin buttons, called up-down controls in the API, are usually paired with another control that indicates a value. Pressing the spin button changes the value (see Figure 6.8).

Figure 6.8   A spin button attached to an edit field

In many ways, spin buttons are programmed like sliding controls:

- They have an orientation, either horizontal or vertical.
- They have a range.
- They have a position within the range.
- They send the specialized scrolling messages.

Sliding controls are described in Section 6.3.5. Look at the Slider dialog in the Control Sampler for spin button examples.

Spin buttons are unique in having a companion, or *buddy*, control. Like a magnet, spin buttons attach themselves to their buddy. When the spin button is clicked, it sends its buddy a WM_SETTEXT message with its new position. Often the buddy is a text or an edit control, which responds to the WM_SETTEXT message by displaying the new value. Other controls can be buddies also, but if they don't respond to WM_SETTEXT they will need to be updated explicitly in response to a scroll message.

There are two ways to specify a buddy. If the spin button has the style UDS_AUTOBUDDY, it will affix itself to the previous control in the dialog, where previous is determined by tab order. Alternatively, the buddy can be set explicitly using CSpinButtonCtrl::SetBuddy. Spin buttons can be given an alignment to specify whether they stick to the left or right side of their buddy.

The Slider dialog illustrates two variations on implementing a spin button (see Figure 6.10). In the simpler case, a vertical spin button is auto-attached to an edit control. Since edit controls respond to WM_SETTEXT, the only programming required is to set the range for the button. The other spin button clings to a slider. Code is required to attach the button, set its range, and update the slider.

A member variable is created for each spin button in the slider dialog:

```
class sliderDlg : public dialog
{
// Construction
public:
    sliderDlg(CWnd* pParent = NULL);   // standard constructor

// Dialog Data
    //{{AFX_DATA(sliderDlg)
    enum { IDD = IDD_Sliders };
    CSpinButtonCtrlm_vertSpin;
    CSpinButtonCtrlm_horzSpin;
```

During initialization, the range for the buttons is set and the horizontal button is attached to the slider:

```
BOOL sliderDlg::OnInitDialog()
{
    dialog::OnInitDialog();
 . . .
    m_horzSpin.SetBuddy(&m_horzSlider);
    m_horzSpin.SetRange(0,MaxVal);
    m_vertSpin.SetRange(0,MaxVal);
```

When clicked, spin buttons send a scroll message to their parent. The horizontal spin button responds by updating its buddy. The value is also displayed in a static text control:

```
void sliderDlg::OnHScroll(UINT nSBCode, UINT nPos,
    CScrollBar *pScrollBar)
{
 . . .
    nPos = m_horzSpin.GetPos();
    m_horzSlider.SetPos(nPos);
    SetDlgItemInt(IDC_HorizontalValue,nPos);
}
```

We'll cover the details of scroll messages in Section 6.3.5.1.

6.3.4.4 Headers

A header is an array of adjacent buttons that can be resized by the user. The individual buttons are drawn by the header; they are not in separate windows. Headers are implemented by the SysHeader32 Win32 class and wrapped by the MFC class CHeaderCtrl. Typically, headers sit on top of columns of text, as in the list view described in Section 6.3.7.6, but they can also appear by themselves as they do at the bottom of the Button dialog shown in Figure 6.6.

Like all the common controls, a header sends notifications to its parent using WM_NOTIFY. The version of MFC I'm using does not include specialized message-map macros for notifications from headers. To catch the notifications, I had to insert an ON_NOTIFY entry into the message map for the dialog. ON_NOTIFY has the form

```
ON_NOTIFY( notification code, control ID, member function )
```

The notification codes for headers are listed in the API manual under "HDN_".

The Button dialog in the Control Sampler illustrates a standalone two-button header. When clicked, the text in the button changes. I coded the header control by hand because the tools I use do not know about headers.[13] Here are the steps:

1. Add a CHeaderCtrl member to the buttonDlg class.
2. Put a STATIC control in the dialog resource as a placeholder for the header.
3. In OnInitDialog, replace the placeholder with the header and initialize the header control.
4. Add an ON_NOTIFY handler to detect header-button presses.

6.3.4.4.1 Using a Placeholder Control

Using a static control as a placeholder is one way to add controls that are unknown to your resource editor. First, position and size the placeholder control in the dialog. Then, in OnInitDialog, use the location and size of the placeholder to generate the parameters for the Create call of the target control. Once its location is known, the placeholder can be removed. Here is the code from the Button dialog for creating the header:

```
BOOL buttonDlg::OnInitDialog()
{
    dialog::OnInitDialog();
. . .
    // Replace place holder by header control
    CWnd *placeHolder = GetDlgItem(IDC_Header);
    CRect rect;
    placeHolder->GetWindowRect(&rect);
    placeHolder->DestroyWindow();
    ScreenToClient(&rect);

    m_headerCtrl.Create(
        WS_CHILD|WS_VISIBLE|WS_TABSTOP|HDS_BUTTONS|HDS_HORZ,
        rect,   // Position and size
        this,   // Parent
        IDC_Header);
. . .
```

It's important to remember that while the rectangle returned by GetWindowRect is in screen coordinates, the rectangle passed to Create must be in client coordinates, since the control has the style WS_CHILD.

---

[13] Of course, tools evolve, so yours may be able to add a header control for you.

6.3.4.4.2 Using a Custom Control

There is an alternative to using a placeholder control that is supported by the resource compiler. Take a look at this excerpt from the Button dialog resource:

```
IDD_Buttons DIALOG DISCARDABLE  0, 0, 207, 125
STYLE DS_MODALFRAME | WS_POPUP | WS_VISIBLE | WS_CAPTION
CAPTION "Buttons"
FONT 8, "MS Sans Serif"
BEGIN
    CONTROL "Right text",IDC_RightRadio,"Button",
            BS_AUTORADIOBUTTON | WS_GROUP | WS_TABSTOP,17,22,48,10
    CONTROL "Left text",IDC_LeftRadio,"Button",
            BS_AUTORADIOBUTTON | BS_LEFTTEXT,20,35,50,10
```

The third parameter to the CONTROL statement is the name of the Win32 class to be instantiated. The code in this example creates two windows from the class Button. For a header control, just change the class name to SysHeader32 and add the appropriate style flags.[14]

6.3.4.4.3 Creating and Responding to Header Buttons

Each header button is described by an HD_ITEM data structure. Like other buttons, header buttons can be text, bitmaps, or owner drawn. In the Button dialog, the header has two buttons, each containing text. Continuing in OnInit-Dialog from Section 6.3.4.4.1:

```
// Create two header buttons
HD_ITEM item = {
    HDI_TEXT|HDI_FORMAT|HDI_WIDTH|HDI_LPARAM,
    rect.Width()/2,         // Initial button width
    NULL,                   // Text, set below
    NULL,                   // Bitmap
    20,                     // Max text length
    HDF_STRING|HDF_CENTER,  // Text format
    0                       // App-defined data
};
item.pszText = _T("zero");
m_headerCtrl.InsertItem(0,&item);
m_headerCtrl.InsertItem(1,&item);
m_headerCtrl.ShowWindow(SW_SHOWNORMAL);

return TRUE;
}
```

---

[14] The Visual C++ resource editor supports custom controls, but has one serious drawback. The style flags for the control must be entered as a single number in either decimal or hex. Besides the obvious inconvenience to write, the style is impossible to read. I prefer to use style flags as macros and therefore use the placeholder technique.

In addition to placing a string on each button, the call to InsertItem initializes a data field reserved for the application. In the Button dialog, when a header button is pressed, its label changes based on the value of the data field.

To detect a button press, the notification from the header control is connected to a handler function using WM_NOTIFY:

```
ON_NOTIFY(HDN_ITEMCLICK,IDC_Header,onHeader)
```

The first parameter to the handler points to a notification data structure. Since all of the common controls use the WM_NOTIFY message, the pointer type is generic. Cast it appropriately for the type of the control. For headers, the type of the structure is HD_NOTIFY:

```
void buttonDlg::onHeader(NMHDR *notifyStruct, LRESULT *result)
{
    HD_NOTIFY *hdn = (HD_NOTIFY *)notifyStruct;
    HD_ITEM item = { HDI_TEXT|HDI_LPARAM };
    headerCtrl.GetItem( hdn->iItem, &item);
    headerCtrl.SetItem( hdn->iItem, incHeader(&item) );
    *result = 0;
}
```

GetItem returns the HD_ITEM for the button. incHeader uses the application-reserved field in the item, lParam, to determine the new button label:

```
HD_ITEM *buttonDlg::incHeader(HD_ITEM *item) // Increment header
button
{
    static TCHAR *text[] = {
        _T("zero"), _T("one"), _T("two"), _T("three"), _T("four"),
        _T("five"), _T("six"), _T("seven"), _T("eight"), _T("nine")
    };

    int next = ++item->lParam % (sizeof(text)/sizeof(text[0]));
    item->pszText = text[next];
    item->lParam = next;
    return item;
}
```

6.3.5 Sliding Controls

Sliding controls come in a variety of forms. All have

- An orientation, either horizontal or vertical
- A range
- A current value within the range, represented either graphically or textually

In addition, as the control is operated by the user, it sends scroll messages to its parent.

6.3.5.1 Scrollbars

Scrollbars were the original Windows slider and in some ways are the most complex. When a scrollbar is manipulated, it generates either a WM_HSCROLL or WM_VSCROLL message, depending on the orientation of the scrollbar. Along with the message is a code that tells how the scrollbar was changed. Figure 6.9 shows the messages associated with clicking on various parts of a scrollbar. Most of the codes should be self-explanatory. The SB_THUMBTRACK code is sent while the scroll box, also known as the *thumb*, is being dragged. SB_THUMBPOS is sent when the user releases the scroll box after dragging it.

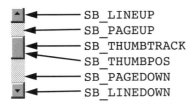

Figure 6.9   Scrollbars send a notification code along with the scroll message. The notification indicates where on the control the mouse was clicked.

The Slider dialog in the Control Sampler illustrates sliders, scrollbars, and spin buttons (see Figure 6.10). It includes two scrollbars, one aligned and one not. *Aligned* scrollbars are drawn the standard width, like the scrollbars on the side of a window. Unaligned scrollbars can be made wider than the standard; they fill the window that defines the control.

In MFC, scrollbars are wrapped by the CScrollBar class. The Slider dialog holds the scrollbar values in integers:

```
int        m_horzScrollbar;
int        m_vertScrollbar;
```

The range for the scrollbars is established in OnInitDialog:

```
BOOL sliderDlg::OnInitDialog()
{
. . .
    CScrollBar *sb = (CScrollBar*)GetDlgItem(IDC_HorizontalScrollbar);
    sb->SetScrollRange(0,MaxVal);
    sb = (CScrollBar *)GetDlgItem(IDC_VerticalScrollbar);
    sb->SetScrollRange(0,MaxVal);
. . .
```

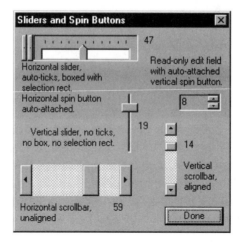

Figure 6.10   The Slider dialog in the Control Sampler illustrates spin buttons, sliders, and scrollbars.

Notifications from the scrollbars are picked up in the member functions OnH-Scroll and OnVScroll. Here is the pertinent code from OnVScroll:

```
void sliderDlg::OnVScroll(UINT nSBCode, UINT nPos,
    CScrollBar* pScrollBar)
{
    switch( pScrollBar->GetDlgCtrlID() ) {
    case IDC_VerticalScrollbar:
        vertScrollbar = computeScrollPos(vertScrollbar,nSBCode,nPos);
        SetDlgItemInt(IDC_VScrollbarValue,vertScrollbar);
        UpdateData(FALSE);
        break;
```

OnVScroll sets the integer variable vertScrollbar based on the notification code (see computeScrollPos below). The new scroll position is put into the associated text control, then the scroll box in the scrollbar is moved by the DDX function for scrollbars. The FALSE parameter to UpdateData tells DoDataExchange to set the dialog controls from the dialog data rather than to set the dialog data from the controls.

computeScrollPos converts a notification code and a current value into a new value:

```
UINT sliderDlg::computeScrollPos(int curPos,UINT nSBCode,UINT nPos)
{
    switch(nSBCode) {
    case SB_LINEDOWN:
        if( curPos<MaxVal ) ++curPos;
        break;
```

```
        case SB_LINEUP:
            if( curPos>0 ) --curPos;
            break;
        case SB_PAGEDOWN:
            if( curPos<=MaxVal-IncVal ) curPos+=IncVal;
            break;
        case SB_PAGEUP:
            if( curPos>=IncVal ) curPos-=IncVal;
            break;
        case SB_THUMBTRACK:
            curPos = nPos;
            break;
        }

        return curPos;
    }
```

Beginning with Windows 95, the size of the scroll box is adjustable. In a typical
scrollbar on the side of a scrolling window, the size of the scroll box indicates
the proportion of a document visible in the window.

The CScrollBar member function SetScrollInfo can change any attribute of a
scrollbar control; using it is the only way to set the size of the scroll box. (Use
CWnd::SetScrollInfo to change the attributes of a window scrollbar.) Set-
ScrollInfo takes as a parameter a SCROLLINFO structure:

```
    struct SCROLLINFO {
        UINT cbSize;        // Size of this structure
        UINT fMask;         // Specify which fields are valid
        int  nMin;          // Low bound of scroll range
        int  nMax;          // High bound of scroll range
        UINT nPage;         // Size of scroll box
        int  nPos;          // Position of scroll box
        int  nTrackPos;     // Position of scroll box during drag
    };
```

The scrollbar sizes the scroll box based on the relative size of nPage to the scroll
range. In the Slider dialog, the scroll-box size for the scrollbars is controlled by
the vertical slider (see Section 6.3.5.2) using the helper function setScrollBox:

```
    void sliderDlg::setScrollBox(UINT id, int size)
    {
        CScrollBar *sb = (CScrollBar *)GetDlgItem(id);
        SCROLLINFO si = { sizeof(SCROLLINFO), SIF_PAGE };
        si.nPage = size;
        sb->SetScrollInfo(&si);
    }
```

Two aspects of calling `SetScrollInfo` are subtle, but important. First, notice that the first field of SCROLLINFO is its size. This may strike you as odd, but it's actually somewhat clever. The size field, easy to compute using `sizeof`, implements a data-structure-specific version tag. If SCROLLINFO were to evolve with the addition of more data fields, Win32 could look at the size field to determine whether the added fields were present, allowing old and new programs to be handled correctly.

The second subtle aspect of calling `SetScrollInfo` relates to a documentation convention used by Win32 and MFC.

6.3.5.1.1 Understanding Win32 Prototypes

Usually, a function prototype type identifies the types of the actual parameters to use in calling the function. For example, given the prototype

```
void f1(int x, TYPE y);
```

you would expect a legitimate call of f1 to be

```
int a;
TYPE b;
f1(a,b);
```

Here is the prototype of `SetScrollInfo` from the reference manual:

```
BOOL SetScrollInfo(LPSCROLLINFO lpScrollInfo, BOOL bRedraw=TRUE);
```

Accordingly, you might be tempted to call `SetScrollInfo` as follows:

```
LPSCROLLINFO si;
SetScrollInfo(si)
```

What you can't see is that LPSCROLLINFO is a Win32 typedef:

```
typedef SCROLLINFO *LPSCROLLINFO;
```

The general rule is that types beginning with LP are long[15] pointers. Since Set-ScrollInfo requires a pointer, the program must allocate a SCROLLINFO data structure and pass a pointer to the structure, as I did in the `setScrollBox` function on the previous page.

---

[15] The convention began with Win16.

6.3.5.2 Sliders

Slider controls, known as *trackbars* in the API, are like scrollbars without the up and down buttons. The MFC class `CSliderCtrl` wraps the Win32 class `msctls_trackbar32`. Sliders come in several styles, so they are more visually versatile than scrollbars. The primary difference in operation is that in addition to sending the `WM_HSCROLL` and `WM_VSCROLL` messages, they send a `WM_NOTIFY` message. For most purposes, it is simpler to ignore `WM_NOTIFY` and respond to the scroll messages.

One complication is that the scroll messages were designed to handle scrollbars, so their prototype contains a pointer to a `CScrollBar`, not a `CSliderCtrl`. Although it is safe to cast the pointer, a better approach is to create a wrapper object for the slider and manipulate the control via the wrapper.

The Slider dialog in the Control Sampler (Figure 6.10) has two slider controls, hence two wrapper objects:

```
CSliderCtrl m_vertSlider;
CSliderCtrl m_horzSlider;
```

As with the scrollbars, the range for the sliders is set during `OnInitDialog`:

```
m_horzSlider.SetRange(0,MaxVal);
m_horzSlider.SetTicFreq(IncVal);
m_vertSlider.SetRange(0,MaxVal);
```

Besides having a range and a position, sliders can have tick marks. `SetTicFreq` sets the distance between tick marks.

As the slider is manipulated, it sends `WM_NOTIFY` before the thumb is updated, and it sends the scroll message after it is updated. Unlike a scrollbar, a slider moves its thumb, so you don't need to. The Slider dialog responds to movement of the sliders by updating an associated text control. Here is the code from `OnHScroll`:

```
void sliderDlg::OnHScroll(UINT nSBCode, UINT nPos,
   CScrollBar* pScrollBar)
{
   switch( pScrollBar->GetDlgCtrlID() ) {
   case IDC_HorizontalScrollbar:
. . .
```

```
        case IDC_HorizontalSlider:
            nPos = m_horzSlider.GetPos();
            m_horzSpin.SetPos(nPos);
            SetDlgItemInt(IDC_HorizontalValue,nPos);
            break;
        case IDC_HorizontalSpin:
            nPos = m_horzSpin.GetPos();
            m_horzSlider.SetPos(nPos);
            SetDlgItemInt(IDC_HorizontalValue,nPos);
            break;
        }
    }
```

Messages from the three horizontal sliding controls in the dialog can be distinguished by looking at the ID of the sender. If the sender is the horizontal slider, its position is retrieved and the associated spin button and text control are updated. If the sender is the spin button attached to the slider, the slider is updated.

The vertical slider controls the size of the scroll boxes for the horizontal and vertical scrollbars, as described in Section 6.3.5.1:

```
    void sliderDlg::OnVScroll(UINT nSBCode, UINT nPos,
        CScrollBar* pScrollBar)
    {
        switch( pScrollBar->GetDlgCtrlID() ) {
    . . .
        case IDC_VerticalSlider:
            SetDlgItemInt(IDC_VerticalValue, m_vertSlider.GetPos());
            setScrollBox(IDC_VerticalScrollbar,
                m_vertSlider.GetPos());
            setScrollBox(IDC_HorizontalScrollbar,
                m_vertSlider.GetPos());
            break;
        }
    }
```

6.3.6 Editable Text

Edit controls create text editors, from a simple numeric field to a multi-page text document. The controls are packed with functionality and, accordingly, have a rich interface. They support left, right, and centered justification; word wrap; undo/redo; scrolling; and clipboard operations.

6.3.6.1 Edit Controls

The basic Win32 edit control, wrapped by the MFC class CEdit, implements a single-font text editor. In its simplest form, it accepts characters until the field on the screen fills up. This is not a very useful property. Because the default font is proportional, the number of characters that fit depends on what characters are entered—five letter I's may fit in the same space as only two W's. To set a reliable input limit, use CEdit::LimitText.

Since the text in even a limited-text edit control may overflow the allotted screen space, edit controls are usually horizontally scrollable. Adding the WS_HSCROLL style to the control enables horizontal scrolling. Multi-line controls can also scroll vertically if they have the style WS_VSCROLL.

Like other input/output controls, an edit control sends notifications to its parent as it is manipulated. Since the control implements all the functions of a simple text editor, the list of notifications is rather long. The notifications are sent as a parameter in a WM_COMMAND message, but MFC has specialized message-map macros for each notification. Here is a partial list of the notifications:

Notification	Description
EN_CHANGE	The text has been changed and displayed.
EN_ERRSPACE	The control cannot allocate the dynamic memory it needs.
EN_HSCROLL	The user has clicked on the horizontal scrollbar.
EN_KILLFOCUS	The control has lost the focus. Perform a value-level check for valid input in response to this notification.
EN_MAXTEXT	The user has attempted to type more than the maximum allowable number of characters.
EN_SETFOCUS	The control has been given the focus.
EN_UPDATE	The text has been changed but not yet displayed. Perform a character-level check for valid input in response to this notification.
EN_VSCROLL	The user has clicked on the vertical scrollbar.

Part of the convenience of edit controls is their inherent ability to cut and paste. Since most programs use edit controls for all text fields, text can be copied from one field to another using the clipboard. The keyboard accelerators for cut, copy, and paste are understood by the control, and the right mouse button triggers a context menu with the clipboard operations. In addition, the control responds to the Win32 messages WM_CUT, WM_COPY, and WM_PASTE. Use the CEdit member functions Cut, Copy, and Paste to send these messages to the control. Chapter 10 implements a text editor using the edit control in the context of the document/view architecture.

Dialog Data Exchange supports representing the contents of an edit control as a CString, making it easy, if somewhat inefficient, to manipulate the control's contents. The CString will contain a copy of the control's contents. The Edit dialog in the Control Sampler represents all the edit controls as CStrings. ClassWizard generated the following declarations in the header file and the DDX calls in the implementation file:

```
class editDlg : public dialog
{
// Construction
public:
    editDlg(CWnd* pParent = NULL);   // standard constructor

// Dialog Data
    //{{AFX_DATA(editDlg)
    enum { IDD = IDD_Edits };
    CStringm_multiLine;
    CStringm_singleLine;
    CStringm_scrollableSingleLine;
    //}}AFX_DATA
. . .
```

In the implementation file:

```
void editDlg::DoDataExchange(CDataExchange* pDX)
{
    dialog::DoDataExchange(pDX);
    //{{AFX_DATA_MAP(editDlg)
    DDX_Text(pDX, IDC_MultiLine, m_multiLine);
    DDX_Text(pDX, IDC_OneLine, m_singleLine);
    DDX_Text(pDX, IDC_OneLineScrollable, m_scrollableSingleLine);
    //}}AFX_DATA_MAP
}
```

The biggest shortcomings of the edit control are the limited amount of text it can hold and the restriction to a single font. That's why the rich-text edit control was invented.

6.3.6.2 Rich-Text Edit Controls

If an edit control implements a simple text editor, a rich-text edit control implements a simple word processor. The control maintains the text in Rich Text

Format (RTF), an ASCII encoding of the word-processing concepts of character and paragraph style.

For most purposes, you can program the rich-text control as you would the edit control. The control provides no interface other than basic mouse and keyboard. To change the format of text, the program must send messages to the control. Surprisingly, unlike the edit control, the rich-text control does not implement a context menu.

The Edit dialog in the Control Sampler shows one way to create and manipulate the rich-text control. My resource editor did not know about rich-text controls, so the code uses the placeholder strategy described above in Section 6.3.4.4:

```
BOOL editDlg::OnInitDialog()
{
    dialog::OnInitDialog();

    CWnd *placeHolder = GetDlgItem(IDC_RichText);
    CRect rect;
    placeHolder->GetWindowRect(&rect);
    placeHolder->DestroyWindow();
    ScreenToClient(&rect);

    m_richEdit.Create(
        WS_CHILD|WS_VISIBLE|WS_TABSTOP|WS_VSCROLL|
        ES_MULTILINE|ES_WANTRETURN|ES_SUNKEN|ES_AUTOVSCROLL,
        rect,
        this,
        IDC_RichText);

    return TRUE; // return TRUE unless you set the focus to a control
                 // EXCEPTION: OCX Property Pages should return FALSE
}
```

The resulting dialog is shown in Figure 6.11. The buttons to the left of the control in the dialog modify the current selection. If there is no selection, they change the style used for new text. The rich-text control uses two data structures to receive and return formatting information: CHARFORMAT for character font and style and PARAFORMAT for paragraph margins and justification. The Edit dialog uses CHARFORMAT.

Each of the button handlers calls on the helper function setCharEffect to set the character style. As an example, pressing the Bold button triggers onBold:

```
void editDlg::onBold()
{
    setCharEffect(CFE_BOLD);
}
```

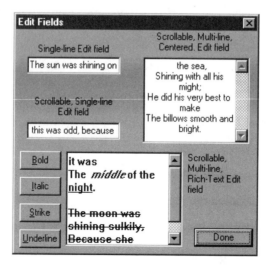

Figure 6.11   The Edit dialog in the Control Sampler illustrates a variety of edit and rich-text controls.

```
void editDlg::setCharEffect(DWORD effect)
{
    CHARFORMAT cf = {
        sizeof(CHARFORMAT),        // cbSize
        CFM_BOLD|CFM_ITALIC|CFM_STRIKEOUT|CFM_UNDERLINE,
                                   // dwMask
        effect                     // dwEffects
    };

    richEdit.SetSelectionCharFormat(cf);
    richEdit.SetFocus();
}
```

The CHARFORMAT structure has mask and effects fields. The mask determines which effects can be set. The effects are flags; they are bitwise OR'd with the mask to generate the format.

In addition to these simple manipulations, the rich-text edit control supports multiple fonts, conversions among a few text formats, stream I/O, and customizable word-wrapping routines. Chapter 7 illustrates how to program many of these capabilities of the rich-text control.

6.3.7 Lists

Win32 supports a wide variety of list styles, from a simple list of values to expandable hierarchies. The basic list types are:

Type	Win32 Class	MFC Class	Description
Simple list	`ListBox`	`CListBox`	Single or multiple columns. The items are always displayed.
Combo box	`Edit` and `ComboLBox`	`CComboBox`	Edit control combined with a single-column list box. The list is always displayed. The edit control can contain a value not in the list.
Drop list	`ComboBox`	`CComboBox`	Text field combined with a list box. The text field can only contain one of the values in the list. The list is displayed only on user request.
Drop-down list	`Edit` and `ComboBox`	`CComboBox`	Edit control combined with a list box. The edit control can contain a value not in the list. The list is displayed only on user request.
Checklist	`ListBox` (owner-draw)	`CCheckListBox`	A check box sits next to each list item. Clicking on an item flips the state of the check box.
List view	`SysListView32`	`CListCtrl`	A list with multiple views. The views are multiple columns of large icons, multiple columns of small icons, single column of small icons, and multi-column report.
Tree	`SysTreeView32`	`CTreeCtrl`	Expandable hierarchical list.

The program interface to a list control varies based on the type of the list and the list style. Most lists support multiple, as well as single, selection. In a multiple-selection list, the user can highlight more than one entry. There are two forms of multiple selection:

Basic	Each click on an entry flips the selection state for the entry. That is, clicking on an entry that is not selected, selects it.
Extended	Mouse clicks are combined with the keyboard Shift and Control keys. A mouse click with neither key down removes any previous selection and highlights the item clicked on. A mouse click with the Control key down selects the clicked-on item. A mouse click with the Shift key down selects all items from the previous item selected to the current item.

6.3.7.1 Simple Lists

The simplest list consists of an array of text items. If the list does not have the style LBS_SORT, the order of the list elements is under program control, so the index of the current selection can be held in an integer member variable. Alternatively, for all types of lists, the current value can be represented by a CString:

The Lists dialog in the Control Sampler illustrates several types of lists (see Figure 6.12). The basic list box in the dialog is unsorted and thus its associated member variable is an integer:

```
class listDlg : public dialog
{
. . .
// Dialog Data
    //{{AFX_DATA(listDlg)
    enum { IDD = IDD_Lists };
    CListBoxm_extended;
    Cstring      m_comboVal;
    Cstring      m_dropDownVal;
    int          m_basicVal;
    Cstring      m_dropListVal;
    //}}AFX_DATA
```

The DDX function DDX_LBIndex transfers data between a list box and its integer representation:

```
void listDlg::DoDataExchange(CDataExchange* pDX)
{
    dialog::DoDataExchange(pDX);
    //{{AFX_DATA_MAP(listDlg)
. . .
    DDX_LBIndex(pDX, IDC_Basic, m_basicVal);
```

Although representing a list box selection with an integer is convenient, it is also potentially dangerous. Should the list style be changed to include LBS_SORT, you

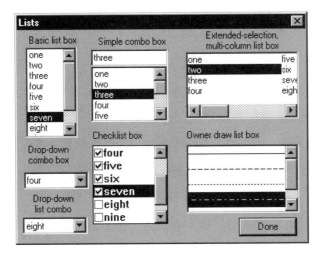

Figure 6.12   The Lists dialog in the Control Sampler illustrates list and combo boxes.

won't get any errors, but the program may not work correctly since the index returned by the list box will refer to the *sorted* list.

When a dialog first appears, users expect controls to show the current values of the corresponding program parameters. For a list, this means highlighting the currently selected item. The DDX function carries out this chore based on the value of the associated member variable. However, before an item can be selected, the list box needs to be filled. Since dialog::OnInitDialog calls CDialog::OnInitDialog, which calls DoDataExchange, initialize the list box *before* calling the base class:

```
BOOL listDlg::OnInitDialog()
{
    initList(IDC_Basic);
    initList(IDC_Extended);
    initCombo(IDC_Combo);
    initCombo(IDC_DropList);
    initCombo(IDC_DropDown);
    dialog::OnInitDialog();
```

initList fills a list box from an array of strings using the CListBox member function AddString:

```
// items to populate lists
static TCHAR *item[] = {
    _T("one"), _T("two"), _T("three"), _T("four"), _T("five"),
    _T("six"), _T("seven"), _T("eight"), _T("nine"), _T("ten")
};

. . .

void listDlg::initList(UINT id)
{
    CListBox *lb = (CListBox *)GetDlgItem(id);

    for( int i=0; i<sizeof(item)/sizeof(*item); ++i )
        lb->AddString(item[i]);
    lb->SetCurSel(0);
}
```

6.3.7.2 Simple Lists with Multiple Selection

In a multiple-selection list, an array of integers represents the selected entries. Again, the integers represent the selection positions in the actual list box on the screen. If the list is sorted, the order probably won't agree with the insertion order. In that case you'll need to use the CListBox::GetText function to convert from an index to the text of an item. Alternatively, 32 bits of data or a pointer can be associated with each item using either SetItemData or SetItemDataPtr.

Dialog Data Exchange doesn't support multiple selection. Use the CListBox functions GetSelItems and SetSel to get and set the selection list. To manipulate the list box, put a CListBox member into the dialog class:

```
class listDlg : public dialog
{
. . .
// Dialog Data
    //{{AFX_DATA(listDlg)
    enum { IDD = IDD_Lists };
    CListBox m_extended;
```

Then get and set the selections in DoDataExchange:

```
void listDlg::DoDataExchange(CDataExchange* pDX)
{
    dialog::DoDataExchange(pDX);
. . .
    if( pDX->m_bSaveAndValidate )
        m_numSelected = m_extended.GetSelItems(MaxSelections,
          m_extendedVal);
    else {
        for( int i=0; i<m_numSelected; ++i )
            m_extended.SetSel(m_extendedVal[i]);
    }
}
```

Recall that DoDataExchange is called to move data both from and to the dialog controls. The m_bSaveAndValidate member of the CDataExchange parameter tells which direction the data is moving. When true, data is moving from the dialog to the associated member variables.

6.3.7.3 Combo Boxes

Combo boxes work much like ordinary lists, but since the value of the combo box may not be one of the list items, the associated member variable should be a CString and the DDX function is DDX_CBString.

From the Lists dialog:

```
class listDlg : public dialog
{
. . .
    CStringm_comboVal;

void listDlg::DoDataExchange(CDataExchange* pDX)
{
. . .
    DDX_CBString(pDX, IDC_Combo, m_comboVal);
```

6.3.7.4 Checklists

Checklists are implemented in MFC. They are owner-draw lists in which the drawing code is in the CCheckBox class. Again, my resource editor did not know about checklists, so I used a placeholder control:

```
CWnd *placeHolder = GetDlgItem(IDC_CheckList);
CRect rect;
placeHolder->GetWindowRect(&rect);
ScreenToClient(&rect);
placeHolder->DestroyWindow();

checkList.Create(
    WS_CHILD|WS_VISIBLE|WS_TABSTOP|WS_VSCROLL|
    WS_BORDER|LBS_HASSTRINGS|LBS_OWNERDRAWFIXED,
    rect,
    this,
    IDC_CheckList);
initList(IDC_CheckList);
```

A checklist is like a multiple-selection list box. Each of the items can be set independently, so you'll need to iterate over the items to read the item states.

6.3.7.4.1 When Things Don't Work

When I first tested the checklist code, it went down in flames. Fortunately, the debugger caught the problem and stopped at the offending code. I want to relate the details of what failed and how I found out. The story has a powerful moral: *Don't even think about removing the* MFC *source code to save space.*

Occasionally when running the Lists dialog, the program would crash in the MFC function CCheckListBox::PreMeasureItem on the statement highlighted below:

```
void CCheckListBox::PreMeasureItem(LPMEASUREITEMSTRUCT
    lpMeasureItemStruct)
{
    int cyItem = CalcMinimumItemHeight();

    MEASUREITEMSTRUCT measureItem;
    memcpy(&measureItem, lpMeasureItemStruct,sizeof(MEASUREITEMSTRUCT));

    measureItem.itemHeight = cyItem;
    measureItem.itemWidth  = (UINT)-1;

    // WINBUG: Windows95 and Windows NT disagree on what this value
    // should be.  According to the docs, they are both wrong
    if (GetStyle() & LBS_OWNERDRAWVARIABLE)
    {
        LRESULT lResult = DefWindowProc(LB_GETITEMDATA,
            measureItem.itemID, 0);
        if (lResult != LB_ERR)
            measureItem.itemData = (UINT)lResult;
        else
            measureItem.itemData = 0;
    }

    if (measureItem.itemData != 0)
    {
        AFX_CHECK_DATA* pState = (AFX_CHECK_DATA*)measureItem.itemData;
        measureItem.itemData = pState->m_dwUserData;
    }
```

The stack trace wasn't particularly surprising:

```
CCheckListBox::PreMeasureItem(
CCheckListBox::OnChildNotify(
CWnd::SendChildNotifyLastMsg(
CWnd::OnMeasureItem(
CWnd::OnWndMsg(
CWnd::WindowProc(
```

But the itemData field of the measureItem structure didn't look right:

```
itemData = 0xe9148920
```

As part of the startup code for an owner-draw list box with fixed-size items, Win32 sends the owner window the message WM_MEASUREITEM to ask how large the items will be. For checklists the message is reflected back to the CCheckBox object. Along with the message is a MEASUREITEMSTRUCT that contains a field named itemData. The API reference manual clearly states that itemData will be zero until the list box is initialized and, in fact, CCheckListBox::PreMeasureItem counts on it being either zero or valid. The reality appears to be that itemData is sometimes garbage. (I must admit that the WINBUG comment a few lines above the fatal line made me feel a little shaky about the documented behavior.)

Having identified the problem, what is the fix?[16] There are two choices:

- Modify PreMeasureItem in the MFC source and recompile the library; or,
- Subclass CCheckListBox and filter PreMeasureItem.

Unless you are responsible for maintaining the MFC library, I hope you agree with me that choice 2 is the correct strategy. One significant strength of C++ is the ease with which specific behavior can be adjusted.

The Lists dialog uses a new class checkListBox:

```
class checkListBox : public CCheckListBox
{
// Operations
public:
    checkListBox();

// Overrides
    // ClassWizard generated virtual function overrides
    //{{AFX_VIRTUAL(checkListBox)
    public:
    virtual BOOL OnChildNotify(UINT message, WPARAM wParam,
        LPARAM lParam, LRESULT* pLResult);
    //}}AFX_VIRTUAL

protected:
    //{{AFX_MSG(checkListBox)
    //}}AFX_MSG

    DECLARE_MESSAGE_MAP()
};
```

Looking from top to bottom at the call stack from PreMeasureItem, the first virtual function is OnChildNotify. Tapping into OnChildNotify, the itemData field can be forced to zero if the message is WM_MEASUREITEM and the list box is empty:

---

[16] The culprit turned out to be Windows 95. MFC release 4.2 includes a patch to avoid the crash.

```
    BOOL checkListBox::OnChildNotify(UINT message, WPARAM wParam,
        LPARAM lParam, LRESULT* pLResult)
{
    if( message==WM_MEASUREITEM ) {
        // On occasion, itemData is non-NULL, even though the listbox
        // has not been initialized yet.  This is counter to the doc
        // and results in a crash in CCheckListBox::PreMeasureItem
        LPMEASUREITEMSTRUCT lp = (LPMEASUREITEMSTRUCT)lParam;
        if( GetCount()==0 )
            lp->itemData = NULL;
    }

    return CCheckListBox::OnChildNotify(message, wParam,
        lParam, pLResult);
}
```

6.3.7.5 Owner-Draw Lists

Like other owner-draw controls, owner-draw lists give the program complete control over the appearance of each list item. Owner-draw lists can have either fixed- or variable-height items. Fixed-height items are slightly simpler to program because the WM_MEASUREITEM message is received only once during initialization. In a list with variable-size items, WM_MEASUREITEM is received repeatedly.

Programming an owner-draw list requires shuffling back and forth between Win32 and MFC, since the messages from Win32 refer to *Win32*, not C++, objects. When the list box needs to draw an item, it will send the dialog box the WM_DRAWITEM message along with a DRAWITEMSTRUCT. The structure will tell the dialog the state of the item, its location, and give a display context in which to draw. This scenario should remind you of an owner-draw button; the control flow is analogous to that shown in Figure 6.7.

As with the owner-draw buttons, I recommend using message reflection to put the drawing code into a CListBox-derived class. The Lists dialog uses an owner-draw list to create a list box of different line styles (see Figure 6.12). The owner-draw list is wrapped by the class ownerDrawList:

```
class ownerDrawList : public CListBox
{
// Construction
public:
    void initList();
    ownerDrawList();

// Attributes
public:
```

```
// Operations
public:

// Overrides
    // ClassWizard generated virtual function overrides
    //{{AFX_VIRTUAL(ownerDrawList)
    public:
    virtual void MeasureItem(LPMEASUREITEMSTRUCT lpMeasureItemStruct);
    //}}AFX_VIRTUAL

// Implementation
public:
    virtual ~ownerDrawList();

    // Generated message map functions
protected:
    //{{AFX_MSG(ownerDrawList)
    afx_msg void DrawItem(LPDRAWITEMSTRUCT lpDrawItemStruct);
    //}}AFX_MSG

    DECLARE_MESSAGE_MAP()
};
```

The Lists dialog includes an instance of an ownerDrawList:

```
class listDlg : public dialog
{
. . .
    ownerDrawList m_ownerDraw;
```

The list is initialized by calling initList:

```
BOOL listDlg::OnInitDialog()
{
. . .
    m_ownerDraw.initList();
```

initList tells the underlying list box control how many items are in the list:

```
void ownerDrawList::initList()
{
    SendMessage(LB_SETCOUNT,sizeof(lineStyles)/sizeof(lineStyles[0]));
}
```

Each item is a line style kept in the array lineStyles:

```
static UINT lineStyles[] = {
    PS_SOLID, PS_DASH, PS_DOT, PS_DASHDOT, PS_DASHDOTDOT
};
```

The list box has the style LBS_OWNERDRAWFIXED, so it's owner will receive one WM_MEASUREITEM message during initialization. CListBox has a virtual function MeasureItem that is called when the owner receives WM_MEASUREITEM. For owner-DrawList, I've set the width to a large number (the size of the screen) and the height to the height of a standard menu bar:

```
void ownerDrawList::MeasureItem(
    LPMEASUREITEMSTRUCT lpMeasureItemStruct)
{
    lpMeasureItemStruct->itemWidth = ::GetSystemMetrics(SM_CXSCREEN);
    lpMeasureItemStruct->itemHeight = ::GetSystemMetrics(SM_CYMENU);
}
```

6.3.7.5.1 *WM_MEASUREITEM in a Fixed-Height List Box*

Handling WM_MEASUREITEM presents a challenge. Consider the sequence of events regarding the list box beginning with the call to DoModal:

1. The program calls DoModal to trigger the dialog.
2. The list box window is created.
3. WM_MEASUREITEM is received by the dialog frame.
4. The frame calls MeasureItem for the corresponding child.
5. WM_INITDIALOG is received by the dialog frame.
6. The C++ wrapper object is connected to the Win32 control.

When WM_MEASUREITEM is received, the wrapper object has not been attached to the underlying list box control. As a result, there is no wrapper object to use in the call to MeasureItem and MFC simply calls DefWindowProc, the Win32 default handler.[17]

To pass control to ownerDrawList::MeasureItem, I intercepted the message in the dialog-box class:

```
void listDlg::OnMeasureItem(
    int nIDCtl, LPMEASUREITEMSTRUCT lpMeasureItemStruct)
{
    ownerDraw.MeasureItem(lpMeasureItemStruct);
}
```

This patch is only needed for fixed-height owner-draw lists. For list boxes with the LBS_OWNERDRAWVARIABLE style, WM_MEASUREITEM is sent just before the list-box item needs to be drawn. This is after the wrapper is attached to the control, so MeasureItem is called as expected.

---

[17] There is no default behavior documented for WM_MEASUREITEM. Empirically, if a list box has zero height, the default, it uses the height of the system font.

6.3.7.5.2 Drawing the Item

When the list box needs to draw an item, it sends the WM_DRAWITEM message to the dialog-box frame. MFC reflects the message to the owner-draw list-box object:

```
void ownerDrawList::DrawItem(LPDRAWITEMSTRUCT lpDrawItemStruct)
{
    CDC *dc = CDC::FromHandle(lpDrawItemStruct->hDC);
    int saveDC = dc->SaveDC();
    CRect rect(lpDrawItemStruct->rcItem);
    int halfHeight = rect.Height()/2;
    int lineStyle = lineStyles[lpDrawItemStruct->itemID];
    CBrush bkBrush;

    if( lpDrawItemStruct->itemState & ODS_FOCUS ) {
        bkBrush.CreateSysColorBrush(COLOR_HIGHLIGHT);
        dc->SetROP2(R2_NOT);
    } else {
        bkBrush.CreateSolidBrush(RGB(255,255,255));
    }

    dc->FillRect(&rect,&bkBrush);

    CPen pen(lineStyle,1,RGB(0,0,0));
    dc->SetBkMode(TRANSPARENT);
    dc->SelectObject(&pen);
    dc->MoveTo(rect.left,rect.top+halfHeight);
    dc->LineTo(rect.right,rect.top+halfHeight);
    dc->RestoreDC(saveDC);
}
```

The DRAWITEMSTRUCT contains the location at which the item should be drawn and a Win32 display context to use for drawing. As I did for the owner-draw button in Section 6.3.4.2, I wrap the display context with a C++ object using CDC::FromHandle.

The background for the line is drawn before the line itself. The itemState flag tells if the item has the focus. If it does have the focus, the user's highlight color is used for the background.[18] Otherwise, white is used. See Chapter 8 for details on drawing and display contexts.

6.3.7.6 List Views

A list-view control displays a list of items along with an icon image and additional associated text fields. At any one time, a list view shows its items in one of four views: a list of large icons, a list of small icons, a list of text, or a report.

---

[18] Highlight color can be set using the Display mini-app of the Windows Control Panel.

Figure 6.13 shows the four views of the List View dialog from the Control Sampler. List views are implemented by the Win32 class `SysListView32` and wrapped by the MFC class `CListCtrl`.

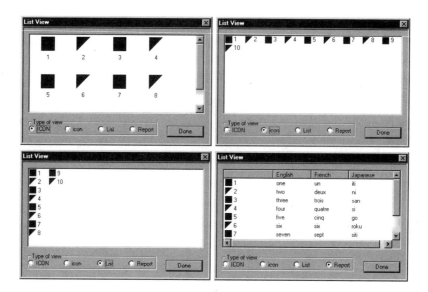

Figure 6.13 The four views of the List View dialog in the Control Sampler: large icons, small icons, list, and report.

To create a list view, you need to work with lists of three types of objects: items, columns, and images.

An *image* list is an array of icons. Image lists are implemented in Win32 and wrapped by the `CImageList` class. In Win32, the icons are represented in a bitmap over which a tile grid is placed. Each image occupies one tile. The bitmap can be created dynamically by adding the icon images to the bitmap one at a time or by statically using a resource editor.[19] For the list view, create two image lists, one for the small icons and one for the large.

The heart of a list view is the *item* list. There is one item per icon in the icon views and one item per row in the report view. Each item has a text label, may refer to an element in the image lists, and may have an associated list of sub-items.

---

[19] In Visual C++, the resource editor has an option to show a tile grid over a bitmap. In a bitmap for an image list, each tile corresponds to one image.

The *column* list forms the basis for the report view. Each column has an index that refers to an element in each item's sub-item list. A column may also have a title which will be displayed in the header control above the column.

Figure 6.14 shows how these lists interact. Setting up a list view takes a bit of work, but once set up, the control operates largely by itself. Here are the steps:

1. Create image lists of large and small icons.
2. Connect the image lists to the list view.
3. Create the list columns and the corresponding headers.
4. Create the list items and corresponding sub-items.

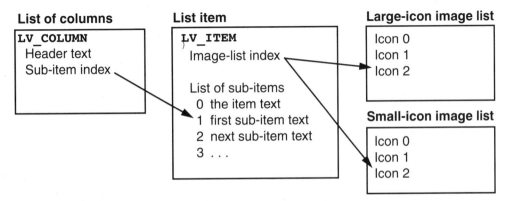

Figure 6.14   A list view consists of a collection of list items. This diagram shows how the items are connected. Each item may have a list of sub-items. The list of columns drives the report view.

Each of these steps is implemented in `OnInitDialog` described below.

6.3.7.6.1 Creating the ImageLlists

The List View dialog has ten items corresponding to the first ten natural numbers. It uses two icons, one for even numbers and one for odd. On initialization, it creates an image list by loading the icon resources:

```
static UINT icons[] = {
    IDI_Odd, IDI_Even,
};
. . .
```

```
BOOL listViewDlg::OnInitDialog()
{
    dialog::OnInitDialog();

    // Create the image lists
    m_largeIcons.Create(::GetSystemMetrics(SM_CXICON),
        ::GetSystemMetrics(SM_CYICON),TRUE,10,10);
    m_smallIcons.Create(::GetSystemMetrics(SM_CXICON)/2,
        ::GetSystemMetrics(SM_CYICON)/2,TRUE,10,10);

    // Initialize the elements
    for( int i=0; i<ELEMCNT(icons); ++i ) {
        m_largeIcons.Add( AfxGetApp()->LoadIcon(icons[i]) );
        m_smallIcons.Add( AfxGetApp()->LoadIcon(icons[i]) );
    }
```

ELEMCNT is a macro I defined that returns the number of elements in an array:

```
#define ELEMCNT(a) (sizeof(a)/sizeof(*a))
```

m_largeIcons and m_smallIcons are CImageList data members of the dialog:

```
class listViewDlg : public dialog
{
. . .
    CImageList m_largeIcons;
    CImageList m_smallIcons;
```

If you look at the icons IDI_Odd and IDI_Even in the resource editor, you'll see that they are large (32 by 32 pixels). CImageList::Create can generate the small icons (16 by 16 pixels) by removing every other line and column of pixels. Alternatively, you can create separate icons for the small images.

6.3.7.6.2 Connecting the Image Lists

The list-view control is wrapped by a member variable of type CListCtrl:

```
class listViewDlg : public dialog
{
. . .
    //{{AFX_DATA(listViewDlg)
    enum { IDD = IDD_ListView };
    CListCtrl m_list;
```

Once the image lists are created, connecting them to the wrapper is easy. Use the SetImageList member function of CListCtrl. Continuing in OnInitDialog:

```
    // Connect the lists to the list view
    m_list.SetImageList(&m_largeIcons,LVSIL_NORMAL);
    m_list.SetImageList(&m_smallIcons,LVSIL_SMALL);
```

6.3.7.6.3 Creating the Columns

Each column in the report view has a format, width, title, and index. The format specifies the justification of the column text. The width is the initial width; the user can change the width by grabbing the dividers in the header control that sits on top of the columns. The title becomes the label in the header control. The index is the index of the sub-item displayed in the column.

Again, continuing in `OnInitDialog`:

```
// Create the columns
LV_COLUMN col;
col.mask = LVCF_ALL;
col.fmt = LVCFMT_LEFT;
col.cchTextMax = 32;
for( i=0; i<ELEMCNT(columns); ++i ) {
    col.pszText = columns[i].text;   // Title
    col.cx = 100;                    // Width
    col.iSubItem = i;                // Index in list of sub items
    m_list.InsertColumn(i,&col);
}
```

In the List View dialog, the report view has four columns. I've put the column titles into the array `columns`:

```
static struct column {
    TCHAR *text;
} columns[] = {
    _T(""),          // Numeric, no need for a title
    _T("English"),
    _T("French"),
    _T("Japanese")
};
```

6.3.7.6.4 Creating the Items

At the top level, a list view consists of a list of items. Each item has an associated text string plus an optional icon and a list of sub-items:

```
// Create the list items
LV_ITEM item;
item.mask = LVIF_TEXT|LVIF_IMAGE|LVIF_PARAM;
item.state = item.stateMask = 0;
for( i=0; i<ELEMCNT(items); ++i ) {
    item.iItem = i;
    item.iSubItem = 0;
    item.pszText = items[i].number;
    item.iImage = idToIndex(items[i].iconID);
    item.lParam = i;
    m_list.InsertItem(&item);
```

```
        // Create the subitems (additional columns)
        m_list.SetItemText(i,1,items[i].english);
        m_list.SetItemText(i,2,items[i].french);
        m_list.SetItemText(i,3,items[i].japanese);
    }
```

SetItemText adds the sub-items. The second parameter is the index of the sub-item. The index corresponds to the index used in the iSubItem field of the associated column.

6.3.7.6.5 Sorting the Report View

In the report view, when a header button is clicked, the list-view control sends the LBN_COLUMNCLICK notification to its parent via the WM_NOTIFY message. Common behavior is to sort the list using the column under the clicked-on header as the primary key. CListCtrl has a sort function, SortItems, that takes a comparison routine and a column number to sort:

```
    void listViewDlg::OnColumnclickList(NMHDR* pNMHDR, LRESULT* pResult)
    {
        NM_LISTVIEW* pNMListView = (NM_LISTVIEW*)pNMHDR;
        m_list.SortItems(colCompare,pNMListView->iSubItem);

        *pResult = 0;
    }
```

The comparison routine is passed the column number being sorted and the sub-item index of the left and right operands to the less-than operator. The return value uses the conventions of the C library routine strcmp:[20]

```
    int CALLBACK listViewDlg::colCompare(
        LPARAM lhs, LPARAM rhs, LPARAM columnNumber)
    {
        TCHAR *s1, *s2;

        switch(columnNumber) {
        case 0:
            return atoi(items[lhs].number) > atoi(items[rhs].number);
        case 1:
            s1 = items[lhs].english;
            s2 = items[rhs].english;
            break;
        case 2:
            s1 = items[lhs].french;
            s2 = items[rhs].french;
            break;
```

---

[20] lstrcmpi is the Win32, case-insensitive version of lstrcmp. It handles narrow and wide characters.

```
    case 3:
        s1 = items[lhs].japanese;
        s2 = items[rhs].japanese;
        break;
    }

    return lstrcmpi(s1,s2);
}
```

colCompare is declared CALLBACK and static since it is called by Win32:

```
class listViewDlg : public dialog
{
. . .
    static int CALLBACK colCompare(LPARAM lhs, LPARAM rhs,
        LPARAM columnNumber);
```

6.3.7.6.6 Changing Views

The method for changing views in a list view is a little strange. The view is controlled by the Win32 window style. To get and set the view, you need to access the data structure that Win32 keeps for the control. The API function ::GetWindowLong gets the Win32 data; ::SetWindowsLong sets it. The style field is referred to by GWL_STYLE.[21]

The List View dialog uses a set of four radio buttons to select the current view. The setView function is called by the handlers for the radio buttons:

```
        afx_msg void onLargeIcon()   { setView(LVS_ICON); };
        afx_msg void onListView()    { setView(LVS_LIST); };
        afx_msg void onReportView()  { setView(LVS_REPORT); };
        afx_msg void onSmallIcon()   { setView(LVS_SMALLICON); };

    void listViewDlg::setView(LONG view)
    {
        LONG state = ::GetWindowLong(m_list.m_hWnd,GWL_STYLE) &
            ~LVS_TYPEMASK;
        ::SetWindowLong(m_list.m_hWnd,GWL_STYLE,state|view);
        m_list.InvalidateRect(NULL);
    }
```

The value returned by ::GetWindowLong includes flags for window attributes such as the border style, window visibility, and activation state. When changing the view, it is important to leave the other flags as they were.

---

[21] A member function to change the view is such an obvious addition to the CListCtrl class that I expect it to materialize any day. Check the MFC reference manual to see if it already has.

6.3.7.7 Trees

Trees, like list views, take considerable work to initialize but then operate mostly by themselves. A tree consists of a hierarchical collection of nodes. Associated with each node is a text string, an optional icon, and optional sub-nodes. Trees are implemented in the Win32 class SysTreeView32 and wrapped by the MFC class CTreeCtrl.

Win32 maintains an internal data structure for each tree node called a TV_ITEM. Associated with each node is a text string, two optional icons, and zero or more sub-nodes. The icons are kept in an image list, just as for list views. The sub-nodes are attached using the CTreeCtrl::InsertItem function. Trees are built from the root down. Use the handle returned by InsertItem to specify the parent node for a new node. Figure 6.15 shows how the data structures are related.

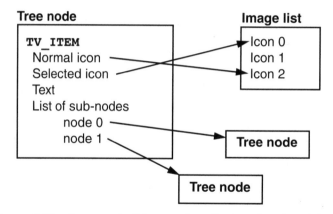

Figure 6.15   Trees are built from nodes. Each node points to images and sub-nodes.

A node can be in one of the following basic states:

Selected	Clicking on a node selects it. The node is shown highlighted.
Expanded	Double-clicking on a node alternately expands and contracts the item.
Changed	Clicking on the selected node triggers an edit control containing the node text. The text can be changed.
Drop highlighted	Trees support drag-and-drop for visual reordering. When nodes are being dragged over a target, the target is drop-highlighted.

Follow these steps to set up a tree control:

1. Create an image list if the tree will show icons.
2. Create the root node.
3. Create the sub-nodes.
4. For each node, specify the node text and icons for the selected and unselected states.

If the tree can be very large, or if it takes a considerable time to retrieve data for the nodes, the sub-trees can be constructed as needed by responding to the TVN_EXPANDING notification.

6.3.7.7.1 Initializing the Tree

The Trees dialog in the Control Sampler builds two directory trees, one just as a hierarchical list and one with icons, buttons, and lines (see Figure 6.16). The basic tree is wrapped by the member variable m_basicTree and the decorated tree by m_fancyTree:

```
class treeDlg : public dialog
{
. . .
// Dialog Data
    //{{AFX_DATA(treeDlg)
    enum { IDD = IDD_Trees };
    CTreeCtrl m_fancyTree;
    CTreeCtrl m_basicTree;
    //}}AFX_DATA
```

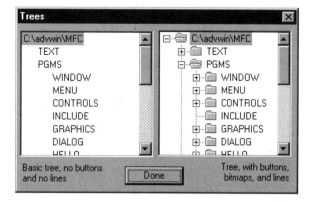

Figure 6.16   The Trees dialog in the Control Sampler contains two tree controls showing directory structure.

`OnInitDialog` initializes the tree. The first step is to create the image list:

```
BOOL treeDlg::OnInitDialog()
{
    dialog::OnInitDialog();

    folderImages.Create(IDB_Folders,16,2,0);
    m_fancyTree.SetImageList(&folderImages,TVSIL_NORMAL);
```

In Section 6.3.7.6.1 I created the image lists from individual icons. Here a single bitmap, called `IDB_Folders`, contains the two images for a node. The bitmap is shown in Figure 6.17.

Figure 6.17   `IDB_Folders` contains two images.

Next, the tree nodes are created. Continuing in `OnInitDialog`:

```
    initTree(m_fancyTree);
    initTree(m_basicTree);
```

The work of walking the directory structure and building the directory tree begins in the member function `initTree`. `initTree` begins by creating a root node for the current directory and then it scans for sub-directories. Arbitrarily, the directory tree begins two levels up the directory hierarchy from the current directory:

```
void treeDlg::initTree(CTreeCtrl &tree)
{
    TCHAR curdir[_MAX_PATH];
    TCHAR path[_MAX_PATH];
    ::GetCurrentDirectory(sizeof(curdir),curdir);
    ::SetCurrentDirectory(_T("..\\.."));
    ::GetCurrentDirectory(sizeof(path),path);

    HTREEITEM root = tree.InsertItem(path,0,0,TVI_ROOT);
    scanDir(tree,root);
    ::SetCurrentDirectory(curdir);
}
```

To distinguish the root to `InsertItem`, pass `TVI_ROOT` for the parent.

`scanDir` walks the directory tree depth first. When it finds a sub-directory, it recurses:

```
void treeDlg::scanDir(CTreeCtrl &tree,HTREEITEM root)
{
    WIN32_FIND_DATA fd;
    HANDLE h = ::FindFirstFile(_T("*.*"),&fd);
    while( FindNextFile(h,&fd) ) {
        if( fd.dwFileAttributes & FILE_ATTRIBUTE_DIRECTORY
          && fd.cFileName[0]!='.' ) {
            HTREEITEM dir = tree.InsertItem(fd.cFileName,0,0,root);
            ::SetCurrentDirectory(fd.cFileName);
            scanDir(tree,dir);
            ::SetCurrentDirectory(_T(".."));
        }
    }
    ::FindClose(h);
}
```

Although it is a bit of an aside, scanDir shows how to walk the directory structure using Win32. MFC does not implement classes for scanning directories.

6.3.7.7.2 Tree Notifications

When the state of a node changes, the tree sends a notification message to its parent. Trees are relatively complex controls and so have several notifications. Here is a partial list:

TVN_BEGINDRAG	The user has begun dragging an item using the left mouse button.
TVN_BEGINLABELEDIT (TVN_ENDLABELEDIT)	The user has started (finished) editing the text of an item.
TVN_DELETEITEM	The user has deleted an item.
TVN_ITEMEXPANDING	A tree item is about to expand or shrink, usually in response to a double click.
TVN_ITEMEXPANDED	The item is done expanding or shrinking.

The tree control delivers a pointer to an NM_TREEVIEW along with the notification. The NM_TREEVIEW gives more information about the event and has a handle to the node being modified:

```
typedef struct _NM_TREEVIEW {
    NMHDR     hdr;        // A common header used in all notifications
                          // Identifies general classes of notifications
    UINT      action;     // Gives more details about the notification
    TV_ITEM   itemOld;    // Some notifications involve two nodes
    TV_ITEM   itemNew;    // The node usually of interest
    POINT     ptDrag;     // The location of the mouse
} NM_TREEVIEW;
```

The Trees dialog responds to only one notification, expansion of a node:

```
BEGIN_MESSAGE_MAP(treeDlg, dialog)
    //{{AFX_MSG_MAP(treeDlg)
    ON_NOTIFY(TVN_ITEMEXPANDED, IDC_FancyTree, onItemexpandedFancyTree)
    //}}AFX_MSG_MAP
END_MESSAGE_MAP()
```

The tree control takes care of expanding and contracting nodes by itself. onItemexpandedFancyTree swaps the icon next to each node, using the open folder when a node is expanded and the closed folder otherwise. The `action` member of NM_TREEVIEW specifies whether the `itemNew` is expanding or collapsing:

```
void treeDlg::onItemexpandedFancyTree(NMHDR* pNMHDR, LRESULT* pResult)
{
    NM_TREEVIEW* pNMTreeView = (NM_TREEVIEW*)pNMHDR;
    int imageIndex = pNMTreeView->action==TVE_EXPAND ? 1 : 0;
    m_fancyTree.SetItemImage(pNMTreeView->itemNew.hItem,imageIndex,
        imageIndex );

    *pResult = 0;
}
```

6.4 Tabbed Dialogs

A tabbed dialog, or *property sheet*, provides convenient access to a set of related sub-dialogs, known as *property pages*. The pages add a layer of hierarchy to the dialog, allowing related dialog items to be shown together. Each page is described by a dialog resource. The pages are displayed in a tab control, implemented by the Win32 class SysTabControl32, and wrapped by the MFC classes CPropertySheet and CPropertyPage. Figure 6.19 shows the Property Sheet dialog from the Control Sampler. Figure 6.18 shows how the pages are related to the whole.

Creating a tabbed dialog involves two major tasks:

1. Create the overall dialog (the property sheet). The property sheet consists of a tab control above an array of buttons.
2. Create the sub-dialogs (the property pages). Each page should be approximately the same size.

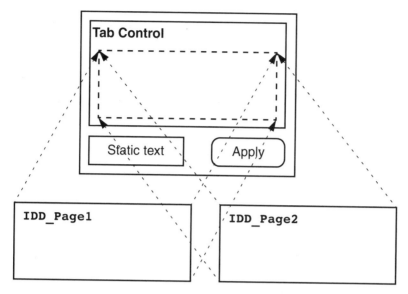

Figure 6.18   A property sheet contains a tab control. The tab control switches between the property pages.

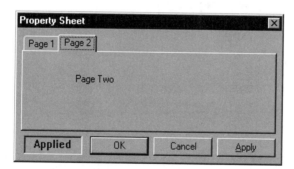

Figure 6.19   The Property Sheet dialog in the Control Sampler triggers this property sheet with a custom text field.

6.4.1 Creating a Property Sheet

The property sheet contains the tab control and top-level buttons. Property sheets have the standard buttons OK and Cancel, and may have Apply and Help. The sheet is generated dynamically based on the size of the largest property page.

A program controls which buttons are present and how the dialog operates through the PROPSHEETHEADER member of CPropertySheet. After initializing PROPSHEETHEADER, call DoModal to run the dialog.

The Dialog Property Sheet command in the Control Sampler triggers the dialog shown in Figure 6.19:

```
void mainFrame::onPropertySheet()
{
    tabDlg dlg("Property Sheet");
    dlg.DoModal();
}
```

The class tabDlg is derived from CPropertySheet. It has one CPropertyPage member for each page:

```
class tabDlg : public CPropertySheet
{
. . .
    CPropertyPage m_page1;
    CPropertyPage m_page2;
```

6.4.2 Creating the Property Pages

Each property page is described by a dialog resource. In effect, you can treat each page as a separate dialog. In creating the dialog resources, keep in mind that the size of the overall dialog frame will be based on the largest of the pages. Property sheets look best when the pages are the same size and have compatible layouts.

If a page has input/output controls, create a CDialog-derived class to hold C++ wrapper objects just as you would for any other dialog. The title of the dialog becomes the label on the tab for the page, so you'll want to keep it short.

Associate the pages with the property sheet using the AddPage member function of CPropertySheet. The tabDlg class does this in its constructor:

```
tabDlg::tabDlg(LPCTSTR pszCaption, CWnd* pParentWnd, UINT iSelectPage)
    :CPropertySheet(pszCaption, pParentWnd, iSelectPage),
    page1(IDD_Page1), page2(IDD_Page2)

{
    AddPage(&page1);
    AddPage(&page2);
}
```

6.4.2.1 Customizing a Property Sheet

For some property sheets, it is useful to have controls that are visible across pages, but since the layout of the sheet is handled dynamically by the control, there is no resource to edit. Modification of the sheet must be done dynamically.

The Property Sheet dialog adds a status indicator to the sheet (see Figure 6.19). Pressing the Apply button flips the state of the indicator between showing "Applied" and "Not Applied". The modifications to the sheet are made in OnInitDialog:

```
BOOL tabDlg::OnInitDialog()
{
    BOOL retval = CPropertySheet::OnInitDialog();
    CRect dlgRect, ctlRect;
    GetClientRect(&dlgRect);
    GetDlgItem(IDOK)->GetWindowRect(&ctlRect);
    ScreenToClient(&ctlRect);
    ctlRect.right = ctlRect.Width() + 10;
    ctlRect.left = 10;

    m_applyText.CreateEx(WS_EX_CLIENTEDGE,
        _T("Static"),
        _T("Not Applied"),
        WS_CHILD|WS_VISIBLE|SS_CENTER,
        ctlRect.left,ctlRect.top,
        ctlRect.Width(), ctlRect.Height(),
        m_hWnd,
        (HMENU)IDC_ApplyText);

    m_page1.SetModified(); // Enable Apply button
    return retval;
}
```

The indicator control is created to be the same size as the OK button and is placed in the lower-left corner, vertically aligned with the button. The control is given the ID IDC_ApplyText. The member variable m_applyText wraps the control:

```
class tabDlg : public CPropertySheet
{
. . .
    CStatic m_applyText;
```

6.4.3 Responding to Commands

The controls on each page are handled in the standard way by creating message-map entries in the page dialogs to pick up WM_COMMAND and WM_NOTIFY messages.

In addition, there are virtual functions in the CPropertyPage class for picking up clicks of the standard OK, Cancel, Help, and Apply buttons, which makes it easy to handle commands within the context of a page.

You can also pick up the standard buttons in the property sheet. The OK and Cancel buttons have the expected IDs IDOK and IDCANCEL. Unfortunately, the IDs for Apply and Help are not documented. You can certainly find out what the IDs are using Spy and then create ON_COMMAND message-map entries for the buttons, but there is no guarantee that the IDs will remain fixed. The Property Sheet dialog illustrates an alternative technique.

The dialog uses the Apply button to change the text in the static control. Presses of Apply are picked up by the tabDlg class in the OnCommand member function. MFC turns WM_COMMAND messages into a call of the virtual function OnCommand. tabDlg overrides OnCommand:

```
BOOL tabDlg::OnCommand(WPARAM wParam, LPARAM lParam)
{
    if( wParam!=IDOK && wParam!=IDCANCEL ) {
        // Must be Apply, so toggle apply text
        CString text;
        m_applyText.GetWindowText(text);
        if( text.Find(_T("Not"))>=0 )
            m_applyText.SetWindowText(_T("Applied"));
        else m_applyText.SetWindowText(_T("Not applied"));
        return TRUE;
    }

    return CPropertySheet::OnCommand(wParam, lParam);
}
```

This chapter has only scratched the surface of tabbed dialogs. See the Wizard Install program in Chapter 14 for an in-depth look at property sheets.

CHAPTER

7 | Common Dialogs

The program in the `ComDlg` directory illustrates the concepts discussed in this chapter. The corresponding executable in the `bin` directory is `ComDlg.exe`.

7.1 Introduction

Nearly every program opens and saves files, many programs print, and lots of programs present text in different fonts. In the early days of Windows, every program had its own implementation of the dialogs that controlled these common tasks. Beginning with Windows 3.1, a handful of standard dialogs have been included as part of the system. Appropriately, these built-in dialogs are known as the Common Dialogs.

Besides making it easier to write Win32 programs, the Common Dialogs promote consistency of operation and appearance across applications. This has an obvious benefit for users. On the other hand, stock dialogs may not fit an application perfectly, thus the Common Dialogs are customizable so that you can modify them as your application requires.

These dialogs are supported:

- Color selection
- File Open and Save
- Find and Replace
- Font selection
- Page Setup
- Print and Print Setup

7.2 Basic Usage

Like all dialogs, each Common Dialog has a dialog resource that specifies the layout of the controls and a dialog procedure that specifies the meaning of operating the controls. At the API level, the interface to each Common Dialog consists of an interface data structure and a function call. The data structure provides two-way communication. A program sets fields in the data structure to guide the dialog and retrieves values from the data structure to find out what the user selected. The function call triggers the dialog. By default, the function uses the predefined resource and dialog procedure, but both can be replaced. All the dialogs except Find and Replace are modal, so the function call doesn't return until the user selects OK or Cancel.

For each Common Dialog, MFC provides a CDialog-derived class that wraps the facility implemented in Win32. Here is the list of classes:

- CColorDialog
- CFileDialog
- CFindReplaceDialog
- CFontDialog
- CPageSetupDialog
- CPrintDialog

7.2.1 Using a Modal Common Dialog

Follow these steps to invoke a modal Common Dialog:

1. Create a dialog object. For the modal dialogs, the object can be created on the stack. Parameters to the dialog constructor direct the initialization of the interface data structure.
2. Optionally, modify the interface data structure. A few fields have been wrapped with member functions, but for most fields you'll need to write directly to the data structure.
3. Call DoModal. When the dialog completes, DoModal will return either IDOK or IDCANCEL. If the return value is IDOK, query the data structure to get the user's selections. A return value of IDCANCEL indicates either that the Cancel or Close button was pressed, or that an error occurred in the dialog. The next section shows how to distinguish the two cases.

Each of the modal Common Dialog classes overrides the CDialog function DoModal. The call to DoModal triggers the dialog, as shown in Figure 7.1. The following code fragment from the ComDlg program shows a simple invocation of the File dialog:

```
CFileDialog dlg(TRUE);   // Parameter indicates Open vs. Save
if( dlg.DoModal()==IDOK )
    readText( dlg.GetPathName(), dlg.GetFileExt() );
```

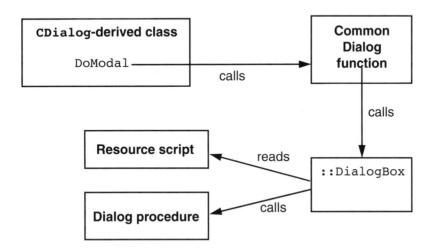

Figure 7.1   Each modal Common Dialog class has a DoModal function that triggers the dialog.

7.2.1.1 Error Handling

Detecting an error from a Common Dialog requires an extra step because the return value from DoModal does not distinguish an error from a press of Cancel. If DoModal returns IDCANCEL, test for an error by calling ::CommDlgExtended-Error. Some dialogs are more likely to return errors than others, but there are many error conditions for which you might want to display recovery information.

The error codes are unique across all the dialogs, so you can use a common error handler.[1] The ComDlg program uses the class commDlgError to encapsulate error handling. For simplicity, the class stores the error messages in a static array; a better implementation would put the messages into a string resource.

---

[1] The list of error conditions is documented with each type of dialog, making it difficult to find the complete list of errors. See the file ComDlg\DlgErr.cpp on the accompanying disk for the complete list.

```
static struct message {
    DWORD id;
    TCHAR *string;
} messages[] = {
    CDERR_FINDRESFAILURE, _T("Cannot find dialog resource"),
    CDERR_INITIALIZATION, _T("Dialog initialization failed"),
. . .
    0
};
```

To test for and post an error using commDlgError, just instantiate the class; the class constructor does the rest:

```
commDlgError::commDlgError(BOOL postMsg)
{
    m_errorNo = ::CommDlgExtendedError();
    if( postMsg && isAnError() )
        postErrorMsg();
}
```

If an error occurred in the last Common Dialog that executed, ::CommDlg-ExtendedError will return nonzero. postErrorMsg formats and displays the error message. getErrorMsg maps error numbers into strings:

```
TCHAR * commDlgError::getErrorMsg()
{
    for( int i=0; messages[i].id!=0; ++i )
        if( messages[i].id==m_errorNo )
            return messages[i].string;

    return _T("");
}

void commDlgError::postErrorMsg()
{
    CString msg;
    msg.Format(_T("Common dialog failed: %s"),getErrorMsg());
    AfxMessageBox(msg);
}
```

As an example that shows error handling, here is the complete File Open command from the ComDlg program. If DoModal does not return IDOK, the function instantiates the commDlgError class:

```
void mainFrame::onFileOpen()
{
    CFileDialog dlg(TRUE);
    if( dlg.DoModal()==IDOK ) {
        readText( dlg.GetPathName(), dlg.GetFileExt() );
    } else commDlgError err;

    editCtrl.SetFocus();
}
```

The constructor parameter defaults to true:

```
class commDlgError
{
// Construction
public:
    commDlgError(BOOL postMsg=TRUE);
    BOOL isAnError() { return m_errorNo!=0; };
    void postErrorMsg();
    TCHAR *getErrorMsg();
private:
    DWORD m_errorNo;
};
```

7.2.2 Using a Modeless Common Dialog

Because they are modeless, the Find and Replace dialogs operate in conjunction with the main message loop of the program. The dialog calls on the program to carry out the text search and replace operations. At the API level, communication is, of course, via messages. When the user asks the dialog to carry out the next find or replace operation, the dialog sends a *registered* message to its owner.

You may recall that each message has a unique integer value. The standard Win32 messages have values less than the defined constant WM_USER. User-defined messages are usually given values that are small offsets from WM_USER. But what about messages from reusable components, such as the Common Dialogs? As the number of components used by a program grows, so does the opportunity for conflicting message numbers. The API function Register-WindowMessage returns a unique systemwide message number given a string name. All calls to ::RegisterWindowMessage with a particular name, even calls in different processes, return the same unique value.[2] See Section 7.4.3 for an example.

As an alternative to catching the registered message from the dialog, you can derive a class from CFindReplaceDialog and respond directly to the controls in the dialog. To do this, you'll need to look at the dialog resource to get the control IDs. Section 7.4.3.4 uses this technique for the customized Find dialog.

---

[2] Of course, this scheme is also flawed since two applications may unwittingly use the same name for the registered message. However, collisions on names are not nearly as likely as collisions on numbers.

7.3   Customization

Most of the Common Dialogs are relatively complex. File Open, Choose Font, and Print have extensive initializations. Color uses a sophisticated custom control. Print can set up a printer device context. These dialogs provide significant functionality, but because of their complexity, nearly every program customizes the dialogs in some way.

The easiest customizations are accomplished by setting flags in the interface data structure, using the `dwFlags` parameter to the constructor. For example, flags control these attributes of the File Open dialog:

- Whether the Read Only, Help, and Network buttons appear
- Whether more than one file can be selected
- Whether the file entered must exist
- Whether the user is prompted before the specified file is created
- Whether long file names are displayed
- Whether a directory change in the dialog persists after the dialog

Other customizations are accomplished by setting values in the interface data structure. For the File Open dialog, there are fields for setting the

- Title of the dialog
- Default extension for file names
- Initial file spec
- Initial directory
- List of file types

Most of these values are simple strings that can be passed to the constructor. The list of file types is somewhat more complex. It is a string of strings, an unusual data structure for C++. Each string is terminated by a null character and the whole string of strings by two null characters. The even-numbered strings are listed in the File Types combo box. The odd strings are the corresponding file specs. Figure 7.2 shows the in-memory layout and one way of creating the data structure. Notice that there aren't any commas in the initializer list, so the adjacent string literals are concatenated.

7.3.1 Changing the Layout

There are two basic techniques for changing the layout of a Common Dialog. Layout is controlled by the dialog resource. A program can replace the resource

```
static TCHAR filters[] = {
    _T("Text\0")        _T("*.txt;*.c;*.cpp;*.h\0")
    _T("Rich text\0")   _T("*.rtf\0")
    _T("Hypertext\0")   _T("*.htm;*.html\0")
    _T("All files\0")   _T("*.*\0")
};
```

```
Text\0*.txt;*.c;*.cpp;*.h\0Rich  ...  All files\0*.*\0\0
```

Figure 7.2   A string of strings is created through concatenation of adjacent string literals, each with its own null terminator.

or add to it. In either case, if the changes create or modify controls, you'll need to derive a new dialog class to manage the changes.

Resource files for the Common Dialogs are delivered in the API header file directory. You can read the resource file into a resource editor to modify it, but beware that some of the resource scripts have conditional sections. The resource editor for Visual C++ silently deletes conditional sections. To preserve the conditional sections, you may need to modify the resource by hand in a text editor, then add the resource file to the list of included resource files.[3] The standard header file dlgs.h defines IDs for the controls.

In modifying the dialog resource, don't remove any controls unless they are static. The dialog procedure for the dialog probably reads and writes each of the dynamic controls. Eliminating the control could cause a crash. Instead of removing a control, try hiding and disabling it or moving it outside the bounds of the dialog frame.

Occasionally, you may want to change the type of a control. For example, in Section 7.4.3.4 the edit control in the Find dialog is replaced by a combo box. It isn't safe to just reuse the ID, since the dialog will expect the control to respond in certain ways to control-specific messages. The sample program hides the edit control but keeps it around to communicate with the dialog procedure.

7.3.1.1 Extending a Dialog

One advantage of using a Common Dialog is that as the dialog evolves, your program will get the new look and feel automatically, without recompiling. One disadvantage of replacing the resource for a Common Dialog is that your

---

[3] In Visual C++, run the View Resource Includes command.

program loses the benefit of automatic upgrading. Beginning with Windows 95, and just for the File Open and Save dialogs, the standard resource can be extended instead of replaced. This allows a program to inherit the basic dialog and add new controls around the edges.

Here are the basic steps for extending the File Open and Save dialogs:

1. Create a new dialog resource containing just the controls you want to add. Give the dialog window the style WS_CHILD and WS_CLIPSIBLINGS.
2. Derive a class from CFileDialog. In the class constructor, set the flags OFN_ENABLETEMPLATE to use a custom dialog resource, and OFN_EXPLORER to have the custom resource extend rather than replace the standard dialog resource.
3. Add handlers for the new controls.

When run, the File dialog will expand the dialog frame to allocate space for the new extension dialog. The extension dialog window will be a child of the Common Dialog frame (see Figure 7.3). As a result, the new controls are nephews of the standard controls, not siblings. This will affect how the extended controls access controls in the standard dialog. For an example, look at the custom File Open Dialog in Section 7.4.2. It adds a file history list that can set the current file name.

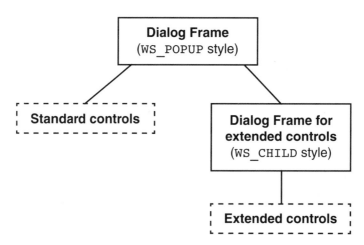

Figure 7.3   The window tree for a customized File Dialog when the flag
OFN_EXPLORER is used

7.4 Example: Common Dialogs and the Rich-Text Control

The ComDlg program fills the client area of its main window with a rich-text edit control (see Figure 7.4). Most of the dialogs illustrated in the program operate on the control. File Open and Save read and write the control. Font and color selection operate on text selected in the control; if nothing is selected, the dialogs change the style of new text. Find and Replace search for strings in the control.

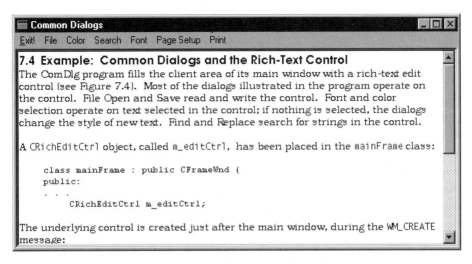

Figure 7.4   The ComDlg program fills the client area of its main program with a rich-text edit control.

A CRichEditCtrl object, called m_editCtrl, has been placed in the mainFrame class:

```
class mainFrame : public CFrameWnd {
public:
. . .
    CRichEditCtrl m_editCtrl;
```

The underlying control is created just after the main window, during the WM_CREATE message:

```
int mainFrame::OnCreate(LPCREATESTRUCT lpCreateStruct)
{
    if (CFrameWnd::OnCreate(lpCreateStruct) == -1)
        return -1;
```

```
        CRect rect;
        GetClientRect(&rect);
        m_editCtrl.Create(
            WS_CHILD|WS_VISIBLE|WS_TABSTOP|WS_VSCROLL|
            ES_MULTILINE|ES_WANTRETURN|ES_SUNKEN|ES_AUTOVSCROLL,
            rect,
            this,
            1);
        m_editCtrl.SetFocus();

        return 0;
    }
```

7.4.1 Font and Color

In most places, Win32 represents the complexities of a font using the logical font data structure, LOGFONT, or one of its derivatives, ENUMLOGFONT and ENUMLOG-FONTEX. (See Chapter 8 for a discussion of font.) The Common Dialog for font selection, ChooseFont, takes a LOGFONT to initialize the dialog and returns a LOG-FONT to indicate the user's selections. Using LOGFONT works well in conjunction with CFont, the MFC wrapper class for fonts.

The rich-text control keeps format information in two data structures, CHARFOR-MAT for character font and style, and PARAFORMAT for text justification and paragraph margins. Unfortunately, CHARFORMAT and LOGFONT are similar but incompatible. The MFC class CFontDialog supports both formats and has member functions to convert between the two formats.

7.4.1.1 The CHARFORMAT Data Structure

A simple use of CHARFORMAT initializes the dialog based on the font of the current selection in the rich-text control. It is illustrated by the Font Choose Font command in the ComDlg program:

```
    void mainFrame::onChooseFont()
    {
        CHARFORMAT cf;
        m_editCtrl.GetSelectionCharFormat(cf);
        CFontDialog dlg(cf);
        m_editCtrl.HideSelection(FALSE,TRUE);

        if( dlg.DoModal()==IDOK ) {
            dlg.GetCharFormat(cf);
            m_editCtrl.SetSelectionCharFormat(cf);
        } else commDlgError err;

        m_editCtrl.SetFocus();
    }
```

GetSelectionCharFormat returns in the CHARFORMAT parameter the format items common to the characters selected in the rich-text control. CFontDialog initializes the dialog box selections based on the CHARFORMAT initializer. HideSelection keeps the text highlighted in the edit control even though the dialog box has the focus. Normally, the highlight would be removed on loss of focus.

GetCharFormat fills in the CHARFORMAT structure based on selections in the dialog.[4] SetSelectionCharFormat changes the attributes of the selected characters. If no characters are selected, it changes the default selection that is used when new text is entered.

Handling color is very similar:

```
void mainFrame::onChooseColor()
{
    CHARFORMAT cf;
    m_editCtrl.GetSelectionCharFormat(cf);
    CColorDialog dlg(cf.crTextColor);
    m_editCtrl.HideSelection(FALSE,TRUE);

    if( dlg.DoModal()==IDOK ) {
        cf.crTextColor = dlg.GetColor();
        cf.dwMask = CFM_COLOR;
        cf.dwEffects = 0; // Make sure CFE_AUTOCOLOR isn't on
        m_editCtrl.SetSelectionCharFormat(cf);
    } else commDlgError err;

    m_editCtrl.SetFocus();
}
```

The Color dialog takes a color reference as an initializer. A *color reference*, represented by the COLORREF type in Win32, specifies on an eight-bit scale the intensity of the red, green, and blue primary colors. (Color is described in more detail in Chapter 8.) The crTextColor field in the CHARFORMAT data structure is the color of the current selection, or if no selection, it is the color used for newly inserted text.

If the user presses OK, GetColor returns the selected color. CFE_AUTOCOLOR tells the edit control to ignore the COLORREF specified in the CHARFORMAT and instead use the color specified by the Window Text entry in the system color palette.[5]

---

[4]Although it is obviously intended to simplify using the Font dialog with a rich-text control, in the version of MFC I am using, GetCharFormat is undocumented.

[5] The system palette can be set using the Display mini-app of the Windows Control Panel.

7.4.1.2 Customizing the Font Dialog

Many dialogs that control formatting have an Apply button to force the current dialog settings to be applied before the dialog is terminated. An Apply button gives a modal dialog limited modeless characteristics. In the ComDlg program, the Font Custom Choose Font command triggers a font dialog with an Apply button and an Auto Apply checkbox (see Figure 7.5). When Auto Apply is checked, text selected in the edit control immediately reflects font changes in the dialog.

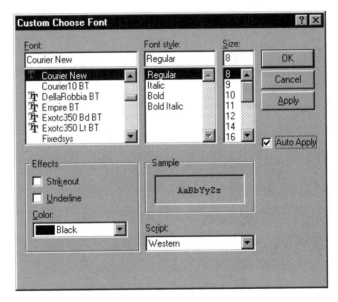

Figure 7.5   The Custom Choose Font dialog has an Auto Apply checkbox.

CFontDialog has an initialization flag to create a dialog with Apply. To process the Apply button, derive a class from CFontDialog. I've called mine fontDlg:

```
class fontDlg : public CFontDialog
{
    DECLARE_DYNAMIC(fontDlg)

public:
    fontDlg(const CHARFORMAT& charformat,
        DWORD dwFlags = CF_SCREENFONTS,
        CDC* pdcPrinter = NULL,
        CWnd* pParentWnd = NULL);

    virtual ~fontDlg();
    . . .
```

To add the Auto Apply checkbox a new dialog template is needed. The dialog constructor adds the flag for Apply and replaces the dialog template by setting the lpTemplateName field in the CHOOSEFONT data structure:

```
fontDlg::fontDlg(const CHARFORMAT& charformat, DWORD dwFlags,
    CDC* pdcPrinter, CWnd* pParentWnd) :
    CFontDialog(charformat, dwFlags, pdcPrinter, pParentWnd)
{
    m_cf.Flags |= CF_ENABLETEMPLATE|CF_APPLY;
    m_cf.lpTemplateName = MAKEINTRESOURCE(IDD_CustomChooseFont);
}
```

By looking at the dialog resource in the API header-file directory, I determined that the Apply button has the ID psh3. I connected the push button to the function onApply by hand:

```
BEGIN_MESSAGE_MAP(fontDlg, CFontDialog)
    //{{AFX_MSG_MAP(fontDlg)
    //}}AFX_MSG_MAP
    ON_COMMAND(psh3,onApply)
END_MESSAGE_MAP()
```

When the Apply button is pressed, onApply reads the dialog controls and applies their values to the rich-text control:

```
void fontDlg::onApply()
{
    CHARFORMAT cf;
    memset(&cf,0,sizeof(cf));
    cf.cbSize = sizeof(cf);

    GetCurrentFont(m_cf.lpLogFont);
    GetCharFormat(cf);
    // Allow any format characteristic to be changed
    // The default is to allow change of only those for
    // which the selected characters have the same value
    cf.dwMask = CFM_BOLD|CFM_COLOR|CFM_FACE|CFM_ITALIC|
        CFM_SIZE|CFM_STRIKEOUT|CFM_UNDERLINE;

    theApp.getMainWnd()->changeFormat(cf);
}
```

onApply changes the rich-text control by calling changeFormat in the mainFrame class. changeFormat calls the SetSelectionCharFormat function used earlier:

```
void mainFrame::changeFormat(CHARFORMAT &cf)
{
    editCtrl.SetSelectionCharFormat(cf);
}
```

When I first tested onApply, nothing happened. Common to many Win32 data structures, CHARFORMAT begins with a field that contains its size (cbSize in the onApply function above). This size field implements a type-specific version tag. Unlike GetSelectionCharFormat which we used earlier for font and color, GetCurrentFont does not set the size field. The invalid size value caused the call to fail. In general for Win32 data structures, it is good practice to initialize the data structure to zeroes and set the size, as illustrated here.

GetCurrentFont reads the dialog controls and fills in the passed LOGFONT by sending the WM_GETFONT_LOGFONT message to the font dialog. GetCharFormat fills in the CHARFORMAT based on the dialog's LOGFONT.

There is one hitch in the current code. Pressing Apply changes the font and style based on current dialog settings, but size and color are not changed. I'll show you the solution, but first I want to explain how I debugged the problem.

7.4.1.2.1 Debugging Strategy

An important step in debugging is to understand the flow of control. Win32's messages and C++'s objects complicate the flow, because many functions are called implicitly. Stepping through a program in the debugger untangles the C++ flow but it doesn't help to understand the message sequence. Since nearly all processing in a program is done in response to messages, the first step is usually to determine what messages are being processed.

Processing for the custom Font dialog begins in response to the Font Custom Choose Font command. The handler in mainFrame triggers the Font dialog:

```
Get current CHARFORMAT
Instantiate fontDlg
    Call fontDlg constructor
        Call CFontDialog constructor
            Create CHOOSEFONT data structure
            Initialize LOGFONT based on CHARFORMAT
Call DoModal to trigger the dialog
```

At this point the flow of control moves into Win32 and tracing in the debugger is futile. To continue tracing, put a breakpoint in a function that will run in response to some event in the dialog. onApply is called when the user presses the Apply button:

```
onApply called
        Call GetCurrentFont to read controls
        Call GetCharFormat to convert from LOGFONT to CHARFORMAT
        Call SetSelectionCharFormat to update rich-text control
```

OnOK is handled by the Common Dialog:

```
User presses OK
        Write CHOOSEFONT based on dialog controls
```

Again, flow is back into Win32. Our code executes next when the call to DoModal returns:

```
Call GetCharFormat to convert from LOGFONT to CHARFORMAT
Call SetSelectionCharFormat to update rich-text control
```

In the algorithm above, I've highlighted the two calls to SetSelectionCharFormat because the call in onApply doesn't change the text size but the call after DoModal returns does. onApply calls GetCurrentFont, which fills in a LOGFONT by reading the controls. It does so by sending the WM_CHOOSEFONT_GETLOGFONT message to the dialog frame window. GetCharFormat then converts the LOGFONT to a CHARFORMAT.

While tracing through GetCharFormat I found that it uses both the LOGFONT and the CHOOSEFONT data structures to set the CHARFORMAT. The API manual points to the source of the problem: Some of the fields in CHOOSEFONT are not set until the dialog terminates (and DoModal returns). Two of those fields happen to be the size and color.

I inserted the fix for size into onApply before the call to GetCurrentFont:

```
        // Size and color lists aren't read until dialog
        // is closed.  Read the size list, punt on color
        CComboBox *cb = (CComboBox *)GetDlgItem(cmb3);
        CString s;
        cb->GetLBText( cb->GetCurSel(), s);
        m_cf.iPointSize = 10 * atoi(s);
```

cmb3 is the ID of the size combo box. The CHOOSEFONT data structure keeps the size, in tenths of a point, in iPointSize.

7.4.1.2.2 Adding an Auto Apply Checkbox
Adding the Auto Apply checkbox required modifying the dialog resource. I copied the resource file font.dlg from the API include directory to the project directory and added the checkbox. The appropriate lines from the resource file are:

```
CONTROL         "Auto Apply",chx3,"Button",
                BS_AUTOCHECKBOX | WS_TABSTOP,
                210,80,50,14
```

To make it easy to refer to the checkbox in the code, I added a wrapper object to the dialog class and connected it to the underlying window using DDX_Control in DoDataExchange. m_autoApply is defined in the class declaration:

```
class fontDlg : public CFontDialog
{
   . . .
      CButton m_autoApply;
```

List boxes and buttons send notifications to the dialog frame via WM_COMMAND messages. All WM_COMMAND messages pass through the virtual function OnCommand. To implement Auto Apply, any WM_COMMAND message (except for that generated by the checkbox itself) simulates pressing the Apply button:

```
BOOL fontDlg::OnCommand(WPARAM wParam, LPARAM lParam)
{
    // Post Apply to guarantee that the response to
    // the command has taken effect
    // Filter out psh3 to prevent infinite recursion
    UINT id = LOWORD(wParam);
    if( id!=psh3 && m_autoApply.GetCheck() )
        PostMessage(WM_COMMAND,psh3);  // Simulate Apply

    return CFontDialog::OnCommand(wParam, lParam);
}
```

7.4.2 File Open and Save

Perhaps the most common of the Common Dialogs are File Open and File Save. In their simplest form, they display a directory tree and a file list. When the Open or Save button is pressed, the dialogs return a file name. File Open was seen earlier; File Save is similar:

```
void mainFrame::onFileSave()
{
    CFileDialog dlg(FALSE,"rtf",NULL,
        OFN_HIDEREADONLY|OFN_EXPLORER|OFN_OVERWRITEPROMPT);
    if( dlg.DoModal()==IDOK )
        writeText( dlg.GetPathName(), dlg.GetFileExt() );
    else commDlgError err;

    m_editCtrl.SetFocus();
}
```

7.4.2.1 Reading and Writing a Rich-Text Control

Rich-text controls read and write their data using a callback function provided by the program. Here are the steps to implementing I/O:

1. Create an EDITSTREAM data structure.
2. Specify the data format.
3. Create a callback function to perform block I/O.
4. Trigger the I/O.

In the ComDlg program, the function writeText writes the data in the rich-text control to the selected file. writeText uses the EDITSTREAM structure to specify the callback function and to pass application-specific data to the callback:

```
static EDITSTREAM editStream = {
    0,              // dwCookie -- app specific
    0,              // dwError
    NULL            // Callback
};
. . .

void mainFrame::writeText(CString fileName, CString fileExt)
{
    CWaitCursor waitCursor;
    CFile file(fileName,CFile::modeWrite|CFile::modeCreate);
    editStream.dwCookie = (DWORD)&file;
    editStream.pfnCallback = writeFunc;

    int format = fileExt.CompareNoCase("rtf")==0
        ? SF_RTF : SF_TEXT;
    m_editCtrl.StreamOut(format,editStream);
}
```

The application-specific data passed to the output function is a pointer to the CFile to write. The rich-text control can write its contents either as raw text or as rich text. Both are ASCII files, but rich text preserves the formatting information. StreamOut tells the control to begin writing. The callback function is called repeatedly by the control with a block of data to write:

```
static DWORD CALLBACK writeFunc(
    DWORD cookie,
    LPBYTE buf,
    LONG bytesToWrite,
    LONG *bytesWritten)
{
    CFile *fp = (CFile *)cookie;
    fp->Write(buf,bytesToWrite);
    *bytesWritten = bytesToWrite;
    return 1;
}
```

The return value from the callback is interpreted by the control as a Boolean; return non-zero to continue writing.

7.4.2.2 Extending the File Open Dialog

Although the layout of the file dialogs can be modified as you would the other Common Dialogs, by replacing the dialog resource, they also use another technique. The problem with replacing the dialog resource is that the dialog appearance won't evolve as the Common Dialog itself evolves. As an implementer, you would need to add your extensions to a new copy of the evolved dialog resource. Instead, you can specify just the additional fields for the file dialogs.

The algorithm for merging new controls with the Common Dialog is far from perfect, but with a little fudging you should get the two to work together. Figure 7.6 shows the File Open dialog with a file-history combo box added. The dialog is triggered by the Custom File Open command in the ComDlg program.

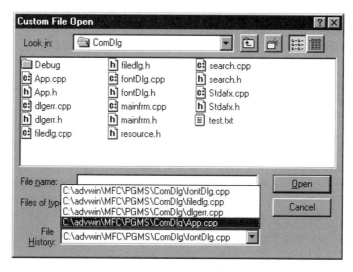

Figure 7.6 A File History combo box has been added to the standard File Open dialog.

When the Open button is pressed in the dialog, the specified file is added to the history list if it is not already there. When a file name is selected from the history list, it is forced into the File Name field to become the current selection.

Here are the steps to customize File Open:

1. Derive a class from CFileDialog.
2. Create a resource with the additional controls.
3. Create wrapper objects for the additional controls.
4. Implement handlers for the controls.

The process begins in response to the File Custom File Open command:

```
void mainFrame::onCustomFileOpen()
{
    fileDlg dlg;

    if( dlg.DoModal()==IDOK )
        readText( dlg.GetPathName(), dlg.GetFileExt() );
    else commDlgError err;

    m_editCtrl.SetFocus();
}
```

7.4.2.2.1 Deriving a Class from CFileDialog

I derived the class fileDlg from the CFileDialog. Its purpose is to set up the OPENFILENAME data structure and handle the history list. The constructor tells the Common Dialog to use an auxiliary dialog resource, called IDD_Custom-FileOpen. By specifying OFN_EXPLORER, the auxiliary resource will merge with, rather than replace, the standard resource:

```
fileDlg::fileDlg(CWnd* pParent /*=NULL*/)
    : CFileDialog(TRUE)
{
    static TCHAR filters[] = {
        _T("Text\0")        _T("*.txt;*.c;*.cpp;*.h\0")
        _T("Rich text\0")   _T("*.rtf\0")
        _T("Hypertext\0")   _T("*.htm;*.html\0")
        _T("All files\0")   _T("*.*\0")
    };

    m_ofn.lpstrFilter = filters;
    m_ofn.Flags |= OFN_ENABLETEMPLATE|OFN_EXPLORER;
    m_ofn.lpTemplateName = MAKEINTRESOURCE(IDD_CustomFileOpen);
    m_ofn.lpstrTitle = "Custom File Open";
}
```

7.4.2.2.2 Creating the Auxiliary Resource

IDD_CustomFileOpen contains just the combo box (and its label) that will be used for the history list:

```
IDD_CustomFileOpen DIALOG DISCARDABLE  0, 0, 219, 26
STYLE DS_3DLOOK | DS_CONTROL | WS_CHILD | WS_CLIPSIBLINGS
FONT 8, "MS Sans Serif"
BEGIN
    RTEXT         "File \n&History:",IDC_STATIC,4,3,32,20
    COMBOBOX      IDC_FileHistory,40,4,171,100,CBS_DROPDOWNLIST |
                  WS_VSCROLL | WS_TABSTOP
END
```

7.4.2.2.3 Creating Wrappers for the Auxiliary Controls

Create wrapper objects for the auxiliary controls just as you would for controls in any other dialog. Add the wrappers to the derived class:

```
class fileDlg : public CFileDialog
{
// Construction
public:
    fileDlg(CWnd* pParent = NULL);   // standard constructor

// Dialog Data
    //{{AFX_DATA(fileDlg)
    CComboBox  m_historyList;
    //}}AFX_DATA
```

Use DoDataExchange to connect the wrapper to the underlying control. Recall that CDialog::OnInitDialog calls DoDataExchange, thus it is important that fileDlg::OnInitDialog inherits behavior before initializing the history list:

```
BOOL fileDlg::OnInitDialog()
{
    CFileDialog::OnInitDialog();

    // Initialize the history list
    for( int i=0; i<MAXHIST && !file[i].IsEmpty(); ++i )
        m_historyList.AddString(file[i]);

    m_historyList.SetCurSel(0);

    return TRUE;  // return TRUE unless you set the focus to a control
                  // EXCEPTION: OCX Property Pages should return FALSE
}
```

The data for the history list is kept in a static array:

```
const int MAXHIST=10;
static CString file[MAXHIST];  // File name history list
```

7.4.2.2.4 Managing the Auxiliary Control

When an item in the history list is selected, it is stuffed into the file-name edit control. Picking up the selection in the history list is easy:

```
BEGIN_MESSAGE_MAP(fileDlg, CFileDialog)
    //{{AFX_MSG_MAP(fileDlg)
    ON_CBN_SELCHANGE(IDC_FileHistory, onSelchangeFileHistory)
    //}}AFX_MSG_MAP
END_MESSAGE_MAP()
```

Notifying the edit control takes a little care. From Figure 7.3, you can see that the edit control is an aunt of the history list:

```
void fileDlg::onSelchangeFileHistory()
{
    int i = historyList.GetCurSel();
    CString pathName;

    if( i!=CB_ERR ) {
        historyList.GetLBText(i,pathName);
        // fileDlg is a child of the common dialog frame
        // as is the edit control.
        GetParent()->SetDlgItemText(edt1,pathName);
    }
}
```

When a file name is selected, it is added to the history list if it isn't already there. `CFileDialog` calls the virtual function `OnFileNameOK` when the Open button is selected:

```
BOOL fileDlg::OnFileNameOK()
{
    CString newFile( GetPathName() );

    // Look to see if file is already in history list
    int i;
    for( i=0; i<MAXHIST; ++i )
        if( newFile==file[i] )
            return CFileDialog::OnFileNameOK();

    // Make room for, then insert, new entry in history list
    for( i=MAXHIST-1; i>0; --i )
        file[i] = file[i-1];

    file[0] = GetPathName();

    return CFileDialog::OnFileNameOK();
}
```

7.4.3 Find and Replace

Programming Find and Replace is more work than programming the other Common Dialogs. Since Find and Replace are modeless, they operate in concert with the rest of the program by sending messages. To implement Find and Replace, follow these steps:

1. Create wrapper objects for the dialog.
2. Register the Find/Replace message used for communication.
3. Implement a handler function to process the message.

In the ComDlg program, the Find and Replace dialogs are triggered by commands on the Search Menu. Figure 7.7 shows the basic Find dialog.

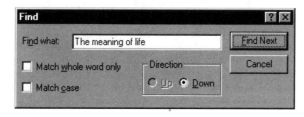

Figure 7.7   The Find Text Common Dialog

7.4.3.1 Creating the Dialog Object

For modal dialogs, we created the dialog object as an automatic variable, then called DoModal on that object. Since DoModal does not return until the dialog completes, using an automatic variable is perfectly safe. In a modeless dialog, the function that triggers the dialog returns while the dialog is still active. Thus, the dialog wrapper object must persist beyond the execution of the command handler.

The ComDlg program uses members in the mainFrame class to point to the dialog objects:

```
class mainFrame : public CFrameWnd {
. . .
protected:
   CFindReplaceDialog *m_findDlg;
   CFindReplaceDialog *m_replaceDlg;
   CFindReplaceDialog *m_customFindDlg;
```

The objects themselves are allocated on the heap using the new operator. Rather than calling DoModal, call Create to trigger the Find dialog:

```
void mainFrame::onFindText()
{
    if( m_findDlg==NULL ) {
        m_findDlg = new CFindReplaceDialog;
        m_findDlg->Create(TRUE,"");
        m_findDlg->GetDlgItem(rad1)->EnableWindow(FALSE);
    } else
        m_findDlg->SetFocus();
}
```

ComDlg searches the rich-text control. Because the rich-text control does not support searching up, the Up radio button, rad1,[6] is disabled.

7.4.3.2 Responding to the Find Dialog Notification

As the Find dialog is manipulated, it sends notifications to its owner—in this case the frame window. The notifications arrive via the registered message "commdlg_FindReplace".

As noted earlier, registered messages provide a way for unrelated processes to share common message numbers. To use a registered message, call the API function RegisterWindowMessage to retrieve a message number:

```
findReplaceMsgID = ::RegisterWindowMessage(_T("commdlg_FindReplace"));
```

Then, create a message-map entry to connect the message number to a handler function:

```
ON_REGISTERED_MESSAGE(findReplaceMsgID,onFindReplace)
```

The handler function has the standard message prototype:

```
LONG mainFrame::onFindReplace(WPARAM,LPARAM lParam)
{
```

For Find/Replace, the lParam parameter is a pointer to a data structure containing the current dialog settings.[7] Use member functions in CFindReplaceDialog to query the structure. The static function GetNotifier returns a pointer to the wrapper object for the current Find/Replace dialog:

```
LONG mainFrame::onFindReplace(WPARAM,LPARAM lParam)
{
    CFindReplaceDialog *dlg = CFindReplaceDialog::GetNotifier(lParam);
```

---

[6] The Search dialog template is in the Win32 include directory in the file findtext.dlg.

[7] The WPARAM parameter is not used, so the formal parameter may be omitted.

```
        if( dlg->IsTerminating() ) {
            if( dlg==m_replaceDlg )
                m_replaceDlg = NULL;
            else if( dlg==m_findDlg )
                m_findDlg = NULL;
            else if( dlg==m_customFindDlg )
                m_customFindDlg = NULL;
        } else if( dlg->FindNext() ) {
            findText(dlg);

        } else if( dlg->ReplaceCurrent() ) {
            replaceText(dlg);
        }

        return 0;
    }
```

The same registered message is used for both Find and Replace. `onFindReplace` uses the pointer value of the wrapper object to determine which dialog is sending the message.

Termination has some subtlety. All Common Dialogs take care of deleting the underlying windows, but `CFindReplaceDialog` goes one step further. It responds to `PostNcDestroy` and *deletes* the C++ wrapper object *even though it didn't create it.* As a result, you must make sure that

- The dialog object is allocated on the heap using `new`; and,
- Your program does not delete the dialog object but must assume that it is gone.

In response to Find Next, `onFindReplace` searches the rich-text control by calling `findText`.

7.4.3.3 Searching a Rich-Text Control

The rich-text control implements forward search. The job of the `findText` function is to read the search string from the dialog and trigger the search. The only tricky piece is converting from the `CString` kept in the dialog object to the `TCHAR *` needed by the control.

To specify a search, fill in a `FINDTEXTEX` data structure. The structure includes the range to search and the string to search for. Since `FINDTEXTEX` is a C data structure, the search string is referenced by a `TCHAR *`. `CFindReplaceDialog::GetFindString`, by contrast, returns a `CString`. The string data in a `CString` is constant, so there is no direct conversion between a `CString` and a

TCHAR *.[8] To get access to the string data, use the GetBuffer and Release-Buffer member functions of CString. Resist the temptation to save a little work by casting away the const property.

```
void mainFrame::findText(CFindReplaceDialog *dp)
{
    DWORD flags = 0;
    if( dp->MatchCase() ) flags|=FR_MATCHCASE;
    if( dp->MatchWholeWord() ) flags|=FR_WHOLEWORD;

    FINDTEXTEX ft;
    CString s(dp->GetFindString());
    ft.lpstrText = s.GetBuffer(0);
    editCtrl.GetSel(ft.chrg);
    ++ft.chrg.cpMin;
    ft.chrg.cpMax = -1;

    editCtrl.HideSelection(FALSE,TRUE);
    if( editCtrl.FindText(flags,&ft)>=0 )
        editCtrl.SetSel(ft.chrgText);
    s.ReleaseBuffer();
}
```

7.4.3.4 Adding a Search-String History List

The Search Custom Find Text command triggers the dialog shown in Figure 7.8. The edit control in the standard dialog has been replaced by a drop-down list that holds the previous search strings. Replacing a control can be delicate because the Common Dialog function reads and writes the control.

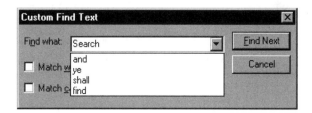

Figure 7.8   In the Custom Find Text dialog, the edit control has been replaced by a drop-down list.

Here are the steps to add the history list:

1. Modify the dialog resource to include the drop-down list and hide the edit control.
2. Initialize the history list on startup.
3. Read the list on Find Next.

---

[8] There is a direct conversion to a const TCHAR *.

onCustomFindText triggers the custom dialog:

```
void mainFrame::onCustomFindText()
{
    if( m_findDlg==NULL )
        m_customFindDlg = new searchDlg;
    else
        m_customFindDlg->SetFocus();
}
```

7.4.3.4.1 Modifying the Dialog Resource

For the dialog to operate properly, the edit control must be preserved. The Find/Replace dialog procedure reads the edit control to fill in the FINDREPLACE data structure, and FINDREPLACE is the source for the GetFindString function. Figure 7.9 shows the relationship between the edit control and the dialog object.

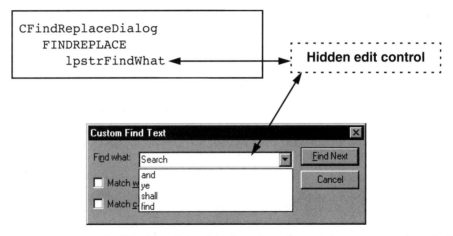

Figure 7.9   The Find/Replace dialog initializes the edit control at startup and reads the control when Find Next is pressed. The arrows represent movement of data.

On the other hand, the edit control does not need to be visible. The Custom Find Text dialog hides the edit control, but uses it to communicate to the rest of the Common Dialog. The Common-Dialog resource file, findtext.dlg, uses #ifdef statements, so I edited the file by hand.[9] Here are the modified lines:

```
EDITTEXT edt1, 0,0,0,0, NOT WS_VISIBLE
COMBOBOX cmb1,43,8,132,80,CBS_DROPDOWN | WS_VSCROLL | WS_TABSTOP
```

---

[9] The Visual C++ resource editor silently removes #ifdef statements.

The modified resource is attached to the dialog in the constructor for the dialog object:

```
searchDlg::searchDlg()
{
    m_fr.Flags |= FR_ENABLETEMPLATE;
    m_fr.lpTemplateName = MAKEINTRESOURCE(IDD_CustomFindText);
    m_fr.hInstance = AfxGetInstanceHandle();
    Create(TRUE,_T("Search"));
}
```

7.4.3.4.2 Initializing the History List

The data for the history list is kept as an array of CStrings:

```
const int MAXHIST=10;
static CString pattern[MAXHIST];   // Search pattern history list
```

As usual, the list is initialized during OnInitDialog:

```
BOOL searchDlg::OnInitDialog()
{
    CFindReplaceDialog::OnInitDialog();

    initComboBox();

    return TRUE;   // return TRUE unless you set the focus to a control
                   // EXCEPTION: OCX Property Pages should return FALSE
}

void searchDlg::initComboBox()
{
    CComboBox *cb = (CComboBox *)GetDlgItem(cmb1);
    for( int i=0; i<MAXHIST && !pattern[i].IsEmpty(); ++i )
        cb->AddString(pattern[i]);

    cb->SetCurSel(0);
}
```

7.4.3.4.3 Managing the History List

Before the Find dialog sends its registered message, it copies the string in the edit control into the FINDREPLACE data structure. The custom dialog needs to set the edit control based on the current selection in the drop-down list.

Looking at the dialog resource, you can see that when the Find Next button is pressed, the dialog generates a WM_COMMAND message with the ID IDOK:

```
CONTROL "&Find Next", IDOK, "button", BS_DEFPUSHBUTTON | WS_CHILD |
        WS_TABSTOP | WS_GROUP,
```

Since OnOK is a virtual function, searchDlg can override it. The overridden version copies the current selection from the combo box to the edit control before inheriting the default behavior:

```
void searchDlg::OnOK()
{
    CComboBox *cb = (CComboBox *)GetDlgItem(cmb1);

    // Common dialog expects edit control to contain search string
    // So, copy combobox text to edit control
    CEdit *edit = (CEdit *)GetDlgItem(edt1);
    CString text;
    cb->GetWindowText(text);
    edit->SetWindowText(text);

    CFindReplaceDialog::OnOK();
```

Finally, if the new search string isn't already in the history list, it is added:

```
    CString newPattern( GetFindString() );

    // Look to see if newPattern is already in history list
    int i;
    for( i=0; i<MAXHIST; ++i )
        if( newPattern==pattern[i] ) return;

    // Make room for, then insert, new pattern
    for( i=MAXHIST-1; i>0; --i )
        pattern[i] = pattern[i-1];

    pattern[0] = newPattern;

    cb->ResetContent();
    initComboBox();
}
```

8 | Graphics, the Mouse, and the Keyboard

The program in the `Graphics\Simple` directory illustrates the concepts discussed in this chapter. The corresponding executable in the `bin` directory is `GraphicsSimple.exe`.

8.1   Introduction

In a graphical environment like Win32, all output is graphical, whether it's line drawings, bitmapped images, or formatted text. This chapter covers the basics of outputting lines, shapes, and text using the Graphics Device Interface (GDI). It also introduces management of the keyboard and mouse.[1]

8.2   The Graphics Device Interface

In most Win32 programs all graphical output goes through GDI.[2] GDI provides a layer of abstraction between a program and a particular device, allowing the same functions to draw on a display screen, fax machine, plotter, or laser printer (see Figure 8.1).

---

[1] MFC wraps GDI with very thin wrappers, adding little new functionality. This chapter surveys the wrapper classes and GDI. For a thorough treatment of GDI, see *Win32 Programming*, by Brent Rector and Joe Newcomer, Addison Wesley Longman, 1997.

[2] Programs that need high-performance output, such as multi-media applications and games, can use the more-direct screen access provided by DirectX.

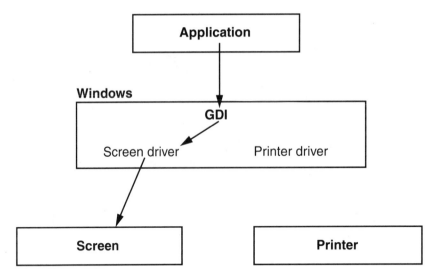

Figure 8.1   GDI isolates a program from differences in devices by allowing the same function calls to draw on a variety of devices.

8.2.1 Device Contexts

To use GDI, a program needs a device context. A *device context* is a data structure that holds the current drawing parameters, such as

- The current pen width for drawing lines
- The current brush color for filling rectangles and ellipses
- The current font for drawing text
- The current coordinate space
- The current clipping rectangle

Drawing functions are always interpreted based on some device context. Device contexts are wrapped in MFC by the classes CDC, CClientDC, CWindowDC, CPaintDC, and CMetaFileDC. Most of the functions for changing attributes of a device context are members of CDC. The actual data structure is maintained inside Win32. Figure 8.2 shows how the classes and data are related.

A device context for the display screen is called a *display* context. The reference manual sometimes uses "display" where it should use the more general term "device". Except for the added concept of a coordinate system tied to a window, display contexts are used just like other types of device contexts.

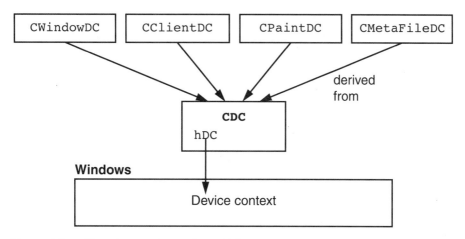

Figure 8.2   The classes derived from CDC wrap the functionality of the Win32 device context.

The basic protocol for using a device context (DC) is

Create a wrapper object for the DC
Output to the DC
Destroy the wrapper object

It has been common practice in Windows programs to create DCs right before use and destroy them right after. This create-as-needed protocol grew out of the scarcity of DCs under 16-bit Windows,[3] but it also has a property desirable in any environment. By creating a new DC each time one is needed, it always begins in a known default state. In effect, create performs a reset.

MFC makes it easy to create and destroy DCs, since the constructor for each CDC-derived wrapper class creates a DC and the destructor destroys it. The different classes reflect the different ways in which a device context can be created and used. The type of wrapper object created determines where output to the DC will go. There are four specialized classes:

CPaintDC	Writes to the invalid rectangle of a WM_PAINT message.
CClientDC	Writes to the client area of a window.
CWindowDC	Writes anywhere in a window, including the nonclient area.

---

[3] Only five DCs were available under Windows 3.1 and Win32S. There is no practical limit under Win32.

CMetaFileDC   Writes to a Windows metafile. A metafile is an encoding of GDI commands, independent of any particular device. The commands can be played back in a device context to recreate the output.

8.2.1.1 Painting the Screen

Most output to the display occurs in response to WM_PAINT and hence is called *painting*. When a program needs to change the image on the screen, rather than immediately drawing, it usually calls InvalidateRect to invalidate the portion of the window to be changed. When no other messages are pending, Win32 generates a WM_PAINT message for any window with an invalid rectangle.

Deferring painting until after all other messages have been processed keeps a program responsive to user input. While a program is painting, it isn't processing messages from the message queue. Also, an operation in a program may cause several changes to the screen. Sometimes the changes may overlap, affecting the same pixels. InvalidateRect accumulates invalid rectangles. When the paint message arrives, the program can paint everything that needs updating in one pass.

To know what to paint, programs maintain data that describes the image on the screen. In response to WM_PAINT, the program walks the data to redraw the image. Before sending WM_PAINT, Win32 creates a paint device context. The paint context includes a clipping rectangle that limits where on the screen the paint code can write. Even if a program naively redraws the complete image for the window, only those pixels in the invalid rectangle will actually be written. This is very convenient. It means that most programs can simply redraw the entire image every time painting is requested. Section 8.7.4.3 illustrates invalidating a rectangle and Section 8.7.2.1 shows the corresponding paint code.

8.2.2 Logical and Physical Objects

As you've seen in earlier chapters, MFC programs manipulate Win32 objects by creating wrapper objects in C++. Win32 uses several different objects to implement drawing, such as pens, fonts, and color palettes. The wrapper classes for the drawing implements are derived from CGDIObject.

GDI itself represents objects on two levels: the ideal and the real. An ideal, or *logical*, object captures how an object would be rendered on a perfect device. You can create a logical object with any combination of attributes, often by instantiating the corresponding MFC class. For example, I'm partial to Bauer Bodoni 17-point red text. Here is the corresponding CFont object for my ideal font:[4]

```
CFont font;
font.CreateFont(
    -1700/ 72,          // Height:  Negative for char height
    0,                  // Width:   Zero so GDI will choose
    0,                  // Escapement:  Verticals are vertical
    FW_REGULAR,         // Weight
    FALSE,              // Italic
    FALSE,              // Underline
    FALSE,              // Strikeout
    ANSI_CHARSET,       // Character set
    OUT_DEVICE_PRECIS,  // Font matching:  Favor device
    CLIP_DEFAULT_PREC,  // Character clipping
    DEFAULT_QUALITY,    // Font matching:  Favor accuracy
    FF_ROMAN,           // Font matching:  Proportional with serifs
    _T("Bauer Bodoni")  // Typeface
);
```

Real devices, of course, aren't perfect. To output text in a particular font, the logical font must be selected into a device context. Upon selection, GDI chooses a real, or *physical*, object that the device can render. The physical object chosen is that which most closely matches the ideal.[5] My printer prints in black at 300 dots per inch. When I select the Bauer Bodoni 17-point text into a device context for the printer and set the text color to red, I get a gray approximation that is actually 16 points high. That is, the physical font is Bauer Bodoni, 16 point, medium weight, printed in gray.

The three layers of representation apply to all GDI drawing objects: pens, brushes, color palettes, and fonts. Figure 8.3 shows the layers in the context of a font. Usually, from MFC you only need to be concerned about the C++ wrapper, although at times you may need to move between the layers. This was the case in the owner-draw list implemented in Chapter 6.

---

[4] Text color is not specified in the logical font; it is an attribute of a device context.

[5] For most objects, "most closely" is easy to compute. For fonts and colors, it is not so easy. In specifying a logical font, several parameters are devoted to guiding the choice. In addition, the function CDC::SetMapperFlags lets you influence the font-selection algorithm.

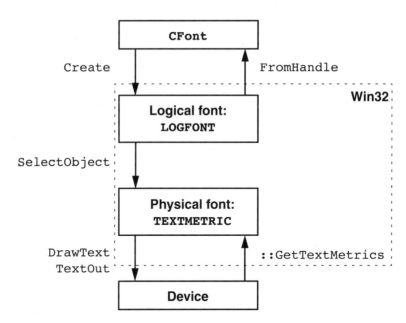

Figure 8.3 GDI objects are represented on four layers—in a C++ class, in logical and physical Win32 objects, and in the device. The labels on the arrows are functions that move between the layers.

The basic procedure for using a GDI object from MFC can be summarized as follows:

1. Instantiate the corresponding MFC class. For some objects, you can give the object's attributes as initializers, in which case the constructor will create the underlying logical object.
2. Create the logical object. If the object has not been created by the constructor, use the Create or CreateIndirect member function.
3. Select the logical object into a device context. This creates the physical object and chooses it as the current setting for the device context.
4. Use member functions of CDC to draw with the object.

8.3 Line-Drawing Graphics

The implements for drawing are pens and brushes.

8.3.1 Pens

A program draws lines using a pen. Lines can be straight or curved, separate or connected. The current pen is also used to draw the outline of shapes like rectangles and ellipses.

Pens have width, style, and color. Pen styles include solid, dotted, and dashed lines. Pens may also have cap and join styles. The cap style specifies what an open end of a line looks like (see Figure 8.4). The join style specifies how the joints of connected lines appear (Figure 8.5). The default pen for a DC is a solid black pen that is one or two pixels wide, depending on the device resolution.

Figure 8.4   Cap styles for pens—A flat cap differs from square in that it terminates at the destination pixel, while a square cap terminates in a square centered on the destination pixel.

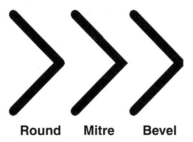

Figure 8.5   Join styles for pens

Objects of the MFC class CPen capture the ideal characteristics of a pen. Depending on the device, some or all of the characteristics may have to be approximated. For example, an ideal pen of red may be represented on a printer as gray.

The actual storage for the attributes of a pen is maintained by Win32. The constructor for CPen, and the Create member function, create a logical pen within

Win32. Use the GetExtLogPen function to get a copy of the logical pen data structure, an EXTLOGPEN. The destructor for CGdiObject deletes the logical pen. When a CPen is selected into a device context, Win32 creates the physical pen based on the attributes of the logical pen and the capabilities of the device.

8.3.2 Brushes

Whereas the current pen controls the outline style of the various shapes, the current brush controls the interior. Brushes fill areas with color and patterns. Built-in patterns include solid colors and several styles of cross hatching. The default brush for a DC is a solid black brush.

As with pens, logical brushes are selected into a device context to get a physical brush. The CBrush class wraps a Win32 logical brush. The following code fragment creates a solid red brush and uses it to fill a rectangle with no outline:

```
void draw(CDC &dc, CRect &rect)
{
    dc.SelectStockObject(NULL_PEN);    // No outine
    CBrush brush( RGB(255,0,0) );      // Red logical brush
    dc.SelectObject(&brush);           // Red physical brush
    dc Rectangle(rect);                // Draw rectangle
```

Custom brush patterns can be created from bitmaps. With a bitmap brush, the top-left eight rows and columns are repeated to tile an area. To create a bitmap brush, first create or load a bitmap, then use that bitmap when creating the brush. For example, this code fragment fills a rectangle with a pattern specified by the bitmap resource IDB_Brush:

```
void draw(CDC &dc, CRect &rect)
{
    CBitmap bitmap;
    bitmap.LoadBitmap(IDB_Brush);
    CBrush brush(&bitmap);
    dc.SelectObject(&brush);
    dc.Rectangle(rect);
```

8.3.3 Color

Pens, brushes, and text come in a variety of colors. Win32 uses the *additive* color model for representing color. Colors are generated by mixing light of the three primary colors: red, green, and blue. To specify a particular color, give the absolute intensity for each of the primaries. The intensities range from 0 to 255. If all intensities are zero, the color is black. If all intensities are 255, the color is white. Here are some other combinations:

Red	Green	Blue	Color
255	0	0	red
255	255	0	magenta
0	255	255	cyan
127	127	127	gray

Use the RGB macro to represent a color in a program. RGB takes as parameters the intensities for red, green, and blue, in that order. Thus RGB(0,255,255) represents the color cyan. The resulting value is called a COLORREF. As with other logical GDI objects, a COLORREF is an ideal; the actual color output depends upon the capabilities of the device.

8.3.3.1 Screen Colors

Most display screens are capable of rendering any color, but there is often a limit to how many colors can be shown at the same time. The amount of graphics memory on a system determines the limit.

Each pixel on a raster display is written 30 or more times per second, depending on the refresh frequency of the device. Win32 stores the color for each pixel in memory dedicated to the display, known as graphics memory. To represent any COLORREF directly would require 24 bits of graphics memory for each pixel, or about 18 megabits for a 1024 by 768 pixel display. Even a VGA screen would require nearly a megabyte of graphics memory. Although these quantities of memory become less intimidating every year, historically they have forced a compromise on the designers of graphics cards. Rather than reserving 24 bits per pixel, graphics devices commonly use just 8 bits plus a color palette. The palette maps the 8-bit numbers stored in graphics memory to 24-bit color values (see Figure 8.6).

If a palette is in use, GDI will evolve the palette based on the program's color requests. Alternatively, a program can take control over the colors in the palette using members of the CPalette class.

8.3.3.2 Printer Colors

The additive color model mirrors how colors form on the display screen. Printers, by contrast, work according to the *subtractive* model. Beginning with white paper, color is generated by applying ink to filter out portions of the spectrum.

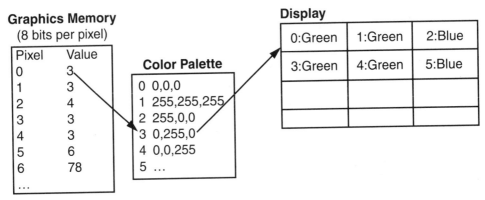

Figure 8.6   The value stored for each pixel is an index into the color palette. For example, the value at pixel 0 is 3. In the color palette, 3 is the index of green, so pixel 0 shows green.

The filters are usually combinations of the subtractive-model primaries, cyan, magenta, and yellow. Paper stock, ink quality, and lighting all affect the printed color.

Mapping from the additive to the subtractive color model is not always straightforward, making it difficult to render colors on paper that exactly match what is seen on screen. GDI uses the concept of logical colors that populate a color space. An end user can fine-tune what physical color a particular logical color maps to. Read about color spaces in the API manual under the heading "Image Color Matching". MFC does not wrap this functionality.

8.3.4 Coordinates and Mapping Modes

The GDI drawing functions take coordinates in a two-dimensional space. The origin of the default coordinate space depends on how the device context was created. For CClientDC, 0,0 is the top-left corner of the window's client area; for a CWindowDC, 0,0 is the top-left corner of the window. All output is clipped at the boundary of the device context.

The location of the origin and the unit dimension in the coordinate space depend additionally upon the mapping mode. The *mapping mode* determines the meaning of one unit horizontally and vertically, as well as the direction of the axes. By changing the mapping mode, a program can use coordinates tied to physical units like inches and meters, leaving it to Win32 to convert the coordinates into an appropriate dimension for the device. For example, by choosing the mapping mode MM_LOMETRIC, a program can specify GDI coordinates in tenths of a millimeter. The following table shows the units for each mapping mode:

Mapping mode	Physical size of one unit
MM_HIENGLISH	.001 inch
MM_LOENGLISH	.01 inch
MM_HIMETRIC	.01 millimeter
MM_LOMETRIC	.1 millimeter
MM_TWIPS	1/1440 inch (1/20th of a point)
MM_TEXT	1 device unit

In addition, there are two mapping modes for setting arbitrary scaling factors, MM_ISOTROPIC and MM_ANISOTROPIC. In the MM_ISOTROPIC mode, the same unit is used for each axis, so the grid is square. MM_ANISOTROPIC has no restriction on the scale for each axis, so it can change the aspect ratio of a drawing. See Chapter 12 for an example of using MM_ANISOTROPIC.

The default mapping mode is MM_TEXT, which has a misleading name since each unit corresponds to one device unit such as a pixel on the screen. It is important to remember that the mapping mode only affects coordinates. Bitmaps and text need to be scaled separately, as is done by the application framework during print preview (see Chapter 13).

There is a subtlety regarding coordinates that shows up especially when the mapping mode is MM_TEXT. To draw a line from pixel a up to and including pixel b, the coordinates given are those of pixel a and those of $b+1$. That is, drawing operations include the first pixel but exclude the last. For a rectangle, the top and left edges are included, but the bottom and right edges are not. This inclusive/exclusive rule is used for coordinates everywhere in GDI.

Another way of thinking about coordinates is to view them as labeling the lines between the pixels and not the pixels themselves. In Figure 8.7, it is clear that drawing a line from 1 to 4 fills in the three intervening pixels

8.3.5 Raster Ops

Using a pen of a selected color, with a specific width, and on a particular coordinate grid has a natural correspondence to objects in the physical world. Device contexts have another attribute, the raster op, that is a bit more abstract. A *raster op* determines how the color of a pen or brush mixes with color on a device.

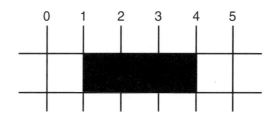

Figure 8.7   Coordinates to GDI functions can be viewed as labeling the lines between the pixels.

The default raster op simply takes the color of the implement and puts it on the device. Other raster ops are used for tasks like drawing stretchable objects, highlighting a region, simple animation, and masking of bitmaps.

When a line is drawn or an area filled, the color of each pixel on the device is the result of applying the current raster op. Raster ops are specified as a bitwise operation. A binary raster op takes as operands the device pixel and the drawing implement's color.[6]   Applying the raster op is like using C++'s bitwise operators. There are 16 binary raster ops, most of which you'll never use. Here are the most important ones:

Raster op	Bitwise operation
R2_COPYPEN	implement
R2_NOT	~device
R2_XORPEN	device ∧ implement
R2_NOTXORPEN	device ∧ ~implement

To see how a raster op works, it's easiest to consider a monochrome device and implement, so that the operands are a single bit. For color, the operands are up to 24 bits wide, but the same principle applies.[7]

R2_COPYPEN is the default. It writes the color of the implement on the device without regard to the color of the device.

---

[6] Win32 also supports ternary raster ops that take a brush and two bitmaps. For details, look up CDC::BitBlt in the reference manual.

[7] On a true-color device (24 bits per pixel), the RGB value can be used as the operand. On devices with a color palette, the palette index is used as the operand for the device.

R2_NOT inverts the color on the device; black becomes white and white becomes black. R2_NOT is used for creating rubber band shapes and highlighting because it is easily reversible (see the sample program in Section 8.7.4.2).

R2_XORPEN and R2_NOTXORPEN have the same reversible property as R2_NOT except that they take the tool color into consideration. Whereas R2_NOT will always draw a black line on a white device, the exclusive OR ops can draw lines of any color.

8.3.6 Shapes

The various drawing functions of CDC cause output to appear based on the settings of the display context. GDI has direct support for drawing a variety of shapes:

Lines	Lines are drawn by controlling the pen. First the pen is moved to the start of the line using MoveTo. Then LineTo draws the line with the current pen attributes.
Rectangles	Rectangles, with sides parallel to the axes, can be drawn by giving the coordinates of the top-left and bottom-right corners. The outline of the rectangle is drawn using the current pen and the interior is filled using the current brush. GDI supports rectangles with square, as well as round, corners.
Polygons	Polygons are specified as an array of points. Lines are drawn between each point and from the last point to the first.
Ellipses	Ellipses are drawn like rectangles, by specifying the diagonal of the bounding rectangle. Also, the outline and interior are controlled by the current pen and brush. A bounding rectangle of a square generates a circle.
Arcs	An arc is an open portion of an ellipse. Arcs can not filled.
Chords	A chord is a closed portion of an ellipse. Chords can be filled.
Pies	A pie is an arc whose center and endpoints are connected by lines. Pies can be filled.
Splines	Win32 draws cubic Bézier splines—curves defined by two endpoints and two control points.

To draw a closed shape without an outline, select the null pen using the `Select-StockObject` member of `CDC`. To draw a closed shape unfilled, select the null brush. Both the outline and the interior of the shape are affected by the current raster op.

If the current pen is wider than one pixel, the whole outline may not fit within the bounding rectangle because the lines are drawn with the pen centered on the edges of the shape. Thus, nearly half the pixels of the pen may lie outside the bounding rectangle. This is an important consideration when computing the invalid rectangle (see Section 8.7.4.3). The pixels of the pen can be forced inside the bounding rectangle by setting the pen style to `PS_INSIDEFRAME`.

8.4 Text

As computers have become expert at showing text in different fonts, what was once an esoteric field has become an interest of many. Tweaking the appearance of the printed page is now a favorite computer pastime. The ability to change the font of text is a capability expected from every program that displays text.

The great divide in fonts is between proportional and fixed-width. In a *proportional* font, like the font you are reading, different characters have different widths. For example, "M" is wide while "I" is narrow. In a *fixed-width* font, each character has the same width as on a typewriter or a line printer. The program listings in this book use a fixed-width font.

Every font has three basic properties:

Style	The characters in a font are designed to look good and read well together, presenting a consistent ink density across the page.
Size	The size of a proportional font is specified as the height of its tallest symbols, usually measured in points. For all practical purposes, there are 72 points per inch. The size of a fixed-width font is usually given as the number of characters per some horizontal unit, such as an inch.
Character set	In addition to the common Roman characters, there are fonts for most of the world's languages and a variety of special symbol sets.

Most fonts can be altered algorithmically to change their style. Traditional modifications, such as <u>underlining</u> and ~~strikethrough~~, don't change the appearance of the characters. Other modifications, such as slanting characters and emboldening strokes, give text a much different look. As programs have become more adept at manipulating character images, it has become more difficult to determine when a font is "new" versus an algorithmic modification of some other font. Consider Figure 8.8. How many fonts are represented? Is it one font algorithmically enlarged, emboldened, and slanted, or is it four different fonts?

Times Roman 10 point

Times Roman 14 point bold

Times Roman 14 point italic

Times Roman 14 point bold italic

Figure 8.8   How many different fonts are shown in the box?

8.4.1 Logical Fonts

GDI represents fonts on two levels, as it does pens and brushes. The logical font describes the ideal characteristics of a font along with its modifications. The text in Figure 8.8 would be represented by four different logical fonts. The LOGFONT data structure, maintained by Win32, describes a logical font:

```
typedef struct tagLOGFONT {
    LONG      lfHeight;        // Cell or character height
    LONG      lfWidth;         // Char width
    LONG      lfEscapement;    // Orientation of base line
    LONG      lfOrientation;   // Orientation of characters
    LONG      lfWeight;        // Thickness of strokes
    BYTE      lfItalic;        // True for italic fonts
    BYTE      lfUnderline;     // True for underlining
    BYTE      lfStrikeOut;     // True for strikethrough
    BYTE      lfCharSet;       // Identifies the character set
    BYTE      lfOutPrecision;  // Guides physical-font matching
    BYTE      lfClipPrecision; // Guides clipping of chars
    BYTE      lfQuality;       // Guides physical-font matching
    BYTE      lfPitchAndFamily; // Rough characterization of font
    WCHAR     lfFaceName[LF_FACESIZE]; // Font name
} LOGFONT;
```

If you look in the API manual, you'll find that there two other data structures for representing fonts, NEWLOGFONT and ENUMLOGFONT. That there are three data structures indicates how difficult it can be to capture all the characteristics of a font and how the Win32 treatment of font has become more sophisticated.

Originally, the fonts used by Win32 were represented by bitmaps, explicit pictures of each character. The problem with using bitmapped fonts is that each device with a different resolution requires a different set of characters.

The NEWLOGFONT data structure was introduced with the TrueType fonts. True-Type fonts are represented by strokes and growth rules rather than bitmaps. These fonts can be scaled to fit different devices and to be presented in different sizes, so only one description is needed regardless of the target output device.[8]

The ENUMLOGFONT data structure was introduced to handle a wider set of languages. It supports Unicode fonts. Unicode is an encoding of nearly every symbol used across all the world's languages, plus numeric symbols from different counting systems and a variety of technical symbols. The set of symbols is large, so Unicode uses 16 bits to encode each symbol.[9]

The CFont class wraps the characteristics of a logical font. It contains a handle to the Win32 logical font data structure.

8.4.2 Physical Fonts

When a logical font is selected into a device context, Win32 chooses a physical font that matches the ideal based on the capabilities of the device. Again, Win32 maintains a data structure to describe the physical font, known as a TEXTMETRIC:

```
typedef struct tagTEXTMETRIC {
    LONG    tmHeight;              // Character height
    LONG    tmAscent;             // Char height above base line
    LONG    tmDescent;            // Char height below base line
    LONG    tmInternalLeading;    // Height of diacritical marks
    LONG    tmExternalLeading;    // Height of space between rows
    LONG    tmAveCharWidth;       // Width of typical char, e.g., x
    LONG    tmMaxCharWidth;       // Width of widest char, e.g., W
```

---

[8] Simple-minded scaling of characters does not produce good results. The growth rules, also known as *hints*, adjust scaling for better appearance.

[9] For more details about Unicode, see *The Unicode Standard, Version 2.0*, The Unicode Consortium, Addison Wesley Longman, 1996.

```
    LONG    tmWeight;              // Thickness of strokes
    LONG    tmOverhang;            // Extra width needed by some chars
    LONG    tmDigitizedAspectX;    // Horz design resolution of font
    LONG    tmDigitizedAspectY;    // Vert design resolution of font
    WCHAR   tmFirstChar;           // First char in char set
    WCHAR   tmLastChar;            // Last char in char set
    WCHAR   tmDefaultChar;         // Char to use for value not in char set
    WCHAR   tmBreakChar;           // Char to mark work breaks
    BYTE    tmItalic;              // True for italic fonts
    BYTE    tmUnderlined;          // True for underlining
    BYTE    tmStruckOut;           // True for strikethrough
    BYTE    tmPitchAndFamily;      // Rough characterization of font
    BYTE    tmCharSet;             // Identifies the character set
} TEXTMETRIC;
```

As with logical fonts, the description of physical fonts has evolved and there is an extended data structure called NEWTEXTMETRIC.

8.4.3 Outputting Text

Once a font is selected, text can be output using that font in a variety of ways. Look at the member functions of the MFC class CDC for operations on text. Two commonly used functions are TextOut and DrawText.

TextOut outputs characters at a specified location. No formatting is performed on the text. The characters are placed one after the other, clipped only by the device context.

In contrast, DrawText outputs text with simple formatting. A bounding rectangle is specified, in which the text can be justified to any edge or corner, or centered. In addition, the text can be wrapped.

All of the text output functions write text in the font currently selected for the device context. Thus, to write text using different fonts requires multiple calls to the output functions interspersed with calls to select the font.

Besides font, there are other attributes of a device context that influences how text will appear:

Text color	Specifies the color of the strokes that make up characters.
Background mode and color	Specifies whether the space around the strokes is filled in with the background color (*opaque*), or whether the characters are drawn on top of an existing background (*transparent*).

Tab settings	Specifies tab settings for the TabbedTextOut function.
Inter-character spacing	Specifies expanded or condensed text.
Text alignment	Specifies top, bottom, left, and right alignment for calls to TextOut.

8.4.4 WYSIWYG Issues

Programs that present on-screen previews of printed output must address the different capabilities of devices. For example, to word-wrap a paragraph, a word processor must know how much space each word will take on the printer. A similar issue arises for text placed next to or inside of graphic elements. For instance, to center text in the rectangles of an organization's hierarchy chart, a program must know how long each text string will be on the printer.

Three basic issues must be considered:

- Font availability
- Device resolution and aspect ratio
- Character kerning

8.4.4.1 Font Availability

Some printers have hundreds of built-in fonts. To use a built-in font, a program selects the font in the printer and then sends strings of characters. The placement of the characters in each string is determined by the printer. If the system does not have the same font for the display screen, then the user will only see an approximation during print preview. The substituted font used on the display is not likely to be the same size as the printer font for each character. Also, the relative character sizes are not likely to be the same. On the printer, for example, an **m** may be four times the width of an **i**, while on the screen it may only be three times wider.

8.4.4.2 Resolution and Aspect Ratio

Even if the same nominal font exists on the system for the display and the printer, the resolution of the display is probably different from that of the printer. Resolution refers to the granularity of the device, measured in dots per linear unit—for instance, dots per inch. Aspect ratio is related to resolution. It is the relative resolution of one axis to the other. A square device has an aspect ratio of 1, so the resolution is the same horizontally and vertically. Some devices are astigmatic; they have higher resolution in one direction.

The result is that if a character width on the printer cannot be represented exactly on-screen because of lower resolution, there will be some round-off error. Depending on the characters, the round-off error can accumulate over a line of text and become significant.

8.4.4.3 Kerning

If you look closely at high-quality typeset text, you'll see that some characters slightly overlap, particularly lower-case letters that follow capitals. This overlap is known as *kerning*. The overall width of a kerned string is less than the sum of the widths of the characters that make up the string.

Kerning is often carried out by the printer. It is controlled by a table that specifies the kerning relationship between pairs of characters. Each character in a font has a kerning relationship to every other character in the font. For a program to represent text accurately on-screen, it must know how the printer will kern each character pair.

8.4.4.4 Strategies

Depending on the requirements of the application, you may find the following strategies helpful.

For graphical applications, in which the placement of individual characters is important, place characters based on the printer widths. A program can retrieve character widths from the printer by using the API function GetCharWidth32, passing a device context for the printer. Then, rather than using functions like DrawText and TextOut to output whole strings, the program can place each character individually. The downside of this approach is that the inter-character spacing on-screen may look odd. Some characters will appear too close together and others too far apart.

Often the placement of individual characters is not as important as the total string length. Programs that wrap text, for example, need to know the total length of a string in order to compute line breaks. Being off by only one device pixel can cause characters to be clipped—for instance, when printing near the edge of the device. The API function GetTextExtentPoint32 retrieves the total length of a string for a specified device context. Once the total length is known on the printer, the on-screen text can be adjusted to occupy the same space. Extra space can be added or eliminated from between words or between characters. The overall appearance using this strategy is better than that of the character-placement strategy, but whole strings may appear squished or spread out.

The best appearance results when the screen and printer use the same font. Another strategy, then, is to give the user the option of only selecting fonts for which both screen and printer versions are available. Using only TrueType or Type I fonts supports this strategy, since they can be scaled to fit nearly any device.

8.5 The Mouse

Pointing is, of course, an integral part of a graphical environment. Although other devices are usable with Win32, pointing is modeled on the mouse.

Compared with the keyboard or the display, the mouse is very simple. There are just a few primary events:

- Pressing a mouse button
- Releasing the button
- Moving the mouse
- Turning the mouse wheel[10]

Operating the mouse over the client area of a window generates these messages:

WM_MOUSEMOVE   Posted after movement is detected over the client area of a window. Only one move message will be on the queue at a time; its coordinates will be updated if the mouse is moved before the message is retrieved.

WM_SETCURSOR   Sent after movement is detected over the client area. A window responds by changing the cursor shape. The default behavior is to set the cursor according to the window class.

---

[10] The mouse wheel appears on top of some mice next to the buttons.

WM_LBUTTONDOWN	Posted when the (nominal) left mouse button is pressed. There are analogous messages for the right and middle buttons, and for clicking in the nonclient area.
WM_LBUTTONUP	Posted when the left mouse button is released.
WM_MOUSEACTIVATE	Sent when a mouse button is clicked over any window other than the current top-level window. A child window will receive this message for *every* mouse click.
WM_LBUTTONDBLCLK	Posted when the left mouse button is pressed, released, and then pressed again within the user-setable double-click time. As with button down and button up, there are analogous messages for the right and middle buttons.
WM_MOUSEWHEEL	Posted when the mouse wheel is turned. Movement of the mouse wheel typically triggers scrolling of the window.

The location of the mouse and the state of the mouse buttons and keyboard shift keys are passed as parameters with most of these mouse messages. The mouse position is given relative to the upper-left corner of the window's client area.

Moving or clicking the mouse over the nonclient area generates analogous NC messages—for example, WM_NCLBUTTONDOWN and WM_NCMOUSEMOVE. The mouse position in a nonclient message is relative to the origin of the display screen.

8.5.1 Capturing the Mouse

Normally, mouse messages are delivered to the window underneath the mouse cursor. There are times when a window needs mouse messages even if the mouse is not over it. For example, a window that tracks a dragged mouse with a highlight or rubber-band shape needs to know when the mouse button is released. To receive all mouse messages, a window can *capture* the mouse. A typical sequence, illustrated by the Graphics program described in Section 8.7.4, is:

1. On button down, capture the mouse.
2. On mouse move, draw a highlight or rubber-band shape.
3. On button up, perform an operation and release the capture.

When you capture the mouse, always make sure you release it. While the mouse is captured, a user will not be able to operate the program's menus, and keyboard accelerators and mnemonics are disabled. In addition, the mouse cursor will not change as the mouse is moved over other windows. Programs take advantage of this last property when posting a temporary cursor. They

1. Capture the mouse.
2. Set a temporary cursor.
3. Release the capture.
4. Restore the previous cursor.

The MFC class CWaitCursor will do this for you automatically.[11]

Capturing the mouse has some additional subtlety. As long as the mouse stays over the application, all mouse messages will go to the window that has the mouse captured. If the mouse is dragged over another application, mouse messages go to the window that has the mouse captured as long as the mouse button is held down. If the mouse button is released, the capture only holds while the mouse is inside the application.

When capture is used in the standard way described above, the window that has captured the mouse also has the focus. It may be possible in an application for a dialog (or message box) to appear while the mouse is captured. It is always possible for the user to switch applications using the systemwide meta keys Alt+Tab. To allow the mouse to work in the dialog or switched-to application, the mouse capture should be released. Win32 sends the WM_CANCELMODE message when the focus changes; the default CWnd response is to release the mouse.

This raises a sticky problem. Often the mouse is captured to guarantee that a program sees the mouse button go up. In response to button-up, the program might clear a highlight or record a command. But if the mouse is released in cancel mode, the program might not see the button go up and, as a result, leave a highlight partially drawn or a command incomplete. The following table summarizes the various events and indicates how a program should respond:

---

[11] To support multi-threaded applications, CWaitCursor doesn't actually capture the mouse, because the capture would lock out all threads. Instead, MFC remembers the current cursor for each thread in private data.

Event	Response
Mouse button pressed	Capture the mouse
Mouse moved	Draw highlight
Mouse button released	Release capture, erase highlight, record operation
Cancel mode	Release capture, erase highlight

As usual, Win32 sends messages for each of the micro-events in this scenario. In addition to the mouse messages, Win32 generates the WM_CAPTURECHANGED message when mouse capture is released. A program can use this message to erase any highlight for all cases, as illustrated in Section 8.7.4.3.

8.6 The Keyboard

The number of events triggered by a single key press on the keyboard is a bit staggering. It is a tribute to the incredible speed of processors that programs seem to respond instantaneously. Figure 8.9 shows the basic flow of control for an ordinary key.

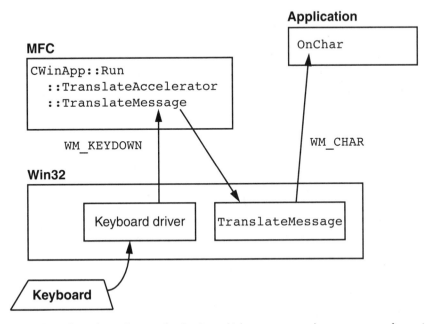

Figure 8.9 Pressing a key on the keyboard triggers a complex sequence of events. The arrows indicate flow of control.

Pressing a key generates a signal that is read by the keyboard driver in Win32. The driver has the job of generating a key-down event indicating that a particular virtual key has been pressed. A *virtual key* represents a key on a "standard" PC keyboard. The job of the keyboard driver is to make the keyboard look standard, regardless of what the hardware really looks like. The key-down event causes a WM_KEYDOWN message to be placed in the message queue for the application. When the key is released, a WM_KEYUP message is posted.

When MFC's message loop picks up the key-down message in CWinApp::Run, it looks to see if the keystroke matches a keyboard accelerator. Recall that there can be an accelerator table associated with a frame window. MFC calls ::TranslateAccelerator to look for a match. If a match is found, ::Translate-Accelerator generates the associated WM_COMMAND message and returns true.

If the keystroke doesn't match an accelerator, CWinApp::Run calls ::Translate-Message to turn the raw keystroke into a character from the current character set being used by the program, such as ASCII. If the keystroke is associated with a character, ::TranslateMessage puts a WM_CHAR message at the head of the message queue.[12] Finally the program picks up the character in OnChar.

As an example, entering the letter **X** might generate the following sequence of messages:

Event	Message
Shift key pressed	WM_KEYDOWN for Shift key
x *key pressed*	WM_KEYDOWN for x key
	WM_CHAR for upper-case X
x *key released*	WM_KEYUP for x key
Shift key released	WM_KEYUP for Shift key

Keystrokes that don't correspond to characters, such as the function and the arrow keys, can be retrieved in response to the key-down message. The Graphics program described below monitors the Ctrl key. See Section 8.7.5 for sample code.

---

[12] A normal call to ::PostMessage places a message at the end of the queue. By contrast, ::TranslateMessage puts the WM_CHAR at the head of the queue to guarantee that the WM_CHAR message will precede WM_KEYUP.

8.6.1 The Caret

Win32 delivers keyboard messages to the window with the focus. At any time, only one window on the system can have the focus. User actions, such as clicking on a window or pressing Ctrl+Tab, change the focus.

To indicate where the next typed character will go, text windows with the focus typically display a flashing box or bar called the *caret*. The term caret is unique to Windows. Many systems call the text-insertion point the *cursor*; Windows, of course, uses cursor to refer to the location of the mouse.

The caret functions are members of CWnd. To start a caret flashing, the caret must be created, using CreateCaret, and then shown, using ShowCaret. When a window loses the focus, it should hide the caret by calling DestroyCaret. Often you will use built-in controls to handle text input, as we did in Chapter 7 with the rich-text edit control, so you won't need to manipulate the caret.

8.7 Graphics: A Program to Create Two-Dimensional Drawings

The Graphics\Simple[13] program goes a long way toward being a complete application. It embodies important aspects of program organization that will be expanded upon in later chapters. It also illustrates

- Line-drawing operations, using pens and brushes with various attributes
- Tracking the mouse
- Monitoring the keyboard
- Modeless dialogs and the concept of a current tool
- Usage of the MFC collection classes

Figure 8.10 shows a screen shot of the Graphics program.

.

---

[13] The Graphics application will evolve from the simple program described here into a fully functional application. For readability in this chapter, I will refer to the Graphics\Simple program simply as the Graphics program.

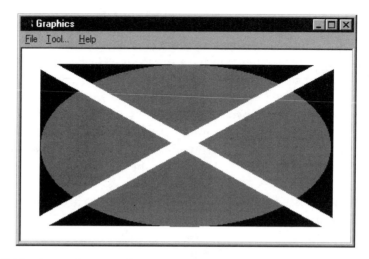

Figure 8.10   A sample screen from the simple Graphics program

8.7.1 Program Organization

The Graphics program displays one drawing at a time. On screen, it has a simple window hierarchy, illustrated in Figure 8.11. This organization is called Single-Document Interface (SDI) and is described fully in Chapter 9.

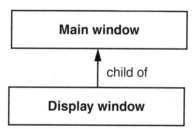

Figure 8.11   The Graphics program consists of two primary windows: a main window with title and menu bars and a display window in which the drawing is rendered.

The menu is managed by the main window, wrapped by the class `mainFrame`. `mainFrame` processes the menu commands. It has commands to erase the drawing, trigger the dialog used to change the current drawing tool, and exit the program.

The program draws in a display window placed on top of the client area of the main window. The display window is an instance of the `display` class. The display class monitors the mouse and keyboard to implement drawing. It also responds to WM_PAINT to draw the picture, as needed.

8.7.1.1 The Concepts of Storage and Display

The data that describes the drawing is managed by a storage class called store. Its job is to store the drawing commands as the user enters them and to play back the commands when the display needs to be redrawn. As shown in Figure 8.12, the tasks of displaying the drawing on-screen and manipulating it in memory are handled by different classes. The separation of storage from display keeps the program flexible. It allows the creation of new display classes that render the drawing in different ways and multiple display objects that show different parts of a single drawing. It also allows the representation of the drawing to be changed without having to modify the code that displays the drawing. We'll use this flexibility to advantage as the Graphics program evolves.

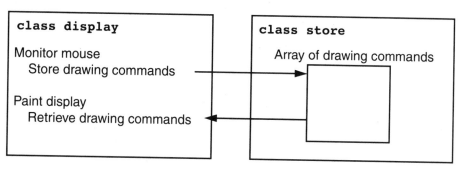

Figure 8.12 The display class handles the on-screen representation of a drawing; the store class manages the in-memory representation. The arrows represent flow of data.

The declarations of the display and store classes reflect their roles and interactions. The display class has handlers for WM_PAINT, mouse operations, and keyboard keystrokes. In this version of Graphics, there is only one display object and one store object, so the display includes the store as a component:

```
class display : public CWnd
{
. . .
    store m_graphics;  // Storage for graphics

    // Generated message map functions
protected:
    //{{AFX_MSG(display)
    afx_msg void OnPaint();
    afx_msg void OnLButtonDown(UINT nFlags, CPoint point);
    afx_msg void OnMouseMove(UINT nFlags, CPoint point);
    afx_msg void OnLButtonUp(UINT nFlags, CPoint point);
    afx_msg void OnKeyDown(UINT nChar, UINT nRepCnt, UINT nFlags);
    afx_msg void OnKeyUp(UINT nChar, UINT nRepCnt, UINT nFlags);
    //}}AFX_MSG
. . .
};
```

The store class presents a program interface to the display for storing and retrieving drawing commands. It holds the commands in a CArray:

```
class store
{
public:
    store();
    BOOL appendCmd(int shape, CRect &rect,
        BOOL fill, int fillColor,
        int outlineColor, int outlineWidth);
    virtual ~store();
    void clear();
    command *getCmd(int i);
    int getCmdCount();
. . .
private:
    CArray <command *,command *> m_cmds;
};
```

8.7.2 Collections

One goal of many programming libraries has been to capture meta algorithms, high-level abstractions of commonly used algorithms. The qsort function in the standard C library is an example. Given a comparison operator, qsort sorts any type array. Abstracting the representation of commonly used data structures is more challenging. This is a primary goal of the Standard Template Library (STL)[14] and of MFC's collection classes.

---

[14] For an introduction to STL, see *C++ Programming with the Standard Template Library*, by David R. Musser and Atul Saini, Addison Wesley Longman, 1996.

Simply put, a *collection* consists of a set of elements. Often the data for an application consists of a collection, such as the list of commands to produce a drawing, the array of text in a document, or the set of records in a database. Regardless of how the data is stored, each collection requires the same basic operations:

- Load and store the collection.
- Add elements to and delete elements from the collection.
- Find a particular element or seek to a particular location in the collection.

In addition, some collections are ordered, such as the array of text in a document. Ordered collections usually require an operation to iterate over the elements.

The idea is to provide a uniform way to manipulate commonly used data structures. Different data structures trade off time and space. By using a collection, the performance decision is decoupled from the implementation algorithm.

MFC supports three types of collections:

Lists (linked lists)	Optimized for insertion and deletion
Arrays	Optimized for access via index
Maps (name-value pairs)	Optimized for access via key

A primary motivation for adding class templates to C++ was to support the creation of collection classes. If you look up collections in the MFC manual, you'll find that there are two implementations, one using generic classes and one using templates.

The generic classes appeared first in MFC, before Microsoft's C++ compiler supported templates. The generic collections consist of lists, arrays, and maps of the basic types. For elements of any particular type, the appropriate generic type is used and the arguments and return values cast. For example, the generic `CPtrList` class was used in the Window program of Chapter 5 to keep track of each CWnd as it was created. The list was `static` data of the `sample` class:

```
class sample : public CWnd
{
. . .
    static CPtrList wnd;
```

When a window was created, it was added to the head of the list:

```
sample::sample()
{
 .  .  .
        wnd.AddHead(this);
```

The Tile command needed to iterate over the elements:

```
void sample::tile()
{
 .  .  .
    POSITION pos = wnd.GetHeadPosition();
 .  .  .
        sample *wp = (sample *)wnd.GetNext(pos);
```

Because the elements in the list are generic pointers, the return value from access functions like GetNext must be cast.

The template implementation does not require casting, since it instantiates a new type with the right kind of elements. There are three class templates, corresponding to the three collection classes: CArray, CList, and CMap.

To use a template, instantiate it to create a new class. In the Window program, the pointer list could have been declared as

```
    static CList <CWnd *,CWnd *> wnd;
```

The template takes two arguments: the type of objects stored and the argument type used in various functions on the collection (see Figure 8.13). In this example, the template creates versions of the AddHead and GetNext functions that take and return a CWnd *. Insertion would thus fail to compile if the parameter were other than a CWnd *, unlike in the generic version where *any* type pointer could be passed to AddHead.

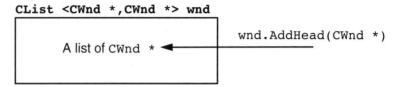

Figure 8.13   The collection templates take two arguments: the type of the elements and the type of the argument to operations on the collection. In this example, both types are CWnd *.

Similarly, GetNext returns a pointer of the correct type, again guaranteeing correct usage:

```
sample *wp = wnd.GetNext(pos);
```

8.7.2.1 A Collection of Commands

The store class in the Graphics program maintains an array of command *:

```
CArray <command *,command *> m_cmds;
```

The class command captures all the details about a drawing element:

```
class command {
public:
    command(
        int shape, CRect &rect,
        BOOL fill, int fillColor,
        int outlineColor, int outlineWidth) {
            cmdShape = shape;
            cmdRect = rect;
            cmdFill = fill;
            cmdFillColor = fillColor;
            cmdOutlineColor = outlineColor;
            cmdOutlineWidth = outlineWidth;
    };

    int cmdShape;
    CRect cmdRect;
    BOOL cmdFill;
    int cmdFillColor;
    int cmdOutlineColor;
    int cmdOutlineWidth;
};
```

The appendCmd function in store appends a drawing command to the array by allocating space for the command, then calling Add. Add grows the array if necessary:

```
BOOL store::appendCmd(int shape, CRect &rect,
    BOOL fill, int fillColor,
    int outlineColor, int outlineWidth)
{
    command *cmd = new command(shape,rect,
        fill,fillColor,outlineColor,outlineWidth);
    m_cmds.Add(cmd);
    return TRUE;
}
```

Two other functions in store support iteration, getCmd and getCmdCount.

```
command *store::getCmd(int i)
{
    return m_cmds[i];
}

int store::getCmdCount()
{
    return m_cmds.GetUpperBound() + 1;
}
```

These functions are used by the display class during painting:

```
void display::OnPaint()
{
    CPaintDC dc(this); // device context for painting
    int count = m_graphics.getCmdCount();

    for( int i=0; i<count; ++i ) {
        command *cp = m_graphics.getCmd(i);
        shape *sp = theTool.getShape(cp->cmdShape);
        COLORREF rgbFill = theTool.getColor(cp->cmdFillColor);
        COLORREF rgbOutline = theTool.getColor(cp->cmdOutlineColor);
        sp->draw(dc,cp->cmdRect,
            cp->cmdFill,rgbFill,
            rgbOutline,cp->cmdOutlineWidth);
    }
    . . .
}
```

Notice that store really doesn't know much about the details of how the array is implemented. The details of growing and indexing are implemented in the library. In Chapter 10, you'll see library support for reading and writing collections.

8.7.3 Basic Drawing Operations

The last section showed the display code for painting. Actual drawing is handled by the shape class; OnPaint gets each shape and calls draw. Here is the declaration of shape:

```
class shape {
public:
    shape();
    virtual void draw(CDC &dc, CRect &rect,
        BOOL fill, COLORREF fillColor,
        COLORREF outlineColor, int outlineWidth);
    virtual void drawShape(CDC &dc, CRect &rect) {};
};
```

shape is the base class for the shapes line, rectangle, and ellipse. The draw function is shared by rectangles and ellipses:

```
void shape::draw(CDC &dc, CRect &rect,
    BOOL fill, COLORREF fillColor,
    COLORREF outlineColor, int outlineWidth)
{
    CPen pen;
    int save = dc.SaveDC();

    if( outlineWidth>0 ) {
        pen.CreatePen(PS_SOLID,outlineWidth,outlineColor);
        dc.SelectObject(&pen);
    } else dc.SelectStockObject(NULL_PEN);

    CBrush brush;
    if(fill) {
        brush.CreateSolidBrush(fillColor);
        dc.SelectObject(&brush);
    } else dc.SelectStockObject(NULL_BRUSH);

    drawShape(dc,rect);
    dc.RestoreDC(save);
}
```

Given a device context, draw

1. Creates a pen to use for the outline, if appropriate;
2. Creates a brush to use for the interior, if appropriate; and,
3. Calls drawShape to output the shape.

ellipse and rectangle have their own versions of drawShape:

```
void ellipse::drawShape(CDC &dc, CRect &rect)
{
    dc.Ellipse(&rect);
}

void rectangle::drawShape(CDC &dc, CRect &rect)
{
    dc.Rectangle(&rect);
}
```

Lines are drawn differently, so line has its own draw code (and no implementation of drawShape):

```
void line::draw(CDC &dc, CRect &rect,
    BOOL, COLORREF,
    COLORREF color, int width)
{
    CPen pen(PS_SOLID,width,color);
    CPen *oldPen = dc.SelectObject(&pen);
    dc.MoveTo(rect.left,rect.top);
    dc.LineTo(rect.right,rect.bottom);
    dc.SelectObject(oldPen);
}
```

8.7.4 Tracking the Mouse

The display class implements interactive drawing using the mouse by following the steps described in Section 8.5 above:

1. On button down, capture the mouse.
2. On mouse move, draw a highlight or rubber-band shape.
3. On button up, perform an operation and release the capture.

8.7.4.1 Capturing the Mouse

Graphics draws a rubber-band shape to indicate where the new shape will appear. The shape is drawn from the location where the left mouse-button was first pressed, m_anchor, to the current location of the mouse, m_cursor. On the button press, the display class remembers the mouse location and captures the mouse:

```
void display::OnLButtonDown(UINT nFlags, CPoint point)
{
    m_anchor = m_cursor = point;
    SetCapture();
}
```

8.7.4.2 Drawing a Rubber-Band Shape

To give the illusion of stretching a rubber band as the mouse moves, shapes are erased and drawn very quickly. Although programs usually draw on a window only in response to WM_PAINT, for interactive input painting will not do. The shape is drawn using the raster op R2_NOT. (theTool holds the user's current choice of shape—see Section 8.7.6.) For a particular pair of m_anchor/m_cursor values, drawing the shape the first time inverts the pixels on the screen; drawing the shape the second time restores the original pixels. Hence for each mouse move, the old shape is erased and the new one drawn:

```
void display::OnMouseMove(UINT nFlags, CPoint point)
{
    if( GetCapture()==this ) {
        CClientDC dc(this);
        dc.SetROP2(R2_NOT);
        theTool.getShape()->draw(dc,
            CRect(m_anchor.x,m_anchor.y,m_cursor.x,m_cursor.y),
            theTool.isFilled(),RGB(0,0,0),
            RGB(0,0,0),theTool.getWidth());
  . . .

        theTool.getShape()->draw(dc,
            CRect(m_anchor.x,m_anchor.y,point.x,point.y),
            theTool.isFilled(),RGB(0,0,0),
            RGB(0,0,0),theTool.getWidth());
        m_cursor = point;
    }
}
```

Of course it is possible for the mouse to be moved over a window when the mouse button is not down. Notice that the drawing code is executed only when this window has the mouse captured.[15] The actual drawing, as during painting, is carried out by the shape class.

8.7.4.3 Releasing Mouse Capture

Releasing the mouse button indicates completion of drawing. The shape is recorded, the mouse capture released, and the screen updated:

```
void display::OnLButtonUp(UINT nFlags, CPoint point)
{
    if( GetCapture()==this ) {
        m_cursor = point;
        adjustPoint(m_cursor);
        CRect rect(m_anchor.x,m_anchor.y,m_cursor.x,m_cursor.y);
        int width = theTool.getWidth();
        m_graphics.appendCmd(
            theTool.getShapeNumber(),
            rect,
            theTool.isFilled(),
            theTool.getFillColorNumber(),
            theTool.getOutlineColorNumber(),
            width);
        ReleaseCapture();
    }
}
```

---

[15] Comparing the CWnd * returned by GetCapture to this would be dicey if GetCapture returned a pointer to a temporary object. For CWnds, MFC always attempts to find the permanent CWnd before creating a temporary.

Recall that there are two paths to releasing mouse capture: button up and cancel mode. The code to update the screen is shared by both; it resides in OnCaptureChanged:

```
void display::OnCaptureChanged(CWnd *pWnd)
{
    if( pWnd!=this ) { // Release
        CRect rect(m_anchor.x,m_anchor.y,m_cursor.x,m_cursor.y);
        int width = theTool.getWidth();
        rect.NormalizeRect();
        rect.InflateRect(width,width);
        InvalidateRect(&rect);
    }
}
```

OnCaptureChanged is called whenever the capture state changes, including when the window first captures the mouse. The test pWnd!=this filters out the initial capture.

The invalid rectangle is computed from the anchor and cursor. Rectangles in Win32 are always specified top-left to bottom-right. Because we don't know the relative locations of the anchor and cursor, I use NormalizeRect to put the rectangle in standard form before calling InvalidateRect. Also, since the current pen may be wider than a single pixel, the invalid rectangle is inflated. By default, the pixels written by a line are centered on the line, so wide pens write outside the nominal rectangle for a shape.

8.7.5 Monitoring the Keyboard

The Graphics program monitors the Ctrl key during drawing. If Ctrl is pressed, the bounding rectangle is constrained to be a square, making it easy to draw squares and circles. To indicate the constraint, the program changes the mouse cursor to a cross-hair.

Recall that keyboard events generate messages on two layers: WM_KEYDOWN for every key press and WM_CHAR for key presses that correspond to characters. Programs process WM_CHAR to pick up user data and WM_KEYDOWN to pick up control keys such as the arrows, the function keys, Home and End, and the shift keys.

Graphics processes WM_KEYDOWN and WM_KEYUP to monitor presses of Ctrl. When Ctrl is pressed or released, the program changes the cursor and triggers a redraw of the rubber-band shape:

```
void display::OnKeyDown(UINT nChar, UINT nRepCnt, UINT nFlags)
{
    if( nChar==VK_CONTROL ) {
        ::SetCursor( theApp.LoadStandardCursor(IDC_CROSS) );
        if( GetCapture()==this && !m_isCtrlKeyDown ) {
            OnMouseMove(MK_CONTROL,m_cursor);
            m_isCtrlKeyDown = TRUE;
        }
    }

    CWnd::OnKeyDown(nChar, nRepCnt, nFlags);
}

void display::OnKeyUp(UINT nChar, UINT nRepCnt, UINT nFlags)
{
    if( nChar==VK_CONTROL ) {
        ::SetCursor( theApp.LoadStandardCursor(IDC_ARROW) );
        if( GetCapture()==this ) {
            CPoint pt;
            ::GetCursorPos(&pt);
            ScreenToClient(&pt);
            OnMouseMove(0,pt);
        }
        m_isCtrlKeyDown = FALSE;
    }

    CWnd::OnKeyUp(nChar, nRepCnt, nFlags);
}
```

Most keys repeat when held down, triggering a stream of WM_KEYDOWN messages. The Boolean variable m_isCtrlKeyDown prevents the stream from flashing the screen. Only the first message triggers redraw.

8.7.6 The Current Drawing Tool

The current tool determines the drawing shape, outline width and color, and fill color. The attributes of the current tool are displayed and set using the modeless Tool dialog shown in Figure 8.14. The tool class controls the dialog. Here is its declaration:

```
class tool : public CDialog
{
// Construction
public:
    tool(CWnd* pParent = NULL);    // standard constructor
    COLORREF getColor(int i);
    BOOL isFilled() { return m_filled; }
    COLORREF getFillColor() { return getColor(m_fillColor); }
    int getFillColorNumber() { return m_fillColor; };
    COLORREF getOutlineColor() { return getColor(m_outlineColor); }
    int getOutlineColorNumber() { return m_outlineColor; };
```

```
            shape *getShape(int i);
            shape *getShape() { return getShape(m_curShape); }
            int getShapeNumber() { return m_curShape; };
            int getWidth() { return m_outlineWidth; };
            BOOL showDialog();

    // Dialog Data
        //{{AFX_DATA(tool)
        enum { IDD = IDD_Tool };
        CSliderCtrlm_widthCtrl;
        int     m_curShape;
        int     m_fillColor;
        int     m_outlineColor;
        BOOL    m_filled;
        //}}AFX_DATA
        int     m_outlineWidth;

    // Overrides
        // ClassWizard generated virtual function overrides
        //{{AFX_VIRTUAL(tool)
        protected:
        virtual void DoDataExchange(CDataExchange* pDX); // DDX/DDV support
        virtual BOOL OnCommand(WPARAM wParam, LPARAM lParam);
        //}}AFX_VIRTUAL

    // Implementation
    protected:
        // Generated message map functions
        //{{AFX_MSG(tool)
        afx_msg void OnClose();
        virtual void OnCancel();
        afx_msg void OnHScroll(UINT nSBCode,UINT nPos,CScrollBar* pScrollBar);
        virtual BOOL OnInitDialog();
        //}}AFX_MSG
        DECLARE_MESSAGE_MAP()
    };
```

The display window queries the tool to determine what shape to draw when the mouse is dragged. Since the Tool dialog does not have to be present during drawing, the data for the tool is decoupled from the dialog; it is kept in a global tool object called theTool:

```
tool theTool;// global tool object
```

theTool is initialized at program startup:

Figure 8.14   The Tool dialog

```
tool::tool(CWnd* pParent /*=NULL*/)
    : CDialog(tool::IDD, pParent)
{
    //{{AFX_DATA_INIT(tool)
    m_curShape = 1;
    m_fillColor = 0;
    m_outlineColor = 0;
    m_filled = FALSE;
    //}}AFX_DATA_INIT

    m_outlineWidth = DfltWidth;
}
```

To display the tool dialog, the program calls showDialog:

```
BOOL tool::showDialog()
{
    if( IsWindow(m_hWnd) ) {
        SetFocus();
        return TRUE;
    } else return Create(IDD);
}
```

If the dialog is not already on the screen, showDialog creates it. The call to Create eventually calls OnInitDialog triggering dialog data exchange. DoData-Exchange transfers data between theTool and the dialog:

```
void tool::DoDataExchange(CDataExchange* pDX)
{
    CDialog::DoDataExchange(pDX);

    //{{AFX_DATA_MAP(tool)
    DDX_Control(pDX, IDC_Width, m_widthCtrl);
    DDX_Radio(pDX, IDC_Ellipse, m_curShape);
    DDX_CBIndex(pDX, IDC_FillColor, m_fillColor);
    DDX_CBIndex(pDX, IDC_OutlineColor, m_outlineColor);
    DDX_Check(pDX, IDC_Filled, m_filled);
    //}}AFX_DATA_MAP

    if( pDX->m_bSaveAndValidate ) {
        m_outlineWidth = m_widthCtrl.GetPos();
        SetDlgItemInt(IDC_WidthText,m_outlineWidth);
    } else {
        m_widthCtrl.SetPos(m_outlineWidth);
    }
}
```

m_widthCtrl wraps the slider. It is manipulated explicitly since there are no DDX functions for handling sliders in the library. IDC_WidthText identifies the text string underneath the slider.

Part II: The Application Framework

CHAPTER

9 | Program Organization

The programs in the `Generic\Sdi` and `Generic\Mdi` directories illustrate the concepts discussed in this chapter. The corresponding executables in the `bin` directory are `GenericSdi.exe` and `GenericMdi.exe`.

9.1 Introduction

In the first part of this book we looked at the objects and concepts that underlie all Win32 programs. You saw how MFC's wrapper classes bring order to the Win32 landscape and provide convenient access to the Win32 API.

In this part I'll concentrate on the bigger picture, the application framework. I'll embed the basic capabilities developed in the last section into the framework. The result will be complete applications with the rich interface Windows users expect.

This chapter lays the groundwork. It addresses the major program styles and the concepts behind the documents and views used by MFC's application framework.

9.2 Program Styles

Although programs vary widely in their look, most fall into one of these two broad categories of operation:

Document-centered	The program provides an interface to a collection of information loosely called a document. The program has operations to manipulate the document. The user drives the sequence of events, selecting from among the operations.
Task-centered	The program has a goal, a task to accomplish. It may interact with the user to carry out its task. The program drives the sequence of events.

9.2.1 Document-Centered Applications

Most programs fall into this category. The concept of a document is borrowed from word processors, where a document typically corresponds to a file. Other programs benefit from the same model. A document may correspond to a Web page, database, spreadsheet, slide show, or interface to a device. Each document is represented on the screen in one or more windows. In terms of overall program operation, a basic design decision is whether more than one document can be displayed at a time.

Single-document interface (SDI) programs display only one document at a time. The window for the document typically fills the main window. To manipulate two documents, two copies of the program are run. WordPad and NotePad are examples of programs that implement SDI.

Multiple-document interface (MDI) programs show more than one document at a time. The main window of an MDI application is a container for the child windows that show the documents. MDI has become the standard for most current personal-productivity applications, such as word processors, spreadsheets, and data base programs.

Even though MDI currently dominates, many people argue for SDI. MDI tends to promote large, monolithic applications. Each MDI application needs meta-keys and menu items for manipulating the various document windows. And, even though the concept of document is central to MDI, a user runs the application and then reads the documents. That is, the usage is application-centered.

In the document-centered model, users open documents, not applications. The application associated in the Win32 registry with the document type is run and the document appears in the application ready to be manipulated. Each newly opened document fires up another instance of the application instead of a new window in a single instance of the application.[1]

Although some people predict the demise of MDI, it is clear that both styles are important. There are times when it is natural to operate on more than one document at a time. The tight integration afforded by a single application facilitates working with multiple document windows—for instance, by providing program commands that work across windows (like tiling and cascading) or by remembering window configurations.

There are also times when running two instances of a program is preferable to manipulating two windows within a single instance. For example, when viewing files in different directories, having separate state information eases navigation.

9.2.1.1 The Single Document Interface

SDI programs tend to be simpler than MDI. They are constructed from a frame window, possible tool and status bars, and a single document window. The document window typically fills, or nearly fills, the frame's client area. The document window may have panes allowing more than one view into the document. Figure 9.1 shows a schematic SDI application.

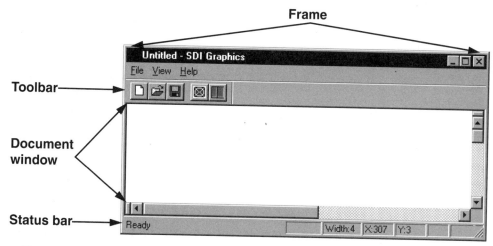

Figure 9.1 The visual components of an SDI application

---

[1] The application itself may be just a shell for invoking a program that know how to deal with the objects contained in the document. This is the component-software viewpoint. For more on Window's component technology, see *Creating Components Using DCOM and C++*, by Don Box, Addison Wesley Longman, 1997; and *Active X Controls*, by Brent Rector, Addison Wesley Longman, 1997.

As there is only one document window, there is no need for a Window submenu, although there may be some control over window panes and a View submenu with commands to hide and show the toolbar and status bar. Although nothing prohibits an SDI application from manipulating different types of documents, they tend to focus on a single type.

Before going on, let me be clear about terminology. A *document* is an abstract concept. As mentioned earlier, it stands for a collection of information, typically stored in a file. A *document window* is an on-screen representation of a document.

9.2.1.2 The Multiple Document Interface

MDI was a program style first described in IBM's *Common User Access* guide;[2] the current description is in *The Windows Interface Guidelines for Software Design* from Microsoft.[3] The basic components should be very familiar:

- The main window is a frame window; it contains the menu bar.
- Each document is represented by a document window contained inside the frame.
- The menu has a Window submenu for managing the document windows.
- When a document window is maximized, its title joins the frame's title bar and a special system menu is prefixed to the menu bar.
- When a document window is minimized, its title-bar is placed at the bottom of the frame window.

Since MDI applications allow more than one document window to be open at a time, they usually allow different views of the same document to be displayed simultaneously. For example, a spreadsheet program may show a sheet view and a graph view of the same spreadsheet. As a result, MDI applications tend to be larger than SDI, not only because they have commands to rearrange the document windows, but also because they contain code to show different types of views and perhaps different types of documents. Figure 9.2 shows the visual components of an MDI application.

The code to implement the MDI protocol is part of Win32, much of it in the Win32 class `MdiClient`. Notice in Figure 9.2 that the document windows are contained inside an `MdiClient` window rather than being direct children of the

---

[2] *Systems Application Architecture, Common User Access: Panel Design and User Interaction*, IBM, December 1987.

[3] *The Windows Interface Guidelines for Software Design*, Microsoft Corp., 1995.

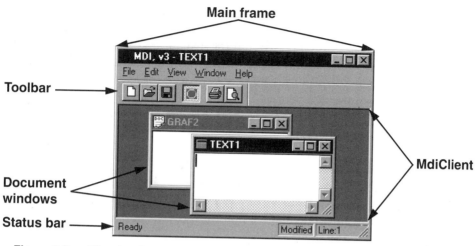

Figure 9.2   The visual components of an MDI application

main frame. By creating the document windows as children of MdiClient, they won't overlap the toolbar or status bar.

From MFC, connecting to the MDI code is just a matter of changing base classes. Use CMDIFrameWnd as the base class for the main frame and CMDIChildWnd as the base class for the child windows. The Mdi program shown later in this chapter uses these classes.

9.2.2 Task-Centered Applications

Task-centered programs guide the user through a sequence of screens and carry out some task based on the user's responses. Installation, set-up, data entry, and some game programs commonly use this style. Often, the screens are dialogs, so the program is a sequence of dialogs. Win32 implements the wizard-mode property sheet to stylize a dialog sequence.

In a dialog-driven application, the main window may be visible, hidden, or non-existent. Sometimes the main window is maximized to provide a controlled background for the dialogs, such as a logo screen or color gradient. Alternatively, the dialog windows may be placed directly on the desktop.

Chapter 14 discusses two task-centered applications: a game and a wizard-mode installation program.

9.3 Documents, Views, Frames, and Templates

The Graphics program developed in Chapter 8 separated the storage of information from its display. The `store` class managed the internal representation of a drawing and presented a program interface to the `display` class. The `display` class managed the on-screen representation of the drawing. Besides encouraging modular design, separating storage from display makes it easy to implement multiple views of the same data.

I have to confess that I didn't invent this design. Like many concepts in GUI programming, it originated at Xerox PARC during the development of Smalltalk.[4] In Smalltalk's Model-View-Controller (MVC) paradigm, programs divvy up functionality among three (or more) objects as follows:

Model	The store—provides a program interface to query and modify the data in the store.
View	The display—represents the data in a window. Views are usually nested.
Controller	Responds to user input—handles the keyboard and the mouse. Tied to a view.

MFC embraces a model similar to MVC. The storage class becomes a *document* and the display class a *view*. Physically, views live inside of *frames,* and the whole package (document, view, and frame) is tied together by an object called a *document template*. Thus, each document window has four associated objects: a document, a view, a frame, and a document template (see Figure 9.3).[5]

The document is instantiated from a `CDocument`-derived class. A document is not a window; `CDocument` is *not* derived from `CWnd`. Its role is to manage the underlying data. For example, a file-based document reads and writes the file. It also presents access functions for manipulating the data. A document object may be shared by several views.

The view is instantiated from a `CView`-derived class. A view is a window; `CView` is derived from `CWnd`. The view contains a representation of the information in

---

[4] The classic reference for Smalltalk is *Smalltalk-80, The Language,* by Adele Goldberg and David Robson, Addison-Wesley Publishing Co., 1989.

[5] Although both MFC and MVC use the term *view,* the MVC concept of view is much simpler than MFC's. An MVC view corresponds more closely to a `CWnd`. For example, both an edit field inside a form and the frame surrounding the form are views to MVC.

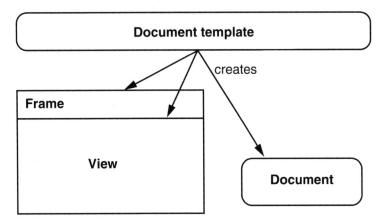

Figure 9.3   When a document window is created, the document template creates a
frame, a view, and a document.

the document. The view uses the document's access functions to manipulate the
information. Views cannot be shared by document windows. There is at least
one view per document window.

The frame is instantiated from `CMDIFrameWnd` for MDI and `CFrameWnd` for SDI.[6]
The frame is a container of views, thus it too is a window. The views typically
cover the client area of the frame. Frames cannot be shared; there is exactly one
per document window.

The document template is instantiated from `CMultiDocTemplate` for MDI and
`CSingleDocTemplate` for SDI. A template is the road map used by the framework. The template has pointers to the document, view, and frame classes. The
framework instantiates those classes pointed to by the template to create a new
document window. In MDI, there is one template object for each type of document window that can be created.

9.3.1 Shared Resource IDs

Consider an MDI application that can handle two types of documents, one graphical and one textual. It could be useful for each type of document window to
have its own menu commands and accelerator keys that reflect the operations
appropriate for the document type. For example, on text documents there might
be operations to control character and paragraph formatting; for graphics documents there might be control over the drawing implement. Also, text documents

---

[6] The frame class can also be a class derived from `CMdiFrameWnd` or `CFrameWnd`, although deriving a
class for the frame is much less common than for documents and views.

would likely be stored in files with a different format from graphics documents, hence the text files should have a different extension than graphics files. The application framework supports switching of menus, accelerators, file extensions, as well as a host of other aspects of a document. Switching is accomplished using the technique of a shared resource ID to connect resources to a document type.

In addition to associating a document, view, and frame, a document template contains a resource ID. The ID specifies

- The *icon* to display in the title bar of a document window
- The *menu* to use when a document window is active
- The *accelerator table* to use when a document is active
- The *document string,* which consists of several substrings that specify the default window title for a document window, the default name for a document file, the file type used in File New list, the file type used in File Open filter list, the default file extension, and a registry file-type ID and name

Previously, our programs used a unique ID for each resource created. Now they will use the same ID for all the resources related to a particular type of document. When the framework needs a resource for the document, it will search for a resource of the appropriate type with the ID specified in the document template.

9.3.1.1 The Document String

The document string specifies a collection of text strings to be associated with a document type. The string consists of several newline-separated fields. Here is a sample along with a description of each field:

```
"App\nDocName\nDocType\nFileType\n.ext\nRegType\nRegName"
```

where

App
  is, for SDI applications, the program name that appears on the title bar. For MDI, the program name is specified in a string resource having the ID associated with the main frame.

DocName
  is used by the framework as the base name for new document windows. A window's name is generated by taking the base name and appending an integer.

DocType   is a descriptive name for the document type. In MDI applications, if there is more than one document type, the File New command places the text in this field in a list box, allowing the user to select the kind of document being created.

FileType   is a descriptive name for the file type. The File Open and Save dialog boxes have a list box of file types that are used to filter the file list. The text in this field is added to the file-types list.

.ext   is the file extension. Each document type can have its own extension. The extension is used as a filter in the File dialog and as the default extension for File Save.

RegType   is the unique systemwide identifier for the file type. For an application to be invoked when the user double clicks on an appropriate file, the application must register its file type.

RegName   is the user-readable name that will be associated, systemwide, with the file type specified in RegType. In a report view, the Windows Explorer shows this name in the file-type field.

9.3.2 The Command Line

Historically, Windows has not used a program's command line for very much. In Windows 3.1, the File Manager was able to invoke an application with a file name if the user double clicked on a file and the Print Manager was able to invoke an application with a print flag and a file name. But that was about it.

As the Windows Shell has become more capable and OLE[7] has evolved, command-line arguments have been added to direct the execution of a program. Although a program can have a unique set of command-line arguments, the following are supported directly by MFC:[8]

/dde   The program is being invoked by a DDE client. The default behavior is to hide the main window.

---

[7] When first introduced, OLE was an acronym for Object Linking and Embedding. As component technology has evolved under Windows, OLE has come to encompass far richer functionality than when it was originally conceived. The name persists but it is no longer thought of as an acronym.

[8] Command-line options are shown with a leading forward slash (/). They can also be introduced with a hyphen (-).

/p	The program is being invoked for printing. The first file-name parameter is the file to print. The default behavior is for the main window to be hidden and the File Print command executed on the named file.
/pt printer	Like /p except that a destination printer name is specified.
/Automation	The program is being invoked as an OLE automation server.
/Embedding	The program is being invoked as an embedded OLE control.
filename	A token that doesn't begin with – or / is taken to be a file name.

You may recall that rather than the argc/argv parameters of a standard C++ environment, the WinMain function receives the command line as a string. It is up to the program itself to break the string into tokens. The CWinApp class has functions for parsing and implementing the standard parameters (see Section 9.3.3.1).

9.3.3 The New Generic

Every MFC program that uses the Document/View model must have certain classes defined. Program generators, such as AppWizard, generate simple versions of these classes. What follows is an AppWizard-generated MDI application stripped down to the bare essentials. It will become our generic program for MDI applications.[9]

The following classes are created:

mdi	Application class
mainFrame	Main window
doc	Underlying data structure for a document
view	Screen representation of a document

Figure 9.4 shows how the classes are related. Let's examine each class in detail.

---

[9] The program described is in the directory Generic\Mdi. A similar program, for SDI applications, is in Generic\Sdi.

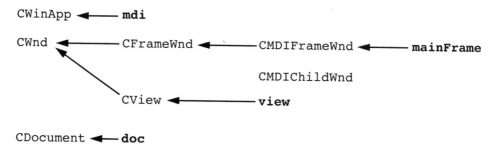

Figure 9.4 These graphs show the derivation tree for the classes created by AppWizard. Class names defined in the application are shown in bold. The arrows represent the relationship "derived from".

9.3.3.1 The Application Class: mdi

The application class, mdi, hasn't changed much from application classes you've seen before:

```
class mdi : public CWinApp
{
public:
    mdi();

// Overrides
    // ClassWizard generated virtual function overrides
    //{{AFX_VIRTUAL(mdi)
    public:
    virtual BOOL InitInstance();
    //}}AFX_VIRTUAL

// Implementation
    //{{AFX_MSG(mdi)
    afx_msg void OnAppAbout();
        // NOTE - the ClassWizard will add and remove member functions here.
        //      DO NOT EDIT what you see in these blocks of generated code !
    //}}AFX_MSG
    DECLARE_MESSAGE_MAP()
};
```

One surprise is that the application class has a message map to connect messages to member functions. Messages are sent to windows. An application object is not a window, so how can it receive messages? Actually, it only receives a few messages; see Chapter 10 for an explanation. mdi has one handler for the Help About command.

The other changes are in `initInstance`. It creates a document template and processes the command line:

```
BOOL mdi::InitInstance()
{
    LoadStdProfileSettings(); // Load standard INI file options

    // Register the application's document templates.  Document
    // templates serve as the connection between documents, frame
    // windows and views.


    CMultiDocTemplate* pDocTemplate;
    pDocTemplate = new CMultiDocTemplate(
        IDR_MDITYPE,                   // Shared resource ID
        RUNTIME_CLASS(doc),            // Document class
        RUNTIME_CLASS(CMDIChildWnd),   // Frame class
        RUNTIME_CLASS(view));          // View class
    AddDocTemplate(pDocTemplate);
```

The Generic application has a single document type and hence a single document template. `AddDocTemplate` appends the template to a list kept in the application class. The parameters to the `CMultiDocTemplate` constructor refer to runtime classes, which are used quite a bit by the framework. They are described in Section 9.4.

Next, the main window class is instantiated and the main window created. Rather than create the window in the constructor as we did in earlier programs, the framework uses a separate creation function, `LoadFrame`. `LoadFrame` will return failure if the window can't be created:

```
    // create main MDI Frame window
    mainFrame* pMainFrame = new mainFrame;
    if (!pMainFrame->LoadFrame(IDR_MAINFRAME))
        return FALSE;
    m_pMainWnd = pMainFrame;
```

If a program uses the standard command-line options, it can take advantage of parsing and processing functions in `CWinApp`:

```
    // Parse command line for standard shell commands, DDE, file open
    CCommandLineInfo cmdInfo;
    ParseCommandLine(cmdInfo);

    // Dispatch commands specified on the command line
    if (!ProcessShellCommand(cmdInfo))
        return FALSE;
```

The CCommandLineInfo data structure holds the result of parsing the command line. ParseCommandLine understands the standard options described in Section 9.3.2. If a program uses different command-line syntax, it can fill in the data structure itself. ProcessShellCommand reads the data structure and implements the default behavior for any specified commands. For example, if the print option is specified, it opens the file and executes a Print command. If no command-line options are specified, ProcessShellCommand executes File New.

Finally, if ProcessShellCommand returns true, the main window is displayed:

```
    // The main window has been initialized, so show and update it.
    pMainFrame->ShowWindow(m_nCmdShow);
    pMainFrame->UpdateWindow();

    return TRUE;
}
```

The order of processing the command line and showing the main window is somewhat problematical. ProcessShellCommand is run first so that it can control whether the main window will be shown. It returns false if it cannot run the command specified on the command line or if the specified command should be run silently, such as for File Print. The difficulty arises if no command is specified. In this case ProcessShellCommand executes File New. In an MDI application, File New pops up a dialog that allows the file type to be selected. Unfortunately, since the main window isn't shown yet, the dialog floats on the desktop.[10]

9.3.3.2 The Main Frame Class: mainFrame

The mainFrame class is a little simpler than it was previously as it no longer creates the main window in its constructor nor handles all the commands. In fact, the generic main frame doesn't do much of anything:

```
class mainFrame : public CMDIFrameWnd
{
    DECLARE_DYNAMIC(mainFrame)
public:
    mainFrame();

// Attributes
public:
```

---

[10] To overcome this problem, our MDI programs will reverse the order of showing the window and processing the command line.

```
    // Operations
    public:

    // Overrides
        // ClassWizard generated virtual function overrides
        //{{AFX_VIRTUAL(mainFrame)
        //}}AFX_VIRTUAL

    // Implementation
    public:
        virtual ~mainFrame();
    #ifdef _DEBUG
        virtual void AssertValid() const;
        virtual void Dump(CDumpContext& dc) const;
    #endif

    // Generated message map functions
    protected:
        //{{AFX_MSG(mainFrame)
            // NOTE - the ClassWizard will add and remove member functions here.
            //    DO NOT EDIT what you see in these blocks of generated code!
        //}}AFX_MSG
        DECLARE_MESSAGE_MAP()
    };
```

We haven't seen the virtual functions `AssertValid` and `Dump` before. Although their default implementations don't do anything, they can be used to assist program development. They can be added to any `CObject`-derived class.

`AssertValid` should perform a validity test on the object to guarantee that it is internally self-consistent. Usually this is done by calling the ASSERT macro:

```
    ASSERT(Boolean expression)
```

If the expression fails when the program is run in the debugger, it will halt the program at the point of failure. `AssertValid` is called at various times by the framework, and you can also call it to test the validity of objects.

`Dump` outputs the contents of an object, usually to the debugger. Where the output goes is controlled by the `CDumpContext` parameter. A dump context can have an associated file; otherwise, output is written using the API function `OutputDebugString`. One global dump context, `afxDump`, is created for debug versions of programs. Use it to dump an object to the debugger, for example

```
    afxDump << this;
```

9.3.3.3 The Document Class: doc

The document class is responsible for managing an application's data and providing an interface to the data. Since the Generic application has no data, there isn't much for the doc class to do. Still, the class must be created. CDocument is an abstract class; the function Serialize is pure virtual, so it must be overridden in a derived class. (Serialize will be discussed in Chapter 10.) The other do-nothing function in the doc class is OnNewDocument. As you no doubt can guess, it will be called to initialize a document.

```
class doc: public CDocument {
protected:  // create from serialization only
    doc();
    DECLARE_DYNCREATE(doc)
. . .
// Overrides
    // ClassWizard generated virtual function overrides
    //{{AFX_VIRTUAL(doc)
    public:
    virtual BOOL OnNewDocument();
    virtual void Serialize(CArchive& ar);  // overridden for document i/o
    //}}AFX_VIRTUAL

// Implementation
public:
    virtual ~doc();

. . .
    DECLARE_MESSAGE_MAP()
};
```

9.3.3.4 The View Class: view

The framework calls on the view class to render in a window the data from the document. The view function OnDraw is called to paint a window, show a print preview, and print. The framework sets up a device context so that, in the simple case, the same code works for all three tasks. In practice, most programs will have to adjust their output depending on where it is going. See Chapter 13 for examples.

The view uses the function GetDocument to get a pointer to its associated document. Using the pointer, it calls on the access functions provided by the document.

A view might want control over its background color, mouse cursor, or window-class style. These are attributes of the Win32 class. In Chapter 5, we called AfxRegisterClass in the call to CWnd::Create to modify these attributes. A program that uses Document/View doesn't call Create itself; the framework does it instead. To get control over a window's Win32 class, override the function Pre-CreateWindow and modify the CREATESTRUCT.

```
class view: public CView
{
protected: // create from serialization only
    view();
    DECLARE_DYNCREATE(view)

// Attributes
public:
    CMdiDoc* GetDocument();
. . .

// Overrides
    // ClassWizard generated virtual function overrides
    //{{AFX_VIRTUAL(view)
    public:
    virtual void OnDraw(CDC* pDC);  // overridden to draw this view
    virtual BOOL PreCreateWindow(CREATESTRUCT& cs);
    protected:
    //}}AFX_VIRTUAL

. . .
    DECLARE_MESSAGE_MAP()
};
```

9.4 Runtime Classes

The runtime class facility of MFC overcomes a significant shortcoming of C++ for programming application frameworks. The implementation of File New illustrates the problem. To implement File New, the framework must create new document, view, and frame objects, along with new view and frame windows. The code must do something like

```
CDocument *pDoc = new docClass;
CMDIFrameWnd *pFrame = new FrameClass;
CView *pView = new viewClass;

if( pFrame->LoadFrame() )
    pView->Create();
```

But what class names should be used in place of the italicized placeholders? For the Generic program, the docClass is doc, but it could just as well have been document or CMyDocument. There is no way for the framework, which has already been compiled, to know what class names I will use in my program.

Virtual functions address exactly this problem, but to call a virtual function the framework needs to have an object of the real type. In the call to new, no object exists yet. There is no virtual new.

9.4.1 The Three Levels of Runtime Class Support

MFC's runtime class support consists of class data and virtual functions. What data and functions are defined depends on the required functionality. There are three levels of functionality:[11]

Dynamic	Implements IsKindOf
DynCreate	Implements virtual new
Serial	Implements virtual I/O

The simplest level answers the question, "Is object x instantiated from class y?" If you look through the MFC source code, you'll see that the framework frequently checks whether objects are really the type they claim to be. The CObject function IsKindOf performs the test. For example, OnFileNew asserts that a pointer to a document template really is a CDocTemplate:

```
ASSERT(pTemplate->IsKindOf(RUNTIME_CLASS(CDocTemplate)))
```

For this expression, IsKindOf returns true if pTemplate was instantiated from CDocTemplate or a class derived from CDocTemplate. To answer the question, MFC recreates the class structure in memory with the help of the class CRuntimeClass and (what else?) macros (see Figure 9.5). A CRuntimeClass object contains the data needed to implement the three levels of runtime-class support:[12]

```
class CRuntimeClass
{
    LPCSTR m_lpszClassName;
    int m_nObjectSize;
    UINT m_wSchema;
    CObject* (PASCAL* m_pfnCreateObject)(); // Pointer to "new"
    CRuntimeClass* m_pBaseClass;
```

---

[11] Support for runtime classes in MFC predates the addition of Run Time Type Information (RTTI) to C++ and templates to the Microsoft C++ compiler.

[12] Here and elsewhere in this discussion, I've simplified the implementation to highlight the architecture. Look in the MFC header file afx.h for all the details.

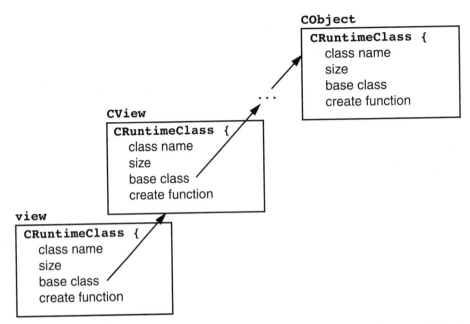

Figure 9.5   Each class can have runtime class data. The data structures are linked together to mimic the C++ class hierarchy.

The runtime class data contains the class name, size, and pointers to a "new" function and the CRuntimeClass structure for the base class. (m_wSchema is used during serialization. It is described in Chapter 10.)

To add Dynamic runtime support for a class, add the macro DECLARE_DYNAMIC(class_name) to the class declaration. The macro declares class data and a virtual function:[13]

```
static const CRuntimeClass class##class_name;
virtual CRuntimeClass* GetRuntimeClass() const;
```

In the implementation file, put the macro IMPLEMENT_DYNAMIC(class_name, base_name) at the external level. It defines the class data and implements the virtual function:

```
CRuntimeClass class_name::class##class_name = {
    #class_name, sizeof(class class_name), wSchema, pfnNew,
        RUNTIME_CLASS(base_name), NULL };
CRuntimeClass* class_name::GetRuntimeClass() const {
    return RUNTIME_CLASS(class_name);
}
```

---

[13] The somewhat obscure preprocessor operator ## pastes a syntactic token to a macro parameter. Thus, if the value of class_name is CView, then class##class_name evaluates to classCView.

RUNTIME_CLASS(class_name) evaluates to a pointer to the CRuntimeClass data structure for the class:

```
&class_name::class##class_name
```

To make all this more concrete, I'll add IMPLEMENT_DYNAMIC to the view class:

```
IMPLEMENT_DYNCREATE(view, CView)
```

which generates the following definitions:

```
CRuntimeClass view::classview = {
    "view", sizeof(class view), wSchema, NULL,
    RUNTIME_CLASS(CView), NULL };
CRuntimeClass* view::GetRuntimeClass() const {
    return RUNTIME_CLASS(view);
}
```

Like message maps, the CRuntimeClass structures are linked together following the class hierarchy. IsKindOf follows the chain to compute its result:

```
BOOL CObject::IsKindOf(const CRuntimeClass* pClass) const
{
    CRuntimeClass* pClassThis = GetRuntimeClass();
    while( pClassThis != NULL ) {
        if( pClassThis == pClass )
            return TRUE;
        pClassThis = pClassThis->m_pBaseClass;
    }
}
```

Notice that IsKindOf calls the virtual function GetRuntimeClass to get the first CRuntimeClass structure. As a result, since CObject has runtime class data, IsKindOf can be called on any object instantiated from a CObject-derived class.

9.4.2 DynCreate

The second level of runtime class support implements the "new" function. The macro DECLARE_DYNCREATE is just like DECLARE_DYNAMIC with the addition of a declaration for the static function CreateObject:

```
static CObject* PASCAL CreateObject();
```

IMPLEMENT_DYNCREATE defines CreateObject as a wrapper for "new":

```
CObject* PASCAL class_name::CreateObject() {
    return new class_name;
}
```

The pointer to the "new" function in the CRuntimeClass structure virtualizes CreateObject. Recall from Section 9.3.3.1 that the document template points to the runtime class structure for the document, frame, and view. Given a pointer to a document template, OnFileNew can begin

```
CDocument *pDoc = pDocTemplate->m_pDocClass->CreateObject();
CMDIFrameWnd *pFrame = pDocTemplate->m_pFrameClass->CreateObject();
CView *pView = pDocTemplate->m_pViewClass->CreateObject();
```

The third level of runtime class support, Serial, is covered in the next chapter.

CHAPTER

10 | Documents and Views

The sample program for this chapter is in the directory `Mdi\V1`. The corresponding executable in the `bin` directory is `MdiV1.exe`.

10.1 Introduction

In this chapter we'll look in more depth at documents and views by examining the primary tasks carried out by document and view objects. The sample program is an MDI application with both a textual and a graphical document type.

10.2 Documents

The primary functions of a document are to

- Provide a programmatic interface for accessing the document data
- Save and restore the data

The view uses the document's interface to show and change the document's data. The framework calls on the document to save and restore the data. The flow of data between the view, the document, and permanent storage is illustrated in Figure 10.1.

Although the operations that make up the interface to a document vary considerably according to the application, some characteristics are always present. Many documents contain lists of items. For such documents, the view needs an operation to iterate over the items. For example, to paint a window, a graphics

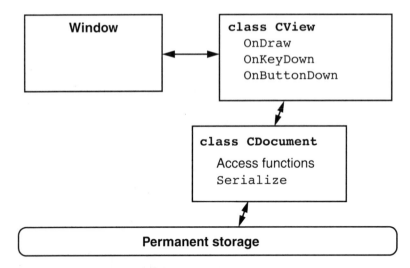

Figure 10.1   The document mediates between permanent storage and the view. The view renders information from the document in a window. The arrows indicate flow of data.

view might iterate over a list of drawing objects and a text view might iterate over lines of text. Record-oriented documents, such as the Address Book program of Chapter 12, need a way to search for a record among the list of records.

Documents that can be modified need insert, delete, and update operations. They also need a way to save and restore their data, a task known as *serialization*. Usually, serialization is accomplished by writing and reading a file, but it could be carried out just as well by accessing a database or querying a device. Serialization is a complex topic. It is covered in detail in the next section.

10.2.1 The CDocument Class

Every document class is derived from the abstract class CDocument. CDocument contains operations and data used by the framework. The operations tell

- Whether the document has been changed and needs to be written
- How to find the associated views
- How to find the associated template
- The path to the associated file
- How to serialize the document's data

Most of these operations are simple. Each document maintains a flag to indicate whether the data in the document has been modified. A document controls the state of the flag using the SetModifiedFlag function. If the flag is true when the user asks to close a document window, the framework will post a message box asking for confirmation. Documents also maintain a list of views, since there can be more than one view pointing to a document. (Section 10.2.3.6.1 shows an example of finding a view from the list.)

From the framework's viewpoint, the most complex task carried out by a document is serialization. The default File Open command is implemented in CWinApp::OnFileOpen. After running the File Open common dialog, if a file is selected, CWinApp::OnFileOpen calls OpenDocumentFile, which eventually calls the document's Serialize function to read the data from the file. Here is the algorithm:

```
virtual CWinApp::OpenDocumentFile
    Choose a Doc Template based on file the extension
    If file is already in a window of same type
        virtual CFrameWnd::ActivateFrame
    else
        virtual CMultiDocTemplate::OpenDocumentFile
            Create CDocument object
            Create Frame object
            CWnd::LoadFrame
                Create Frame window
                    Create Client (view) window
            virtual CDocument::OnOpenDocument
                CFile::Open
                Create CArchive object
                virtual CObject::Serialize
```

If the file has already been opened using the chosen template, the framework activates the corresponding window. Otherwise, the framework creates the associated objects and windows, opens the selected file, and calls Serialize.

By the time Serialize is called, all of the parts of the document window have been created: the view object and window, the frame object and window, and the document object. For file-based documents, the file to read from has been opened with the appropriate access and a CArchive object has been created. The archive plays a key role in serialization.

10.2.2 The CArchive Class

The CArchive class is modeled on the iostream class from the standard C++ library. The class defines binary insertion (<<) and extraction (>>) operators to write and read a document's data. Here are the prototypes:

```
CArchive & operator<<(CArchive &, Type &);
CArchive & operator>>(CArchive &, Type &);
```

Notice that, like an iostream, the return value of the operators is a reference to the left-hand operand. As a result, insertion and extraction can be concatenated:

```
CArchive ar;
Type t1, t2;

ar << t1 << t2;
```

The implementation of insertion and extraction are sometimes friends of *Type,* because the operators may need access to private members to read and write instances of *Type.* Friends are declared within the class declaration:

```
class Type {
. . .
friend CArchive &operator<<(CArchive *, Type &);
```

Even though the operator is declared within the class, it is *not* a member function. It has no this pointer and so access to the *Type* object is through a parameter.

CArchive has operators for inserting and extracting the "portable" basic types. The portable types are those that do not change size across current systems. Here is the list:

BYTE	An unsigned 8-bit value
WORD	An unsigned 16-bit value
LONG	A signed 32-bit value
DWORD	An unsigned 32-bit value
float	A single-precision floating-point value
double	A double-precision floating-point value
CString	An array of characters

In addition, CArchive has operators for some system-specific types, like int and unsigned, but you should use these with caution as their sizes differ under different implementations of Windows. There are also operators for some of the basic Win32 data structures:

SIZE	Two ints
POINT	Two LONGs
RECT	Four LONGs

Note that the SIZE structure is built from ints, so it is not portable. Finally, insertion and extraction have been defined for some general classes, such as CString, CTime, and CTimeSpan.

CArchive also has two member functions for reading and writing objects of any class derived from the CObject. The functions ReadObject and WriteObject take care of reading and writing the C++ bookkeeping information needed to describe an object.

10.2.3 Serialization

The complexity of serialization derives from the divided responsibility for its implementation. Part of the task is carried out by MFC and part by the application; control flows back and forth between the application and the library. The role of the application depends on the format of the persistent data and the kind of objects being serialized.

MFC provides the most support for documents in which the file format is unconstrained. In this case, serialization reads and writes whole *objects*. If the file has a specified format—for example, pure text—the application must do more work. During serialization the program reads and writes the *data* contained inside of objects.

Before looking at these two forms of serialization in detail, let's revisit MFC's runtime class support.

10.2.3.1 Runtime Class Information

Recall from Chapter 9 that MFC provides three levels of runtime-class support:

Dynamic	Implements support for IsKindOf
DynCreate	Implements virtual new
Serial	Implements virtual I/O

Serializing data requires the DynCreate support; serializing objects requires Serial. To use a runtime class:

1. Put a runtime-class DECLARE_ macro in the class declaration.
2. Put a runtime-class IMPLEMENT_ macro in the class implementation file.

Making a class DynCreate adds an implementation of CreateObject to the class. CreateObject is called by the framework to instantiate the class; it implements the virtual "new" operator, as described in Chapter 9. CreateObject will be called from the library on classes you create—classes the library couldn't possibly have known about when it was compiled.

10.2.3.2 Serializing Objects

When a program serializes objects, it reads and writes whole C++ objects. The stored data is self-descriptive, allowing the objects to be recreated when retrieved. CArchive and CObject provide much of the underlying support for serialized objects.

To reconstruct an object when it is read, CArchive must write out C++ book-keeping information about the object. CArchive's WriteObject function outputs this information for an object, followed by the object's data. The application does not control the format of the bookkeeping information—the format is controlled by the library—but it can control the format and content of the object's data.

If an object's data consists only of the portable types, it can be read and written using the built-in extraction and insertion operators. If an object is more complex, the program may have to define more forms of << and >>. Consider a document that contains data consisting of a CString, a data structure, and a pointer to a data structure:

```
class document : public CDocument {
. . .
    CString string;
    Data data;
    Data *pData;
```

The Serialize function for the document might look like this:

```
void document::Serialize(CArchive &ar)
{
    CDocument::Serialize(ar);

    if( ar.IsStoring() ) {
        ar << string;
        ar << data;
        ar << pData;
    } else {
        ar >> string;
        ar >> data;
        ar >> pData;
    }
}
```

The CArchive object maintains a flag that specifies whether data is being read or written. IsStoring returns true for writing. The insertion and extraction operators for string come from the library because string is a CString. But what about data and pData? Since the class Data is defined by the program, the operators must be defined by the program. Suppose Data contains two floats:

```
class Data : public CObject {
    float f1, f2;
};
```

Extraction for the instance of Data could be defined simply as

```
CArchive operator>>( CArchive &ar, Data &data )
{
    ar >> data.f1;
    ar >> data.f2;
    return ar;
}
```

As an alternative to creating specialized insertion and extraction operators, many programs override Serialize for embedded objects. For example, Serialize could be defined for Data:

```
void Data::Serialize(CArchive &ar)
{
    CObject::Serialize(ar);

    if( ar.IsStoring() ) {
        ar << f1;
        ar << f2;
    } else {
        ar >> f1;
        ar >> f2;
    }
}
```

and document::Serialize changed to

```
void document::Serialize(CArchive &ar)
{
    CDocument::Serialize(ar);
    data.Serialize(ar);

    if( ar.IsStoring() ) {
        ar << string;
        ar << pData;
    } else {
        ar >> string;
        ar >> pData;
    }
}
```

The use of a single function both to read and write may strike you as odd, but it has the virtue of keeping the two operations close together. The order in which the components are read must match *exactly* the order in which they are written.

The extraction of pData, the pointer to Data, must first allocate an instance of a Data so that the pointer can point to it. It could be written like this:

```
CArchive operator>>( CArchive &ar, Data * &pData)
{
    pData = new Data;
    pData->Serialize(ar);
    return ar;
}
```

The basic rule for using serialization can be summarized as follows:

- To serialize an embedded object: If the object is of a basic type, use the insertion or extraction operator for the object. Otherwise call the Serialize function for the class.
- To serialize a pointed-to object: Use the insertion or extraction operator for the object.

10.2.3.3 DECLARE_SERIAL and IMPLEMENT_SERIAL

Although you could write insertion and extraction operators for each type of pointed-to object in your documents, it is not necessary to do so. The runtime-class macros can do it for you if the classes to be serialized are derived from CObject. The DECLARE_SERIAL macro declares, and IMPLEMENT_SERIAL implements, an extraction operator for the class. CArchive has a generic insertion operator for a CObject * that can be inherited. Using runtime class support, the declaration of class Data looks like this:

```
class Data: public CObject{
    void Serialize(Carchive &ar);
    DECLARE_SERIAL(Data);
    float f1, f2;
};
```

DECLARE_SERIAL declares and IMPLEMENT_SERIAL defines the following function:

```
CArchive& operator>>(CArchive& ar, Data * &pOb) \
{
    pOb = (Data *) ar.ReadObject(RUNTIME_CLASS(Data));
    return ar;
}
```

ReadObject reads the bookkeeping information for the object, allocates an instance of Data, and then calls Serialize on the object to read the data from the archive. The rather convoluted flow of control is shown in Figure 10.2.

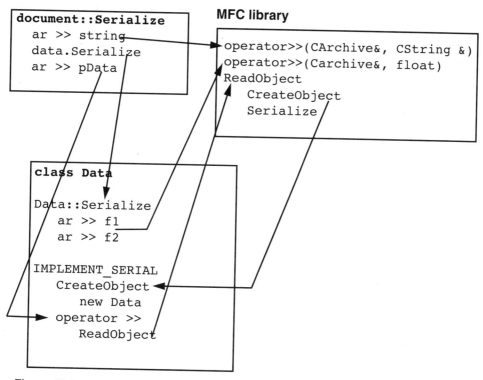

Figure 10.2   The arrows indicate the flow of control during extraction. Execution begins in document::Serialize. Extraction of string is handled by the library. Extraction of data is handled first by the program and then by the library. Extraction of pData bounces back and forth between the library and the program.

10.2.3.4 Serializing Collections

Usually, a document doesn't consist of a single object, but rather a collection of objects. MFC's collection classes implement serialization for arrays of embedded and pointed-to objects.

In an embedded collection, the objects are stored inside the collection, as shown in Figure 10.3 for an embedded array. If, in addition, the collection is a component of the document (as in grafDoc, Section 10.2.3.4.1), the document's Serialize function is straightforward:

```
document::Serialize
    Call Collection::Serialize
        Read/write any Collection data
        Will call virtual Collection::SerializeElements
```

The collection's Serialize function writes private data maintained by the collection, such as the number of elements in the collection, and then calls the global function SerializeElements. The implementation of SerializeElements for CArray performs a block write of the memory occupied by the elements. For CList, SerializeElements walks the list, serializing each element in turn. If the default behavior is not appropriate, you can override SerializeElements in any collection class, as shown in the next section.

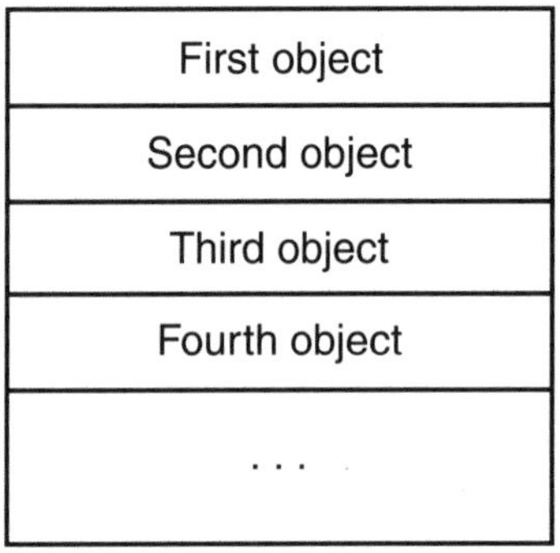

First object
Second object
Third object
Fourth object
. . .

Figure 10.3   In an embedded collection, the objects are stored inside the collection.

As with all objects, if the collection is not part of the document, it must be allocated before being serialized. The collection's IMPLEMENT_SERIAL macro defines an insertion operator that calls ReadObject. As described in Section 10.2.3.3, ReadObject will allocate the collection object and then call the collection's Serialize function. For example, here is a document class that points to a collection:

```
class document : public CDocument {
    . . .
    CArray <Item, Item &> *itemPtr;
```

Accordingly, its Serialize function calls insertion and extraction instead of Serialize:

```
void document::Serialize(Carchive *ar)
{
    if( ar.IsStoring() ) {
        ar << itemPtr;
    } else {
        ar >> itemPtr;
    }
}
```

Instead of holding the actual objects, a collection can contain pointers to dynamically allocated objects as in Figure 10.4. In this case, each object in the collection needs to be allocated on extraction. The easiest way to do this is to override the global function SerializeElements. Here is an example using an array of pointers:

```
SerializeElements(CArchive &ar, Type **pObjs, int cnt)
{
    if( ar.IsStoring() ) {
        for( int i=0; i<cnt; ++i )
            ar << pObjs[i];
    } else {
        for( int i=0; i<cnt; ++i )
            ar >> pObjs[i];
    }
}
```

Type must be derived from CObject and declared Serial so that the extraction operator constructs the elements. Since SerializeElements is global, it is chosen based on the types of its parameters.

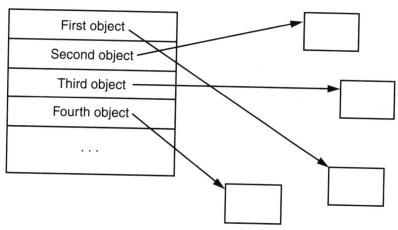

Figure 10.4 A collection can consist of pointers to objects rather than the objects themselves.

10.2.3.4.1 Example: Serializing Graphics

The Mdi program (in the directory Mdi\V1) handles two types of documents, graphical and textual. Graphical documents are based on the Graphics program from Chapter 8. The store class from Graphics forms the basis for the document class grafDoc and the display class the basis for the view class graf-View. Figure 10.5 illustrates the relationship between the document and the view in the Mdi program. These classes are specified to the framework in InitInstance:

```
BOOL mdi::InitInstance()
{
. . .
    CMultiDocTemplate* grafTemplate;
    grafTemplate = new CMultiDocTemplate(
        IDR_GrafType,                    // Shared resource ID
        RUNTIME_CLASS(grafDoc),          // Document class
        RUNTIME_CLASS(CMDIChildWnd),     // Frame class
        RUNTIME_CLASS(grafView));        // View class
    AddDocTemplate(grafTemplate);
```

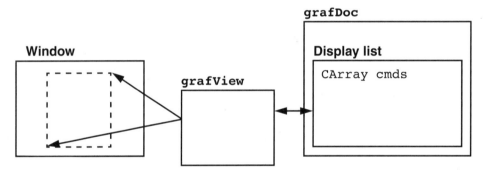

Figure 10.5   The grafDoc class contains the display list that describes a drawing. grafView reads the display list and renders the drawing.

As before, the display list is stored in the document as a CArray of pointed-to drawing commands:

```
class grafDoc : public CDocument
{
. . .
private:
    CArray <command *,command *> m_cmds;
```

Serialize in grafDoc calls on CArray::Serialize, which in turn calls SerializeElements:

```
void grafDoc::Serialize(CArchive& ar)
{
    CDocument::Serialize(ar);
    m_cmds.Serialize(ar);
}
```

SerializeElements walks through the display list and serializes each command:

```
void AFXAPI SerializeElements(CArchive &ar, command **pCmds, int cnt)
{
    if( ar.IsStoring() ) {
        for( int i=0; i<cnt; ++i )
            ar << pCmds[i];
    } else {
        for( int i=0; i<cnt; ++i )
            ar >> pCmds[i];
    }
}
```

The details of each drawing command are encapsulated by the class command. command is declared Serial to generate the extraction operator:

```
class command : public CObject {
public:
    command(
        WORD shape, CRect &rect,
        WORD outlineColor, WORD outlineWidth) {
            cmdShape = shape;
            cmdRect = rect;
            cmdOutlineColor = outlineColor;
            cmdOutlineWidth = outlineWidth;
    };
    command() {};
    void Serialize(CArchive &);
    DECLARE_SERIAL(command)

    WORD cmdShape;
    CRect cmdRect;
    WORD cmdOutlineColor;
    WORD cmdOutlineWidth;
};
```

Ultimately, command's Serialize function is responsible for reading and writing the low-level data:

```
void command::Serialize(CArchive &ar)
{
    CObject::Serialize(ar);
```

```
        if( ar.IsStoring() ) {
            ar << cmdShape;
            ar << cmdRect;
            ar << cmdOutlineColor;
            ar << cmdOutlineWidth;
        } else {
            ar >> cmdShape;
            ar >> cmdRect;
            ar >> cmdOutlineColor;
            ar >> cmdOutlineWidth;
        }
    }
```

10.2.3.5 Schemas

Once you understand the serialization model, you can read and write complex objects with little programming effort. Unfortunately, there is one problem with the serialized data; the sequence of read-objects must match the sequence of writes *exactly*. Making even a tiny change, such as adding a new field, renders the data incompatible.

This is not a minor concern. As a program evolves, its data structures will undoubtedly also evolve. But making a change in the representation of any serialized object makes old files unreadable. To address this problem, serialization uses a version number called a *schema*. A schema in database parlance defines the structure of the data, for example, the layout of tables in a relational database. Analogously, the schema number for an object specifies the layout of the fields in the object.

The schema number is specified in the IMPLEMENT_SERIAL macro for a class and stored as a data member in the CRuntimeClass object associated with the class. When you change the data members of a serializable object, change the schema, usually by incrementing it. On output, CArchive::WriteObject will write the schema number with the rest of the class information. On input, CArchive::ReadObject compares the schema number in the file against the current number for the class. If the two don't agree, it raises the CArchiveException exception.

For backward compatibility, you can use the schema number to read and write old objects formats. Unfortunately, like many things in MFC, the more you dig the more subtleties you find.

10.2.3.5.1 Versionable Schemas

The first thing to observe about schema numbers is that they are class, not file, specific. This allows a program to bury all the details about different versions of a class in the class itself. To implement backward compatibility for a class:

1. Add the VERSIONABLE_SCHEMA flag to the schema number in the IMPLEMENT_SERIAL macro by using the bitwise OR operator.
2. Call CArchive::GetObjectSchema during serialization to retrieve the schema number that was retrieved from a file.

To illustrate backward read capability, I'll modify the representation of graphical documents written by grafDoc. When first implemented, grafDoc did not support filled shapes. When filled shapes were added, I added the VERSIONABLE_SCHEMA flag to the command class used by grafDoc and bumped the schema number:

```
const int SchemaNumber=1;
IMPLEMENT_SERIAL(command, CObject, VERSIONABLE_SCHEMA|SchemaNumber)
```

Then I added the new fields to the class:

```
class command : public CObject {
public:
    command(
        WORD shape, CRect &rect,
        BYTE fill, WORD fillColor,
        WORD outlineColor, WORD outlineWidth) {
            cmdShape = shape;
            cmdRect = rect;
            cmdOutlineColor = outlineColor;
            cmdOutlineWidth = outlineWidth;
            cmdFill = fill;
            cmdFillColor = fillColor;
    };
    . . .
    WORD cmdOutlineColor;
    WORD cmdOutlineWidth;
    BYTE cmdFill;
    WORD cmdFillColor;
```

The Serialize function writes the new fields:

```
void command::Serialize(CArchive &ar)
{
    CObject::Serialize(ar);
```

```
        if( ar.IsStoring() ) {
            ar << cmdShape;
            ar << cmdRect;
            ar << cmdOutlineColor;
            ar << cmdOutlineWidth;
            ar << cmdFill;
            ar << cmdFillColor;
        } else {
```

Old files won't have the last two fields, so on input, Serialize looks at the schema number:

```
        if( schema==(UINT)-1 )
            schema = ar.GetObjectSchema();

        ar >> cmdShape;
        ar >> cmdRect;
        ar >> cmdOutlineColor;
        ar >> cmdOutlineWidth;

        if( schema == SchemaNumber ) {
            ar >> cmdFill;
            ar >> cmdFillColor;
        } else { // Backwards compatibility
            cmdFill = 0;
            cmdFillColor = 0;
        }
    }
}
```

GetObjectSchema returns a valid value only once per serialization of each class, *after* the first object of that class is read. This is because, in the file, the class information precedes the data for the first instance of the class. Somehow, then, a class must know when the first object has been read so that it can call Get-ObjectSchema. For high-level classes, like grafDoc, that is easy since it triggers the serialization. Low-level classes, like command, need a different technique.

I chose to add a static initSchema function to command.[1] It sets the class variable schema to an invalid value:

```
class command : public CObject {
public:
    .  .  .
    static void initSchema() { schema=(UINT)-1; };
    .  .  .
private:
    static UINT schema;
};
```

---

[1] I admit that this is not a wonderful solution. The alternative is to create a less flexible file-based schema.

SerializeElements calls initSchema before the array of commands is serialized:

```
void AFXAPI SerializeElements(CArchive &ar, command **pCmds, int cnt)
{
    if( ar.IsStoring() ) {
        for( int i=0; i<cnt; ++i )
            ar << pCmds[i];
    } else {
        command::initSchema();
        for( int i=0; i<cnt; ++i )
            ar >> pCmds[i];
    }
}
```

When command::Serialize is called (after the class information for the first command is read), it can test schema against -1 as shown above. If schema==-1, it reads the schema number by calling GetObjectSchema. Here is the whole picture beginning with the framework calling on the document to serialize itself:

```
grafDoc::Serialize()
    Call m_cmds.Serialize
        m_cmds is implemented as a CArray, thus
        CArray::Serialize()
            Call SerializeElements(CArchive &,command **)
                SerializeElements()
                    Call command::initSchema
                    command::initSchema()
                        schema = -1
                ar >> pCmds[i]
                    IMPLEMENT_SERIAL creates >> operator
                    operator>>(CArchive&,command*&)
                        Read class info
                        pObj = new command (using virtual "new")
                        pObj->Serialize
                            command::Serialize
                                if( schema==-1 )
                                    schema = GetObjectSchema()
```

10.2.3.6 Serializing Data

Frequently, the file for the document's data must adhere to a specific format, either for compatibility with past versions of a program or for compatibility with other programs. For example, text editors write pure text files so that they can be read by any program that reads text.

The document object can take complete control over the file format in the `Serialize` function. Rather than calling on objects to serialize themselves, the document can read and write objects using the block transfer functions defined in `CArchive`, `Read` and `Write`. In the Mdi program, text documents are stored in raw text files.

10.2.3.6.1 Example: Serializing Text

Text documents in the Mdi program are implemented using a Win32 edit control. Although this is very convenient, it does force an inflexible architecture. Edit controls manage both a window and the underlying data. Because the control is a window, it is wrapped by a view class (see Figure 10.6). As a result, the data is effectively stored in the view rather than in the document, making it difficult to have multiple views of the same data since each edit control would need to have its own copy of the data.

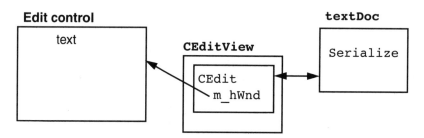

Figure 10.6   The edit control manages its own text. The document must query the view to read and write the text.

To serialize the text, the document class `textDoc` must retrieve the data stored in the edit control. The document accesses the edit control through the view. As there can be more than one view associated with a document, documents maintain a list of the associated views. Figure 10.7 shows what functions to use to find the various objects associated with a document. The `Serialize` function can iterate through its list of views using `GetFirstViewPosition` and `GetNextView`:

```
void textDoc::Serialize(CArchive& ar)
{
    // CEdit's view is intertwined with its storage
    POSITION pos = GetFirstViewPosition();
    CView *view = GetNextView(pos);
```

`GetFirstViewPosition` retrieves a pointer to the list. `GetNextView` retrieves successive items on the list, beginning with the first. Each item is a pointer to an object of class CView, or a class derived from CView. Since textDoc can have only one associated view, the first view retrieved must be the one to query. Continuing in textDoc::Serialize:

```
CString text;
if( ar.IsStoring() ) {
    view->GetWindowText(text);
    ar.WriteString(text);
} else {
    ar.ReadString(text);
    view->SetWindowText(text);
}
}
```

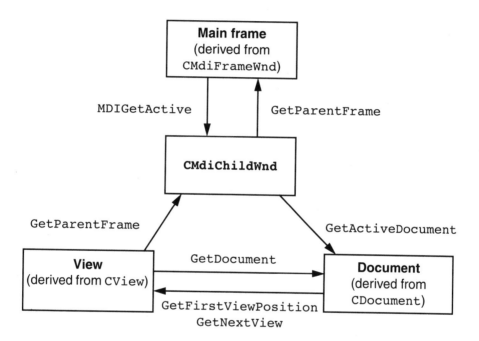

Figure 10.7   Four objects are associated with each document window. This diagram shows how to find the associated objects, given any one of the objects. The labels on the arrows indicate what functions to call to find the object at the end of the arrow.

CArchive has member functions for reading and writing raw text strings. The text in the edit control is transferred by way of a CString. I didn't write

```
view->GetWindowText(text);
ar << text;
```

as this would write out the complete CString object, rather than just the text inside the object.

10.2.3.6.2 *Finding Needles in the MFC Haystack*

Although textDoc::Serialize presented in the last section is not long, there is actually a simpler way to read and write the data from the edit control. It turns out that MFC has a function to do that very task:

```
POSITION pos = GetFirstViewPosition();
CEditView *view = (CEditView *)GetNextView(pos);
ASSERT( view->IsKindOf(RUNTIME_CLASS(CEditView)) );
view->SerializeRaw(ar);
```

GetNextView returns a pointer to a CView, but we know that the view is really a CEditView. (Just in case it's not, I've put in an assertion to verify the class.[2]) There is a member of CEditView called SerializeRaw that serializes the text from an edit control. Perfect! But how could you have found such a function?

It's not too likely that you'd have guessed the function name, but you certainly did know the class name. Finding functions in the reference manual is an important skill for programming with MFC. The manual is organized by class. When browsing for a function, start first by identifying the class of object you're operating on and then look up the operations on that class. Don't forget to browse the operations defined in the base classes, as well.

10.2.4 Communicating with the Views

The data in a document will often be changed by a view. For example, drawing in a graphics window or typing in a text window causes the underlying document to change. Sometimes the document's data will change and the view or views will need to be notified. For example, the File New command clears the document and then notifies the view.

In the case of multiple views, when one view changes the document, the other views need to be updated. This is the case when two windows have been opened on the same file. (Chapter 12 illustrates another case of multiple views: split windows.)

---

[2]Another needle: The DYNAMIC_DOWNCAST macro is a useful alternative to ASSERT. It returns true if the cast is safe based on runtime type information.

As you've seen, the document object contains a list of its associated views. The function CDocument::UpdateAllViews calls CView::OnUpdate for each view. The default implementation of OnUpdate invalidates the view window, forcing a complete redraw. A common optimization is to limit the invalid rectangle to the portion of the view that has changed. UpdateAllViews takes two parameters that can be used to pass optimization hints. Optimized update is illustrated in Chapter 12.

10.3 Views

The primary roles of a view are to

- Present the data in the document on screen
- Print the document
- Provide a GUI that allows the user to manipulate and, perhaps, edit the document

Recall that view windows live inside of frame windows. The frame displays the border, title, and perhaps scrollbars; while the view displays the window contents. This arrangement allows more than one view to appear in a document window, as is the case in a split view. The frame window is the direct parent of each view.

The framework calls the function OnDraw to request that a view draw its representation of the document. The same function is used regardless of where the output is going. That is, OnDraw is called for painting, printing, and previewing. The framework sets up the device context to adjust the output appropriately.[3] In response to OnDraw, the view typically queries the document and outputs to the device context passed in as an argument.

10.3.1 Drawing

In order to render a document, the view must access the document's data. The CView function GetDocument returns a pointer to the corresponding document object. The view uses the access functions provided by the document to guide the drawing.

---

[3] Printing often requires different output than painting. Chapter 13 shows how to specialize drawing during printing and previewing.

10.3.1.1 Example: Drawing Graphics

grafDoc presents a simple interface to the view:

```
class grafDoc : public CDocument
{
protected: // create from serialization only
. . .
    command *getCmd(int i);
    int getCmdCount();
```

getCmd(i) retrieves the *i*th drawing command; getCmdCount returns the number of commands. grafView iterates over the drawing commands calling (as in Chapter 8) on the shape class to carry out the actual drawing:

```
void grafView::OnDraw(CDC* pDC)
{
    grafDoc* pDoc = GetDocument();
    ASSERT_VALID(pDoc);

    int count = pDoc->getCmdCount();

    for( int i=0; i<count; ++i ) {
        command *cp = pDoc->getCmd(i);
        shape *sp = theTool.getShape(cp->cmdShape);
        COLORREF rgbFill = theTool.getColor(cp->cmdFillColor);
        COLORREF rgbOutline = theTool.getColor(cp->cmdOutlineColor);
        sp->draw(pDC,cp->cmdRect,
            cp->cmdFill,rgbFill,
            rgbOutline,cp->cmdOutlineWidth);
    }
}
```

The tool class has functions to map shape numbers into the corresponding shape object and color numbers into the corresponding COLORREF.

10.3.2 Handling User Input

Most views also provide a user interface for editing the document by responding to mouse and keyboard events. The degree of interaction between the view and document depends on the complexity of the operation and the nature of the data.

In the Mdi program, the grafView class uses the same mouse handlers as the display class in the Graphics program. When the mouse button is released, it stores a new drawing command by calling grafDoc::appendCmd:

```
void grafView::OnLButtonUp(UINT nFlags, CPoint point)
{
    if( GetCapture()==this ) {
        grafDoc* pDoc = GetDocument();
        ASSERT_VALID(pDoc);

        m_cursor = point;
        adjustPoint(m_cursor);
        CRect rect(m_anchor.x,m_anchor.y,m_cursor.x,m_cursor.y);
        int width = theTool.getWidth();
        pDoc->appendCmd(
            theTool.getShapeNumber(),
            rect,
            theTool.isFilled(),
            theTool.getFillColorNumber(),
            theTool.getOutlineColorNumber(),
            width);
        ReleaseCapture();
    }
}
```

10.3.3 Handling Commands

Just as C++ implements overloading of functions and operators based on the
type of parameters, Windows users expect certain commands to be overloaded.
For example, if the current window is a text window, Edit Copy should copy the
selected text to the clipboard. If the current window is a graphics window, Edit
Copy should copy graphics. Thus, the Edit Copy command is polymorphic.

In the programs you've seen so far, all of the command handlers have been
members of the main window class, since the main window receives all
WM_COMMAND messages from menu selections. To implement Edit Copy in main-
Frame would require a switch based on the currently active window—for
instance,

```
void mainFrame::onEditCopy()
{
    if( current window is graphics )
        call onEditCopy for graphics
    else if( current window is text )
        call onEditCopy for text
```

Although simple, this organization forces the mainFrame class to be aware of the
types of document windows it contains. Each time a new document type is
added, the handler will need to be changed.

A better organization is to put the handlers for Edit Copy directly in the class that will ultimately implement the command. For example, if both `textView` and `grafView` had handlers for Edit Copy, there would be no need for `mainFrame` to be involved at all. The only problem is how to call the right handler. Fortunately, the document/view framework can help.

10.4   Commands

Recall that every Win32 message has a window as its destination. The standard MFC window procedure searches the message map for the class associated with the target window. If a handler is not found, the window procedure follows the chain of pointers to base-class message maps all the way up to the top of the class hierarchy. The linked message maps implement inheritance that mimics the C++.

10.4.1 Command Routing

When using documents and views, this simple search path is not sufficient for commands. Many commands take the current window or a selection in the window as an operand. The natural place to put the command is in the class responsible for the window or its data. The framework routes WM_COMMAND messages to allow just that.

Routing a message to an object means giving that object an opportunity to catch the message. In MFC, an object catches a message if its message map, or a base-class message map, has an entry for the message. The actual route a message travels is determined by the virtual function OnCmdMsg. Each class in the framework has its own implementation of OnCmdMsg. The implementation may hand the message off to another class by calling OnCmdMsg for that class or search its own message map by calling CCmdTarget::OnCmdMsg.

The menu is owned by the main frame, so the WM_COMMAND message is first routed to CMDIFrameWnd:

```
CMDIFrameWnd
    Call CMDIChildWnd::OnCmdMsg for currently active child
    CMDIChildWnd
        Call CView::OnCmdMsg for currently active view
        CView
            Search View message map
            Call CDocument::OnCmdMsg
            CDocument
                Search Document message map
                Call CDocTemplate::OnCmdMsg
                CDocTemplate
                    Search Template message map
        Search Child Frame message map
        Call CWinApp::OnCmdMsg
        CWinApp
            Search Application message map
    Search Main Frame message map
```

You can see that the message map for each of the objects associated with the currently active document window, plus the message maps for the application and the main frame are searched! This allows you to put the command handler in any of these classes. As a result, you'll find that rather than being the usual place commands are implemented, the main frame is often the last place. For example, Edit Cut and Edit Copy are often implemented in the view, Edit Paste in the document, and File New in the application.

10.4.2 Sharing Menus

In Chapter 9 you saw that each kind of document window can have its own menu bar. If there is a menu resource with the shared ID for the document type, the framework will display the menu when a document of that type has the focus. It is often the case, however, that different document types have identical, or nearly identical, menus. That is the case for the Mdi program.

Creating two nearly identical menus is wasteful and errorprone. Each resource occupies space in the executable file, as well as in memory. Also, since there is no way to share submenus in a resource, each time a command is added to one menu it must be added (in the right place) to other menus, where appropriate.

An alternative is to tell the framework to use the same menu for all of the document types. The Mdi program uses one menu for the main frame and one for the document windows. When there are no document windows open, the main frame's menu is displayed. When a document window is activated, the framework posts the menu specified by the m_hSharedMenu field in the corresponding template. In mdi::InitInstance, the templates for graphics and text share the same value:[4]

```
CMultiDocTemplate* grafTemplate;
grafTemplate = new CMultiDocTemplate(
    IDR_GrafType,                    // Shared resource ID
    RUNTIME_CLASS(grafDoc),          // Document class
    RUNTIME_CLASS(CMDIChildWnd),     // Frame class
    RUNTIME_CLASS(grafView));        // View class
AddDocTemplate(grafTemplate);

CMultiDocTemplate* textTemplate;
textTemplate = new CMultiDocTemplate(
    IDR_TextType,                    // Shared resource ID
    RUNTIME_CLASS(textDoc),          // Document class
    RUNTIME_CLASS(CMDIChildWnd),     // Frame class
    RUNTIME_CLASS(CEditView));       // View class
textTemplate->m_hMenuShared = grafTemplate->m_hMenuShared;
AddDocTemplate(textTemplate);
```

10.4.3 Controlling Menu State

An important property of a well-designed GUI program is that it limits a user's choice of commands to those appropriate for the current state of the program. For menu items, this usually means enabling and graying items. When the user clicks on the menu bar, Win32 sends the WM_INITMENUPOPUP message to the main window before it displays the popup menu. This is an ideal time to change the state of the items on the popup.

It usually makes sense for the code that controls the state of a menu item to be in the same class as the code that implements the command associated with the item. MFC supports this code organization by turning the WM_INITMENUPOPUP message into a call of a *user-interface update handler*. Update handlers have the prototype

```
void Class::UpdateHandler(CCmdUI *ui)
```

Each menu item can have its own handler. Connect a handler to a menu item by adding a message-map entry to the appropriate class:[5]

```
ON_UPDATE_COMMAND_UI(Menu ID, UpdateHandler)
```

---

[4] If you share menus in this way, the debug version of your program will issue a warning that can be safely ignored: Warning: no shared menu for document template. The warning indicates that while creating the document template, the framework did not find a menu resource with the shared ID.

[5] ClassWizard will do this for you when you select UPDATE_COMMAND_UI in the Messages box.

The framework searches message maps for UI update handlers following the same algorithm that it uses to search for commands. That is, it starts looking in the message map for the current view, then the document, the child frame, the document template, the application, and, finally, the main frame.

The handler sets the state of a menu item by operating on the CCmdUI pointer passed in as a parameter. For an example, watch the Edit menu in the Mdi program when a text window is active. If there is text on the Clipboard, the Paste command will be enabled. If you highlight text in the window, the Copy and Cut commands will be active. Control over Cut, Copy, and Paste is inherited from the CEditView class:

```
BEGIN_MESSAGE_MAP(CEditView, CCtrlView)
    //{{AFX_MSG_MAP(CEditView)
    ON_UPDATE_COMMAND_UI(ID_EDIT_CUT, OnUpdateNeedSel)
    ON_UPDATE_COMMAND_UI(ID_EDIT_PASTE, OnUpdateNeedClip)
    ON_UPDATE_COMMAND_UI(ID_EDIT_COPY, OnUpdateNeedSel)
```

The update handler for Paste asks the Clipboard if there is any text stored. CCmdUI::Enable takes a Boolean argument to set the menu-item state:

```
void CEditView::OnUpdateNeedClip(CCmdUI* pCmdUI)
{
    ASSERT_VALID(this);
    pCmdUI->Enable(::IsClipboardFormatAvailable(CF_TEXT));
}
```

The handler for Cut and Copy asks the edit control if anything is selected, then sets the menu item accordingly:

```
void CEditView::OnUpdateNeedSel(CCmdUI* pCmdUI)
{
    ASSERT_VALID(this);
    int nStartChar, nEndChar;
    GetEditCtrl().GetSel(nStartChar, nEndChar);
    pCmdUI->Enable(nStartChar != nEndChar);
}
```

The graphics classes do not support Clipboard operations. When a graphics window is active, the framework will find neither an update handler nor a command handler. Appropriately, the framework will gray the corresponding menu items.

If the update handlers for the Edit menu had been put in the frame class, they would always be found during a search. By putting the commands closer to the data, in CEditView, not only is there less inter-class communication, but inappropriate commands are disabled automatically. What a nice confirmation that the design choice was a good one.

CHAPTER

11 | Toolbars and Status Bars

The sample program for this chapter is in the directory `Mdi\V2`. The corresponding executable in the `bin` directory `MdiV2.exe`.

11.1 Control Bars

As display screens have gotten larger, program designers have used more space for buttons and status information, making their programs easier to use. Win32 has built-in window classes for creating toolbars and status bars. Collectively, MFC refers to these items as control bars.[1]

Control bars are usually placed directly onto the client area of the main frame and are direct children of the frame. Typically, control bars are attached to an edge of the frame, although they can float in a window with a half-size title bar, called a miniframe. Figure 11.1 shows a toolbar and status bar in a common arrangement. Figure 11.2 shows the window tree for an MDI application.

11.1.1 The CControlBar Class

CControlBar is the base class for the three types of control bars: status, button, and dialog. It implements operations to control the position and size of the bars, such as resizing a bar to fit inside a parent frame. It also implements docking, allowing the user to drag a bar from one edge of the frame to another (see Section 11.3.4).

---

[1] Prior to Windows 95, control bars were implemented in MFC, not in Windows.

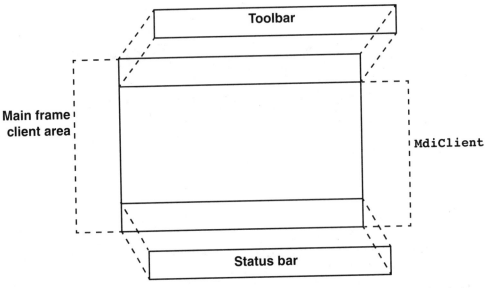

Figure 11.1 The toolbar and status bar are placed in the client area of the main window.

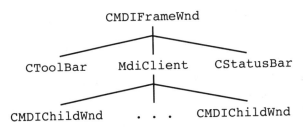

Figure 11.2 The window tree shows parent-child relationships for an MDI application with tool and status bars. Each document window is contained inside a CMDIChildWnd frame.

All control bars have a defining window. Thus, CControlBar is derived from CWnd and control bars are created on two levels, as is any other CWnd. On the other hand, you won't usually use CWnd members to manipulate a control bar. For example, hiding, showing, and moving a control bar all affect the frame and may cause the bar to reconfigure itself. Change visibility with CControl-Bar::ShowControlBar rather than CWnd::ShowWindow. Move a docked control bar with CFrameWnd::DockControlBar instead of CWnd::MoveWindow.

Status and button bars are implemented as Win32 controls, so it is possible to put them in any window and, in particular, in a dialog. MFC has classes that directly wrap the controls, but manipulating them at that level takes considerable programming. Look at the documentation for CStatusBarCtrl and CToolBarCtrl for details. MFC provides the most support for control bars that are children of a CFrameWnd. Much of the support is in three classes derived from CControlBar:

CStatusBar	An array of output-only panes
CToolBar	An array of bitmap buttons
CDialogBar	An array of Win32 controls

Both CToolBar and CDialogBar implement what are generally called toolbars. To avoid confusion, I'll refer to the toolbar generated by CToolBar as *button* bars and the toolbar generated by CDialogBar as *dialog* bars.

11.2 Status Bars

A status bar is divided into display regions called *panes*. A pane can be either fixed or variable size. A status bar may have one variable pane, usually the leftmost pane. As the status bar is resized in response to a change in the size of its parent, the variable pane shrinks and grows. The status bar in Figure 11.3 has a variable pane and seven fixed panes. The panes in a status bar are static in that they don't respond to keyboard or mouse input.

Figure 11.3   A status bar with eight panes

To create a status bar:

1. Create the status-bar object, an instance of CStatusBar.
2. Create the status-bar window using CStatusBar::Create.
3. Create the panes and specify their sizes.

Once the status bar is created, you'll need to write update handlers to keep the panes current.

11.2.1 Creating the Status-Bar Object

Programs usually create the status-bar object once and then hide and show the underlying window, as appropriate. If you use AppWizard to generate a status bar for your application, it will embed the CStatusBar object in the main frame class. Alternatively, you can create the status bar on the heap or as a global object.

The Mdi\V2 program embeds the status bar in mainFrame:

```
class mainFrame : public CMDIFrameWnd
{
. . .
    CStatusBar m_statusBar;
```

11.2.2 Creating the Status-Bar Window

The status-bar window is an instance of the Win32 class msctrls_statusbar32. CStatusBar::Create creates the window and lets you specify its style and location relative to the frame. In addition, the status-bar window, like all child windows, may have a control ID. The CFrameWnd class assumes that the ID will be AFX_IDW_STATUS_BAR, which is the default value for the ID parameter to Create. If you want the framework to hide and show the status bar in response to commands on the View menu, you'll need to use the default ID.

A good time to create the status-bar window is during the creation of the frame window but before the frame has been displayed. Recall that the WM_CREATE message is received during window creation. Accordingly, AppWizard puts the call to Create in OnCreate:

```
int mainFrame::OnCreate(LPCREATESTRUCT lpCreateStruct)
{
. . .
    if( !m_statusBar.Create(this) ) return -1;
```

11.2.3 Creating the Panes

The CStatusBar function SetIndicators tells the status bar how many panes to create and how large they should be. SetIndicators takes an array of IDs as a parameter. For each element in the array, if the ID matches a string resource, then the size of the string determines the size of the pane. The first ID in the array is often zero, indicating the variable-size pane.

The use of a string resource to size the pane may seem odd, but it is actually very convenient. In designing a status bar, you'll need to decide what text will be displayed. View the string resource as a template string; it should be the widest string that will be displayed. By widest, I don't necessarily mean the string with the most characters. Since status-bar panes use a proportional font, the widest string is the one that takes up the most space. W's are very wide compared to I's. Also, the space character tends to be quite thin. Don't reserve space for five letters by entering five spaces!

Often, a pane will contain numbers. The template string for numbers should consist of digits. All digits are the same width, so you don't have to worry which to choose.

The status bar for a graphics window in the Mdi\V2 program is illustrated in Figure 11.3. The three right-most panes are for Caps Lock, Num Lock, and Scroll Lock. The panes will appear in the order of the IDs in the array:

```
static UINT grafIndicators[] = {  // Graf status bar
    0,
    IDS_Modified,
    IDS_Width,
    IDS_Xpos, IDS_Ypos,
    ID_INDICATOR_CAPS, ID_INDICATOR_NUM, ID_INDICATOR_SCRL

m_statusBar.SetIndicators(grafIndicators,sizeof(grafIndicators));
```

The template strings are defined in a string resource:

```
STRINGTABLE DISCARDABLE
BEGIN
    ID_INDICATOR_CAPS      "CAP"
    ID_INDICATOR_NUM       "NUM"
    ID_INDICATOR_SCRL      "SCRL"
    IDS_Xpos               "X:1234"
    IDS_Ypos               "Y:1234"
    IDS_Width              "Width:12"
    IDS_Modified           "Modified"
END
```

11.2.4 Updating the Panes

You might recall from Chapter 5 that painting a window is a low-priority task; Win32 generates WM_PAINT only if there are no other messages pending. That's because painting is relatively slow and a pending message might alter what should be painted. Painting prematurely can reduce a program's responsiveness to user input and may write to the screen more than is necessary.

The same reasoning can be applied to the user interface maintained by the framework. MFC updates status-bar panes, menu-bar help, docking configuration, and toolbar bitmaps only when no messages are pending.

11.2.4.1 Idle-Time Processing

The implementation of the main message loop in `CWinApp::Run` is not as simple as I indicated in Chapter 2. Run calls `CWinThread::Run`, which in turn calls `CWinThread::OnIdle` if there aren't any messages on the message queue. In `OnIdle`, `CWinThread` adjusts various aspects of a program's interface, such as the current menu, the application's title bar, and the layout of the control bars. In addition, it sends the message `WM_IDLEUPDATECMDUI` to every descendent of the main frame. For the status bar window, `CControlBar` picks up the message and calls `CStatusBar::OnUpdateCmdUI`, which in turn calls update handlers for each pane.

Here is the algorithm:

```
CWinApp::Run
    Call CWinThread::Run
        Call CWinThread::OnIdle
            Send WM_IDLEUPDATECMDUI to all children of frame
                Received by CControlBar::OnIdleUpdateCmdUI
                    for status bar
                Call CStatusBar::OnUpdateCmdUI
                    Search for update handler for each pane
```

By the way, `OnIdle` is a virtual function and, somewhat unintuitively, `CWinApp` is derived from `CWinThread`. As a result, you can add idle-time processing to your program by overriding `OnIdle` in the application class. (Just make sure you call `CWinApp::OnIdle`, or you'll wipe out the default processing.) We'll do exactly that in Section 11.2.5.

11.2.4.2 User Interface Update Handlers

The algorithm for updating status bar panes in the previous section ends somewhat vaguely. Just where does `CStatusBar` search?

If you think about status-bar panes, they are in some ways similar to menu commands. For some panes, the data to be displayed depends on the currently active window, like polymorphic commands. For other panes, the data is independent of the current window. Consider the status bar in Figure 11.3. The mouse position depends on data in the graphics window while the lock keys do not. It makes sense for the code that updates the mouse position to be in a graphics class, but the code for the lock keys should be elsewhere.

As described in Chapter 10, the search path for menu update handlers is identical to that for commands. Status-bar update handlers follow the same route. `CStatusBar::OnUpdateCmdUI` calls `OnCmdMsg` for the frame. In this case, `OnCmdMsg` looks for a message-map entry of the form

```
ON_UPDATE_COMMAND_UI(Pane ID, UpdateHandler)
```

The update handler is passed a pointer to the status-bar pane in the form of a `CCmdUI`:

```
void Class::UpdateHandler(CCmdUI *ui) {
```

The handler operates on the pane indirectly through the pointer. `CCmdUI::SetText` writes a text string to the pane. The pane is smart enough not to redraw itself if it already is displaying the correct text.

11.2.4.2.1 Example: Graphics Status Bar

The handlers for the graphics status bar shown in Figure 11.3 are distributed over a few classes. The mouse position is kept in the `grafView` data member `m_cursor`, so `grafView` is the natural place to put update handlers for the X and Y coordinates. One member function is created for each pane:[2]

```
class grafView : public CView
{
. . .
    CPoint m_cursor;
. . .
    afx_msg void onUpdateXpos(CCmdUI *);
    afx_msg void onUpdateYpos(CCmdUI *);
```

The member function is bound to a pane by adding an `ON_UPDATE_COMMAND_UI` entry to the message map for the class:

```
BEGIN_MESSAGE_MAP(grafView, CView)
    ON_UPDATE_COMMAND_UI(IDS_Xpos,onUpdateXpos)
    ON_UPDATE_COMMAND_UI(IDS_Ypos,onUpdateYpos)
```

The implementation creates a string and sets the pane using `SetText`:

---

[2] Adding update handlers for status-bar panes is one task ClassWizard isn't up to. The member-function declarations and the message-map entries must be added by hand.

```
void grafView::onUpdateXpos(CCmdUI *ui) {
    CString buf;
    buf.Format("X:%d",m_cursor.x);
    ui->SetText(buf);
    ui->Enable();
}
```

The call to Enable guarantees that the text is visible. Calling Enable(FALSE) clears the pane.

The handler for the line-width pane is also in grafView. The pane to indicate whether the document has been modified, however, depends on the modified flag in the document object. Therefore, it is implemented in grafDoc:

```
void grafDoc::onUpdateModified(CCmdUI *ui) {
    CString s;

    if( IsModified() ) s.LoadString(IDS_Modified);
    else s.Empty();

    ui->SetText(s);
    ui->Enable();
}
```

The LoadString function retrieves a string from a string resource. grafDoc displays the text **modified** in the pane if the document has been modified since it was last written.

Finally, update handlers for the lock keys are general and needed by many applications. They are implemented in CFrameWnd and are inherited implicitly by mainFrame.

11.2.4.3 Menu-Item Help

The sample program does not have an update handler for the variable-size status-bar pane. That pane is updated automatically by the framework. During idle time, the pane usually displays the string specified in the string resource AFX_IDS_IDLEMESSAGE. When a menu item is highlighted, however, the pane often shows a string that describes the item.

In Chapter 3, we discussed the messages generated by the Win32 menu handler. While a menu item is highlighted, Win32 sends the message WM_MENUSELECT, telling which item is highlighted, and then WM_ENTERIDLE. CFrameWnd::OnEnterIdle posts the help text for the current menu item.

The help text for a menu item is a string resource with the same ID as the item.[3] Program generators like AppWizard define help strings for commonly used menu items. As you extend a menu in an application, it is a good idea to see if there is already a string resource that describes the item. If there is, give the menu item the same ID as the string resource.

11.2.5 Swapping Status Bars

It is ironic that the framework supports separate menus for different types of documents but not separate status bars. Since menu bars for different document types are often identical, or nearly so, sharing is common. Chapter 10 showed how to override the default menu behavior and share menus across document types. By contrast, status bars often have fields that pertain specifically to the current window. This section shows how to manage multiple status bars.

Two strategies can be used to implement multiple status bars:

- Create multiple status bars, then hide and show them.
- Create one status bar and reconfigure it.

The framework works best with a single status bar, so I've chosen to use the second strategy in the sample program.

11.2.5.1 Example: Three Status Bars

The Mdi\V2 program has three status bars:

- A simple, standard status bar if there are no documents open;
- A status bar for text documents that shows the current line and column; and,
- A status bar for graphic documents, discussed earlier in Section 11.2.4.2.1.

As before, the status-bar object is embedded in the main frame. In addition, a data member has been defined to point to the list of desired status-bar pane IDs:

```
class mainFrame : public CMDIFrameWnd
{
. . .
    UINT *m_curIndicators;// Current status bar indicators
```

---

[3] From inside the resource editor of Visual C++, help text is specified in the Prompt field on the property page for a menu item.

As the focus changes among the views, `m_curIndicators` is modified appropriately and the status bar is reconfigured, if necessary (see Figure 11.4). `mainFrame::setIndicators` performs the reconfiguration:

```
void mainFrame::setIndicators(UINT *indicators,int count)
{
    if( indicators== m_curIndicators ) return; // Nothing to do
    m_curIndicators = indicators;

    // Set new indicators
    m_statusBar.SetIndicators(indicators,count);

    // Disable indicators until View class has a chance to
    // update them
    for(int i=count-1; i>=0; --i ) {
        UINT id, style;
        int width;
        m_statusBar.GetPaneInfo(i,id,style,width);
        m_statusBar.SetPaneInfo(i,id, SBPS_DISABLED,width);
    }
    m_statusBar.Invalidate(); // Redraw background
}
```

You've seen `CStatusBar::SetIndicators` before. It establishes one pane per ID, with the pane size determined by a string with the same ID. Once the new panes have been specified, the status bar needs to be redrawn. Since a status bar is a window, calling `CWnd::Invalidate` will trigger repainting. However, the panes are initialized to the text in the template strings; the panes won't have real data until idle time, when the update handlers are called. To avoid flashing the template text, the panes are disabled by calling `SetPaneInfo`. In `CStatusBar::OnPaint`, the status-bar background and the pane outlines will be drawn. When the update handlers are called, the pane contents will be shown.

If there are no documents open, we want to show the default status bar. We'll detect this case during idle time, before the update handlers are called. To add idle time processing, override the virtual function `OnIdle` in the application class:

```
BOOL mdi::OnIdle(LONG lCount)
{
    mainFrame *pMain = (mainFrame *)m_pMainWnd;
    if( pMain->MDIGetActive()==NULL ) // No active document window
        pMain->setIndicators();
    return CWinApp::OnIdle(lCount);
}
```

The parameter to `OnIdle` tells how many times `OnIdle` has been called since the last time there was a message. The return value tells the framework whether it should continue calling OnIdle. Since most aspects of the user interface won't change unless there is a message, there is no need to keep running the idle-time code. If idle-time processing includes polling for external events, such as the arrival of some data over a network, then you might want to continue to poll even though there is no activity in the program.[4]

If there isn't an active document window, mdi::OnIdle specifies the default status bar by calling setIndicators with no arguments:

```
void mainFrame::setIndicators()
{
    static UINT defaultIndicators[] = {  // Default status bar
        0,ID_INDICATOR_CAPS, ID_INDICATOR_NUM, ID_INDICATOR_SCRL
    };
    setIndicators(defaultIndicators,
        sizeof(defaultIndicators)/sizeof(UINT));
}
```

Each view class has its own array of indicators so that when a view is activated, the status bar can be reconfigured appropriately. For example, when a grafView window gets the focus:

```
void grafView::OnSetFocus(CWnd* pOldWnd)
{
    CView::OnSetFocus(pOldWnd);

    static UINT grafIndicators[] = {  // Graf status bar
        0,
        IDS_Modified,
        IDS_Width,
        IDS_Xpos, IDS_Ypos,
        ID_INDICATOR_CAPS, ID_INDICATOR_NUM, ID_INDICATOR_SCRL
    };
    theApp.setStatusBar(grafIndicators,sizeof(grafIndicators));
}
```

theApp refers to the application object, an instance of the mdi class. mdi::set-StatusBar passes the array of indicators onto the mainFrame:

```
void mdi::setStatusBar(UINT *newIndicators,int byteLength) {
    ((mainFrame *)m_pMainWnd)->setIndicators(
        newIndicators,byteLength/sizeof(UINT));
}
```

---
[4] Using a timer to trigger polling for external events gives you better control over the frequency of polling. Putting the timer in a low-priority thread will improve overall system performance. Threads are discussed in Chapter 16.

Figure 11.4 illustrates the flow of control.

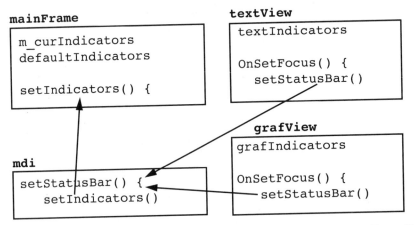

Figure 11.4   As the focus shifts, each view class calls `mdi::setStatusBar` with indicators appropriate for the view. The arrows represent flow of control.

11.3   Toolbars

A toolbar provides graphical shortcuts to executing commands. MFC supports two types of toolbars: button bars and dialog bars. Dialog bars are more versatile than button bars. They are layed out in a resource editor and can contain any Win32 control. By contrast, button bars are limited to same-size bitmap buttons. The tradeoff is that a button bar draws the buttons, in contrast to a dialog bar, in which the controls draw themselves. Besides being more efficient with system resources, button bars can configure themselves automatically to be arranged vertically, horizontally, or as a matrix.

11.3.1 Button Bars

Button bars are implemented using the Win32 toolbar control, `ToolWindow32`, and are wrapped by the MFC class `CToolBar`. Figure 11.5 shows a simple button bar with standard bitmaps for the File New, Open, and Save commands and one custom bitmap for View Graphics Tool.

Figure 11.5   A simple button bar

Button bars are created with a procedure similar to that for status bars:

1. Create the button-bar object, an instance of `CToolBar`.
2. Create the button-bar window using `CToolBar::Create`.
3. Create and load the bitmap images and specify their IDs.

The bitmap-button images are specified in a single bitmap consisting of fixed-size tiles. Each tile defines a button (see Figure 11.6). Use `CToolBar::SetSizes` to specify the size of each tile. Be careful when creating the bitmap, as there is nothing in the bitmap itself that identifies the boundaries between buttons. The image on a button will be a copy of the pixels that lie within the corresponding tile.[5]

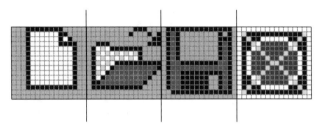

Figure 11.6   The buttons for a button bar are specified in a single bitmap. The bitmap is partitioned into tiles.

From Figure 11.6 you can see that the bitmap contains the image for the normal state of the buttons. The two other states, button down and disabled, are generated algorithmically from the normal state. Also, a button can be either alternate action, like the Caps Lock key, or momentary, like regular keys. The action of a button is controlled by its style. The default style is `TBBS_BUTTON`; use `CToolBar::SetButtonStyle` to set the style to `TBBS_CHECKBOX` for an alternate-action button.

The `CToolBar` function `SetButtons` associates an ID with each tile in the bitmap. When the button is pressed, the button bar will generate a `WM_COMMAND` message with the associated ID. The command can be picked up in the same way as a menu selection—in fact, because most buttons correspond to menu commands, no additional code is required beyond creating the button bar.

---

[5] From Visual C++, use the Image Grid Settings command and select Tile Grid to see a tile overlay on a bitmap. As an alternative to creating a single bitmap directly, the Visual C++ resource editor has a toolbar resource that lets you manipulate the images separately. It then combines the images to form the required bitmap.

Here is the code from the Mdi\V2 program that creates the button bar in Figure 11.5:

```
int mainFrame::OnCreate(LPCREATESTRUCT lpCreateStruct)
{
. . .
    static UINT buttons[] = { // Must match toolbar bitmap
        ID_FILE_NEW,
        ID_FILE_OPEN,
        ID_FILE_SAVE,
        ID_SEPARATOR,
        IDM_GrafTool
    };
    if( !toolBar.Create(this)
     || !toolBar.LoadBitmap(IDR_MAINFRAME)
     || !toolBar.SetButtons(buttons,sizeof(buttons)/sizeof(buttons[0])))
        return -1;
. . .
```

Notice that the space between the third and fourth buttons in Figure 11.5 is specified by inserting ID_SEPARATOR into the array of button IDs, not by putting space in the bitmap resource. MFC 4 introduced a slightly more convenient way to create button bars. If you create a button bar as a toolbar resource, use LoadToolBar to call the LoadBitmap and SetButtons functions.

11.3.2 Dialog Bars

A dialog bar is a bit of a hybrid. Like a dialog, it consists of Win32 controls and can be designed in a resource editor. Like a control bar, it is a child of a frame and sends command messages to the frame. As a result, programming a dialog bar borrows from both dialogs and control bars.

The steps for creating a dialog bar reflect its dual heritage:

1. Create a dialog resource.
2. Create a dialog-bar object, an instance of CDialogBar.
3. Create the dialog-bar window using CDialogBar::Create and initialize the controls.

I'll use the Graphic-tool dialog bar from the Mdi\V2 program to illustrate how to program a dialog bar. The tool has the same functionality as the modeless Tool dialog presented in Chapter 8. Figure 11.7 shows the dialog bar. Figure 11.8 shows the corresponding window tree.

Figure 11.7   The Graphic-tool dialog bar

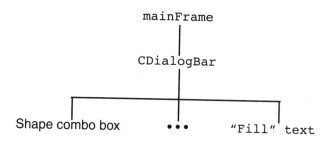

Figure 11.8   The window tree for the Graphic-tool dialog bar

11.3.2.1 Creating the Dialog Resource

There are a couple of unusual aspects of the dialog resource for a dialog bar. Unlike "real" dialogs, dialog bars are child windows and so must have the style WS_CHILD. Also, because they will be integrated into a control-bar ribbon, they should have neither a frame nor a title bar. Compare the styles of the About dialog and the dialog bar from the Mdi\V2 program:

```
IDD_ABOUTBOX DIALOG DISCARDABLE  0, 0, 217, 55
STYLE DS_MODALFRAME | WS_POPUP | WS_CAPTION | WS_SYSMENU
CAPTION "About MDI"
. . .

IDD_Tool DIALOG DISCARDABLE  0, 0, 248, 20
STYLE WS_CHILD
```

When creating the resource, keep in mind the orientation of the bar. Unlike button bars, dialog bars must be designed to appear either horizontally or vertically. They will not reconfigure themselves. For horizontal bars, keep the height to a minimum so that the bar will work well with other toolbars.

11.3.2.2 Creating the Dialog-Bar Object

Like a dialog, the dialog-bar object is usually an instance of a class with data members that correspond to the values of the child controls. The dialog bar can even use DDX to move the data between the object and the controls. Unlike a dialog, the dialog-bar class is not derived from `CDialog`. Instead, it is derived from `CDialogBar`.

The graphic-tool object is an instance of the `tool` class:

```
class tool : public CDialogBar
{
// Construction
public:
    tool();
. . .
```

Notice that unlike a dialog, the constructor for a dialog bar does not refer to the dialog resource. That binding will be left to the `Create` call.

As in the earlier version of the Mdi\V2 program, the tool is created as a global object (in `tool.cpp`):

```
tool theTool;  // global tool object
```

11.3.2.3 Creating the Dialog-Bar Window

`CDialogBar::Create` plays the same role as `CDialog::Create`. It creates the dialog frame window and then the dialog controls. However, unlike a real dialog, dialog bars do not receive the `WM_INITDIALOG` message. The program must trigger initialization of the controls itself.

The `tool` class has the function `showDialog` to show and hide the dialog bar:

```
void tool::showDialog()
{
    CMDIFrameWnd *main = (CMDIFrameWnd *)AfxGetMainWnd();
    if( !IsWindow(m_hWnd) ) {
        if( Create(main,IDD_Tool,CBRS_TOP,AFX_IDW_CONTROLBAR_FIRST+32) ) {
            UpdateData(FALSE);
. . .
}
```

The first time `showDialog` is called, it will create the dialog bar. The `Create` call takes as parameters

- The parent window, in this case the main frame
- The ID of the dialog resource
- Where the dialog bar will be docked
- The ID of the control-bar window

If you want the dialog bar to be positioned by the framework, the ID of the control-bar window must be between AFX_IDW_CONTROLBAR_FIRST and AFX_-IDW_CONTROLBAR_FIRST+255. The first 32 values are reserved by the framework for MFC-defined control bars like the one shown during Print Preview.

The call to UpdateData triggers DDX, which calls DoDataExchange to initialize the controls:

```
void tool::DoDataExchange(CDataExchange* pDX)
{
    //{{AFX_DATA_MAP(tool)
    DDX_Control(pDX, IDC_Width, m_widthCtrl);
    DDX_CBIndex(pDX, IDC_Shape, m_curShape);
    DDX_CBIndex(pDX, IDC_FillColor, m_fillColor);
    DDX_CBIndex(pDX, IDC_OutlineColor, m_outlineColor);
    DDX_Check(pDX, IDC_Filled, m_filled);
    //}}AFX_DATA_MAP

    if( pDX->m_bSaveAndValidate ) {
        m_outlineWidth = m_widthCtrl.GetPos();
    } else {
        m_widthCtrl.SetRange(MinWidth,MaxWidth);
        m_widthCtrl.SetPos(m_outlineWidth);
    }
}
```

One subtlety of dialog bars arises in the handing of notifications from the controls. In a dialog, the notifications are received by the dialog frame window; for a dialog bar we sometimes want the notifications sent to the main frame so that they can be treated like commands. Other notifications, such as the scroll messages from sliding controls, shouldn't be passed on as they could interfere with the scroll messages from the frame's scrollbars. The default behavior for a dialog bar is to pass the notification messages WM_COMMAND and WM_NOTIFY on to the parent frame, but a program can intercept any message in the dialog-bar class and override the default behavior.

As before in the Mdi\V2 program, the tool class uses the scroll and command messages to trigger updates of the dialog data:

```
void tool::OnHScroll(UINT nSBCode, UINT nPos, CScrollBar* pScrollBar)
{
    UpdateData();
}
```

Unfortunately, the dialog bar generates a WM_COMMAND message before the controls are created. If the program calls UpdateData before the controls are created, the program will crash in the DDX functions. The `tool` class overrides the virtual function `OnCommand` to filter out the initial message:

```
BOOL tool::OnCommand(WPARAM wParam, LPARAM lParam)
{
    if( ::IsWindow(widthCtrl.m_hWnd) )
        // Filter out initial WM_COMMANDs
        UpdateData();

    return CDialogBar::OnCommand(wParam, lParam);
}
```

11.3.3 Tool Tips and Fly-By Help

Although the intent of adding a toolbar is to make a program easier to use, users new to a program invariably ask, "What does that button do?" Tool tips, the small popup windows that appear when the mouse is left motionless over a toolbar item, were invented to answer the question.[6]

Recall the technique for adding status-bar help for menu items. If you add a string resource with the same ID as the menu item, the framework will post the string to the status bar during menu idle time. This approach is extended for tool tips.

If you add an additional field to the string resource with the same ID as a button-bar button or a dialog-bar control, the framework will post a tool tip with the specified text. The text is specified in the string using a newline to separate the fields:

```
Help-Text\nTool-Tip
```

For example, here are some strings for the button and dialog bars in the Mdi\V2 program:

```
ID_FILE_NEW     "Create a new document\nNew"
ID_FILE_OPEN    "Open an existing document\nOpen"
IDM_GrafTool    "Show or hide graphics toolbar\nGraphics Tool"
IDC_Shape       "Current drawing shape\nShape"
IDC_Width       "Width of pen used for shape outline\nOutline width"
```

In the case of the button bar, the text for the tool tip is just appended to the help text used by the menu because the buttons have the same IDs as menu commands. For the dialog bar, the strings have IDs that correspond to controls. But

---

[6] Tool tips were implemented in MFC before they appeared in Windows 95. Chapter 6 describes the underlying Win32 tool-tip control.

what is the first field for if there is no menu item? That text won't go to waste. If fly-by help is enabled, when the mouse is moved over a toolbar item, the framework displays the help text in the status bar just as it does for menu items.

Tool tips and fly-by help are styles for toolbars. In the Mdi\V2 program, both styles are set when the dialog bar is created:

```
void tool::showDialog()
{
    CMDIFrameWnd *main = (CMDIFrameWnd *)AfxGetMainWnd();
    if( !IsWindow(m_hWnd) ) {
        if( Create(main,IDD_Tool,CBRS_TOP,AFX_IDW_CONTROLBAR_FIRST+32) ) {
            UpdateData(FALSE);
            SetBarStyle(GetBarStyle()|CBRS_TOOLTIPS|CBRS_FLYBY);
```

11.3.4 Docking

One of the slickest properties of a toolbar is its ability to be ripped off one side of a frame and stuck to another or left floating in its own window. When a toolbar is stuck to the side of a frame, it is said to be *docked*.

Docking requires work on the part of both the frame and the toolbar. The frame is responsible for allocating space in its client area to be used by the control bars. The CFrame function RecalcLayout shrinks and grows the client area as required.

Dockability is a property of both the toolbar and the frame, specified with the EnableDocking function. For a toolbar to stick to a particular side, both the toolbar and the frame must allow docking on that side. For example, in the Mdi\V2 program, the main frame allows docking on any side and the toolbar will dock on any side:

```
int mainFrame::OnCreate(LPCREATESTRUCT lpCreateStruct)
{
. . .

    EnableDocking(CBRS_ALIGN_ANY); // Any frame border will accept toolbar
    m_toolBar.EnableDocking(CBRS_ALIGN_ANY); // Makes toolbar dockable
    DockControlBar(&m_toolBar);
```

By contrast, the dialog bar will dock only at the top or bottom of the frame:

```
void tool::showDialog()
{
    CMDIFrameWnd *main = (CMDIFrameWnd *)AfxGetMainWnd();
. . .
            EnableDocking(CBRS_ALIGN_TOP|CBRS_ALIGN_BOTTOM);
            main->DockControlBar(this,AFX_IDW_DOCKBAR_BOTTOM);
```

After the docking has been enabled, the program explicitly docks both the button bar and the dialog bar. Contrast the two calls to `DockControlBar` in the last two code fragments above. The docking location for the dialog bar is explicitly the bottom of the frame, since `AFX_IDW_DOCKBAR_BOTTOM` is given as the optional second parameter. The button bar will be docked at the top of the frame, since that is the first border that can accept it. The order of consideration is top, bottom, left, then right.

To float, rather than dock, a toolbar, call `CFrameWnd::FloatControlBar`.

11.4   Hiding, Showing, and Updating Control Bars

If you generate an application with control bars, add a View menu for showing and hiding the bars, and use the correct IDs (`ID_VIEW_TOOLBAR` and `ID_VIEW_STATUS_BAR`), you'll find that the View commands work with no coding on your part. `CFrameWnd` has default support for showing and hiding one toolbar and one status bar.

If you add additional tool and status bars, you'll need to manage them yourself by taking the following steps:

1. For each control bar, add a command to hide and show the control bar. Conventionally, the commands are placed on the View menu.
2. Add an update handler to modify the command based on the control bar's visibility. Again, convention is to place a checkmark next to the menu item if the bar is visible.

The Mdi\V2 program performs both of these tasks for the graphics-tool dialog bar. The command View Graphics Tool toggles the visibility of the dialog bar:

```
void grafView::onGrafTool()
{
    theTool.showDialog();
}
```

We've already looked at most of `tool::ShowDialog`. The first time it is called, it creates the dialog bar. After that, it hides and shows the bar by calling `CFrameWnd::ShowControlBar`:

```
void tool::showDialog()
{
    CMDIFrameWnd *main = (CMDIFrameWnd *)AfxGetMainWnd();
    if( !IsWindow(m_hWnd) ) {
    . . .
```

```
        } else main->ShowControlBar(this,!IsWindowVisible(),FALSE);
    }
```

Previously, you saw update handlers for menu items, so you probably have a good idea of how grafView could put a checkmark next to the View Graphics Tool menu item. Here is the update handler:[7]

```
    void grafView::onUpdateGrafTool(CCmdUI* pCmdUI)
    {
        pCmdUI->SetCheck( theTool.IsWindowVisible() );
    }
```

It would be very nice if the View Graphics Tool button (the right-most button in Figure 11.5) also indicated whether the tool was already on the screen. The button style has been set to alternate action; one click presses the button and the next releases it. We can use the pressed state to indicate that the tool is on-screen. This sounds like a task for an update handler, but we've already created a handler for IDM_GrafTool to control the checkmark on the menu item. How can we create another handler with the same ID to control the button-bar button?

It turns out that we don't have to—the *same* handler that controls the menu item will do just what we want for the button bar. CCmdUI is the base class of three types of user-interface objects: menu items, button-bar buttons, and status-bar panes. The CCmdUI functions Enable, SetText, and SetCheck are virtual. The update handler is called at different times for the different user-interface objects, with the CCmdUI parameter pointing to the object. In the update handler, calling SetCheck when the CCmdUI is a menu item puts a checkmark next to the item; calling SetCheck when the CCmdUI is a button-bar button puts the button in the down state.

As with menu items, if the framework doesn't find a command or update handler for an ID on the button bar, it grays and disables the button. In the Mdi\V2 program, when a graphics window is not active, the View Graphics Tool button is automatically grayed.

11.4.1 Saving Location and State

A nice touch for a program with control bars is to remember their locations when the program exits so that they can be restored the next time the program

---

[7] The tool is created at startup, so the handler doesn't need to check if the tool window exists. See Section 11.4.1 for the startup code.

is run. MFC makes this easy by providing two functions in the CFrameWnd class to perform the chore. The trickiest part of using the functions is knowing where to place them.

SaveBarState saves the location and state of each control bar. It takes a single parameter, the name of the section in which to store the information. The section will be in either an initialization file or the Registry, depending on where the program saves its startup information.[8] Call SaveBarState during program shutdown but before the control bars and main frame window have been destroyed. OnDestroy is too late because CFrameWnd::OnClose hides any floating toolbars. The Mdi\V2 program saves control-bar state before it inherits the default OnClose behavior:

```
void mainFrame::OnClose()
{
    SaveBarState("Control Bars");
    CMDIFrameWnd::OnClose();
}
```

Restore the control bars by calling LoadBarState, passing the section name that was used in the save. The call should be placed after the main frame and the control bars have been created, but before they are shown. mainFrame::OnCreate might seem like the logical place, since that is where the control bars are created. But in OnCreate, the creation of the main frame window is not complete and calling LoadBarState there will fail. The first place that the program gets control after creation of the main window is in InitInstance:

```
BOOL mdi::InitInstance()
{
    ...
    // create main MDI Frame window
    mainFrame* pMainFrame = new mainFrame;
    if (!pMainFrame->LoadFrame(IDR_MAINFRAME))
        return FALSE;
    m_pMainWnd = pMainFrame;

    theTool.showDialog();
    pMainFrame->LoadBarState("Control Bars");
```

---

[8] The default location used by MFC is a file in the Win32 directory named App.ini, where App is the name of the application. By calling CWinApp::SetRegistryKey, MFC will use the Registry instead.

Notice that the program now must force creation of the graphics toolbar before LoadBarState can restore its location.[9] showDialog takes care of creating the toolbar.

CHAPTER

12 | Specialized Views

The sample programs for this chapter are in the directories `Graphics\Views` and `AddrBook`. The corresponding executables in the `bin` directory are `Graphics-Views.exe` and `AddrBook.exe`.

12.1 Introduction

The presentation of documents varies widely, depending on the type of data in a document and what is being done with the data. MFC has specialized view classes to support some of this diversity. In this chapter, we'll look at views that can be scrolled and split, views that consist of a collection of fields, and views based on trees and lists.

12.2 Scrolling Views

Scrolling makes sense for nearly every type of view. The model for scrolling consists of two coordinate spaces: a *logical* coordinate space, in which the document is stored, and a *physical* (or *device*) coordinate space, in which the document is rendered.[1] The document class works only with logical coordinates, but the view class, unfortunately, must work with both. Figure 12.1 shows the relationship of the view and document spaces.

---

[1] The terms *logical* and *physical* are common usage, although they could also be called *virtual* and *real*. Programs operate on virtual coordinates that eventually get mapped to real pixel locations.

283

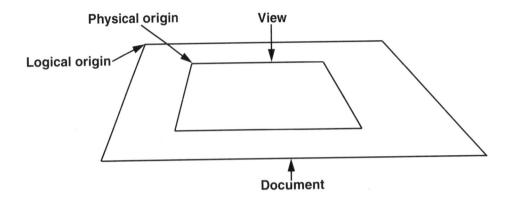

Figure 12.1   The view floats on top of the document.

12.2.1 Mapping Modes

Win32 provides some support for managing the two coordinate spaces needed to implement scrolling. A device context can present a logical coordinate space that is scaled and offset from the physical coordinate space of the window. The mapping from logical to physical coordinates is controlled by the device context's mapping mode. The mapping mode specifies the scale factor and origin of the transformation from logical to physical coordinates. Once the mapping mode is set, each logical coordinate x_l given to GDI will be transformed into the physical x_p as follows:

$$x_p = x_l * x_{scale} + x_{origin}$$

As described in Chapter 8, Win32 has mapping modes that allow a program to specify coordinates in real-world units, such as hundredths of an inch, and then have GDI transform the coordinates into physical-device units. Additionally, the isotropic and anisotropic mapping modes allow a program to specify arbitrary scaling factors and origins.

Scrolling doesn't require scaling, but it does utilize translation of the origin. Mapping modes can be set using the API functions `SetViewportExtEx` and `SetWindowExtEx` or by using the `CScrollView` class.

12.2.2 The CScrollView Class

`CScrollView` simplifies the implementation of scrolling by setting the mapping mode and managing the scrollbars. After the view sets the size of the logical coordinate space, `CScrollView` will display proportional scrollbars and handle the scrollbar notification messages.

To add scrolling to a view:

1. Derive the view class from `CScrollView`.
2. In the view's `OnCreate` function, specify the relationship between the logical and physical spaces using `SetScrollSizes`.
3. Before writing to the view window, call `OnPrepareDC`.

Although `CScrollView` handles many of the details of scrolling, it doesn't completely insulate a program from having to know about physical coordinates and thus using a scrolling view is a bit tricky. The trickiness arises because a mapping mode is an attribute of a device context. There are times when a program communicates with a window without a device context—for instance, while receiving mouse input or to invalidate a rectangle. As a result, when using a scrolled view, you sometimes use physical coordinates, but at other times you use logical coordinates.

The basic rules are simple:

- If you are operating on a device context, call `OnPrepareDC` and use logical coordinates. Otherwise, use physical coordinates.
- Always store logical coordinates.

Writing to a window always uses a device context, so drawings can be specified using logical coordinates. For example, the `OnDraw` function uses logical coordinates:

```
void view::OnDraw(CDC* pDC)
{
    pDC->MoveTo(logicalX,logicalY)
```

Before calling `OnDraw`, the framework sets the mapping mode appropriately by calling `OnPrepareDC`.

By contrast, input never has a device context. Mouse position, for example, is always in physical coordinates:

```
void view::OnLButtonDown(UINT nFlags, CPoint point)
{
    point is physical
```

If a program must correlate the mouse position with an object stored in the document, it must convert the physical coordinate to logical. In general, the conversion requires an offset and scaling. The offset is the scroll position; determine the offset in logical units using GetScrollPosition. The scaling is the ratio of the size of a logical unit to the size of a physical unit. The function toLogical converts its argument from physical to logical coordinates (Figure 12.2 illustrates the conversion problem):

```
void view::toLogical(CPoint *physical)
{
    SIZE physicalSz;
    CPoint scrollPosition = GetScrollPosition();

    physical->x = physical->x * LogicalSizeX/physicalSz.cx
        + scrollPosition.x;
    physical->y = physical->y * LogicalSizeY/physicalSz.cy
        + scrollPosition.y;
}
```

See Section 12.2.3 for an example of a scaled scrolling view.

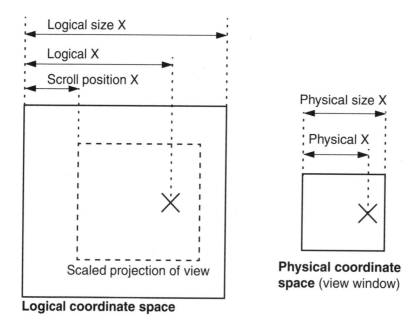

Figure 12.2 Conversion between physical to logical coordinates requires scaling and offsetting. The offset is based on the scroll position and the scale factor is based on the relative size of the units.

12.2.2.1 Scale-to-Fit

Scrolling allows the user to view a document that is larger than the view window. Scaling can sometimes be a useful alternative to scrolling. CScroll-View::ScaleToFit sets the mapping mode to MM_ANISOTROPIC, then scales each axis so that the entire logical coordinate space fits within the view window.[2] The size of the logical space is passed as an argument. Obviously, scale-to-fit only works if the logical coordinate space can be bounded, as in showing a page of text or showing the extent of the current drawing.

12.2.3 Example: Using CScrollView

The Graphics\Views program adds scrolling and scaling to the earlier Graphics\Simple program described in Chapter 8. The View menu's Static Splitter command switches between a single pane and two panes. In the single pane, logical and physical units are the same size. The dimensions of the logical coordinate space are set, arbitrarily, to the size of the display screen, guaranteeing that a drawing can be larger than any view. Scroll bars are added so that the whole logical space can be seen.

In the two-pane configuration, shown in Figure 12.3, the right pane shows the drawing with logical and physical coordinates the same size and the left pane shrinks the drawing so that it fits completely within the pane. Thus, the right pane scrolls and the left is scaled to fit.

To use the framework support for scrolling, the view class is derived from CScrollView:

```
class view : public CScrollView
{
```

When the view window is created, the size of the logical coordinate space is specified.

---

[2] MFC uses a bogus mapping mode internally to identify scale-to-fit. If you retrieve the mapping mode, for example via GetDeviceScrollSizes, you will get a warning at runtime about the bogus value for the mapping mode.

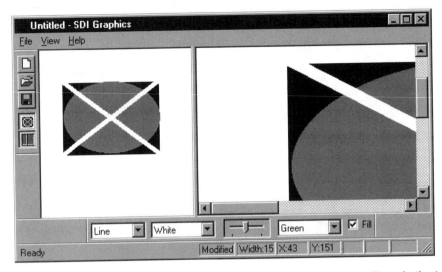

Figure 12.3 The Graphics\Views program implements scaling and scrolling. In the two-pane configuration, the left pane scales the drawing to fit in the pane. The right pane shows the drawing full size, adding scroll bars to move around the drawing.

```
int view::OnCreate(LPCREATESTRUCT lpCreateStruct)
{
    if (CScrollView::OnCreate(lpCreateStruct) == -1)
        return -1;

    SetScrollSizes(MM_TEXT,CSize(
        ::GetSystemMetrics(SM_CXSCREEN),
        ::GetSystemMetrics(SM_CYSCREEN)));

    return 0;
}
```

The Win32 function GetSystemMetrics returns various systemwide constants. SM_CXSCREEN and SM_CYSCREEN are the sizes of the display screen in the X and Y directions.

Based on the dimensions specified to SetScrollSizes, CScrollView will post and manage scrollbars for the view window. For painting, OnDraw will be called with a device context already adjusted for scrolling and scaling, so the original code from the Graphics\Simple program needs no change to paint a scrolled view.

Handling mouse input is a different story. When the left mouse button is pressed, the location of the mouse is given in physical coordinates. The anchor and cursor are kept in logical coordinates:[3]

```
void view::OnLButtonDown(UINT nFlags, CPoint point)
{
    toLogical(&point);
    m_anchor = m_cursor = point;
    SetCapture();
}
```

The function toLogical, described in Section 12.2.2, performs the conversion:

```
void view::toLogical(CPoint *pt)
{
    int mapMode;
    SIZE physicalSz, dontCare;
    GetDeviceScrollSizes(mapMode,physicalSz,dontCare,dontCare);
    CPoint origin = GetScrollPosition();

    pt->x = pt->x * ::GetSystemMetrics(SM_CXSCREEN)/physicalSz.cx
        + origin.x;
    pt->y = pt->y * ::GetSystemMetrics(SM_CYSCREEN)/physicalSz.cy
        + origin.y;
}
```

As the mouse is moved, the program draws a rubber-band shape. Unlike OnDraw, OnMouseMove creates its own device context in which to draw, so it must adjust the device context itself:

```
void view::OnMouseMove(UINT nFlags, CPoint point)
{
    toLogical(&point);
    if( GetCapture()==this ) {
        CClientDC dc(this);
        dc.SetROP2(R2_NOT);
        OnPrepareDC(&dc);   // Adjust dc for scroll origin
        theTool.getShape()->draw(&dc,
            CRect(m_anchor.x,m_anchor.y,m_cursor.x,m_cursor.y),
            theTool.isFilled(),RGB(0,0,0),
            RGB(0,0,0),theTool.getWidth());
    . . .
```

After OnPrepareDC is called, all drawing functions take logical coordinates.

---

[3] The *anchor* is the location where the mouse button was pressed; the *cursor* is the current mouse location. See Chapter 8 for more details.

When the left button is released, the shape is recorded and the view updated. The shape is stored in logical coordinates, but the invalid rectangle is physical:[4]

```
void view::OnLButtonUp(UINT nFlags, CPoint point)
{
    if( GetCapture()==this ) {
        document* pDoc = GetDocument();
        ASSERT_VALID(pDoc);

        toLogical(&point);
        m_cursor = point;
        adjustPoint(m_cursor);
        CRect rect(m_anchor.x,m_anchor.y,m_cursor.x,m_cursor.y);
        int width = theTool.getWidth();
        pDoc->appendCmd(
            theTool.getShapeNumber(),
            rect,
            theTool.isFilled(),
            theTool.getFillColorNumber(),
            theTool.getOutlineColorNumber(),
            width);

        toPhysical( &rect.TopLeft() );
        toPhysical( &rect.BottomRight() );
        rect.NormalizeRect();
        rect.InflateRect(theTool.getWidth()/2+1,
            theTool.getWidth()/2+1);
        InvalidateRect(&rect);

        ReleaseCapture();
    }
}
```

We're not yet ready to look at the commands that switch between the single and two-pane configurations, since they involve splitter windows. Those commands are covered in Section 12.3.3. However, specifying whether any particular view is scrolled or scaled is easy. Two functions have been added to the view class to make a view either scaleable or scrollable:

```
void view::makeScalable()
{
    SetScaleToFitSize(CSize(
        ::GetSystemMetrics(SM_CXSCREEN),
        ::GetSystemMetrics(SM_CYSCREEN)));
}
```

---

[4] OnLButtonUp in the Graphics\Views program is actually slightly different than shown here because it handles multiple views. See Section 12.2.5.

```
void view::makeScrollable()
{
    SetScrollSizes(MM_TEXT,CSize(
        ::GetSystemMetrics(SM_CXSCREEN),
        ::GetSystemMetrics(SM_CYSCREEN)));
}
```

To make a view scrollable, call `SetScrollSizes`. It can be called repeatedly to establish scrolling and to change the bounds of the logical coordinate space. `SetScaleToFitSize` marks a view as scaled. Whenever the size of the frame window is changed, the view will adjust the scaling factor so that the specified logical coordinate space just fits. Since the aspect ratio of the view window may be different than that for the logical space, the drawing may appear distorted, either squashed or elongated.

12.3   Splitters

Split, or multi-pane, windows put more than one view into a single frame-window. Multi-pane windows are an alternative to multiple child windows. They have become popular, particularly in SDI applications. I find it ironic that multi-pane windows have become a mark of a "modern" application, since panes are similar to tiled windows. A few years ago, a windowing system was considered modern if it supported overlapped windows instead of the tiled windows of the early systems.

There are two basic types of splitters: dynamic and static. Dynamic splitters are often used in conjunction with scrolling to allow distant parts of a document to be seen at the same time. Dynamic splitters can be created and deleted by the user, as needed, using a splitter box that sits at the top of the vertical scrollbar and to the left of the horizontal scrollbar.[5] Dynamic splitters are limited to two panes along each axis. Each pane may have its own set of scrollbars.

Static splitters are generally used to display two different types of views—for example, the tree and file views in Explorer windows, or the scaled and scrolled views in the Graphics\Views program. The number and organization of static splitters is fixed, although the user may be able to resize the panes by dragging the divider bar.

---

[5] The scrollbars in a splitter window are not window scrollbars in the usual sense. They are scrollbar controls placed on the client area of the splitter window. The splitter window posts the scrollbar controls and draws the splitter box. Try double clicking on a splitter box.

Splitters are implemented by the `CSplitterWnd` class. To split a frame window, create a `CSplitterWnd` window as a child of the frame. In each pane, put a view. Figure 12.4 shows the window tree for the Graphics\Views program displayed in Figure 12.3. Notice that the views are no longer direct children of the frame.

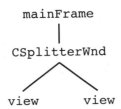

Figure 12.4   The client area of the frame contains the splitter. Each pane in the splitter contains a view.

12.3.1 Dynamic Splitters

Dynamic splitters are easier to use than static because the framework does nearly all the work. Here are the steps:

1. Create the frame window.
2. In `OnCreateClient`, create the splitter window by calling `Create`. The splitter will create the views as needed.

Before the splitter window can be created, there must be a `CSplitterWnd` object. Often, the `CSplitterWnd` object is a member of the frame class. In that case, the splitter window can be created in `OnCreateClient` by acting on the component. That is, if

```
class mainFrame : public CFrameWnd
{
. . .
    CSplitterWnd m_splitterWnd;
```

then

```
BOOL mainFrame::OnCreateClient(LPCREATESTRUCT lpcs,
    CCreateContext* pContext)
{
    return m_splitterWnd.Create(this,2,2,CSize(1,1),pContext);
}
```

The call to `Create` above creates a 2 by 2 dynamic splitter with each pane having a minimum size of 1 pixel square. Initially, the splitter created by `CSplitterWnd::Create` will show only one pane. When the user drags the splitter box to create new panes, CSplitterWnd calls CreateView using the class information passed in the CCreateContext object. The framework pulls this information out of the document template before it calls OnCreateClient.

If a view supports scrollbars, then the splitter window will create one scrollbar for each row of panes and one for each column. Manipulating a scrollbar at the end of a row sends scroll messages to each view in that row. Likewise for manipulating a scrollbar at the bottom of a column. CSplitterWnd does not support separate scrollbars for each pane.

12.3.2 Static Splitters

With a static splitter, the user cannot change the number of panes. It is up to the program to create and remove panes as needed. Since the panes usually show different types of views, it is also up to the program to create the views. Here is the procedure:

1. Create the frame window.
2. In OnCreateClient, create the splitter window by calling CreateStatic.
3. Create each view by calling CreateView.

A static splitter can have up to four rows and four columns of panes. The panes are referred to by their row and column index, beginning at index zero.

The program must create a view for each pane, even if the view isn't visible. CSplitterWnd::CreateView creates the view window. Here is its prototype:

```
virtual BOOL CreateView(
    int row, int col,
    CRuntimeClass* viewClass,
    SIZE size,
    CCreateContext* pContext );
```

To call CreateView, you'll need to get the runtime-class structure for the view. To do so, use the RUNTIME_CLASS macro or the virtual function GetRuntimeClass. After a view is created, use the GetPane function to get a pointer to the view in a particular pane.

12.3.3 Example: Swapping Between Dynamic and Static Splitters

The View Static Splitter command in the Graphics\Views program switches between static and dynamic splitters. The static splitter is shown in Figure 12.3; the dynamic splitter is illustrated by Figure 12.5.

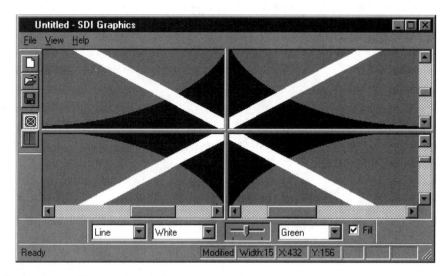

Figure 12.5   The drawing of Figure 12.3 shown in a dynamic splitter with four panes

Changing the dynamic/static attribute of a splitter is not directly supported in CSplitterWnd, so we'll need to poke around. The implementation is in main-Frame. I've added a flag to indicate the splitter configuration, a pointer to the CSplitterWnd object, and functions to handle the command:

```
class mainFrame : public CFrameWnd
{
. . .
    afx_msg void onViewStaticSplitter();
    afx_msg void onUpdateViewStaticSplitter(CCmdUI* pCmdUI);
. . .
    CSplitterWnd *m_splitterWnd;
. . .
    BOOL m_isStaticSplitter;
```

onViewStaticSplitter changes the configuration of the splitter in both directions. It's a long function, so I'll treat it in pieces. Its basic tasks are to

1. Prepare the create context that will be used by CSplitterWnd to create views;
2. Create the new splitter and its associated views;
3. Delete the old splitter and its associated views; and,
4. Adjust the layout of the frame.

Rather than tweaking the internals of the splitter object, the program destroys and then recreates the splitter:

```
void mainFrame::onViewStaticSplitter()
{
    CCreateContext context;
    memset( &context, 0, sizeof(context) );
    CRect rect;
    GetClientRect(&rect);
    CView *curView = (CView *)m_splitterWnd->GetPane(0,0);
    context.m_pCurrentDoc = curView->GetDocument();

    CSplitterWnd *newSplitter = new CSplitterWnd;
```

mainFrame creates the CSplitterWnd object as needed. Unlike the case of creating the splitter in OnCreateClient described earlier, onViewStaticSplitter needs to create its own CCreateContext. The context structure contains quite a few fields, most of which can be set to NULL; memset handles that job. So that the new views will be connected to the document, I've set the m_pCurrentDoc field to point to the current document.

Next, the function branches based on whether we're creating a static or dynamic splitter:

```
    if(m_isStaticSplitter) {
        // Create dynamic splitter
        context.m_pNewViewClass = RUNTIME_CLASS(view);
        newSplitter->Create(this,2,2,CSize(1,1),&context);

        // Remove right-hand pane from static splitter
        m_splitterWnd->DeleteView(0,1);
```

m_isStaticSplitter is true if the current configuration uses a static splitter. To switch to a dynamic splitter, the view class for the panes is specified in the create context and then the splitter window is created. Creating the splitter creates the first view. A document must always have at least one view, so I don't delete the old views until the new ones have been created.

Creating the static splitter is more work. First, the dynamic splitter might have up to four panes, and hence four views, that must be removed. Also, creating a static splitter requires creating the views explicitly:

```
    } else {
        // Create static splitter
        newSplitter->CreateStatic(this,1,2);
```

```
        // Create views as children of splitter
        newSplitter->CreateView(0,0,RUNTIME_CLASS(view),
            CSize(rect.right/3,rect.bottom),&context);
        newSplitter->CreateView(0,1,RUNTIME_CLASS(view),
            CSize(0,0),&context);

        // Make left pane scale-to-fit, right scrollable
        ((view *)newSplitter->GetPane(0,0))->makeScalable();
        ((view *)newSplitter->GetPane(0,1))->makeScrollable();

        // Remove all but first pane from dynamic splitter
        if( m_splitterWnd->GetRowCount()>1 )
            m_splitterWnd->DeleteRow(1);
        if( m_splitterWnd->GetColumnCount()>1 )
            m_splitterWnd->DeleteColumn(1);
    }
```

The static splitter consists of two panes side-by-side. The left pane is scaled, the right is scrolled. The calls to `CSplitterWnd::DeleteRow` and `DeleteColumn` remove all but the first pane and view.

Deleting the last pane and view from a splitter is tricky. `DeleteRow` and `Delete-Column` call `CSplitterWnd::DeleteView`. After `DeleteView` removes a view, it tries to guarantee that there is still an active pane. If `DeleteView` removes the last view, there is no pane to make active, causing `DeleteView` to fail. Instead of using `DeleteView`, I use the lower-level function `CDocument::RemoveView`. I'll remove the last view by first removing it from the document and then deleting the view window. Once the last view is gone, the old splitter itself can be removed:

```
        // Delete old splitter, remember new
        context.m_pCurrentDoc->RemoveView(curView);
        m_splitterWnd->DestroyWindow();
        delete m_splitterWnd;
        m_splitterWnd = newSplitter;

        m_splitterWnd->SetActivePane(0,0);
        OnUpdateFrameTitle(TRUE);
        RecalcLayout();
        m_isStaticSplitter = !m_isStaticSplitter;
    }
```

Finally, the new splitter is attached to the frame and the frame is updated. `RecalcLayout` computes the size and location of the control bars and the new splitter, and then triggers redrawing.

There is a minor error in the way MFC handles the frame's title bar. If you switch back and forth between static and dynamic views, you may notice the title flash (it's easiest to see using the toolbar button to switch between the views). The CFrameWnd class provides two ways to update the title bar: immediate and delayed (that is, during idle time). Unfortunately, when a view is removed, the title bar is updated immediately. Since the call to RemoveView removes the last view for the splitter, it removes the document name from the title bar. onView-StaticSplitter calls OnUpdateFrameTitle to reinsert the document name into the title. It would be better if CDocument used the delayed version of updating the frame title; then we wouldn't have to trigger another update and the title bar wouldn't flash.

12.3.4 Setting the Active Pane

Depending on the nature of the views, the concept of "current pane" may be important. For example, in text windows, the caret position may be pane-specific, so the current pane would determine where new text would be inserted. In the Address Book program of Chapter 13, the current pane determines the form of the printed output. The function CSplitterWnd::ActivateNext activates the next or previous pane. You can call it in response to a menu command or keyboard accelerator. CView has built-in support for handling commands with the IDs ID_NEXT_PANE and ID_PREV_PANE.

In a more graphical application, it might make sense for the pane underneath the mouse to be the active pane. The Graphics\Views program changes activation based on mouse position. If the user isn't drawing, and thus if the mouse isn't captured, the view under the mouse activates itself. The code is in the view class:

```
void view::OnMouseMove(UINT nFlags, CPoint point)
{
    toLogical(&point);
    if( GetCapture()==this ) {
. . .
    } else {
        // If not drawing, have activation follow the mouse
        CFrameWnd *main = (CFrameWnd *)AfxGetMainWnd();
        main->SetActiveView(this);
    }

    cursor = point;
}
```

One nice side effect of changing activation based on the cursor is that the status bar coordinates track the mouse better, since the coordinates represent the cursor position in the current view.

12.3.5 Synchronizing the Panes

In Chapter 10 we addressed the problem of updating a view after modifying its document. A similar problem occurs whenever there is more than one view referring to the same document, as is the case for multiple panes. In both cases, one or more views need to be updated. The basic algorithm is

```
Document or view calls UpdateAllViews
    UpdateAllViews calls OnUpdate for each view
        OnUpdate calls Invalidate() on the view
```

The default behavior of calling `Invalidate` causes the whole of every view to be redrawn. Although this is adequate, in many instances it is far from optimal. Consider the Graphics\Views program with multiple panes. Drawing in one pane should be reflected immediately in any others that show the same portion of the picture. Redrawing each pane may be unnecessary, depending on the portion of the drawing shown in the pane. The result of the default behavior is excessive screen flashing. A better strategy is to limit the invalid rectangle to just the affected portion of the drawing.

`UpdateAllViews` allows the program to send update hints to each view. A view can use the hints to minimize the area updated. The hints are passed through generic parameters. Here is the prototype:

```
void UpdateAllViews(
    CView* pSender,
    LPARAM lHint = 0L,
    CObject* pHint = NULL );
```

If it is a view calling `UpdateAllViews`, it can exclude itself from the update, since it may have already redrawn itself. It does so by passing its `this` pointer as the first parameter. The other parameters are program-specific.

The Graphics\Views program optimizes update by passing an invalid rectangle to each view. The procedure begins when the mouse button is released. The view records the new drawing command:

```
void view::OnLButtonUp(UINT nFlags, CPoint point)
{
    if( GetCapture()==this ) {
        document* pDoc = GetDocument();
        ASSERT_VALID(pDoc);
```

```
        toLogical(&point);
        m_cursor = point;
        adjustPoint(m_cursor);
        CRect rect(m_anchor.x,m_anchor.y,m_cursor.x,m_cursor.y);
        int width = theTool.getWidth();

        pDoc->appendCmd(
            theTool.getShapeNumber(),
            rect,
            theTool.isFilled(),
            theTool.getFillColorNumber(),
            theTool.getOutlineColorNumber(),
            width);
        ReleaseCapture();
    }
}
```

The logical coordinates for the drawing command are passed as a rectangle to the document function appendCmd. appendCmd adds the command to the display list and then updates the views:

```
BOOL document::appendCmd(int shape, CRect &rect,
    BOOL fill, int fillColor,
    int outlineColor, int outlineWidth)
{
    command *cmd = new command(
        shape,rect,fill,fillColor,outlineColor,outlineWidth);
    m_cmds.Add(cmd);

    UpdateAllViews(NULL,0,(CObject *)&rect);
    SetModifiedFlag();
    return TRUE;
}
```

UpdateAllViews calls OnUpdate for each view, passing the hint:

```
void view::OnUpdate(CView* pSender, LPARAM lHint, CObject* pHint)
{
    // Hint rect is logical so that it can be adjusted for
    // each view.  InvalidateRect takes physical coords
    if( pHint!=NULL ) {
        CRect rect((CRect *)pHint);
        toPhysical( &rect.TopLeft() );
        toPhysical( &rect.BottomRight() );
        rect.NormalizeRect();
        rect.InflateRect(theTool.getWidth()/2+1,
            theTool.getWidth()/2+1);
        InvalidateRect(&rect);
    } else CScrollView::OnUpdate(pSender,lHint,pHint);
}
```

The invalid rectangle is copied from the pHint parameter and then converted into physical coordinates for the view.[6] Since every view is optimized, there is no benefit to treating the current view differently. Also, notice the test for pHint!=NULL. OnUpdate is called by the framework from places other than UpdateAllViews. In these calls there will be no hints.

12.4 Form Views

Programs that collect and present data are often organized around a form. An MFC form view merges properties of dialogs and views. Like a dialog, a form view is constructed from a collection of controls and thus can be designed using a resource editor. Also like a dialog, the view can use Dialog Data Exchange to read and write the controls. Like a view, a form view can be managed by the framework; it lives inside a frame and has an associated document.

12.4.1 Creating the Form

In many ways, a form view looks and acts like a modeless dialog. Because the view is not modal, there is no need for an OK or Cancel button, but there may be other buttons that trigger commands. Commands will be routed, so they can be processed in the view, document, frame, or application object.

Unlike a dialog, the form won't reside in a popup window. Since it lives inside a frame, it must be a child and shouldn't have a border. Compare the attributes of the form resource for the AddrBook program with the About box:

```
IDD_ABOUTBOX DIALOG DISCARDABLE  34, 22, 217, 55
STYLE DS_MODALFRAME | WS_POPUP | WS_CAPTION | WS_SYSMENU
CAPTION "About AddrBook"
FONT 8, "MS Sans Serif"
BEGIN

IDD_FORM DIALOG DISCARDABLE  0, 0, 256, 184
STYLE WS_CHILD
FONT 8, "MS Sans Serif"
BEGIN
```

Creating a dialog resource for a form view should remind you of creating a resource for a dialog bar (see Chapter 11), since they have the same style. Unlike a dialog bar but like other dialogs, there is no restriction on the layout of

---

[6] Since pHint *points* to the logical rectangle, it is important that the rectangle be copied before being converted. Otherwise toLogical would operate on the original rectangle defined in OnLButtonDown.

the controls. Also like a dialog, you can reorganize the controls in a form and change their sizes at runtime.

A large form may not fit inside the frame window. There are a couple of different strategies you can use to show all of the form. Simplest is to do nothing. The form-view class, CFormView, is derived from CScrollView. If the frame is not large enough to show the whole form, scrollbars will be posted allowing the form to be scrolled.

If the form will fit on a typical screen, you might want to take control of the size of the frame window. The easiest way is to call CScrollView::ResizeParent-ToFit once you know the size of the form view. You can also change the size of the frame window by calling CWnd::MoveWindow. To prevent the user from changing the frame size, remove the WS_THICKFRAME attribute from the frame window. Overriding PreCreateWindow for the frame will let you control these and other attributes of the form.

12.4.1.1 Overriding PreCreateWindow

You might recall from Chapter 5 that after the call to Create, but before the call to the Win32 function CreateWindow, the framework calls the virtual function PreCreateWindow. By intercepting this call, a program can control the appearance and behavior of the new window.

PreCreateWindow is passed a CREATESTRUCT. The structure contains the initial size and location of the window, as well as the window style flags. As we discussed in Chapter 5, the style flags let you specify the type of border for the window, as well as whether the window has a title bar and system buttons.

As an example, consider an SDI application that uses a form view. To remove the resizable border from the frame window, add a PreCreateWindow function to the main frame class and change the class style:

```
BOOL mainFrame::PreCreateWindow(CREATESTRUCT& cs)
{
    cs.style &= ~WS_THICKFRAME;
    return CFrameWnd::PreCreateWindow(cs);
}
```

12.4.2 Displaying the Data

Using CFormView is similar to using any other view. To specify the form view, put a pointer to its runtime class into the document template using the

RUNTIME_CLASS macro. Since the controls in the view draw themselves, form views don't usually need an OnDraw function (at least not until you want to print the form; see Chapter 13). Form views often benefit from an OnUpdate function to optimize repainting, as shown in Section 12.6.2.2.

DDX can transfer data between the controls and the CFormView object. You'll need to trigger the exchange explicitly by calling UpdateData. Although a form view can use the dialog technique of creating one member variable in the C++ wrapper object for each control, this can become unwieldy for lots of data. An alternative is to package the data in a structure or class.

12.4.3 Edit Fields Within a Form

One control you'll likely use in every form is the edit control. Besides providing basic text input, edit controls implement simple text formatting, single-level undo/redo, as well as cut, copy, and paste. Unfortunately, the rich keyboard interface to an edit control can conflict with the overall program interface.

Consider a form like that in Figure 12.7. Suppose that the text in the First Name field is highlighted. Should pressing Ctrl+C copy to the clipboard just the highlighted name or the complete form? Should pressing Ctrl+V copy the text on the clipboard to the current edit control or should the text be interpreted as a form? CFormView and AppWizard conspire to make the latter the default in both cases.

When it generates an application, AppWizard creates an accelerator table with the standard keys, something like:

```
IDR_MAINFRAME ACCELERATORS PRELOAD MOVEABLE PURE
BEGIN
    "N",           ID_FILE_NEW,        VIRTKEY, CONTROL
    "O",           ID_FILE_OPEN,       VIRTKEY, CONTROL
    "S",           ID_FILE_SAVE,       VIRTKEY, CONTROL
    "Z",           ID_EDIT_UNDO,       VIRTKEY, CONTROL
    "X",           ID_EDIT_CUT,        VIRTKEY, CONTROL
    "C",           ID_EDIT_COPY,       VIRTKEY, CONTROL
    "V",           ID_EDIT_PASTE,      VIRTKEY, CONTROL
    VK_BACK,       ID_EDIT_UNDO,       VIRTKEY, ALT
    VK_DELETE,     ID_EDIT_CUT,        VIRTKEY, SHIFT
    VK_INSERT,     ID_EDIT_COPY,       VIRTKEY, CONTROL
    VK_INSERT,     ID_EDIT_PASTE,      VIRTKEY, SHIFT
    VK_F6,         ID_NEXT_PANE,       VIRTKEY
    VK_F6,         ID_PREV_PANE,       VIRTKEY, SHIFT
END
```

Before a keystroke is inspected by a control in a form view, the accelerator tables for the enclosing frame windows are searched. If the keystroke combination matches an accelerator, the corresponding command is generated and the keystroke eaten, never to be seen by the control. Thus if the main frame has the above accelerator table, Ctrl+C would send WM_COMMAND(ID_EDIT_COPY) to the main window and nothing to the current control.

If you want Ctrl+C, Ctrl+Z, and the others to be interpreted by the edit control, remove the corresponding accelerators from the table for the frame window.

12.5 Control Views

A complex Win32 control can provide lots of functionality for little work. Chapter 10 used the edit control to build most of a text editor. Chapter 7 has the beginnings of a word processor built from a rich-text control. Both of these controls, as well as the list view and tree controls, are wrapped by view classes derived from CCtrlView.

In a control view, the control *is* the view. That is, the control window fills the client area of a frame window or the pane of a splitter. When the frame is resized, the control is resized. The view operates like the control, although it is easy to extend the control's behavior by deriving a class from the wrapper class.

CEditView and CRichEditView are complete enough to be used as-is in many programs. Just put the view class into the document template as we did in Chapter 10:

```
textTemplate = new CMultiDocTemplate(
    IDR_TextType,                   // Shared resource ID
    RUNTIME_CLASS(textDoc),         // Document class
    RUNTIME_CLASS(CMDIChildWnd),    // Frame class
    RUNTIME_CLASS(CEditView));      // View class
```

CListView and CTreeView need support for getting data into and out of the control. To use them:

1. Derive a view class from CListView or CTreeView.
2. In OnInitialUpdate, put data into the control.
3. Respond to notifications from the control.

Handling notifications raises an interesting problem. A control sends notifications to its parent. The parent for the control view is the frame window. It would be ugly to put response code for the view into the frame.

12.5.1 Message Reflection

CWnd handles notifications from controls differently than it does other messages. (Recall that notifications are usually delivered via WM_COMMAND or WM_NOTIFY messages.) Before searching the message map for the current window, the window procedure for CWnd gives the wrapper class of the sender an opportunity to handle the message.

It's perhaps easiest to see the flow of control with a simple example. Figure 12.6 shows a frame window with a view. In the example, the view is a CTreeView, but the type of the view is irrelevant. When an item in the tree is selected, the tree control sends the notification TVN_SELCHANGED to the frame window. The window procedure for the frame, CWnd's window procedure, first searches the view class for a message-map entry of the form:

```
ON_NOTIFY_REFLECT(TVN_SELCHANGED, Handler)
```

If one is found, the handler is called and processing for the notification terminates. If no handler is found, then the window procedure searches the message map for the frame, as usual.

12.5.2 Example: Using a List Box as a View

Using the CCtrlView class, any control can be turned into a view by following these steps:

1. Derive a wrapper class for the view from CCtrlView.
2. In the constructor for the class, initialize the constructor for CCtrlView with the Win32 class name and window style.
3. For ease of use, create a GetCtrl function to return a pointer to the control.

As an example, I've created the view listView based on the Win32 list box control. listView is derived from CCtrlView:

```
class listView : public CCtrlView
{
```

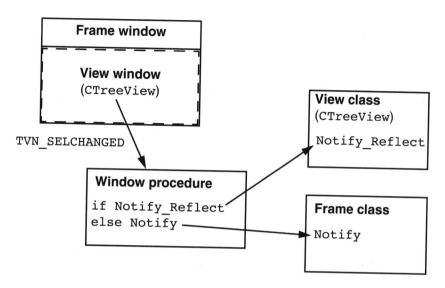

Figure 12.6 The tree view sends notifications to its parent frame. The window procedure for the parent looks to see if the wrapper class for the tree has a reflect handler for the notification. The arrows represent flow of control.

So that CCtrlView can create the correct kind of Win32 window, its constructor is given the Win32 class name:

```
listView::listView() :
    CCtrlView("LISTBOX",
      WS_CHILD|WS_VISIBLE|WS_VSCROLL|LBS_EXTENDEDSEL|LBS_NOINTEGRALHEIGHT)
{
}
```

The second parameter in the constructor is the style flags. Always include WS_CHILD and WS_VISIBLE, plus other control-specific flags that should be set in the call to create the window. For listView, I've enabled vertical scrolling and extended list-selection. The style LBS_NOINTEGRALHEIGHT tells the control that it may need to display a partial item at the bottom of the list. List boxes in dialogs are usually sized to be a multiple of the height of an item. In a view, the size of the list is determined by the frame window, so it may not be a multiple of the item height. A user of listView can modify the window style by overriding PreCreateWindow.

To populate the list box, override OnInitialUpdate. Since the view window is the control, m_hWnd for the view is the window handle of the control window. To get a pointer to the wrapper class for the control, you can just cast the `this` pointer for the view to the type of the control, as in:

```
void listView::OnInitialUpdate()
{
    CCtrlView::OnInitialUpdate();

    CListBox *lb = (CListBox *)this;
    lb->AddString( . . .
```

It would be better style, perhaps, to create a `getCtrl` function:

```
CListBox * listView::getCtrl() {
    return (CListBox *)this;
}
```

12.6   Example: An Address Book

The AddrBook program is an SDI application for creating and maintaining an address book. The main frame contains a static splitter with two panes. The left pane contains a tree view of the address book and the right pane a form view of the current address. Figure 12.7 shows the program's appearance and Figure 12.8 is the window tree for the view windows.

The main frame creates the splitter and the splitter creates the views at startup in `OnCreateClient`:

```
BOOL mainFrame::OnCreateClient(LPCREATESTRUCT lpcs,
    CCreateContext* pContext)
{
    CRect rect;
    GetClientRect(&rect);
    CSize sz(rect.Width()/4,rect.Height());

    m_splitterWnd.CreateStatic(this,1,2);
    m_splitterWnd.CreateView(0,0,RUNTIME_CLASS(treeView),sz,pContext);
    return m_splitterWnd.CreateView(0,1,RUNTIME_CLASS(formView),sz,
        pContext);
}
```

The tree view occupies the first quarter of the frame and the form view the rest. It is not necessary to compute what "the rest" is as the last pane will automatically fill in whatever is left over. Also, when the frame is resized horizontally only the form view will grow and shrink. The same algorithm would apply to vertical growth if the panes had been stacked—the bottom pane would be variable-size.

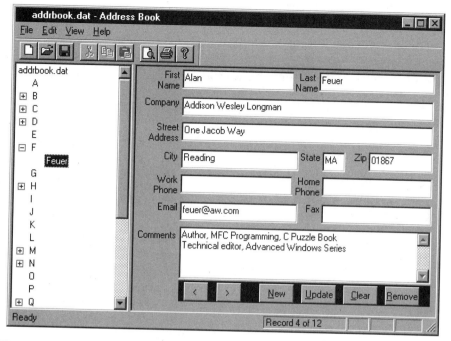

Figure 12.7   The address book uses a two-pane static splitter. The left pane contains a tree view, the right a form view.

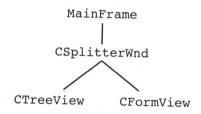

Figure 12.8   The window tree for the address book

12.6.1 The Document and the Views

The document, of course, manages the data for the address book. When a book is opened, all the data is read into an array in memory. At all times, one address in the array is considered the current address. The details of what an address looks like are buried in a helper class called address.

The document class provides operations to

• Retrieve, modify, and remove the current address

- Iterate over the addresses
- Read a new address book into memory and save an address book to a file
- Clear the in-memory address book

Its class declaration reflects these operations:

```
class document : public CDocument
{
. . .
// Operations
public:
    void deleteCurrentAddr();
    void getCurrentAddr(address &);
    int getCurrentIndex() { return currentAddr; };
    void newAddr(address &);
    BOOL nextAddr();
    BOOL prevAddr();
    BOOL setCurrentIndex(int i);
    void updateCurrentAddr(address &);

// Overrides
    // ClassWizard generated virtual function overrides
    //{{AFX_VIRTUAL(document)
    public:
    virtual void DeleteContents();
    virtual BOOL OnOpenDocument(LPCTSTR lpszPathName);
    virtual BOOL OnNewDocument();
    //}}AFX_VIRTUAL
. . .
protected:
    CArray <address *,address *> m_addrBook;
    int m_currentAddr;
. . .
};
```

The AddrBook program defines two view classes. formView, derived from CFormView, provides the user interface to an address. In addition to the fields that display the data, it has buttons to manipulate the book. treeView, derived from CTreeView, implements an index into the address book based on last names. Clicking on an entry in the tree puts the corresponding record into the form view.

The implementation of the formView class reflects its dual heritage. It has "dialog" data and uses DoDataExchange. The current address being displayed is kept in an address variable named m_a. The view also responds to OnUpdate to optimize screen painting:

```
class formView : public CFormView
{
. . .
    //{{AFX_DATA(formView)
    enum { IDD = IDD_FORM };
    //}}AFX_DATA
. . .

// Overrides
    // ClassWizard generated virtual function overrides
    //{{AFX_VIRTUAL(formView)
    protected:
    virtual void DoDataExchange(CDataExchange* pDX);   // DDX/DDV support
    virtual void OnUpdate(CView* pSender, LPARAM lHint, CObject* pHint);
    //}}AFX_VIRTUAL
. . .

// Generated message map functions
protected:
    //{{AFX_MSG(formView)
    afx_msg void onNew();
    afx_msg void onUpdate();
    afx_msg void onRemove();
    afx_msg void onClear();
    afx_msg void onNext();
    afx_msg void onPrevious();
    //}}AFX_MSG
    DECLARE_MESSAGE_MAP()
private:
    address m_a;
};
```

treeView is considerably simpler. Data flows only one way, into the tree. The tree is built in response to OnInitialUpdate or OnUpdate, so there is no need for DDX. The tree control operates mostly by itself. The program only needs to know when a new item has been selected. Here is the class declaration:

```
class treeView : public CTreeView
{
. . .
// Overrides
    // ClassWizard generated virtual function overrides
    //{{AFX_VIRTUAL(treeView)
    public:
    virtual void OnInitialUpdate();
    protected:
    virtual void OnUpdate(CView* pSender, LPARAM lHint, CObject* pHint);
    virtual BOOL PreCreateWindow(CREATESTRUCT& cs);
    //}}AFX_VIRTUAL
. . .
```

```
        // Generated message map functions
        //{{AFX_MSG(treeView)
        afx_msg void onSelchanged(NMHDR* pNMHDR, LRESULT* pResult);
        //}}AFX_MSG
        DECLARE_MESSAGE_MAP()
    };
```

12.6.2 Program Operation

The action begins in InitInstance. The program attempts to open the file in use the last time the program was run. The file name is stored in the recent-file list by the framework kept either in the Registry or in an initialization file. CWinApp::GetProfileString retrieves a string from the initialization data. The data is partitioned into sections and fields. If the "File1" field is found in the "Recent File List" section, the remembered file is opened; otherwise the default addrbook.dat file is opened:

```
    BOOL application::InitInstance()
    {
    . . .
       CSingleDocTemplate* pDocTemplate;
       pDocTemplate = new CSingleDocTemplate(
           IDR_MAINFRAME,
           RUNTIME_CLASS(document),
           RUNTIME_CLASS(mainFrame),  // main SDI frame window
           RUNTIME_CLASS(formView));
       AddDocTemplate(pDocTemplate);

       // Open the most recent address book
       CString bookName = GetProfileString(
           _T("Recent File List"),_T("File1"),_T("addrbook.dat"));
       if( OpenDocumentFile(bookName)==NULL )
           OnFileNew();

       return TRUE;
    }
```

Take a look at the document template in the code above. I've specified the view to be a formView, but the class put here is not important since the framework doesn't create the formView for us. We create it explicitly in OnCreateClient.

12.6.2.1 Serialization

If the address book is found, OpenDocumentFile calls OnCreateClient, which creates the views and eventually calls Serialize on the document. The document keeps the address book data in the CArray member m_addrBook. To serialize the data, the document tells the m_addrBook to serialize itself:

```
void document::Serialize(CArchive& ar)
{
    CDocument::Serialize(ar);
    addrBook.Serialize(ar);
}
```

Since m_addrBook is a CArray of pointers, we override SerializeElements to handle each element:

```
void AFXAPI SerializeElements(CArchive &ar, address **pAddrs, int cnt)
{
    if( ar.IsStoring() ) {
        for( int i=0; i<cnt; ++i )
            ar << pAddrs[i];
    } else {
        for( int i=0; i<cnt; ++i )
            ar >> pAddrs[i];
    }
}
```

The address class implements each field in the form as a CString. The class is declared Serial to implement >> and it implements Serialize to read and write its data:

```
class address : public CObject
{
public:
    CString  city;
    CString  comments;
    CString  company;
. . .
    CString  workPhone;
    CString  zip;

    address() {};
    address(address&);
    address& operator=(address&);

    void Serialize(CArchive &);
    DECLARE_SERIAL(address)

    void clear();
};
```

Serialize relies on the CString operators provided by CArchive:

```
void address::Serialize(CArchive &ar)
{
    CObject::Serialize(ar);
```

```
        if( ar.IsStoring() ) {
            ar << firstName;
            ar << lastName;
            ar << company;
   . . .

            ar << fax;
            ar << comments;
        } else {
            ar >> firstName;
            ar >> lastName;
            ar >> company;
   . . .

            ar >> fax;
            ar >> comments;
        }
    }
```

12.6.2.2 Managing the Form

Once the data is read, the framework calls OnInitialUpdate for the views. The default implementation of OnInitialUpdate simply calls OnUpdate. In OnUpdate, formView retrieves the current address and then invalidates the data fields:

```
void formView::OnUpdate(CView* pSender, LPARAM lHint, CObject* pHint)
{
    if( lHint!=ClearItem ) GetDocument()->getCurrentAddr(m_a);
    UpdateData(FALSE);

    GetDlgItem(IDC_City)->Invalidate();
    GetDlgItem(IDC_Comments)->Invalidate();
    GetDlgItem(IDC_Company)->Invalidate();
   . . .
    GetDlgItem(IDC_WorkPhone)->Invalidate();
    GetDlgItem(IDC_Zip)->Invalidate();
}
```

Notice that OnUpdate uses one hint, passed through lHint. Normally, the form displays the current address in the document. But if the user clears out the form, perhaps before creating a new entry, we don't want to get the current address. That is, the onClear function clears the address variable m_a then updates the screen:

```
void formView::onClear()
{
    m_a.clear();
    OnUpdate(NULL,ClearItem,NULL);
    GetDlgItem(IDC_FirstName)->SetFocus();
}
```

Next, OnUpdate calls UpdateData to trigger DDX. Before looking at DoData-Exchange, I want to comment on the series of calls to Invalidate that make up the bulk of OnUpdate. The default OnUpdate behavior is to call Invalidate for the view window, which would accomplish the same thing as the list of calls. But if you look at the form in Figure 12.7, you'll see that besides the data fields, the form contains lots of labels. Invalidating the view would redraw the labels as well as the data, causing the whole form to jiggle. The tedious calls to Invalidate are an optimization, redrawing only the controls that can actually change.

DoDataExchange moves data back and forth between the edit fields and the address variable. It is very convenient to keep the data for the form in its own class. Unfortunately, ClassWizard cannot handle the class references in the DDX calls, so the calls were added by hand:

```
void formView::DoDataExchange(CDataExchange* pDX)
{
    CFormView::DoDataExchange(pDX);
    //{{AFX_DATA_MAP(formView)
    //}}AFX_DATA_MAP

    DDX_Text(pDX, IDC_City, m_a.city);
    DDX_Text(pDX, IDC_Comments, m_a.comments);
    DDX_Text(pDX, IDC_Company, m_a.company);
    . . .
    DDX_Text(pDX, IDC_WorkPhone, m_a.workPhone);
    DDX_Text(pDX, IDC_Zip, m_a.zip);
}
```

The rest of formView consists of functions to handle the button commands. You've already seen onClear; the other functions are just as simple, calling on the underlying support in the document class:

```
void formView::onNew()
{
    UpdateData();
    GetDocument()->newAddr(m_a);
    GetDocument()->SetModifiedFlag();
    GetDocument()->UpdateAllViews(this,AddItem);
}

void formView::onUpdate()
{
    UpdateData();
    GetDocument()->updateCurrentAddr(m_a);
    GetDocument()->SetModifiedFlag();
}
```

```
void formView::onRemove()
{
    GetDocument()->deleteCurrentAddr();
    GetDocument()->SetModifiedFlag();
}

void formView::onNext()
{
    if( !GetDocument()->nextAddr() )
        ::MessageBeep(MB_ICONHAND);
}

void formView::onPrevious()
{
    if( !GetDocument()->prevAddr() )
        ::MessageBeep(MB_ICONHAND);
}
```

12.6.2.3 Managing the Tree

There are two tasks that need to be coded to implement the tree view: initialization of the tree control and response to a tree selection. Initialization is the more complex; it begins at OnInitialUpdate:

```
void treeView::OnInitialUpdate()
{
    initTree();
}
```

initTree carries out the initialization. The tree consists of a root node and one subnode for each letter of the alphabet. initTree walks the address-book data attaching each name to a letter node based on the first letter of the last name.

First it creates the root:[7]

```
void treeView::initTree()
{
    TV_INSERTSTRUCT is = {
        TVI_ROOT,TVI_LAST
    };
    document *pDoc = GetDocument();

    // Establish root
    is.item.mask = TVIF_TEXT;
    CString title = pDoc->GetTitle();
    is.item.pszText = title.GetBuffer(1);
    title.ReleaseBuffer();
    is.hParent = GetTreeCtrl().InsertItem(&is);
```

---

[7] Trees are complex to set up. Before reading further, you might want to review the discussion of the tree control in Chapter 6.

Each node has a text field, pszText, that is displayed in the tree. For the root node, the text is the data file name. The GetBuffer/ReleaseBuffer calls are needed to get a pointer to the data inside the CString returned by GetTitle. You would be correct to question passing a pointer to the data inside a C++ object; in general, this is a dicey operation. It is safe here because the tree control, like all controls, creates its own copy of the data.

initTree walks the address book using the operations provided by the document. First, the current address index is saved so that it can be restored later. Then, the current address index is set to the first entry, index zero, in preparation for the iteration:

```
// Establish list
address addr;
TCHAR s[] = _T("X");
int saveIndex = pDoc->getCurrentIndex();
pDoc->setCurrentIndex(0);
```

The document maintains the address book in alphabetical order, so populating the tree proceeds as follows:

```
For each letter from A to Z
    Create the subnode for the letter
    Get the address at the current index
        If it begins with the current letter
            Create a subnode for the address
            Increment the index
```

Here is the code:

```
for( TCHAR ch='A'; ch<='Z'; ++ch ) {
    s[0] = ch;
    is.item.mask = TVIF_TEXT|TVIF_PARAM;
    is.item.pszText = s;
    is.item.lParam = -1;
    HTREEITEM item = GetTreeCtrl().InsertItem(&is);

    do { // Look for entries beginning with ch
        pDoc->getCurrentAddr(addr);
        if( addr.lastName.IsEmpty()
          || (TCHAR)::CharUpper((LPSTR)addr.lastName[0]) != ch )
            break;
        TV_INSERTSTRUCT is2 = { item, TVI_LAST };
        is2.item.mask = TVIF_TEXT|TVIF_PARAM;
        is2.hParent = item;
        is2.item.pszText = addr.lastName.GetBuffer(1);
        is2.item.lParam = pDoc->getCurrentIndex();
        GetTreeCtrl().InsertItem(&is2);
        addr.lastName.ReleaseBuffer();
    } while( pDoc->nextAddr() );
}
```

To create a tree node, fill in a TV_INSERTSTRUCT. It has three fields:

```
typedef struct {
    HTREEITEM hParent;
    HTREEITEM hInsertAfter;
    TV_ITEM item;
} TV_INSERTSTRUCT;
```

The first two fields specify where in the tree to add the node: the parent and left-most sibling. The data for the node goes in the third field, the TV_ITEM:

```
typedef struct {
    UINT        mask;
    HTREEITEM   hItem;
    UINT        state;
    UINT        stateMask;
    LPWSTR      pszText;
    int         cchTextMax;
    int         iImage;
    int         iSelectedImage;
    int         cChildren;
    LPARAM      lParam;
} TV_ITEM;
```

The lParam field in the TV_ITEM is a place where you can put 32 bits of node-specific information. initTree initializes the field to the corresponding index of the address book entry. TV_ITEM uses a mask to specify which data fields are being used. While the mask eliminates the need to initialize unused fields, it requires that the desired flag bits be set.

Once the tree is created, the root node is expanded to show the letter nodes. Finally, the current address in the document is restored.

```
        GetTreeCtrl().Expand(is.hParent,TVE_EXPAND);
        pDoc->setCurrentIndex(saveIndex);
    }
```

initTree is also called on update. OnUpdate uses lHint to guide the update. Considerably less than optimal, the tree is rebuilt whenever a change is made in the document:

```
void treeView::OnUpdate(CView* pSender, LPARAM lHint, CObject* pHint)
{
    switch(lHint) {
    case AddItem:
    case ChangeItem:
    case DeleteItem:
        // TODO: optimize for each kind of update
        SetRedraw(FALSE);   // Keep tree quiet
        GetTreeCtrl().DeleteAllItems();
        initTree();
        SetRedraw(TRUE);
        UpdateData(FALSE);
        break;

    case DeleteAllItems:
        GetTreeCtrl().DeleteAllItems();
        UpdateData(FALSE);
        break;
    }

    return;
}
```

The use of SetRedraw adds polish to the program. Win32 maintains a redraw
flag for each window. When the flag is false, the window will not be repainted.
Besides speeding up the tree initialization, turning off redraw during update will
display the tree in a single paint. The update of any control that accepts lots of
data can benefit from using SetRedraw.

When a leaf of the tree is selected, the tree control sends a notification to its parent. As described in Section 12.5.1, the view will catch the reflected notification
if you insert an ON_NOTIFY_REFLECT macro into its message map:

```
ON_NOTIFY_REFLECT(TVN_SELCHANGED, onSelchanged)
```

The handler sets the current address index to correspond to the selection and
then updates the form view:

```
void treeView::onSelchanged(NMHDR* pNMHDR, LRESULT* pResult)
{
    NM_TREEVIEW* pNMTreeView = (NM_TREEVIEW*)pNMHDR;
    if( GetDocument()->setCurrentIndex(pNMTreeView->itemNew.lParam) )
        GetDocument()->UpdateAllViews(NULL);

    *pResult = 0;
}
```

12.6.2.4 Managing the Document

In addition to serialization, described in Section 12.6.2.1, the document implements the operations on the address book used by the views. The document, in turn, relies on CArray, so none of the operations are very complex. We'll look at the most interesting ones.

When a new address is created, formView calls newAddr to put the address in the book. newAddr keeps the data sorted:

```
void document::newAddr(address &addr)
{
    int cnt = m_addrBook.GetSize();
    int i;

    // Keep list sorted
    for( i=0; i<cnt; ++i ) {
        if( addr.lastName.CompareNoCase(m_addrBook[i]->lastName) < 0 )
            break;
    }

    m_addrBook.InsertAt(i,new address(addr));
    m_currentAddr = i;
}
```

The Remove button in the form view calls deleteCurrentAddr to remove the current address from the book:

```
void document::deleteCurrentAddr()
{
    if( m_currentAddr>=0 && m_currentAddr<m_addrBook.GetSize() ) {
        delete m_addrBook[m_currentAddr];
        m_addrBook.RemoveAt(m_currentAddr);
        if( m_currentAddr > m_addrBook.GetUpperBound() )
            m_currentAddr = m_addrBook.GetUpperBound();
        UpdateAllViews(NULL,DeleteItem);
    }
}
```

formView uses getCurrentAddr to retrieve the address data for the current index:

```
void document::getCurrentAddr(address &addr)
{
    if( i>=0 && i<m_addrBook.GetSize() )
        addr = *m_addrBook[i];
    else addr.clear();
}
```

treeView uses setCurrentIndex to change the current index:

```
BOOL document::setCurrentIndex(int i)
{
    if( i>=0 && i<m_addrBook.GetSize() ) {
        m_currentAddr = i;
        UpdateAllViews(NULL,NoChange);
        return TRUE;
    }

    return FALSE;
}
```

CHAPTER

13 | Printing and Previewing

The sample programs for this chapter are in the directories Mdi\V3 and Addr-Book. The corresponding executables in the bin directory are MdiV3.exe and AddrBook.exe.

13.1 Introduction

Printing has always been a complex topic. The myriad of printing devices; the potential for error conditions, such as the printer being out of paper; and the desire for accurate on-screen preview contribute to the complexity of printing. Win32 and MFC offer considerable support to simplify the printing task.

Win32 simplifies access to printers by isolating applications from device peculiarities. Programs write to printers using the same GDI functions that write to the screen. The Win32 Print common dialog simplifies printer selection and adjustment. MFC addresses printing by providing high-level print procedures in the framework. Accurate previewing is addressed by both GDI and the MFC class CDC.

For the simplest type of printing, the code that paints a window can also draw on the printer. This is, in fact, the default behavior for CView-derived classes. However, most applications need to supplement the window-drawing code—for example, to add page headers or footers. Form-based programs, so easy to create in a resource editor, need completely separate printing code since the on-screen fields are drawn by the controls that make up the form.

Other reasons to customize printing are

- To add support for adjusting printing margins, paper size, and page orientation
- To scale the output, perhaps to cover the page
- To handle multi-page documents

Each of these features will be discussed and illustrated in this chapter.

13.2 Support for Printing and Previewing

One benefit of programming with MFC is that printing and previewing can largely use the same code. During Preview, the framework adjusts the device context and overrides GDI functions so that output based on the printer is drawn proportionately in a preview window. Nevertheless, printing and previewing are complex, so even though both procedures are similar, I'll treat them separately.

13.2.1 Printing

Responsibility for printing is divided among Win32, MFC, and the application. The basic algorithm for a typical print job is coded in CView::OnFilePrint:

```
CView::OnFilePrint()
    virtual CView::OnPreparePrinting(CPrintInfo* pInfo)
        Set valid range for pages
        virtual CView::DoPreparePrinting(CPrintInfo* pInfo)
            Run print common dialog
                Get printer selection and pages to print
            Get device context for printer

virtual CView::OnBeginPrinting(CDC* pDC, CPrintInfo* pInfo)
        Allocate GDI objects such as fonts
        Set printer attributes such as orientation or paper tray
    Post Print-status dialog

CDC::StartDoc
        For each page
            Update status dialog
            CDC::StartPage
            virtual CView::OnPrepareDC(CDC* pDC, CPrintInfo* pInfo)
                Can signal terminate of printing here
            virtual CView::OnPrint(CDC* pDC, CPrintInfo* pInfo)
                Print page header
                Select objects
                For WYSIWYG, call virtual OnDraw
                Print page footer
            CDC::EndPage
```

```
CDC::EndDoc
    virtual CView::OnEndPrinting(CDC* pDC, CPrintInfo* pInfo)
        Delete GDI objects
        Remove Print-status dialog
```

Most of the steps are implemented as virtual functions in CView. I've highlighted those functions in the algorithm above. Depending on the particular type of view being printed, you'll need to override none, some, or all of the functions. Each function is discussed below.

Although OnFilePrint is a member function of CView, it isn't hooked up to the Print command in CView's message map. To trigger the default printing algorithm, add a message map entry in the view class to bind the Print command to OnFilePrint:

```
ON_COMMAND(ID_FILE_PRINT,CView::OnFilePrint)
```

The first step in the print procedure is to get details about the print job from the user. The Print common dialog allows selection of the printer; setting of printer attributes, such as print quality and page size; and specification of which pages to print.

The primary job of OnPreparePrinting is to gather the print-job information, usually by calling DoPreparePrinting which triggers the Print dialog. Your view class must implement its own OnPreparePrinting, as the default in CView doesn't do anything. OnPreparePrinting receives a pointer to a CPrintInfo object that holds details about the print job, such as the range of valid page numbers. If an application knows how many pages are in the document, it can set the maximum page number using CPrintInfo::SetMaxPage before calling DoPreparePrinting.

Here are the important members of CPrintInfo:

```
struct CPrintInfo // Printing information structure
{
    CPrintDialog* m_pPD;       // Pointer to print dialog
    BOOL m_bPreview;           // TRUE if in preview mode
    BOOL m_bDirect;            // TRUE if bypassing Print Dialog
    BOOL m_bContinuePrinting;// Set to FALSE to end printing
    UINT m_nCurPage;           // Current page
    UINT m_nNumPreviewPages; // Desired number of preview pages
    CString m_strPageDesc;     // Format string for page number display
    LPVOID m_lpUserData;       // Pointer to user created struct
    CRect m_rectDraw;          // Current usable page area
```

```
                // Access functions
                void SetMinPage(UINT nMinPage);
                void SetMaxPage(UINT nMaxPage);
                UINT GetMinPage() const;
                UINT GetMaxPage() const;
                UINT GetFromPage() const;
                UINT GetToPage() const;
        };
```

DoPreparePrinting runs the Print dialog. Besides setting the range of page numbers in the CPrintInfo object, DoPreparePrinting can exert modest control over the dialog by setting fields, such as Flags, in the PRINTDLG structure embedded within CPrintInfo. If the dialog is confirmed, it returns a device context for the selected printer.

OnBeginPrinting initializes the print cycle. It is a good place to allocate GDI objects needed for printing. It is also the first time you can get your hands on the device context for the printer. (But don't select objects into the device context here because the context will be reset at the start of each page.) If the application has a Page Setup command, OnBeginPrinting can set the requested printer attributes. See Section 13.4 for a discussion of Page Setup.

The Print-status dialog tells the user which page is being printed. In Win32, printing is spooled to a temporary file, so the dialog relates the state of spooling rather than the actual state of the printer.

The CDC functions StartDoc, StartPage, EndPage, and EndDoc are thin wrappers for Win32 calls to the printer driver. The driver sends the appropriate commands to the printer.

OnPrepareDC can play two roles: It can adjust the device context for the page and it can signal termination of printing. It is called during both printing and painting (that is, normal window update). Although you can distinguish between the two events by calling CDC::IsPrinting, OnPrint can be used for adjusting the device context specifically for printing.

Using OnPrepareDC to indicate print termination may strike you as slightly odd. Sometimes, an application doesn't know how many pages there are in a print job until it actually goes through the printing algorithm, since printer selection, page orientation, paper size, and margins all affect the length of a document. CPrintInfo has a flag member, m_bContinuePrinting, that is checked in OnFilePrint after calling OnPrepareDC. The default implementation of OnPrepareDC sets the flag to false if the maximum number of pages has not been set.

This forces printing to terminate after one page. For multiple-page documents, you'll need to set m_bContinuePrinting to true *after* calling the base class OnPrepareDC, for all but the last page.[1] See Section 13.5 for an example of multi-page printing.

Output begins in OnPrint. This is the appropriate place to select objects and adjust the device context specifically for printing, since OnPrint is called only during printing and previewing. This is also the place to output print-specific items like page headers.

For WYSIWYG (what-you-see-is-what-you-get) printing, OnPrint can call OnDraw and thus share code between printing and painting. Non-WYSIWYG and form-based applications need code specifically to draw during printing. For multi-page printing, get the current page being printed from CPrintInfo::m_nCurPage.

After all the pages are printed, OnEndPrinting gives the program an opportunity to clean up. In particular, GDI objects created in OnBeginPrinting should be deleted in OnEndPrinting.

13.2.2 Previewing

Even though it does not deal explicitly with the printer, previewing is considerably more complex than printing. To begin with, Preview juggles two devices—it renders an image on the screen based on attributes of the printer. It must also implement the preview window and its associated commands.

The process involves a few classes and objects internal to MFC, including the view class CPreviewView. The preview window is an instance of CPreviewView. During Preview, the preview window will be the currently active view, replacing the application's view window. Here is the beginning of the algorithm for a typical preview (again I've highlighted the virtual functions that you might override):

```
CView::OnFilePrintPreview()
    Create a CPreviewView object
    virtual CFrameWnd::OnSetPreviewMode
        Delete app's toolbars and views
        Create the preview window
    Create preview toolbar
    Make the CPreviewView object the current view
```

---

[1] You might expect setting the maximum page number by calling CPrintInfo::SetMaxPage would terminate printing automatically when the last page is reached. SetMaxPage is only effective if called before calling DoPreparePrinting.

```
CPreviewView::SetPrintView(CView* pPrintView)
    virtual CView::OnPreparePrinting(CPrintInfo* pInfo)
        virtual CView::DoPreparePrinting(CPrintInfo* pInfo)
            Set valid range for pages
            Get device context for default printer
            Set device context for preview window
    virtual CView::OnBeginPrinting(CDC* pDC, CPrintInfo* pInfo)
        Allocate GDI objects such as fonts
        Set printer attributes such as orientation or paper tray
Invalidate view window
```

Like OnFilePrint, OnFilePrintPreview exists in CView buts needs to be connected to a command via a message map. OnFilePrintPreview begins by creating the view object, the associated preview window, and the toolbar that sits above the window. The frame-class function OnSetPreviewMode deletes and restores the application's views and toolbars.[2]

Next, OnFilePrintPreview creates two device contexts, one for the current printer and one for the view. Preview needs both so that it can mimic the printer in the window.

OnBeginPrinting plays the same role during previewing that it does during printing. However, unlike printing, not all pages are output at once. Preview allows either one or two pages to be seen at a time. OnBeginPrinting invalidates the view window to trigger painting of the preview pages. The response to the WM_PAINT message begins in OnPaint:

```
CView::OnPaint
    CPreviewView::OnDraw(CDC* pDC)
        virtual CView::OnPrepareDC(CDC* pDC, CPrintInfo* pInfo)
        For each preview page
            Determine target rectangle
            Draw empty page
            Adjust mapping mode and clipping rectangle for paint DC
            virtual CView::OnPrint(CDC* pDC, CPrintInfo* pInfo)
                Print page header
                Select objects
                For WYSIWYG, call virtual CView::OnDraw
                Print page footer
```

---

[2] Prior to MFC 4.2, in an MDI application OnFilePrintPreview created the preview window as a child of the main frame. Beginning with 4.2, the preview window replaces the current view and thus is a child of the currently active frame window.

As usual, CView::OnPaint calls OnDraw for the current view, in this case CPreviewView. The device context passed to OnDraw is for the whole preview window. Each preview page is drawn within that window. The rectangle that defines the print area on the page is passed in CPrintInfo::m_rectDraw.

To scale the output so that it fits on the page, CPreviewView::OnDraw adjusts the mapping mode allowing OnPrint to proceed as it does for printing. Here is where previewing does its most intricate dance. When OnPrint makes a query about the device context, the answer should be given based on the printer. But when OnPrint draws on the device context, the output should go into the preview window. Seemingly, the same device context must refer to two devices.

MFC handles this division of behavior by having a CDC actually refer to two Win32 device contexts; the contexts are stored in m_hDC and m_hAttribDC. Usually, both of these members refer to the same device context, but during Preview, m_hAttribDC refers to the printer while m_hDC refers to the screen. Queries of the CDC use m_hAttribDC, but output commands use m_hDC. You can ignore this detail of CDC unless you need to query about the preview window or select an object based on the printer. The example of Section 13.5.1 illustrates one such case.

Usually, OnPrint executes the same code during previewing as during printing. If an application needs to distinguish printing from previewing, it can query the CPrintInfo::m_bPreview flag.

When the user exits Preview, the function CPreviewView::OnPreviewClose restores the application's views and toolbars:

```
CPreviewView::OnPreviewClose
    Destroy preview toolbar
    virtual CView::OnEndPrintPreview
        virtual CView::OnEndPrinting(CDC* pDC, CPrintInfo* pInfo)
            Delete GDI objects
        virtual CFrameWnd::SetPreviewMode
            Restore app's toolbars and views
    Destroy preview window
```

13.2.3 Printing and Previewing Edit Controls

As in using a CFormView, using a view based on CCtrlView is convenient since the control does most of the work (CCtrlView is described in Chapter 12). In particular, the control manages the data and paints the window. When it comes to printing, however, the standard algorithm needs modification.

The text-editor views, CEditView and CRichEditView, provide most of the needed modifications by overriding the virtual functions used for printing. Both types of views operate in a similar manner, although the implementation details are different. (See Section 13.5.1 for an example of printing a CCtrlView that does not have built-in support.)

To trigger printing or previewing, connect the message map entry for the command to the appropriate CView member function:[3]

```
ON_COMMAND(ID_FILE_PRINT, CEditView::OnFilePrint)
ON_COMMAND(ID_FILE_PRINT_PREVIEW, CEditView::OnFilePrintPreview)
```

CEditView overrides OnPreparePrinting with the necessary call to DoPreparePrinting:

```
BOOL CEditView::OnPreparePrinting(CPrintInfo* pInfo)
{
    return DoPreparePrinting(pInfo);
}
```

To print a CRichEditView you'll need to create your own copy of OnPreparePrinting.

Both of the editor views implement OnBeginPrinting. CEditView creates a printer font that corresponds to the font used in the control window. A rich-text control can display text in different fonts and with different attributes, so rendering the text on the printer is more complex. The rich-text control has built-in support for outputting formatted text to a device context. CRichEditView relies on that built-in functionality.

Both CEditView and CRichEditView trigger pagination in OnPrepareDC and set the CPrintInfo::m_bContinuePrinting flag appropriately. Both classes also override OnPrint to trigger printing. CRichEditView sets up the device context and then calls on the control to print. CEditView implements printing itself, since the basic edit control offers no support for printing.

One common extension to printing is support for print margins. (See Section 13.4 for a description of the Page Setup dialog for setting margins.) Adding margins is handled slightly differently for the two editor classes.

---

[3] Actually, CEditView does have a message-map entry for ID_FILE_PRINT but not for ID_FILE_PRINT_PREVIEW. CRichEditView has neither message-map entry. In any case, it is always safe to add the entries to an application's view class.

To set the margins for a CRichEditView, use the member function SetMargins. If the margins come from the Page Setup dialog, they'll be in thousandths of an inch or hundredths of a millimeter. You'll need to convert the margins to twips,[4] the unit required by SetMargins.

To set margins for a CEditView, override OnPrint. The CPrintInfo object passed to OnPrint contains the bounding rectangle, m_rectDraw, for output. Adjust the bounding rectangle by subtracting the margins from each edge. The rectangle is specified in device units, so again the margins may need to be transformed.

The Mdi\V3 program applies margins to a text view, which is constructed using CEditView. CPageSetupDialog::GetMargins retrieves the margins for the view in thousandths of an inch. OnPrint converts the margins to device units, sets the bounding rectangle for output, and then calls on the view to print:

```
void textView::OnPrint(CDC* pDC, CPrintInfo* pInfo)
{
    // Get margins
    CRect margins;
    m_pageSetupDlg.GetMargins(&margins,NULL);

    // Subtract converted margins from drawing area
    int horzRes = pDC->GetDeviceCaps(LOGPIXELSX);
    int vertRes = pDC->GetDeviceCaps(LOGPIXELSY);
    pInfo->m_rectDraw.left += ::MulDiv(horzRes,margins.left,1000);
    pInfo->m_rectDraw.right -= ::MulDiv(horzRes,margins.right,1000);
    pInfo->m_rectDraw.top += ::MulDiv(vertRes,margins.top,1000);
    pInfo->m_rectDraw.bottom -= ::MulDiv(vertRes,margins.bottom,1000);

    // Draw the text
    CEditView::OnPrint(pDC, pInfo);
}
```

pDC->GetDeviceCaps returns information about the attribute device—in this case, the printer. LOGPIXELSX and LOGPIXELSY are the number of pixels per inch along the X and Y axes. ::MulDiv multiplies its first two parameters to generate a 64-bit product, then divides that product by the third parameter. Thus, ::MulDiv(horzRes,margins.left,1000) computes the number of pixels for the left margin:

```
pixels-per-inch * left-margin-in-thousandths-of-an-inch / 1000
```

---

[4] A *twip* is nominally 1/20th of a point and thus about 1/1440th of an inch.

13.3 Example: WYSIWYG Printing

The framework provides the most support for single-page WYSIWYG printing. The same OnDraw function that paints on the screen draws the print preview and print output. If OnDraw uses a mapping mode other than MM_TEXT, the output will be scaled correctly for previewing and printing. However, because MM_TEXT specifies one logical unit per pixel, default printing using MM_TEXT will usually be too small, since printers typically have many more pixels per inch than displays.

The Mdi\V3 program implements WYSIWYG printing for graphics, scaling the image appropriately. The same function, grafView::OnDraw, outputs the drawing during previewing and printing:

```
void grafView::OnDraw(CDC* pDC)
{
    grafDoc* pDoc = GetDocument();
    ASSERT_VALID(pDoc);

    int count = pDoc->getCmdCount();

    for( int i=0; i<count; ++i ) {
        command *cp = pDoc->getCmd(i);
        shape *sp = theTool.getShape(cp->cmdShape);
        COLORREF rgbFill = theTool.getColor(cp->cmdFillColor);
        COLORREF rgbOutline = theTool.getColor(cp->cmdOutlineColor);
        sp->draw(pDC,cp->cmdRect,
            cp->cmdFill,rgbFill,
            rgbOutline,cp->cmdOutlineWidth);
    }
}
```

13.3.1 Scaling the Output to Fit

grafView draws using MM_TEXT mapping, so with no adjustment, the print and preview output would appear too small on the page. To compensate during printing, grafView scales the drawing so that the current view fills the output page. The result is that the printed image fills the page to the same extent that it fills the view (see Figure 13.1), but if the view window and the page have different aspect ratios, the image will appear distorted.

The device context used in OnDraw can be adjusted in any of three functions: OnPrepareDC, OnPrint, and OnDraw itself. OnPrepareDC and OnDraw are always called to render the view, regardless of the destination; OnPrint is called just during printing and previewing. Since grafView scales its output only during printing and previewing, OnPrint performs the adjustment:

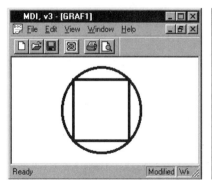

Figure 13.1   The image in the view is mapped to a page. If the aspect ratios of the view and page differ, the view will be distorted in the mapping, as in this picture.

```
void grafView::OnPrint(CDC* pDC, CPrintInfo* pInfo)
{
    CRect viewPort = m_pageSetupDlg.computeDrawRect(&pInfo->m_rectDraw);

    pDC->IntersectClipRect(&viewPort); // Clip to viewport

    // Scale drawing to fit in print rectangle
    pDC->SetMapMode(MM_ANISOTROPIC);
    pDC->SetWindowExt(m_clientRect.Width(),m_clientRect.Height());
    pDC->SetViewportExt(viewPort.Width(),viewPort.Height());
    pDC->SetViewportOrg(viewPort.TopLeft());

    CView::OnPrint(pDC, pInfo);
}
```

By setting the mapping mode to MM_ANISOTROPIC, the X and Y axes can be scaled independently. The coordinates of the view window, held in m_clientRect, are mapped to the coordinates that make up a page, represented by viewPort (see Figure 13.2).

In addition to scaling, one further refinement is necessary. Since the view window might not be showing the whole drawing, the output during printing may need to be clipped so that it doesn't overflow into the page margins. CDC::IntersectClipRect creates a new clipping rectangle for a device context that is the intersection between a specified rectangle and the current clipping rectangle.

The rectangles m_clientRect and viewPort both have their subtleties. m_clientRect is set to the size of the client area of the view window before printing or previewing begins:

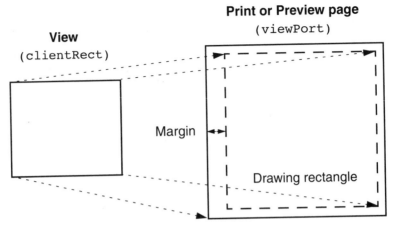

Figure 13.2 The client area of the view (clientRect) is mapped to the drawing rectangle inside the printed page or preview window (viewPort). The drawing rectangle is the page size less the margins.

```
void grafView::onFilePrintPreview()
{
    GetClientRect(&m_clientRect);
    CView::OnFilePrintPreview();
}
```

Why not just call GetClientRect in OnPrint? During Preview, the toolbar is changed to the Preview toolbar. When a toolbar is added or removed, existing views are resized since the amount of space left in the client area of the main frame may have changed. During Preview, therefore, GetClientRect may return a different rectangle than before Preview, even though the resized view is never seen.

viewPort contains the bounding rectangle for drawing. The CPrintInfo object passed to OnPrint also contains the bounding rectangle for the output, in m_rectDraw but we don't use it directly. computeDrawRect, called in OnPrint, adjusts the bounding rectangle for margins and paper size. The next section covers the details.

13.4 Example: Page Setup

The Page Setup common dialog presents a sample page that allows the user to select the paper, specify portrait or landscape orientation, and adjust the margins (see Figure 13.3).

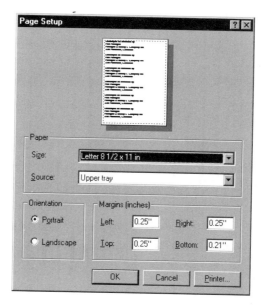

Figure 13.3 The Page Setup common dialog allows selection of paper and orientation, as well as adjustment of print margins.

The dialog partially duplicates the Print Setup dialog; both allow specification of paper size and orientation. Mdi\V3 uses the settings from Page Setup. It keeps separate settings for textView and grafView, allowing each type of document to have its own paper selection, margins, and orientation. The page setup settings are kept in a CPageSetupDialog member:

```
class textView : public CEditView
{
. . .
private:
   CPageSetupDialog m_pageSetupDlg;
};
```

The File Page Setup command runs the Page Setup dialog to get the paper selection and margins:

```
void textView::onFilePageSetup()
{
   m_pageSetupDlg.DoModal();
}
```

grafView has similar m_pageSetupDlg and onFilePageSetup members. It uses the class grafPageSetupDlg to extend CPageSetupDialog. Recall that for printing, grafView scales the drawing based on the size of the view window, the print rectangle, and the margins. The computation of the viewport is carried out in computeDrawRect:

```
CRect grafPageSetupDlg::computeDrawRect(LPRECT rawRect)
{
    // Get margins
    CRect margins;
    GetMargins(&margins,NULL);

    // Subtract converted margins from viewport
    CRect viewPort(rawRect);
    CSize pageSize = GetPaperSize();
    int viewWidth = viewPort.Width();
    int viewHeight = viewPort.Height();
    viewPort.left += ::MulDiv(viewWidth,margins.left,pageSize.cx);
    viewPort.right -= ::MulDiv(viewWidth,margins.right,pageSize.cx);
    viewPort.top += ::MulDiv(viewHeight,margins.top,pageSize.cy);
    viewPort.bottom -= ::MulDiv(viewHeight,margins.bottom,pageSize.cy);

    return viewPort;
}
```

Figure 13.4 illustrates the computation. rawRect is the drawing rectangle in logical units. Both the margins and the page size are kept in inches. computeDrawRect determines what fraction of the page is taken up by each margin and subtracts that fraction from each side of the drawing rectangle. viewPort thus contains the drawing rectangle, in logical units, after adjustment for margins.

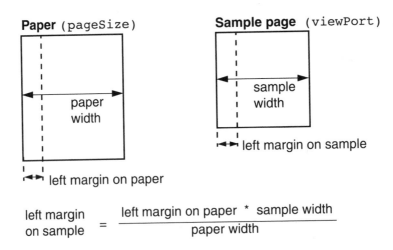

$$\text{left margin on sample} = \frac{\text{left margin on paper * sample width}}{\text{paper width}}$$

Figure 13.4   Margins for the sample page are determined by computing what fraction the margin occupies on the paper.

There is one potential problem with basing the drawing rectangle on values in
m_pageSetupDlg. It is important to make sure that m_pageSetupDlg contains
reasonable settings even if the setup dialog has not been run. The Mdi\V3 program initializes m_pageSetupDlg based on the current default printer:

```
textView::textView() :
    m_pageSetupDlg(PSD_MARGINS|PSD_INTHOUSANDTHSOFINCHES|PSD_RETURNDEFAULT)
{
    m_pageSetupDlg.DoModal(); // Get default printer attributes
    m_pageSetupDlg.m_psd.Flags &= ~PSD_RETURNDEFAULT;
}
```

When the PSD_RETURNDEFAULT flag is set, calling DoModal retrieves settings for the
default printer without actually running the Page Setup dialog.

13.4.1 Changing Printer Attributes

In addition to setting the margins, Page Setup allows changing attributes of the
current printer, such as paper size and page orientation. Attributes for a printer
are stored in a Win32 DEVMODE structure. If the user confirms the Page Setup
dialog, the dialog saves a pointer to the DEVMODE structure with the selected
attributes.

The standard File Print and Preview commands normally use the default
attributes for the printer. CDC::ResetDC changes the printer attributes for a
device context to those in its DEVMODE argument:

```
void grafView::OnBeginPrinting(CDC* pDC, CPrintInfo* pInfo)
{
    DEVMODE *devMode = pageSetupDlg.GetDevMode();
    if( devMode!=NULL )
        pDC->ResetDC(devMode); // Adjust printer attributes

    CView::OnBeginPrinting(pDC, pInfo);
}
```

13.4.2 Customizing Page Setup

Notice in Figure 13.3 that the sample window shows a page of text. While this is
an appropriate sample for textView, it is misleading for grafView. The graf-
View class illustrates a useful customization of Page Setup, taking control of
drawing the sample page.

The Page Setup common dialog can call an application-supplied function to draw the sample page. From MFC, derive a class from CPageSetupDialog and override the virtual function OnDrawPage to get control of the sample:

```
UINT grafPageSetupDlg::OnDrawPage(CDC *pDC,UINT nMessage,LPRECT lpRect)
{
    CRect sample = computeDrawRect(lpRect);

    pDC->Rectangle(&sample); // Show margins on sample page
    pDC->IntersectClipRect(&sample); // Clip output at margins

    // Scale drawing to fit on sample page
    pDC->SetMapMode(MM_ANISOTROPIC);
    CRect rect;
    m_curView->GetClientRect(&rect);
    pDC->SetWindowExt(rect.Width(),rect.Height());
    pDC->SetViewportExt(sample.Width(),sample.Height());
    pDC->SetViewportOrg(sample.TopLeft());

    m_curView->OnDraw(pDC);
    return 1;
}
```

As in printing and previewing, drawing the sample takes the page size, margins, and orientation into consideration by calling the computeDrawRect function described in Section 13.4. OnDrawPage shows the margins as a dotted rectangle and clips the output to the drawing area. Then it adjusts the device context to scale the drawing to the drawing rectangle of the sample page, allowing the sample image to be generated by calling OnDraw, just as for painting, printing, and previewing (see Figure 13.5).

13.5 Example: Multiple-Page Output

Multi-page printing requires a couple of extra considerations:

- How to control the printing loop
- How to control the Next Page, Prev Page, One Page, and Two Pages buttons during Preview (Figure 13.1 shows the layout of Print Preview)

If the page count is known in advance, call SetMaxPage in OnPreparePrinting to set the page range. The print loop in CView::OnFilePrint will terminate when the last page is reached. During Preview the UI update handlers for the preview buttons will test m_nCurPage against the first and last page to be printed, setting the Next and Previous buttons accordingly.

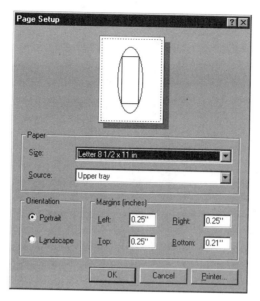

Figure 13.5 By overriding `CPageSetupDialog::OnDrawPage`, a program can customize the sample page.

If the page count isn't known in advance, you'll need to set `m_bContinuePrinting` in `OnPrepareDC` to control the print loop. Also, during Preview, set the maximum page as soon as it is known, to control the Preview buttons.

13.5.1 Printing a Control View

The Address Book program described in Chapter 12 uses a tree control to provide quick access to the address records. Like all controls, the tree control manages its own data and display. Unfortunately, tree controls offer no support for printing. When the focus is in the tree view, AddrBook responds to a Print or a Preview command by generating a complete dump of the address book (see Figure 13.6).

Printing and previewing are driven by the default command handlers:

```
BEGIN_MESSAGE_MAP(treeView, CTreeView)
    ON_COMMAND(ID_FILE_PRINT, CView::OnFilePrint)
    ON_COMMAND(ID_FILE_PRINT_PREVIEW, CView::OnFilePrintPreview)
    . . .
```

The implementation of printing and previewing for `treeView` requires overriding each of `CView`'s virtual functions for printing.

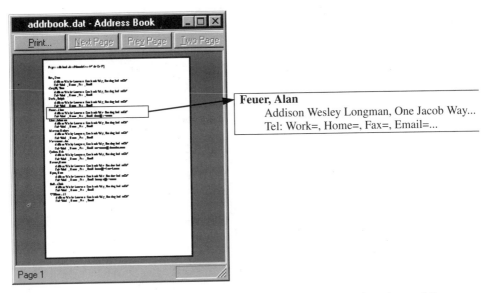

Figure 13.6   Printing or previewing the tree view generates a complete dump of the address book.

13.5.1.1 OnPreparePrinting

OnPreparePrinting does the minimal:

```
BOOL treeView::OnPreparePrinting(CPrintInfo* pInfo)
{
    return CTreeView::DoPreparePrinting(pInfo);
}
```

At this point, treeView doesn't know how many pages of output there will be, so it cannot set the page count.

13.5.1.2 OnBeginPrinting

Two fonts are used during printing, one for record titles and one for record bodies (see Figure 13.6). Corresponding CFont data members of treeView, m_bodyFont and m_titleFont, wrap the fonts. OnBeginPrinting creates the fonts appropriate for the printer:

```
void treeView::OnBeginPrinting(CDC* pDC, CPrintInfo* pInfo)
{
    // CreatePointFont interprets point size based on DC
    // Want size based on printer, so use printer DC
    CDC *printerDC = CDC::FromHandle(pDC->m_hAttribDC);
    m_bodyFont.CreatePointFont(120,_T("Times New Roman"),printerDC);
    LOGFONT logFont;
    m_bodyFont.GetLogFont(&logFont);
    logFont.lfWeight = FW_BOLD;
    m_titleFont.CreateFontIndirect(&logFont);

    m_recsPerPage = 0; // Don't know yet
    CTreeView::OnBeginPrinting(pDC, pInfo);
}
```

The body font is Times New Roman 12 point. CFont::CreatePointFont simplifies the task of creating a font of a given logical size. It uses the specified device context to determine what size the physical font needs to be—that is, it computes the size of the font in pixels. However, we can't use pDC for the device context, since pDC refers to the *screen* during printing. To guarantee the font is chosen correctly for the printer, and thus scaled correctly during Preview, the attribute device context is used. printerDC is a temporary CDC wrapper for the attribute device context.

The title font is a bold version of the body font. To create the title font, first the logical font for the body is retrieved, the font weight set to bold, and then the new font is created from the modified logical font by calling Create-FontIndirect.

The treeView member m_recsPerPage will hold the number of address records that fit on a page. At this point we don't know the size of the print rectangle, since CPrintInfo::m_rectDraw hasn't been set yet. m_recsPerPage is set to zero to indicate "not known".

13.5.1.3 OnPrepareDC

Because the program didn't set the page count in OnPreparePrinting, OnPrepareDC will be responsible for terminating the print loop:

```
void treeView::OnPrepareDC(CDC* pDC, CPrintInfo* pInfo)
{
    CTreeView::OnPrepareDC(pDC, pInfo);
    pInfo->m_bContinuePrinting =
        pInfo->m_nCurPage <= pInfo->GetMaxPage();
}
```

In the normal case, we want to continue printing as long as the current page is a valid page number. (OnPrepareDC is called *before* m_nCurPage is printed.) But if we don't know how long the document is, how do we know if the current page is valid?

An assumption is made that there is at least one page. Since the program hasn't set the maximum page yet, GetMaxPage returns its initial value of 0xFFFF. In OnPrint, the size of the drawing rectangle will finally be known, so we can compute the page count there.

Notice one last thing about OnPrepareDC. It sets m_bContinuePrinting after calling the base class OnPrepareDC. This is important as the default behavior for OnPrepareDC is to set m_bContinuePrinting to true or false, depending on whether the maximum page number has been set.

13.5.1.4 OnPrint

Printing a tree view is not WYSIWYG, so OnPrint creates the output. It's a long function, so I'll treat it in sections. OnPrint begins by outputting a page header containing the page number, data-file name, and current date:

```
void treeView::OnPrint(CDC* pDC, CPrintInfo* pInfo)
{
    CTime now = CTime::GetCurrentTime();
    CString buf;

    // Output page header
    buf.Format(_T("Page %d %s (Printed %s)"),
        pInfo->m_nCurPage,
        GetDocument()->GetTitle(),
        now.Format(_T("%c")));
    CFont *prevFont = (CFont *)pDC->SelectObject(&m_bodyFont);
    pDC->TextOut(0,0,buf);
```

The output will be printed a line at a time, so we need to compute the height of each line. The physical font determines the line height in device units:

```
    document *pDoc = GetDocument();

    // Compute the height of each line
    TEXTMETRIC tm;
    pDC->GetTextMetrics(&tm);
    int lineHeight = tm.tmHeight+tm.tmExternalLeading;
    int indent = tm.tmAveCharWidth*5;
    int y = 3*lineHeight;
```

The local variable y holds the current Y position on the page. It starts three lines down to reserve space for the page header.

Now that we know the line height, the number of records per page and the page count can be computed:

```
if( m_recsPerPage==0 ) {  // Compute number of records per page
    m_recsPerPage = pInfo->m_rectDraw.Height() / (3*lineHeight) -1;
    pInfo->SetMaxPage( pDoc->getRecCount()/m_recsPerPage + 1);
}
```

Finally, the records themselves can be output. The variable i holds the record number to output and limit contains one greater than the last record for the page:

```
int i = (pInfo->m_nCurPage-1) * m_recsPerPage;
int limit = i+m_recsPerPage;
if( limit > pDoc->getRecCount() ) {
    limit = pDoc->getRecCount();
}
```

Outputting the records is a matter of formatting each line of text, selecting the correct font, and writing the text using CDC::TextOut:

```
// Output records
address ad;
for( ; i<limit; ++i ) {
    pDoc->getAddr(i,ad);
    buf.Format(_T("%s, %s"),ad.lastName,ad.firstName);
    pDC->SelectObject(&m_titleFont);
    pDC->TextOut(0,y,buf);
    y += lineHeight;

    buf.Format(_T("%s, %s, %s %s %s"),
        ad.company, ad.streetAddress, ad.city, ad.state, ad.zip);
    pDC->SelectObject(&m_bodyFont);
    pDC->TextOut(indent,y,buf);
    y += lineHeight;

    buf.Format(_T("Tel: Work=%s, Home=%s, Fax=%s, Email=%s"),
        ad.workPhone, ad.homePhone, ad.fax, ad.email);
    pDC->TextOut(indent,y,buf);
    y += lineHeight;
}

pDC->SelectObject(prevFont);
}
```

When OnPrint completes, it is important that the current font selected for pDC be neither m_titleFont nor m_bodyFont. Both fonts will be deleted before the device context is destroyed. A basic commandment of Win32 programming is: Thou shall not delete a currently selected GDI object.

13.5.1.5 OnEndPrinting

The primary job of OnEndPrinting is to delete the GDI objects created in OnBeginPrinting:

```
void treeView::OnEndPrinting(CDC* pDC, CPrintInfo* pInfo)
{
    bodyFont.DeleteObject();
    titleFont.DeleteObject();
    CTreeView::OnEndPrinting(pDC, pInfo);
}
```

13.6   Example: Printing a Form

When the focus is in the form view of AddrBook, Print and Preview output the current address in the upper-left corner of the printed page (suitable for printing on a note card; see Figure 13.7). As for the tree view, during painting the address is output by the controls in the form; during printing and previewing the address must be output by the application.

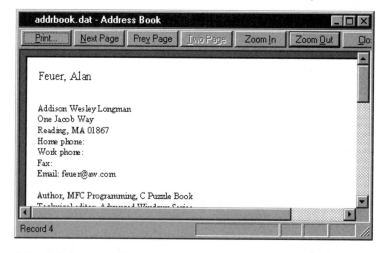

Figure 13.7   Printing or previewing the form view puts the current record in the upper-left corner of the page.

In many ways, printing the form is similar to printing the report illustrated in the previous section. Accordingly, rather than show all the details, I'll just point out the highlights.

Like treeView, formView uses the standard Print and Preview command handlers. However, OnPreparePrinting has a few new wrinkles.

13.6.1 OnPreparePrinting

formView prints one record per page. As it can query the document to determine how many records are in the address book, it knows the page count right from the start. In addition, it sets the current page to correspond to the record shown on the form:

```
BOOL formView::OnPreparePrinting(CPrintInfo* pInfo)
{
    pInfo->SetMaxPage(GetDocument()->getRecCount());
    pInfo->m_nCurPage = GetDocument()->getCurrentIndex()+1;
. . .
```

During Preview, the Next Page and Prev Page buttons pull up the next and previous records. A nice touch is to change the status-bar text to say "Record" instead of "Page". Continuing in OnPreparePrinting:

```
    BOOL retval;
    if( pInfo->m_bPreview || pInfo->m_bDirect ) {
        // Preview or shell command
        retval = CFormView::DoPreparePrinting(pInfo);
        pInfo->m_strPageDesc = _T("Record %u\nRecord %u-%u\n");
. . .
```

You can see that CPrintInfo.m_strPageDesc contains a text string with two fields separated by a newline. The first field is used for single-page preview, the second for two-page preview.

Although users of AddrBook might want occasionally to print all the records, a more common alternative is to print only the current record. To make printing the current page the default, set both the From and To fields in the Print dialog to the current page number and select the Pages radio button in the Print Range group box (see Figure 13.8). Again, continuing in OnPreparePrinting:

```
    } else {
        // For printing, set initial page range to current page
        pInfo->m_pPD->m_pd.nFromPage = pInfo->m_pPD->m_pd.nToPage
            = pInfo->m_nCurPage;
        pInfo->m_pPD->m_pd.Flags |= PD_PAGENUMS;
        retval = theApp.DoPrintDialog(pInfo->m_pPD)==IDOK;
    }

    return retval;
}
```

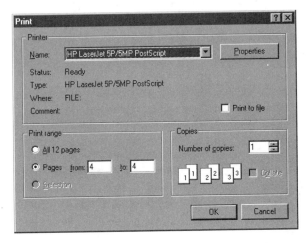

Figure 13.8 The Print range in the Print dialog is initialized to the current page.

During printing, `CView::DoPreparePrinting` invokes the Print dialog by calling a public but undocumented function in `CWinApp` called `DoPrintDialog`. Unfortunately, `DoPreparePrinting` also clobbers `nFromPage` and `nToPage`, so it must be circumvented to print just the current page.

13.6.2 OnPrint

Like `treeView`, `formView` uses two fonts in its print output: one for the page title and one for the page body. `OnBeginPrinting` creates the fonts and `OnEndPrinting` deletes them.

`OnPrint` queries the document for the current record and then outputs the record text. Again, the code is similar to that for `treeView`:

```
    void formView::OnPrint(CDC* pDC, CPrintInfo* pInfo)
{
    address ad;
    GetDocument()->getAddr(pInfo->m_nCurPage-1,ad);

    // Output card title
    CString buf;
    buf.Format(_T("%s, %s"),ad.lastName,ad.firstName);
    CFont *prevFont = (CFont *)pDC->SelectObject(&m_titleFont);
    pDC->TextOut(0,0,buf);

    pDC->SelectObject(&m_bodyFont);
    TEXTMETRIC tm;
    pDC->GetTextMetrics(&tm);
    int lineHeight = tm.tmHeight+tm.tmExternalLeading;
    int y = 3*lineHeight;

    // Output card details
. . .
```

One way in which printing differs from painting is in the comments field. In the address structure, the comment is stored as a CString. On-screen, comments are kept in an edit control. formView relies on the edit control to break the string into lines. CDC::DrawText has similar functionality, so OnPrint uses it instead of TextOut:

```
    CRect rect(0,y,pInfo->m_rectDraw.Width(),
        pInfo->m_rectDraw.Height());
    pDC->DrawText(ad.comments,&rect,
        DT_EXPANDTABS|DT_WORDBREAK|DT_NOCLIP);

    pDC->SelectObject(prevFont);
}
```

As before, the local variable y holds the current line position and m_rectDraw contains the bounding rectangle for output.

13.6.3 Controlling the Status Bar During Preview

In Section 13.6.1, you saw code in OnPreparePrinting for changing the text on the status bar during previewing. Since the current view is the CPreviewView, status bar panes for the application's views will be disabled automatically if there are default handlers in the main frame as described in Chapter 11. However, the application's document remains active. Any update handlers in the current document will continue to be called during Preview.

In AddrBook, the document puts the current record number in the status bar. Preview has a different notion of record number, so it would be confusing for the document's number to appear on the status bar as well. Somehow, the document needs to know that the current view is a preview window instead of a formView or treeView.

One solution is to move the update handler for the record number out of document and into the views, but this would require duplicating the code in each view. Another solution is to override the virtual function CFrameWnd-::OnSetPreviewMode.

CView calls OnSetPreviewMode to take over and give up drawing of the frame's client area. Unfortunately, the frame doesn't keep track of whether it is in preview mode. By intercepting the call to OnSetPreviewMode, the application can keep its own flag:

```
void mainFrame::OnSetPreviewMode(BOOL bPreview,
    CPrintPreviewState* pState)
{
    theApp.m_previewMode = bPreview;
    CFrameWnd::OnSetPreviewMode(bPreview, pState);
}
```

When the preview flag is set, the document disables its record-indicator pane:

```
void document::onUpdateRecordUI(CCmdUI *pCmdUI)
{
    if( m_currentAddr>=0 && !theApp.m_previewMode ) {
        CString buf;
        buf.Format(_T("Record %d of %d"),
            m_currentAddr+1,
            m_addrBook.GetSize());
        pCmdUI->SetText(buf);
        pCmdUI->Enable(TRUE);

    } else pCmdUI->Enable(FALSE);
}
```

Part III: Extended Examples

CHAPTER

14 | Dialog-Based Applications

The programs in the `Hangman` and `Wizard` directories illustrate the concepts discussed in this chapter. The corresponding executables are `Hangman.exe` in the `bin` directory and `Install.exe` in the root directory.

14.1 Introduction

Some programs are most easily implemented as a collection of dialogs. Task-centered applications, such as installation and data-entry programs fit this model. Other programs with a simple internal structure can also be built from dialogs. Games often fall into this category, such as the Hangman game illustrated in this chapter.

Once you learn how easy it is to create programs from dialogs, you may be tempted to force all your programs into the dialog mold. This is a poor decision for many programs. Dialogs do not have much framework support for command handling and they encourage a simplistic treatment of data. Furthermore, when a dialog-based program becomes unmanageably complex, you'll get little help from the standard development tools to reorganize the program to use documents and views.

A dialog-based program runs in `CWinApp::InitInstance`. Here is the top-level flow of control:

```
::WinMain
    Call CWinApp::InitInstance
        Create dialog object
        Initialize dialog data
        Call DoModal
            Dialog runs
            May carry out tasks based on user choices
        If user presses OK
            May carry out tasks based on data
```

Unlike all other MFC programs we've looked at, dialog programs never execute CWinApp::Run. They still have a message loop; they use the one triggered by DoModal.

To create a dialog-based program, create the initial structure using a program generator, such as AppWizard. It should generate two classes, an application class and a dialog class. In the application, class you'll need to modify Init-Instance, filling in behavior based on whether the dialog was confirmed or canceled.

The bulk of the application code resides in the dialog class or classes. From here on, writing the program consists of creating dialogs. The program generator will create a simple dialog resource to get you started. Add controls and corresponding member variables, compile the program, and execute![1]

14.2 Hangman: A Dialog-Based Game

The Hangman program chooses a word randomly from a word list, displays one empty slot for each letter in the word, and then accepts guesses. The player's goal, of course, is to guess the chosen word. For each guessed letter that appears in the word, Hangman places the letter in the corresponding slot or slots. Each guess that is not in the word results in adding another piece to the hanging man. Figure 14.1 shows a game in progress.

Overall, the program is typical of a dialog-based program. There is an application class and one dialog class, and the program runs in InitInstance. The

---

[1] The code generated by AppWizard for the dialog class includes handlers for two messages that may surprise you: WM_PAINT and WM_QUERYDRAGICON. They are included for compatibility with the old Program Manager interface in which programs are responsible for drawing their own icons.

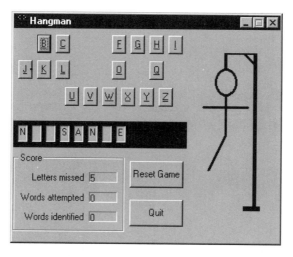

Figure 14.1   A game of Hangman in progress

word list is kept in the application class and the game statistics are kept as class variables in the dialog.

Here is the top-level algorithm:

```
InitInstance
    Read words from file
    Choose a word
    Loop: Create dialog object, initialize word to guess
        Call DoModal
            Play the game
        If the player wants to play again, goto Loop
        else quit
```

14.2.1 The Application Class

The application class, hangmanApp, reads the word list and then triggers the dialog. Here is its declaration:

```
class hangmanApp : public CWinApp
{
public:
    hangmanApp();

// Overrides
    // ClassWizard generated virtual function overrides
    //{{AFX_VIRTUAL(hangmanApp)
    public:
    virtual BOOL InitInstance();
    virtual int ExitInstance();
    //}}AFX_VIRTUAL
```

```
// Implementation
 . . .
private:
    CStringArray m_words;
    BOOL readWords();
}
```

The words are stored as a collection using the class CStringArray. Since the word list can be long, we'll get much better performance if we tell the array how to grow:

```
hangmanApp::hangmanApp()
{
    m_words.SetSize(0,24000);
}
```

The parameters to SetSize specify the initial size of the array and the number of elements to grow by. When the first word is added, the array will grow to 24,000 elements.[2] Specifying a smaller number could require that the list be reallocated several times. Depending upon the implementation of the collection, reallocation can be an expensive undertaking if it requires destructing and constructing each element.

Most of the action is in InitInstance. First, the word list is read from a text file, one word per line:

```
BOOL hangmanApp::InitInstance()
{
    if( !readWords() ) {
        AfxMessageBox(_T("Cannot read word list"));
        return FALSE;
    }
```

We haven't used standard I/O before, so I'll describe it briefly. The MFC class CStdioFile wraps the ANSI C file functions. CStdioFile is derived from the more general CFile, which defines an enumeration of file types and modes, such as typeText and modeRead used in readWords.

readWords opens the word-list file as text, then reads the file one line at a time. If the text read is longer than two characters but not longer than MaxLetters, it is added to the array of words:

---

[2] The word list in the Hangman directory contains about 22,000 words.

```
BOOL hangmanApp::readWords()
{
    try {
        CStdioFile file(_T("words.txt"),CFile::typeText|CFile::modeRead);
        CString word;
        while( file.ReadString(word) ) {
            if( word.GetLength()<=MaxLetters && word.GetLength()>2 )
                m_words.Add(word);
        }
    } catch(CException *e) {
        e->Delete();
    }

    m_words.FreeExtra();
    return m_words.GetSize();
}
```

As mentioned above, the words array grows by chunks. After the word list has been read, words won't grow any further, so the excess memory is freed by the call to FreeExtra.[3]

In the unlikely case that the program cannot get memory to grow the array, the call to Add may trigger a memory exception. The exception is caught, so rather than aborting, Hangman will continue as long as some words were read. Exceptions in MFC generate CException objects on the heap. Unless the exception is rethrown, free the object by calling Delete.

A word is chosen from the array of words based on the system time. The chosen word is passed in the constructor to the dialog:

```
BOOL hangmanApp::InitInstance()
{
. . .
    DWORD i = ::GetTickCount() % words.GetSize();

    for(;;) {
        hangmanDlg dlg(words[i],frame);
        CString buf;
```

We'll look at initializing and running the dialog in the next section. The dialog returns one of four values through DoModal. Continuing in InitInstance:

---

[3] If you run Hangman in the debugger, you may notice that it takes a while to start up and shut down. MFC keeps track of operations in dynamic memory so that it can detect memory leaks. As a result, the word list takes a noticeable amount of time to construct and delete. On my system, Hangman loads outside the debugger in one fourth the time it takes inside the debugger.

```
                hangmanDlg dlg(m_words[i],NULL);
                CString buf;

                switch( dlg.DoModal() ) {
                case IDCANCEL:                  // Exit
                    return FALSE;

                case IDYES:                     // Success, next word
                    i = ::GetTickCount() % m_words.GetSize();
                    break;

                case IDC_NewWord:               // Failure, next word
                    buf.Format(_T("The word was %s"),(LPCTSTR)m_words[i]);
                    AfxMessageBox(buf,MB_ICONINFORMATION);
                    i = ::GetTickCount() % m_words.GetSize();
                    break;

                case IDC_Restart:               // Same word again
                    break;
                }

        return FALSE;  // Never reached
    }
```

If the user pressed Quit, DoModal returns IDCANCEL and InitInstance returns false to tell WinMain to quit. Before exiting, WinMain calls the virtual function CWinApp::ExitInstance. ExitInstance is overloaded to clean up the array of words:[4]

```
    int hangmanApp::ExitInstance()
    {
        m_words.RemoveAll();
        return CWinApp::ExitInstance();
    }
```

For all other return values from DoModal, the dialog is restarted, perhaps with a different word. A program optimization would be to create a reinitialization function in the dialog class to reset the controls and data structures without having to destroy and recreate the dialog. This would yield slightly crisper performance and the dialog frame wouldn't flash when changing words.

---

[4] Although not strictly necessary because the memory will be freed when the process terminates, it is good practice for a program to free what it allocates.

14.2.2 The Dialog Class

The heart of the program code resides in the dialog class, hangmanDlg. It

- Responds to the controls
- Maintains game statistics
- Evaluates the current game state, detecting success or failure when either occurs
- Updates the gallows, letters guessed, and letters identified

The game statistics are maintained in the dialog class. Some of the variables are declared static so that they persist across instantiations of the dialog:

```
class hangmanDlg : public CDialog
{
. . .
// Dialog Data
private:
    static int wordsIdentified;
    static int wordsAttempted;
    static int lettersMissed;
    CBitmap m_bitmap;    // Current gallows bitmap
    CString m_word;      // The word to be guessed
    BOOL m_letter[26];   // The letters that have been guessed
    int m_misses;        // The number of incorrect guesses
    int m_hits;          // The number of letters found
```

The static variables are defined and initialized in the implementation file:

```
int hangmanDlg::wordsAttempted = 0;
int hangmanDlg::wordsIdentified = 0;
int hangmanDlg::lettersMissed = 0;
```

14.2.2.1 The Dialog Resource

Before looking deeper into the implementation, I want to point out a few things about the dialog resource. Here are some excerpts from hangman.rc:

```
IDD_HANGMAN DIALOGEX 0, 0, 227, 162
. . .
BEGIN
    PUSHBUTTON      "&A",IDC_A,4,4,12,14
    PUSHBUTTON      "&B",IDC_B,20,4,12,14
. . .

    PUSHBUTTON      "&Y",IDC_Y,108,44,12,14
    PUSHBUTTON      "&Z",IDC_Z,124,44,12,14
    CONTROL         "",IDC_STATIC,"Static",SS_BLACKRECT,0,70,148,20
. . .
```

```
        CONTROL      "",IDC_Gallows,"Static",SS_BITMAP,160,10,15,13
        CTEXT        "",IDC_Word1,4,74,8,12,SS_SUNKEN
        CTEXT        "",IDC_Word2,16,74,8,12,SS_SUNKEN
    . . .

        CTEXT        "",IDC_Word11,124,74,8,12,SS_SUNKEN
        CTEXT        "",IDC_Word12,136,74,8,12,SS_SUNKEN
        GROUPBOX     "Score",IDC_STATIC,0,94,95,60
        RTEXT        "Letters missed",IDC_STATIC,5,109,55,8
        LTEXT        "Static",IDC_LettersMissed,65,109,24,8,SS_SUNKEN
    . . .
    END
```

The button for each alphabetic letter has an ID that corresponds to the letter using the formula

```
    ID = 'x' - 'a' + IDC_A
```

for the letter x. Notice that the label for each button contains an ampersand (&), making the letter a mnemonic for the button. As a result, the game can be played by typing letters on the keyboard.

The slots for the letters in the word to guess have a similar relationship; they are sequential from IDC_Word1 through IDC_Word12. Each slot is a static text control and all the slots sit on top of a black rectangle.

The game statistics are also displayed in text controls and surrounded by a group box. The gallows is a static control with the style SS_BITMAP. The bitmap will be wholly replaced in response to incorrect guesses.

14.2.2.2 Initialization

The target word is held in the CString variable m_word. On construction of the hangmanDlg object, the target word is recorded and converted to upper case. Also, the icon for the application is loaded and its handle put in a data member of the dialog so that it can be attached to the dialog frame window:

```
hangmanDlg::hangmanDlg(CString s,CWnd *parent)
    : m_word(s), CDialog(hangmanDlg::IDD,parent)
{
    //{{AFX_DATA_INIT(hangmanDlg)
        // NOTE: the ClassWizard will add member initialization here
    //}}AFX_DATA_INIT
    // Note that LoadIcon doesn't require subsequent DestroyIcon in Win32
    m_hIcon = AfxGetApp()->LoadIcon(IDR_MAINFRAME);
    m_word.MakeUpper();
}
```

Initialization of the dialog is a little messy, although the icon and most of the menu code was generated by AppWizard. It starts off by adding an About menu item to the system menu, since the dialog box does not have a menu bar. I added code to remove the Maximize menu item, since the Hangman dialog doesn't benefit from being maximized:

```
BOOL hangmanDlg::OnInitDialog()
{
    CDialog::OnInitDialog();

    // Add "About..." menu item to system menu.
    // IDM_ABOUTBOX must be in the system command range.
    ASSERT((IDM_ABOUTBOX & 0xFFF0) == IDM_ABOUTBOX);
    ASSERT(IDM_ABOUTBOX < 0xF000);

    CMenu* pSysMenu = GetSystemMenu(FALSE);
    CString strAboutMenu;
    strAboutMenu.LoadString(IDS_ABOUTBOX);
    if (!strAboutMenu.IsEmpty())
    {
        pSysMenu->AppendMenu(MF_SEPARATOR);
        pSysMenu->AppendMenu(MF_STRING, IDM_ABOUTBOX, strAboutMenu);
    }

    // Delete Maximize menu item
    pSysMenu->DeleteMenu(SC_MAXIMIZE,MF_BYCOMMAND);
```

Next, OnInitDialog sets the large and small icons for the dialog frame window. Since the dialog frame *is* the main window, the small icon for the dialog will be shown on the task bar:

```
    // Set the icon for this dialog. The framework does this automatically
    // when the application's main window is not a dialog
    SetIcon(m_hIcon, TRUE);      // Set big icon
    SetIcon(m_hIcon, FALSE);     // Set small icon
```

The dialog maintains an array of guessed letters. When a letter is guessed, its button is hidden. Initially, no letters have been guessed, so all the buttons are visible:

```
    for( int i=0; i<26; ++i ) {
        m_letter[i] = FALSE;
        CWnd *button = GetDlgItem(IDC_A+i);
        button->ShowWindow(SW_SHOWNORMAL);
    }
    m_hits = m_misses = 0;
```

The dialog displays one slot for each letter in the target word. This loop establishes the correct number of empty slots:

```
        for( i=0; i<MaxLetters; ++i ) {
            CWnd *slot = GetDlgItem(IDC_Word1+i);
            slot->ShowWindow( i<m_word.GetLength() ?
                SW_SHOWNORMAL : SW_HIDE);
        }
```

Finally, the initial score is displayed:

```
        updateScore();

        return TRUE; // return TRUE  unless you set the focus to a control
    }
```

14.2.2.3 Handling a Guess

Like all buttons, a letter button generates a WM_COMMAND message when it is pressed. I could have created 26 ON_COMMAND message-map entries to handle the letter buttons, but since the buttons have sequential IDs, it's easier to pick off the commands using the ON_COMMAND_RANGE macro:

```
    BEGIN_MESSAGE_MAP(hangmanDlg, CDialog)
    . . .
        ON_COMMAND_RANGE(IDC_A,IDC_Z,onLetter)
    END_MESSAGE_MAP()
```

The handler onLetter receives the ID of the pressed button as a parameter:

```
    void hangmanDlg::onLetter(UINT letterID)
    {
        CWnd *button = GetDlgItem(letterID);
        button->ShowWindow(SW_HIDE);
        button->EnableWindow(FALSE);  // Disable keyboard key
```

The first thing onLetter does is hide the button that was pressed because that letter cannot be entered again. It also disables input to the button window, which eliminates the mnemonic for the letter.

The next job is to test whether the letter guessed is in the target word:

```
        if( test('A' + letterID-IDC_A) ) {  // A hit
```

The function test compares the guessed letter with each letter in the target word. Since the letter may appear more than once in the word, the loop iterates over all the letters in the word:

```
    BOOL hangmanDlg::test(char guess)
    {
        BOOL anyHits = FALSE;
```

```
    for( int i=0; i<m_word.GetLength(); ++i ) {
        if( guess == m_word[i] ) {
            CWnd *slot = GetDlgItem(i+IDC_Word1);
            slot->SetWindowText( CString(guess) );
            slot->UpdateWindow();
            anyHits = TRUE;
            ++m_hits;
        }
    }
    return anyHits;
}
```

If a match is found, the text for the corresponding slot is set to the letter and the slot is redrawn. test returns true if the guessed letter was found in the target word.

Back in onLetter, if the guess was successful, a check is made to see if all the letters in the word have been guessed:

```
if( test('A' + letterID-IDC_A) ) {  // A hit
    if( solved() ) {
        ++wordsAttempted;
        ++wordsIdentified;
        updateScore();
        int response = AfxMessageBox(
            _T("Congratulations!\nWould you like to play again?"),
            MB_YESNO|MB_ICONQUESTION);
        if( response==IDYES ) EndDialog(IDYES);
        else EndDialog(IDCANCEL);
    }
```

If solved returns true, the statistics are updated and the user is offered the option of trying another word.

If the guessed letter is not in the word, the next piece of the gallows is drawn. The gallows is represented by a series of bitmaps drawn in a static control. To draw the bitmap, two data members were added to the dialog: a CBitmap to hold the current bitmap and a CStatic wrapper for the control:

```
class hangmanDlg : public CDialog
{
. . .
    CBitmap bitmap;  // Current gallows bitmap
. . .
    //{{AFX_DATA(hangmanDlg)
    enum { IDD = IDD_HANGMAN };
    CStaticm_gallows;
    //}}AFX_DATA
```

The variable m_gallows is attached to the underlying control in DoDataExchange:

```
void hangmanDlg::DoDataExchange(CDataExchange* pDX)
{
    CDialog::DoDataExchange(pDX);
    //{{AFX_DATA_MAP(hangmanDlg)
    DDX_Control(pDX, IDC_Gallows, m_gallows);
    //}}AFX_DATA_MAP
}
```

Back in onLetter, to draw the gallows, the bitmap data is loaded and then attached to the static control:

```
void hangmanDlg::onLetter(UINT letterID)
{
    . . .
    if( solved() ) {
    . . .
    } else {  // A miss
        ++lettersMissed;
        updateScore();

        m_bitmap.DeleteObject();
        if( m_bitmap.LoadBitmap(IDB_Gallows + m_misses++) ) {
            m_gallows.SetBitmap((HBITMAP)m_bitmap.m_hObject);
            m_gallows.UpdateWindow();
        }
```

Like the letter buttons and the word slots, the gallows bitmaps have sequential IDs so that they can be addressed using an offset from the first ID, IDB_Gallows.

If enough wrong guesses have been made to hang the man, the score is updated and the user given an option to try again, attempt a new word, or quit:

```
        if( m_misses>=MaxMisses ) {  // Man is hung
            ++wordsAttempted;
            updateScore();
            int response = AfxMessageBox(
                _T("Too bad\nWould you like to try again?"),
                MB_YESNO|MB_ICONQUESTION);
            if( response==IDYES ) EndDialog(IDC_Restart);
            else EndDialog(IDC_NewWord);
        }
    }
}
```

The parameter to EndDialog becomes the return value from DoModal in hangmanApp::InitInstance.

14.3 Wizard: A Dialog-Based Installation Program

Wizard is a simple installation program.[5] It asks the user for a destination
directory and a set of programs to install, then it copies the programs to the
specified directory. It is task-centered—the program decides the sequence of
events. Wizard is implemented using a collection of dialogs embedded in a
property sheet. The property sheet operates in *wizard mode,* with the familiar
Back, Next, and Finish buttons at the bottom of the dialog. Each step through
the property sheet is implemented as a property page. Figure 14.2 shows the
opening page of the dialog.

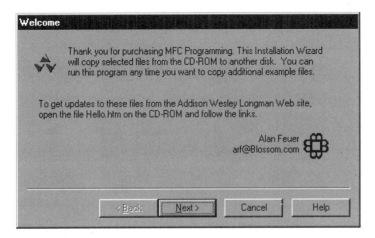

Figure 14.2   The opening page of the Wizard property sheet

Even though the operation of Wizard is much simpler than Hangman, the implementation is more complex. Wizard uses these classes:

wizard	The application
mainFrame	The main window, used for coloring the background
wizardSheet	The property sheet
start, installDir, select, end	The property pages
checkListBox	Implements a safe check-list box
browseDlg	Implements a directory browser
data	Holds data to drive the installation process

---

[5] Wizard is the install program for the programs in this text. It is in the root directory of the
accompanying disk as the file Install.exe.

14.3.1 The Application Class

The purpose of the dialog is to gather information that will be used to guide the installation. The global data resides in the application class, `wizardApp`:

```
class wizardApp : public CWinApp
{
public:
    wizardApp();
    int getTopic(int index) { return selected[index]; }
    int getTopicCnt()       { return selected.GetSize(); }
    void clearTopics()      { selected.RemoveAll(); }
    void addTopic(int index){ selected.Add(index); }

// Overrides
    // ClassWizard generated virtual function overrides
    //{{AFX_VIRTUAL(wizardApp)
    public:
    virtual BOOL InitInstance();
    //}}AFX_VIRTUAL
. . .

// Implementation
    CString m_destDir;      // Destination for files to be copied
. . .
    CUIntArray m_selected;  // Indexes of selected topics
};
```

The class data, described in Section 14.3.1.1, contains an array of programs that can be installed. The indexes of the selected topics are kept in the CUint-Array m_selected. The access functions getTopic, getTopicCnt, clearTopics, and addTopic manipulate the array of selected topics.

The application class also contains the program's "main" function, InitInstance:

```
BOOL wizardApp::InitInstance()
{
    m_pMainWnd = new mainFrame;
    m_pMainWnd->PostMessage(WM_NCACTIVATE,TRUE);
        // Normally, when a modal dialog is posted, the parent
        // is drawn inactive.  This call makes it look active
```

Wizard covers the screen with its own background. InitInstance creates a main window whose sole job is to draw the background. The PostMessage call tells the main window to make its title bar look active.

Next, InitInstance creates the property sheet and turns on wizard mode. The property pages are added in the constructor of the sheet (see Section 14.3.1.1).

```
wizardSheet sheet(_T("Source Code Installation"));
sheet.SetWizardMode();
```

Once the sheet is created, it can be run by calling DoModal:

```
sheet.DoModal();

m_pMainWnd->DestroyWindow();
// Since the dialog has been closed, return FALSE so
// that we exit the application, rather than start the
// application's message pump.
return FALSE;
}
```

If the user presses Finish on the last page of the dialog, the selected files are copied. By the time DoModal returns, there is nothing left to do except destroy the main window.

14.3.1.1 The Data Class

To make it easy to create installation wizards, specific details for the program are kept in a separate class. The data class contains an array of topics, a default installation directory, and a product title:

```
class data {
    static Topic topics[];      // The array of topics.
        // The topics are presented in the order
        // they appear in the array.
    static int numTopics;       // Elements in topics array
    static TCHAR * defaultDest;  // Default installation directory
    static TCHAR * title;        // The product title
```

A topic is the unit of selection. It has a name that is displayed in a topic list, a detail string that describes the topic, and a path to the directory that corresponds to the topic:

```
struct Topic {
    TCHAR *name;      // The topic name
    TCHAR *detail;    // A description of the topic
    TCHAR *path;      // The relative path for the directory
};
```

The implementation file initializes the data. If the path is NULL, as in these initializers, Wizard uses the name field as the directory name:

```
TCHAR * data::title = _T("MFC Programming");
TCHAR * data::defaultDest = _T("C:\\MFC Programming");
. . .
Topic data::topics[] = {
    { _T("AddrBook"),
      _T("Address book.  An SDI Document/View application . . ."),
    },
    { _T("ComDlg"),
      _T("Illustrates most of the common dialogs . . ."),
    },
. . .
};

int data::numTopics = sizeof(topics)/sizeof(Topic);
```

The data class also defines several access functions:

```
class data {
. . .
// Access functions
    static const int getCount() { return numTopics; }
    static const TCHAR *getName(int i) { return topics[i].name; }
    static const TCHAR *getDetail(int i) { return topics[i].detail; }
    static const TCHAR *getPath(int i) {
        return topics[i].path!=NULL ?
            topics[i].path : topics[i].name;
    }
    static const TCHAR *getDefaultDest() { return defaultDest; }
    static const TCHAR *getTitle() { return title; }
};
```

14.3.2 The Property Sheet

The property sheet is the container for the property pages. It has the pages as components. Since each page is treated like a dialog, each page has its own CDialog-derived class:

```
class wizardSheet : public CPropertySheet
{
. . .
    start m_startPage;
    installDir m_installDirPage;
    select m_selectPage;
    end m_endPage;
```

The constructor for the property sheet adds the pages to the sheet:

```
wizardSheet::wizardSheet(LPCTSTR pszCaption, CWnd* pParentWnd,
  UINT iSelectPage)
    :CPropertySheet(pszCaption, pParentWnd, iSelectPage)
{
    AddPage(&m_startPage);
    AddPage(&m_installDirPage);
    AddPage(&m_selectPage);
    AddPage(&m_endPage);
}
```

Most of the behavior for the dialog is inherited from CPropertySheet or coded in the pages. WizardSheet responds to just one command, Help:

```
void wizardSheet::onHelp()
{
    CDialog dlg(IDD_ABOUTBOX);
    dlg.DoModal();
}
```

14.3.3 The Property Pages

The dialog consists of four property pages displayed in the following order:

Instance Name	Class Name	Task
m_startPage	start	Puts up the welcome screen
m_installDirPage	installDir	Gets the installation directory
m_selectPage	select	Gets the list of programs to install
m_endPage	end	Gets the confirmation for installation

Each page consists of a dialog resource and a dialog class. Although the pages are created using standard dialog techniques, creating a smoothly working wizard dialog involves some subtleties.

Foremost to remember is that control between the pages flows forwards *and* backwards. The dialog window for a page is created the first time the page is displayed. After that, the dialog is hidden and redisplayed as needed. Data on one page may affect others. When a page is revisited, data entered on another page may cause the information displayed on this page to change.

To guarantee that the user has entered required information, a page may need to disable the Next and Finish buttons. In wizard mode, the buttons are the only way to leave a page.

The following virtual functions enable a page to handle these issues:

OnInitDialog	Called once when a page is first created.
OnSetActive	Called before a page is shown. Some controls should be initialized here so that they reflect changes made on other pages.
OnWizardNext, OnWizardBack, OnWizardFinish	Called after the associated button (Next, Back, and Finish) is pressed but before control passes on to another page. Return zero to allow control to pass to the next page or -1 to keep the current page active.

Each page in Wizard is described below in turn.

14.3.3.1 The Start Page

The Start page is illustrated in Figure 14.2. Since the page is static, there isn't much underlying code. One thing to notice is that, as this is the first page, the Back button has been disabled. The CPropertySheet function SetWizard-Buttons provides control over the buttons. Whenever startPage is activated, it enables Next but not Back:

```
BOOL start::OnSetActive()
{
    ((CPropertySheet *)GetParent())->SetWizardButtons(
        PSWIZB_NEXT);
    return CPropertyPage::OnSetActive();
}
```

14.3.3.2 The Installation-Directory Page

Wizard asks for the installation directory using the dialog shown in Figure 14.3. The installation directory is kept in the CString m_destDir of the application class. m_installDirPage represents the string on the screen as an edit control. It uses DDX to transfer the data back and forth between the application and the control:

```
void installDir::DoDataExchange(CDataExchange* pDX)
{
    CPropertyPage::DoDataExchange(pDX);
    //{{AFX_DATA_MAP(installDir)
    //}}AFX_DATA_MAP
    DDX_Text(pDX, IDC_InstallDir, theApp.m_destDir);
}
```

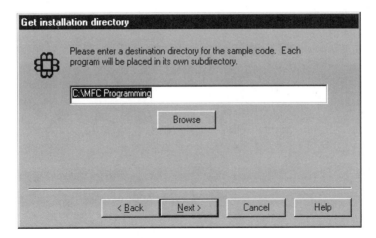

Figure 14.3 The Installation-directory page gets the installation directory.

Whenever the edit control is modified, m_destDir is updated by calling UpdateData:

```
void installDir::onChangeInstallDir()
{
    UpdateData();
    setButtons();
}
```

setButtons takes care of the wizard buttons. The Next button appears whenever m_destDir is nonempty:

```
void installDir::setButtons()
{
    DWORD buttons;

    if( theApp.m_destDir.IsEmpty() )
        buttons = PSWIZB_BACK;
    else buttons = PSWIZB_BACK|PSWIZB_NEXT;

    ((CPropertySheet *)GetParent())->SetWizardButtons(buttons);
}
```

When the Next button is pressed, m_installDirPage attempts to guarantee that the specified directory exists, creating the directory if necessary:

```
LRESULT installDir::OnWizardNext()
{
    // Return 0 to move on to next page
    // Return -1 to stay on current page
```

```
        CString msg;
        UpdateData();

        CFileStatus status;
        if( CFile::GetStatus(theApp.m_destDir,status) ) {
            if( status.m_attribute & CFile::directory )
                return 0;
            else {
                msg.Format(_T("A file with the name \"%s\" already exists"),
                    theApp.m_destDir);
                AfxMessageBox(msg);
            }
        } else {
            msg.Format(_T("The directory \"%s\" does not exist."
                "Create it now?"),
                theApp.m_destDir);
            if( AfxMessageBox(msg,MB_YESNO|MB_ICONQUESTION)
                == IDYES ) {
                if( _mkdir(theApp.m_destDir)==0 )
                    return 0;
                else {
                    msg.Format(_T("Cannot create the directory \"%s\""),
                        theApp.m_destDir);
                    AfxMessageBox(msg);
                }
            }
        }
        return -1;
    }
```

If the specified directory cannot be created, OnWizardNext returns -1, preventing control from leaving the page.

To help the user select a destination directory, the page includes a Browse button that triggers a directory tree. The Browse dialog is described in Section 14.3.4.

14.3.3.3 The Select Page

The Select page presents a checklist containing the list of topics and a detail window that describes the currently highlighted topic (Figure 14.4). The data for the list and detail box comes from the data class described in Section 14.3.1.1.

When the dialog is created, the checklist replaces a placeholder (placeholders are described in Chapter 6):

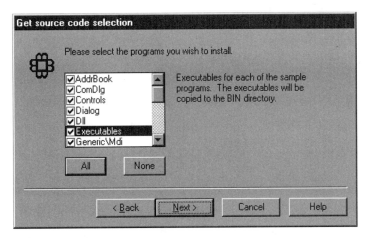

Figure 14.4 The Select page gets the list of programs to install.

```
BOOL select::OnInitDialog()
{
    CPropertyPage::OnInitDialog();

    // Setup checklist
    CWnd *placeHolder = GetDlgItem(IDC_TopicList);
    CRect rect;
    placeHolder->GetWindowRect(&rect);
    ScreenToClient(&rect);
    CFont *font = placeHolder->GetFont();
    placeHolder->DestroyWindow();

    m_topicList.Create(
        WS_CHILD|WS_VISIBLE|WS_TABSTOP|WS_VSCROLL|
        WS_BORDER|LBS_HASSTRINGS|LBS_OWNERDRAWFIXED|
        LBS_NOTIFY,
        rect,
        this,
        IDC_TopicList);

    m_topicList.SetFont(font,FALSE);
    m_topicList.init();
    m_topicList.SetCurSel(0);
    m_details.SetWindowText( data::getDetail(0) );

    return TRUE;  // return TRUE unless you set the focus to a control
                  // EXCEPTION: OCX Property Pages should return FALSE
}
```

The default font for a checklist is larger than the font in the other controls, so OnInitDialog sets the font explicitly. Next, the highlight is placed on the first list item and the corresponding detail text is displayed.

When the page is activated, the wizard buttons are set:

```
BOOL select::OnSetActive()
{
    setButtons();
    return CPropertyPage::OnSetActive();
}
```

`setButtons` enables Next if at least one topic has been chosen:

```
void select::setButtons()
{
    int selectCnt = 0;
    DWORD buttons = PSWIZB_BACK;

    for( int i=0; i<data::getCount(); ++i ) {
        if( m_topicList.GetCheck(i)==1 ) {
            buttons = PSWIZB_BACK|PSWIZB_NEXT;
            break;
        }
    }

    ((CPropertySheet *)GetParent())->SetWizardButtons(buttons);
}
```

`m_selectPage` responds to four commands:

```
BEGIN_MESSAGE_MAP(select, CPropertyPage)
    //{{AFX_MSG_MAP(select)
    ON_LBN_SELCHANGE(IDC_TopicList, onTopicChange)
    ON_BN_CLICKED(IDC_All, onAll)
    ON_BN_CLICKED(IDC_None, onNone)
    //}}AFX_MSG_MAP
    ON_CLBN_CHKCHANGE(IDC_TopicList, onSelectChange)
END_MESSAGE_MAP()
```

Movement of the highlight triggers the list-box notification LBN_SELCHANGE. In response, the handler onTopicChange changes the detail text:

```
void select::onTopicChange()
{
    m_details.SetWindowText( data::getDetail(m_topicList.GetCurSel()) );
}
```

Changing the check state of a list item triggers the checklist notification CLBN_CHKCHANGE. The handler sets the wizard buttons appropriately:

```
void select::onSelectChange()
{
    setButtons();
}
```

The All and None buttons set and clear the item checkmarks by iterating over the list of topics:

```
void select::onAll()
{
    for( int i=0; i<data::getCount(); ++i )
        m_topicList.SetCheck(i,1);
    setButtons();
}

void select::onNone()
{
    for( int i=0; i<data::getCount(); ++i )
        m_topicList.SetCheck(i,0);
    setButtons();
}
```

When the Next button is pressed, the indexes of the selected items are copied to the application:

```
LRESULT select::OnWizardNext()
{
    theApp.clearTopics();
    for( int i=0; i<data::getCount(); ++i ) {
        if( m_topicList.GetCheck(i)==1 ) {
            theApp.addTopic(i);
        }
    }
    return CPropertyPage::OnWizardNext();
}
```

14.3.3.4 End Page

As the last step, m_endPage asks for confirmation of the installation selections. The list of topics is displayed in a multi-column list box (see Figure 14.5). To get multiple columns, the list-box control was given the style LBS_MULTICOLUMN. The control takes care of formatting the columns.

The contents of the list box are initialized each time the page is activated, since the selected topics may change. ResetContent clears out the list box from the previous activation:

```
BOOL end::OnSetActive()
{
    ((CPropertySheet *)GetParent())->SetWizardButtons(
        PSWIZB_BACK|PSWIZB_FINISH);
```

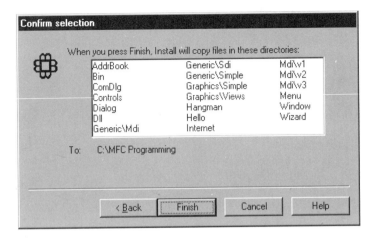

Figure 14.5 The End page gets the confirmation for installation.

```
    m_installDir.SetWindowText(theApp.m_destDir);

    m_topicList.ResetContent();
    for( int i=0; i<theApp.getTopicCnt(); ++i )
        m_topicList.AddString( data::getPath(theApp.getTopic(i)) );

    return CPropertyPage::OnSetActive();
}
```

Pressing the Finish button triggers copying of the files:

```
BOOL end::OnWizardFinish()
{
    copyDlg dlg(this);
    BOOL success = dlg.doCopy();

    if(success) {
        AfxMessageBox(_T("Installation successful"));
        return TRUE;
    } else {
        AfxMessageBox(_T("Installation wasn't completed successfully"));
        SetFocus();
        return FALSE;
    }
}
```

The work of actually copying directories of files is handled by the class `copyDlg` described in Section 14.3.5.

14.3.4 The Browse Dialog

The Browse dialog is based on the directory tree control described in Chapter 6. In addition to the tree, it uses a bitmap button for the parent-directory command, a drop-down list to switch drives, and a text control to show the current directory. The dialog is shown in Figure 14.6.[6] If the dialog exits with IDOK, the selected directory can be retrieved via the getDirectory member function:

```
class browseDlg : public CDialog
{
// Construction
public:
    browseDlg(LPCTSTR dir);
    CString &getDirectory() { return m_curDir; }
. . .
```

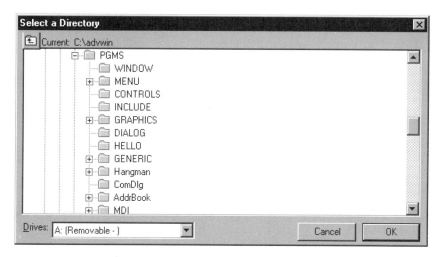

Figure 14.6   The Browse dialog implements graphical directory selection.

In Chapter 15 the dialog is placed in a dynamic link library so that it can be included in an application without having to include the source code.

14.3.5 The Copy Dialog

The Copy dialog copies the selected source directories to the installation directory. The function doCopy triggers the copy. An interesting wrinkle in the installation process is that copying can take considerable time, so the program should let the user know that it is working. Different programs have solved this

---

[6]A useful improvement to the dialog would be to sort the directory names.

problem in different ways. In order of user kindness, possible strategies include:

- Display a wait cursor.
- Post a modeless dialog. Copy files in the run loop for the dialog.
- Post a modeless dialog. Copy files in a separate thread.

Displaying a wait cursor locks out interaction with the program. In particular, it prevents the addition of a Cancel button to terminate copying, so this strategy should be avoided.

A Cancel button can be implemented in a modeless dialog, but the button may be unresponsive in a single-threaded application. Win32 has a convenient API function, CopyFile, to copy a file. The thread that calls CopyFile must wait for the function to return. Since copying a large file can take a long time, a press of the Cancel button may not take effect immediately. Performing the copy in a separate worker thread keeps the interface active.

doCopy posts a dialog and triggers a worker thread to copy files. It performs these steps:

1. Find the root of the source tree. The directory containing the executable is assumed to be the root.
2. Count the number of files to be copied. doCopy walks the source directories twice—first to count the files and later to perform the copy.
3. Post and update the status dialog. The status dialog, shown in Figure 14.7, displays a progress bar and contains a Cancel button. The progress bar data is updated by the worker thread; the bar is repainted by the primary thread. Progress is based on file count.
4. Spawn a worker thread to perform copying. To keep the user interface active, a non-GUI thread copies the files.
5. Monitor the worker thread and the Cancel button. doCopy terminates because either the worker thread has terminated or the user presses the Cancel button.
6. Terminate the status dialog. On termination, doCopy removes the status dialog and returns an indication of whether the installation was successful.

Each of these steps is described below.

Figure 14.7   The status dialog is posted while files are being copied in a worker thread.

14.3.5.1 Finding the Root of the Source Tree

The API function GetModuleFileName returns the full pathname of a program's executable file. doCopy strips off the last component to get the root of the source tree:

```
BOOL copyDlg::doCopy()
    // Entry point to post the copy dialog and begin copying files
{
    if( ::GetModuleFileName(AfxGetInstanceHandle(),
      m_srcRoot,sizeof(m_srcRoot))==0 ) {
        AfxMessageBox(_T("Cannot determine path of Wizard executable."));
        return FALSE;
    }

    TCHAR *p;
    if( (p=_tcsrchr(m_srcRoot,'\\'))!=NULL )
        *p = '\0';
```

_tcsrchr is the language-neutral wrapper for the standard library function strrchr.

14.3.5.2 Counting the Number of Files to be Copied

copyDlg has three member variables that maintain the state of copying:

```
BOOL m_justCounting; // True during counting, rather than copying, files
int m_fileCnt;       // The number of files to copy
BOOL m_stop;         // When set to true, copying stops
```

To count the files, the variables are initialized and the copy process is triggered. Back in doCopy:

```
    // First pass: Determine the number of files to copy
    m_stop = FALSE;
    m_justCounting = TRUE; // Flag prepass
    m_fileCnt = 0;
    copyTopics();
    m_justCounting = FALSE;
```

copyTopics initiates a depth-first traversal of the directories selected on the
Select page. The same code both counts and copies. We'll look at the details in
Section 14.3.6.

14.3.5.3 Posting and Updating the Status Dialog

The Status dialog could have been implemented as either modal or modeless. I
chose to use a modeless dialog so that the program could monitor the worker
thread in its message loop. The dialog is triggered by calling Create:

```
if( !m_stop ) {
    // Second pass: Copy the files
    Create(IDD_CopyDlg);
```

Section 14.3.5.5 describes the message loop that monitors the worker thread.
Alternatively, I could have used a modal dialog and foregone the message loop.
Instead of having doCopy monitor the worker, the worker thread could send a
message to the modal dialog when copying completes. A WM_COMMAND message
would suffice. The modal dialog would respond by exiting, allowing doCopy to
terminate.

14.3.5.4 Spawning a Worker Thread to Perform Copying

A worker thread is a path of execution through a program that does not manipulate GUI objects. It carries out a task in parallel with the primary GUI thread of
a program. Since the thread executes independently of the GUI, it can perform
time-consuming operations without shutting down the interface. See Chapter
16 for a more complete discussion of threads.

AfxBeginThread starts the thread executing at the function specified in the first
parameter—bkgndCopy in the example (see Figure 14.8)—returning a pointer to
a CWinThread object:

```
CWinThread *bkgnd = AfxBeginThread(bkgndCopy,this,
    THREAD_PRIORITY_NORMAL,0,CREATE_SUSPENDED);
bkgnd->m_bAutoDelete = FALSE;
bkgnd->ResumeThread();
```

doCopy creates the thread *suspended*, so that the thread does not begin executing right away. Normally, the CWinThread object created by AfxBeginThread
would be deleted when its underlying thread terminates. The thread handle,
needed to monitor and terminate the thread, is a data member of CWinThread.
doCopy needs the thread object to persist beyond the lifetime of the thread so
that it can detect when the thread has exited. doCopy sets m_bAutoDelete to

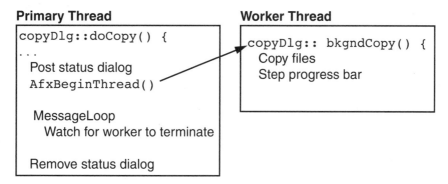

Figure 14.8 doCopy spawns a worker thread to copy files. It monitors the worker in an ad hoc message loop.

false to prevent the CWinThread object from being deleted when the thread dies, then it calls ResumeThread to start the thread.

14.3.5.5 Monitoring the Worker Thread and the Cancel Button

The message loop in doCopy waits for the worker thread to terminate or the user to press the Cancel button. (Pressing Cancel sets m_stop to true.) While the thread is executing, ::GetExitCodeThread will set exitCode to STILL_ACTIVE:

```
DWORD exitCode;
while( ::GetExitCodeThread(bkgnd->m_hThread,&exitCode)
  && exitCode==STILL_ACTIVE ) {
  if( !AfxGetThread()->PumpMessage() )
      m_stop = TRUE;
  if( m_stop ) // Stop a long copy in worker thread
      ::TerminateThread(bkgnd->m_hThread,0);

}
```

To keep the user interface active, the loop must give MFC a chance to process messages. PumpMessage processes the message at the head of the queue, if any.

One flaw in this program is that if the worker is terminated by calling ::TerminateThread, it will leave any heap objects it created still allocated. The worker doesn't get any indication that it is going away, so it has no chance to clean up. As a result, it is always best to let threads terminate themselves.

14.3.5.6 Terminating the Status Dialog

When the message loop terminates, the dialog and the thread object are no longer needed. AfxBeginThread allocates the CWinThread object on the heap, so doCopy deletes it by calling `delete`. Modeless dialogs are terminated by calling `DestroyWindow`:[7]

```
        delete bkgnd;
        DestroyWindow( );
    }

    return !m_stop;
}
```

14.3.6 The Worker Thread

The real work in this program is carried out by the worker thread. The thread begins executing at `bkgndCopy`, as specified in the call to `AfxBeginThread` and described in Section 14.3.5.4. `bkgndCopy` is a static function that receives a generic pointer. It cannot be an ordinary member function, since it will not receive a `this` pointer. Instead, the `this` pointer of the dialog object is passed through the generic pointer:[8]

```
UINT copyDlg::bkgndCopy(PVOID param)
{
    copyDlg *dlg = (copyDlg *)param;
    dlg->copyTopics( );
    return 0;
}
```

`copyTopics` walks the directory tree for the selected topics, creating directories under the installation directory and copying files to the corresponding places. Although its job is interesting, it has little to do with either MFC or GUI programming. Accordingly, it and the functions it calls are presented below without comment.

```
void copyDlg::copyTopics( )
    // Trigger copy of each selected topic
{
    for( int i=0; !m_stop && i<theApp.getTopicCnt( ); ++i ) {
        LPCTSTR relPath = data::getPath(theApp.getTopic(i));
        CString src, dest;
        src.Format(_T("%s\\%s"),m_srcRoot,relPath);
        dest.Format(_T("%s\\%s"),theApp.m_destDir,relPath);
        copyDir(src,dest);
    }
}
```

---

[7] If you look at the source code carefully, you'll find that copyDlg does not override PostNcDestroy as is typical in a modeless dialog. The copyDlg object is actually *automatic*; created and destroyed in end::OnWizardFinish. This simpler memory allocation technique works since doCopy does not return until the dialog is done. That is, to OnWizardFinish, copyDlg looks like a modal dialog.

[8] An alternate strategy is to make bkgndCopy a friend of the copyDlg class.

```
void copyDlg::copyDir(LPCTSTR srcDir, LPCTSTR destDir)
    // Copy all files in srcDir to destDir
    // Recurse through subdirectories
{
    char curDir[_MAX_PATH];

    ::GetCurrentDirectory(sizeof(curDir),curDir);
    if( ::SetCurrentDirectory(srcDir) ) {
        if( m_justCounting || makeDir(destDir) ) {
            WIN32_FIND_DATA finfo;
            HANDLE h;
            if( (h=FindFirstFile(_T("*.*"),&finfo))!=INVALID_HANDLE_VALUE ) {
                do {
                    if( finfo.cFileName[0]!='.' ) {
                        CString dest;
                        dest.Format(_T("%s\\%s"),destDir,finfo.cFileName);
                        if( finfo.dwFileAttributes & FILE_ATTRIBUTE_DIRECTORY )
                            copyDir(finfo.cFileName,dest);
                        else copyFile(finfo.cFileName,dest);
                    }
                } while( !m_stop && FindNextFile(h,&finfo) );
                FindClose(h);
            }
        }

    } else {
        CString buf;
        buf.Format(_T("Cannot change to source directory \"%s\"."),srcDir);
        AfxMessageBox(buf);
        m_stop = TRUE;
    }

    ::SetCurrentDirectory(curDir);
}

BOOL copyDlg::makeDir(LPCTSTR dir)
    // Dreate dir, if it doesn't already exist
{
    if( !isaDir(dir) ) {
        // First make sure parent dir exists
        PSTR p, path = _strdup(dir);
        if( (p=strrchr(path,'\\')) || (p=strrchr(path,'/')) ) {
            // The parent is a dir, not a drive
            *p = '\0';
            if( !makeDir(path) ) { // Can't create parent
                free(path);
                return FALSE;
            }
        }
        free(path);
```

```
            if( !::CreateDirectory(dir,NULL) ) {
                CString buf;
                buf.Format(_T("Cannot create directory \"%s\".\n"
                  "Would you like to continue anyways?"),dir);
                if( AfxMessageBox(buf,MB_ICONQUESTION|MB_YESNO)==IDNO )
                    m_stop = TRUE;
                return FALSE;
            }
        }

    return(TRUE);
}

void copyDlg::copyFile(LPCTSTR src, LPCTSTR dest)
    // Copy src file to dest
    // Update on-screen dialog
{
    if( m_justCounting ) { // Prepass, just increment file count
        ++m_fileCnt;
        return;
    }

    CString buf;
    buf.Format(_T("Copying %s to %s"),src,dest);
    m_copyFile.SetWindowText(buf);

    if( !::CopyFile(src,dest,FALSE) ) {
        buf.Format(_T("Copy to \"%s\" failed: %s.\n"
          "Would you like to continue anyways?"),dest,
            getErrorString());
        if( AfxMessageBox(buf,MB_ICONQUESTION|MB_YESNO)==IDNO ) {
            m_stop = TRUE;
            return;
        }
    }

    m_copyProgress.StepIt();
}

CString copyDlg::getErrorString()
    // Get a string description of the last Win32 error
    // Error strings are kept in a string resource
    // The resource has the same ID as the error number
{
    int errorNum = GetLastError();
    CString buf;
    if( !buf.LoadString(errorNum) )
        buf.Format(_T("Error number %d"),errorNum);
    return buf;
}
```

```
BOOL copyDlg::isaDir(LPCTSTR name)
    // return TRUE if name refers to a directory
{
    DWORD attr = ::GetFileAttributes(name);
    return attr!=-1 && (attr&FILE_ATTRIBUTE_DIRECTORY);
}
```

CHAPTER

15 | Dynamic Link Libraries

The program and DLLs in the Dll directory illustrate the concepts discussed in this chapter. The corresponding executable in the bin directory is Dll.exe.

15.1 Introduction

Dynamic link libraries (DLLs) have been a part of Windows from the early days, although their usage and nature has changed considerably. Originally, they were a messy hybrid of shared library and server. They were tricky to use but indispensable given the scarcity of memory.

Under Win32, DLLs look very much like the shared libraries supported on other operating systems, such as UNIX and VMS. A DLL is structured like an executable file. It contains code, data, and resources. It can be loaded and unloaded independently from an application. When it is loaded into an application, references from the application to the DLL are connected dynamically. The DLL executes in the address space of the application.

15.2 How DLLs Are Used

Dynamic linking is a basic facility provided by Win32 that finds use in different contexts:

- It provides the basis for sharing libraries to save space on disk and in memory.
- It allows dynamic loading of resources and functions.

383

- It underlies the implementation of in-process servers, providing server behavior without the overhead of interprocess communication and context switching.

First we'll look at each of these uses of dynamic linking from the viewpoint of program architecture and then we'll look at the programming details.

15.2.1 Shared Libraries

A shared library plays the same role as an ordinary statically-linked library. It allows functions and data to be packaged separately from the programs in which they are used. When a program links to a static library, the object code referenced is included as part of the program's executable image. As a result, if a library function is used in several applications, a copy of the function will appear multiple times on disk and in memory. When libraries were small, the space occupied by these copies was not significant. But with mega-libraries like the Win32 API and MFC, static linking has become very costly.

When a program links dynamically to a library, it retains references to library functions rather than copies of the functions. The references are resolved when the library is loaded. Ideally, it should make no difference to the program whether the library is linked statically or dynamically, the choice being a packaging optimization.

Figure 15.1 contrasts static and dynamic linking to the C library function sprintf.

15.2.2 Dynamic Data and Code

When a program takes control over loading of a library, it can swap data and functions based on user preferences. One common example is to switch the presentation language of a program, as illustrated by Figure 15.2. A resource DLL contains just resource data. In the example, each resource DLL might contain strings and dialogs for a particular language. After the correct DLL is loaded, the remainder of the program will operate in whichever language was chosen.

Another important usage of dynamic loading is selective update of functionality. A good example is Win32 itself. Since the functionality of Win32 is provided largely in DLLs, the system can be upgraded incrementally by installing later DLLS.

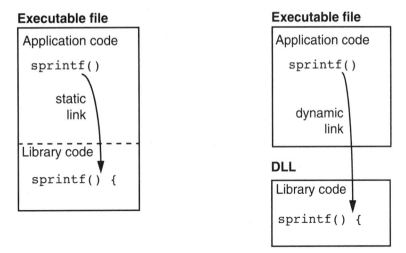

Figure 15.1 With static linking, code and data in the library become part of the application's executable file. With dynamic linking, the application and library are stored separately.

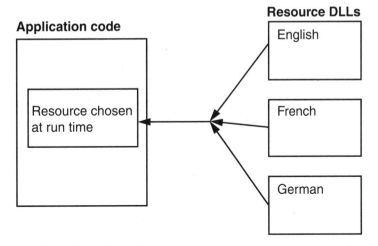

Figure 15.2 Using dynamic loading, a program can load resources based on user preference.

15.2.3 In-Process Servers

On most operating systems, servers run as independent processes. When a client needs service, it communicates with the server process via some interprocess communication (IPC) mechanism such as a pipeline or a socket. IPC is relatively expensive because function calls and data must be shuttled back and forth between the address spaces of the two processes. Also, if the client and server are on the same machine, the operating system must switch between the two processes contexts.

In the case where the client and server run on the same machine, placing the server within the client process is more efficient, since no shuttling of data is necessary nor is a process switch required. Each client accesses the server via ordinary function calls (Figure 15.3).

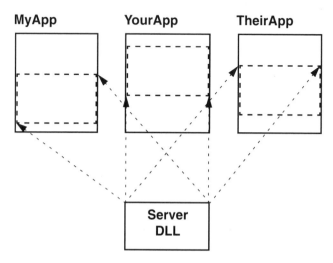

Figure 15.3   An in-process server appears in the address space of each of its clients. The server may maintain shared storage for its own purposes. The DLL stays in memory as long as any client is active.

One attribute typical of a server is that it maintains state information for all of its clients, doling out service to the clients, in turn. To implement a server in-process, the server state information needs to be visible to each process in which the server is running. Typically, these server "threads" use Win32 file mapping to share memory.[1] The increased efficiency achieved by putting servers in-process is not without cost. When an in-process server crashes, it brings down the application it is serving, unlike an out-of-process server.

---

[1] To learn more about shared memory, look up the Win32 functions `CreateFileMapping`, `OpenFileMapping`, and `MapViewOfFile`. For a detailed discussion of shared memory, see *Win32 Systems Programming* by Johnson Hart, Addison Wesley Longman, 1997.

15.3 Using a DLL

This section examines the programming protocol for using dynamic linking.

15.3.1 Implicit and Explicit Loading

There are two fundamental protocols for using DLLs: *implicit* and *explicit* loading. Implicit loading is the simpler to use—the library is accessed as is a static library, using ordinary function calls. An *import* library for the DLL is specified at link time, telling the link editor what symbols the DLL resolves and the name of the DLL file that contains the implementation.[2] References into the DLL point into a table of pointers, much like references to virtual functions in C++. At runtime, Win32 searches for the DLL, and, if the DLL is found, fills in the table of pointers.

Explicit loading takes a bit more work. The program loads the DLL by calling the function AfxLoadLibrary and then wires its own pointers—with explicit loading, functions can only be called through pointers. The extra work has some rewards:

Implicit Loading	Explicit Loading
Requires that an import library exist at link time to resolve references into the DLL.	Cannot refer to DLL exports by name, so an import library is not required.
Requires that the DLL be found before the program can run.	The DLL isn't needed to run the program. AfxLoadLibrary returns failure if the DLL can't be found, allowing the program to recover.
DLL remains in memory until the program exits.	The DLL can be unloaded to save space or it can be replaced to change functionality.

15.3.2 Example: Explicit Loading

The Dll program is a simple, dialog-based application that illustrates both implicit and explicit loading. The opening dialog is shown in Figure 15.4. The Get Directory button triggers a directory-tree dialog wrapped by the getDirDlg class. The program loads the getDirDlg class implicitly from the dirtree DLL.

---

[2] Import libraries have a .lib extension just like static libraries. Import libraries are created by the link editor.

Use of getDirDlg is the same as if the class were defined in the application. The export library dirtree.lib is added to the link line to resolve references to getDirDlg. Implementation of the DLL is described in Section 15.4.2.

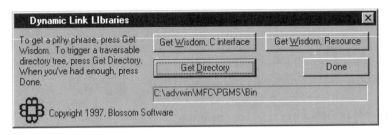

Figure 15.4   The Dll program links to two DLLS. It loads the directory-tree DLL implicitly and the wisdom DLL explicitly.

In response to the Get Wisdom buttons, the Dll program loads the Wisdom library explicitly to generate a message box containing a pithy phrase, as illustrated by Figure 15.5. The library resides in the file wisdom.dll. There are two versions of the Get Wisdom command. The button "Get Wisdom, C Interface" uses a C function to query static data in the DLL. "Get Wisdom, Resource" retrieves a string resource from the DLL.

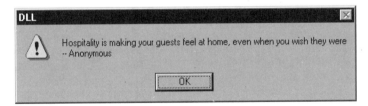

Figure 15.5   When a Get Wisdom button is pressed, the program takes a pithy phrase from wisdom.dll and displays it in a message box.

15.3.2.1 C Function Interface

To call a function in an explicitly loaded DLL, the caller retrieves the address of the function, then calls indirectly through the address to reach the function. The API function GetProcAddress takes the name of the function and returns its address. At runtime, C++ functions are known by their mangled names, making them particularly inconvenient to call. By contrast, the names of C functions can be used directly in the call to ::GetProcAddress.

The wisdom DLL implements an access function in C called getWisdom. (See Section 15.4.3 for the implementation of getWisdom.) Given an integer, getWisdom returns a string. The Get Wisdom, C Interface command:

1. Loads the Wisdom library;
2. Retrieves a pointer to getWisdom in the library;
3. Calls getWisdom through the pointer passing a random number;
4. Puts the string returned by getWisdom in a message box; and,
5. Frees the library.

Here is the code:

```
void dialog::onGetWisdomC()
{
    HINSTANCE hLib = AfxLoadLibrary(_T("wisdom.dll"));

    if( hLib!=NULL ) {
        GetWisdom pGetWisdom =
            (GetWisdom) ::GetProcAddress(hLib,"getWisdom");
        if( pGetWisdom!=NULL ) {
            SYSTEMTIME time;
            ::GetLocalTime(&time);
            TCHAR *msg = pGetWisdom(time.wSecond);
            AfxMessageBox(msg);
            AfxFreeLibrary(hLib);
            return;
        }

        AfxMessageBox(_T("Cannot find \"getWisdom\" function"
          " in \"wisdom.dll\""),
            MB_OK|MB_ICONSTOP);
        AfxFreeLibrary(hLib);
        return;
    }

    AfxMessageBox(_T("Cannot find \"wisdom.dll\""),MB_OK|MB_ICONSTOP);
}
```

The pointer returned by ::GetProcAddresss is generic. To call the function with the appropriate parameter list, the pointer must be defined with the correct function prototype. Wisdom.h makes the job simpler by declaring the type GetWisdom:

```
// Header file for usage with wisdom.dll

// If application is linked with wisdom.lib, then
// getWisdom can be called directly using the following
// prototype
```

```
extern "C" {
    TCHAR *getWisdom(int);
};

// If wisdom.dll is loaded explicitly, then use
// GetProcAddress("getWisdom") to retrieve a
// pointer to the following type

typedef TCHAR *(__stdcall *GetWisdom)(int);
```

AfxFreeLibrary tells Win32 that the application is finished with the library. When all users of a DLL are finished, Win32 removes the library from memory.

15.3.2.2 Resources in a DLL

Programs often keep strings in resources. Normally, an MFC program can use CString::LoadString to retrieve a string resource. CString::LoadString relies on the API function LoadString, which takes, among other things, a module instance handle and a resource ID. But, which module instance handle does CString::LoadString use? The application and each DLL explicitly loaded have their own instance handles.

To make it easier to use DLLs, MFC searches through a list of modules for a resource, beginning with the application module and continuing with any DLLs that have been attached. This strategy is very convenient if you implement both the DLL and the application, since you can adhere to a convention for naming resources to avoid conflicts. If the application happens to use the same resource identifier as a DLL, the DLL's resource will be hidden.

To eliminate the possibility of naming conflicts, when looking up a resource you can restrict the search to just the DLL by calling ::LoadString (or more generally, ::FindResource) directly. The Get Wisdom, Resource command does exactly that by using the library instance handle returned from AfxLoadLibrary:

```
void dialog::onGetWisdomRes()
{
    static int id=0;
    HINSTANCE hLib = AfxLoadLibrary(_T("wisdom.dll"));
```

```
if( hLib!=NULL ) {
    TCHAR msg[256];
    if( ::LoadString(hLib,++id,msg,sizeof(msg))==0 ) {
        // At end of table, restart and try again
        id = 0;
        if( ::LoadString(hLib,++id,msg,sizeof(msg))==0 ) {
            AfxMessageBox(_T("Cannot find string resources"
               " in \"wisdom.dll\""),
                MB_OK|MB_ICONSTOP);
            AfxFreeLibrary(hLib);
            return;
        }
    }

    AfxMessageBox(msg);
    AfxFreeLibrary(hLib);
    return;
}

AfxMessageBox(_T("Cannot find \"wisdom.dll\""),MB_OK|MB_ICONSTOP);
}
```

The string resources in `wisdom.dll` are numbered from 1 to n. `onGetWisdomRes` cycles through the strings. It doesn't know the value of n, so when `::LoadString` fails, it starts over again with the first string.

15.4   Creating DLLs

DLLs have come a long way. In the early years of Windows, programming a DLL required adhering to strict conventions imposed by the system. Violating the conventions would usually lead to a program crash. In Win32, programming a DLL is, for the most part, like programming the other parts of an application.

You've seen from the previous discussion that a dynamic link library consists of code and data, like an executable file. When a DLL is loaded, it begins executing at a specifiable entry point, by default `DllMain` for Win32 programs.[3] `DllMain` is called whenever the DLL is attached to or detached from a process. The code needed in `DllMain` depends on how the DLL is to be used. A minimal `DllMain` might have the following structure:

---

[3] By using the API function `LoadLibraryEx`, a DLL can be loaded as data only, in which case no code executes.

```
extern "C" int APIENTRY
DllMain(HINSTANCE hInstance, DWORD dwReason, LPVOID lpReserved)
{
    switch(dwReason) {
    case DLL_PROCESS_ATTACH:
        Initialize DLL
        break;
    case DLL_PROCESS_DETACH:
        Cleanup DLL
        break;
    }

    return 1;    // ok
}
```

If the DLL is not implemented using MFC and has no internal state that needs initializing, it may not need an explicit DllMain. The Win32 library provides a default DllMain that does nothing. DLLs with a C interface, such as the wisdom.dll described in Section 15.4.3, can use the default DllMain.

If a DLL is written using MFC there are additional considerations that affect its implementation:

- Will the DLL be used only with applications that also use MFC?
- Does the DLL require explicit initialization, as is typical with an in-process server?
- Does the DLL export class names?
- How will resources in the DLL be accessed?

DLLs can be implemented in one of two styles, known as *regular* and *extension*. Use a regular DLL for use with applications not written using MFC. MFC provides a DllMain that calls upon a CWinApp object, just as WinMain does in an MFC application. The DLL can override InitInstance and ExitInstance to implement startup and shutdown behavior.

A regular DLL can also be used with MFC-based applications, but some care must be taken. As described in Section 15.3.2.2, MFC will search for resources beginning with the application module. To prevent an accidental conflict, insert the AFX_MANAGE_STATE macro at the start of any function that load resources.

Extension DLLs are simpler to use than regular DLLs. They use a simplified DllMain and do not have their own application object. DllMain, written by AppWizard, inserts the instance handle of the DLL into the list of modules to search when loading resources. Thus, naming conflicts are possible, but

AFX_MANAGE_STATE cannot be used.[4]   You can use two strategies to avoid conflicts:

- Load resources explicitly using the API functions as shown above in Section 15.3.2.2.
- Name resources using unlikely names. The dirTree DLL described in Section 15.4.2 is an extension DLL that uses a *string* name rather than an integer for the dialog resource to minimize the chance of a conflict with the application.[5]

15.4.1 Exporting Names

As with any C++ module or class, some names in a DLL are private and some public. Public names must be so declared using a special syntax. Global names are, by default, private.

To make a name visible to a user of the DLL, export the name. The import library for a DLL contains the list of exported names, allowing the link editor to resolve reference to those names. Similarly, ::GetProcAddress can see only those names in a DLL that have been exported.

There are two techniques you can use to export a name. The simpler is to use the __declspec storage class. For example,

```
__declspec(dllexport) TCHAR * getWisdom(int number)
```

exports the function getWisdom. Alternatively, you can create a module definition file and provide a list of exported names. So, getWisdom could be declared simply as

```
TCHAR *getWisdom(int number)
```

if the module definition file, wisdom.def, listed its name:

---

[4] The problem with using AFX_MANAGE_STATE arises from a library packaging problem in current versions of MFC. The usual parameter to AFX_MANAGE_STATE is AfxGetStaticModuleState. AfxGetStaticModuleState is defined in the MFC library in the same module as DllMain. Because extension DLLs have their own DllMain, the link editor sees two definitions for the function and the link fails.

[5] In looking for resource ID conflicts, you need to consider only top-level resources. For example, the IDs used inside of a dialog resource do not have to be unique since they are always interpreted in the context of the dialog. The ID for the dialog resource itself, however, must be unique.

```
; Wisdom.def : Declares the module parameters for the DLL.

LIBRARY        "WISDOM"
DESCRIPTION    'Wisdom Dynamic Link Library'

EXPORTS
    ; Explicit exports can go here
    getWisdom
```

Any global object can be exported, including whole classes. The dirTree DLL exports the getDirDlg class:

```
class AFX_EXT_CLASS getDirDlg : public CDialog
{
```

where the macro AFX_EXT_CLASS expands to __declspec(dllexport). Why not use __declspec(dllexport) directly in the class declaration?

To use the class getDirDlg in an application, the class must be declared in the application. It's always preferable to share the same class declaration between the user and the implementer of a class, but __declspec(dllexport) isn't correct for the user. Accordingly, MFC defines AFX_EXT_CLASS based on the macro _AFXEXT:

```
#ifdef _AFXEXT
    #define AFX_EXT_CLASS        AFX_CLASS_EXPORT
. . .
#else
    #define AFX_EXT_CLASS        AFX_CLASS_IMPORT
. . .
#endif

#define AFX_CLASS_EXPORT __declspec(dllexport)
#define AFX_CLASS_IMPORT __declspec(dllimport)
```

As you undoubtedly inferred, _AFXEXT should be defined only during compilation of the extension library.

Using __declspec is simpler and less errorprone than using a module definition file. Still, there are situations for which an explicit list of exports is necessary. Consider a DLL that implements a shared library. An application accesses the exported objects in the library indirectly via a table of pointers, as illustrated in Figure 15.6. The order of the entries in the table is not important as long as the application and the DLL agree. When __declspec is used to export names, the table order is generated by the link editor. If the library evolves and more functions are added, the order may change. For the library to be backward compatible, the order of the entries at the beginning of the table must be kept constant. If they aren't, the application will point to the wrong objects (see Figure 15.7.)

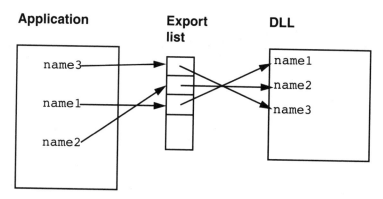

Figure 15.6 An application accesses exported objects in a DLL via a table of pointers.

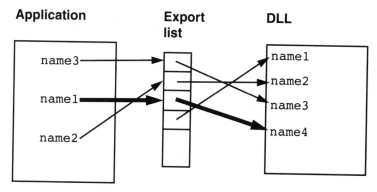

Figure 15.7 When a DLL is modified, the order of the names in the export list may change. An application relying on the order in a previous version of the DLL may have pointers bound incorrectly.

Using a module definition file, names can be given explicit slots in the export list. For example, the DLL in Figure 15.6 could use a module definition file with the statements

```
EXPORTS
    name1 @1
    name2 @2
    name3 @3
```

to keep the locations of particular names constant.

15.4.2 Example: MFC Extension DLL

The Dll program introduced in Section 15.3 uses a CDialog-derived class implemented in an extension DLL. The class, getDirDlg, is based on the directory browser described in Chapter 14 and shown in Figure 15.8. getDirDlg retrieves a directory path by allowing the user to browse a directory tree. To use the class, instantiate it and call DoModal, as illustrated by the Get Directory command in the Dll program:

```
void dialog::onGetDirectory()
{
    getDirDlg dlg(m_directory);
    if( dlg.DoModal()==IDOK ) {
        m_directory = dlg.getDirectory();
        UpdateData(FALSE);
    }
}
```

The member variable m_directory contains the current directory. It is updated if the user confirms the dialog.

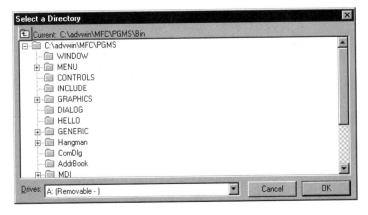

Figure 15.8   The getDirDlg class implements a directory tree browser.

The implementation of getDirDlg is in the directory Dll\DirTree. It consists of implementation files for the class and an AppWizard-generated DllMain. The class is declared AFX_CLASS_EXPORT, as described in Section 15.4.1.

Other than exporting the class, getDirDlg is implemented just as it would be if it were placed in the application. One minor change was made to reduce the possibility of a resource conflict. The library is general purpose and can be used widely, so any numeric ID chosen for the dialog resource could easily conflict with an ID used in the application. To reduce the chance of conflict, the dialog resource was given the string name "getDirDlg":

```
getDirDlg::getDirDlg(LPCTSTR dir)
    : curDir(dir), CDialog(_T("getDirDlg"), NULL)
{
```

15.4.3 Example: Dynamic Resources

The Get Wisdom commands of the Dll program load the Wisdom library dynamically, as described in Section 15.3.2. The Wisdom DLL contains a C interface to static data and a string resource. It exports the C interface, the getWisdom function.

The implementation of the Wisdom library is in the directory Dll\wisdom. wisdom.c contains the static data and getWisdom:

```
#include <tchar.h>
#define ELEMCNT(array) (sizeof(array)/sizeof(*array))

static char * wisdom[] = {
. . .
    _T("Comedy is tragedy, plus time\n-- Carol Burnett"),
. . .
};

__declspec(dllexport) TCHAR *
getWisdom(int number)
{
    return( wisdom[number % ELEMCNT(wisdom)] );
}
```

The string resource resides in the resource script, wisdom.rc.

CHAPTER

16 | A Simple Internet Browser

The program in the `Internet` directory illustrates the concepts discussed in this chapter. The corresponding executable in the `bin` directory is `ibrows.exe`.

16.1   Introduction

And now, for my last trick, I'll create an MDI-based Internet browser. The browser displays Internet files as text, highlighting anything that looks like a Uniform Resource Locator (URL). Double clicking on an URL[1] causes the browser to open the URL and read the named document into a new window. Figure 16.1 shows the browser in action.

Although the program is not long, it uses many of the concepts we've covered in the text plus introduces a few more. The browser is based on the document/view framework, integrating network access with the document class. To communicate with the Internet, the document uses the Internet classes `CInternetSession` and `CInternetFile`, based on the WinInet API. Connecting to the network introduces lots of potential for failure and significant time delays. Accordingly, the browser uses exception handling to catch some failures and it spawns worker threads to communicate with the Internet without shutting down the browser's user interface.

---

[1] Although convention varies, I usually pronounce URL to sound like Earl.

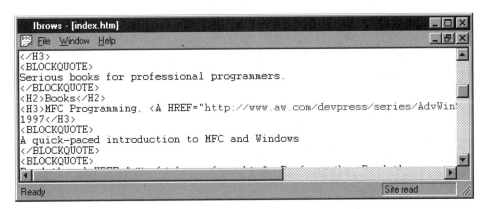

Figure 16.1 Ibrows reads files and displays them as raw text, highlighting URLs.

16.2 Overview

The program structure is typical document/view. Here are the primary classes:

ibrows
: The application class. The default behavior on startup is to open the last file that was opened.

mainFrame
: The main window. Ibrows has a status bar that is created during the initialization of the mainFrame.

doc
: The document class. It implements the storage of and access to text. The text is stored in a CArray collection. doc serializes files stored locally and files stored on the Internet.

view
: The view class. It displays ordinary text in black and URLs in red. The view takes control of the cursor shape to display the hand pointer when the mouse is over an URL. Clicking on an URL highlights it; double clicking opens it.

The document class gets help from two support classes:

line
: A line of text. line handles the details of parsing text to find URLs. A document consists of an array of lines.

netFile   A file stored on the Internet. MFC's Internet classes are still evolving and lack some important functionality. Nevertheless, they are very convenient to use, particularly since they can be integrated with serialization. The netFile class adds important functionality to the CInternetFile class.

16.3 Initialization

InitInstance has an interesting twist. Usually MDI programs start by displaying an empty document. Documents in Ibrows are read-only, so an empty document is quite useless. The default behavior, then, is to show the main window and then open the last file browsed the previous time Ibrows was run:

```
BOOL ibrows::InitInstance()
{
. . .

    CMultiDocTemplate* pDocTemplate;
    pDocTemplate = new CMultiDocTemplate(
        IDR_TEXTTYPE,                    // Shared resource ID
        RUNTIME_CLASS(doc),              // Document class
        RUNTIME_CLASS(CMDIChildWnd),     // Frame class
        RUNTIME_CLASS(view));            // View class
    AddDocTemplate(pDocTemplate);

    // create main MDI Frame window
    mainFrame* pMainFrame = new mainFrame;
    if (!pMainFrame->LoadFrame(IDR_MAINFRAME))
        return FALSE;
    m_pMainWnd = pMainFrame;

    // Show the main window
    pMainFrame->ShowWindow(m_nCmdShow);
    pMainFrame->UpdateWindow();

    // Parse command line for standard shell commands, DDE, file open
    CCommandLineInfo cmdInfo;
    ParseCommandLine(cmdInfo);

    // If no file name on command line, open last file if any
    if( cmdInfo.m_nShellCommand == CCommandLineInfo::FileNew ) {
        cmdInfo.m_strFileName = GetProfileString(
            _T("Recent File List"),_T("File1"),NULL);
        if( !cmdInfo.m_strFileName.IsEmpty() )
            cmdInfo.m_nShellCommand = CCommandLineInfo::FileOpen;
    }
```

```
        // Dispatch commands specified on the command line
        // But don't allow File New
        if( cmdInfo.m_nShellCommand != CCommandLineInfo::FileNew )
            ProcessShellCommand(cmdInfo);

        return TRUE;
    }
```

If Ibrows was invoked without any command-line arguments, ParseCommandLine sets m_nShellCommand to FileNew. InitInstance changes the FileNew to File-Open if the first name on the Recent File list isn't empty. ProcessShellCommand will then attempt to open the file.

You might notice that the order of operations in InitInstance has been changed a bit. This problem was discussed in Chapter 14. AppWizard doesn't display the main window until after calling ProcessShellCommand, since some operations, such printing and automation, run without the application being displayed. But to delay showing the main window doesn't work well for programs that try to restore a file. If ProcessShellCommand cannot open the file, it posts a message box. Without the main window displayed, the message box floats on top of whatever application happens to be on the screen, potentially misleading the user into thinking some other application is posting the message.

16.4   Displaying the Text

Once a file is opened, it is read into the document and displayed in a view. I have derived the view class from CScrollView to implement scrolling. I didn't use an edit view because of the fine level of control needed over the display to highlight URLs and change the cursor.[2]

At initialization, the view computes the size of a character cell and stores it in the CSize variable m_cellSize. For simplicity, the text is drawn using the constant-width font ANSI_FIXED_FONT:

---

[2] A rich-text edit view could handle coloring and highlighting the text, but manipulating the cursor would not be easy.

```
void view::OnInitialUpdate()
{
    // Compute size of a character cell
    CClientDC dc(this);
    dc.SelectStockObject(ANSI_FIXED_FONT);
    TEXTMETRIC tm;
    dc.GetTextMetrics(&tm);
    m_cellSize.cx = tm.tmAveCharWidth;
    m_cellSize.cy = tm.tmHeight + tm.tmExternalLeading;

    CView::OnInitialUpdate();
}
```

To support scrolling, the mapping mode and scrollbar ranges must be set.
OnUpdate calls the helper function setScrollSizes to compute the scroll ranges:

```
void view::OnUpdate(CView* pSender, LPARAM lHint, CObject* pHint)
{
    setScrollSizes();
    CScrollView::OnUpdate(pSender, lHint, pHint);
}

void view::setScrollSizes()
{
    doc *pDoc = GetDocument();
    int lineCnt = pDoc->getLineCount();

    if( lineCnt==0 ) // Empty document
        SetScrollSizes(MM_TEXT,CSize(1,1)); // Anything but zero

    else { // compute number of whole rows and columns
        CRect clientRect;
        GetClientRect(&clientRect);
        int rows = clientRect.Height()/m_cellSize.cy;
        int cols = clientRect.Width()/m_cellSize.cx;

        SetScrollSizes(MM_TEXT,
          CSize( pDoc->getLongestLineWidth()*m_cellSize.cx,
            lineCnt*m_cellSize.cy),
          CSize( cols*m_cellSize.cx, rows*m_cellSize.cy),
          CSize( m_cellSize.cx, m_cellSize.cy));
    }
}
```

The height of the document is the number of lines and the width is the width of
the longest line. The program uses the MM_TEXT mapping mode, so the height
and width are converted to pixels by multiplying by the height and width of a
character.

Although resizing doesn't change the number of rows and columns in a document, it may change the need for scrollbars and does change the size of the

proportional scroll box. Accordingly, setScrollSizes is called when the view window is resized:

```
void view::OnSize(UINT nType, int cx, int cy)
{
    CScrollView::OnSize(nType, cx, cy);
    setScrollSizes();
}
```

The work of displaying the text falls to OnDraw. It's kind of long, so I'll treat it in parts. It begins by setting the font, getting the size of the client rectangle, and computing the offset in document coordinates to the first character on the screen. Remember, before OnDraw is called, OnPrepareDC has adjusted the device context, requiring that OnDraw use document coordinates.

```
void view::OnDraw(CDC* pDC)
{
    doc* pDoc = GetDocument();
    ASSERT_VALID(pDoc);
    pDC->SelectStockObject(ANSI_FIXED_FONT);

    CRect clientRect;
    GetClientRect(&clientRect);
    CPoint origin = GetScrollPosition();
```

As an optimization, OnDraw only outputs those lines that will be wholly (or partially) visible:

```
    // Determine first and last visible lines
    // (first and last may be partial)
    int i = origin.y / m_cellSize.cy;
    int last = clientRect.Height()/m_cellSize.cy + 2 + i;
    int y = i * m_cellSize.cy;
    line *lp;

    for( ; i<last && (lp=pDoc->getLine(i))!=NULL; ++i ) {
```

Each line consists of one or more segments, where a segment is a sequence of characters all in the same color. URLs are drawn red, non-URLs black. Each line has an associated array of UINTs (unsigned ints) that contains the column index for the start of each segment. Section 16.5 describes the structure of a line of text; Figure 16.2 illustrates the data structure.

OnDraw walks through the segments, outputting the text in the appropriate color:

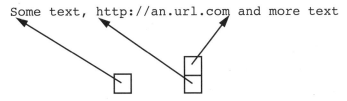

```
class line { m_text, m_breaks, m_isFirstUrl=FALSE
```

Figure 16.2   A document consists of an array of lines. A line contains a pointer to the text and an array of indexes that mark the boundaries between URLs and non-URLs.

```
int segCnt = lp->getSegCount();
CUIntArray &a = lp->getBreaks();
BOOL isUrl = lp->m_isFirstUrl;
INT tabSpace = 4 * m_cellSize.cx;

for( int j=1; j<segCnt; ++j ) {
    pDC->SetTextColor( isUrl ? RGB(255,0,0) : RGB(0,0,0) );
    pDC->TabbedTextOut( a[j-1]*m_cellSize.cx, y,
        lp->getText().Mid(a[j-1],a[j]), // Extract URL
        1, &tabSpace, 0 );
    isUrl = !isUrl;
}
```

Finally, the vertical position of the next line is computed and the loop continues:

```
    y += m_cellSize.cy;
}
```

Clicking on an URL highlights it. The view remembers the row and column boundaries of the highlighted area in a CRect called m_selectRect. OnDraw must restore any highlight:

```
    highlight(pDC);  // Restore highlight, if any
}
```

highlight inverts the color of the selection rectangle. It can be called with or without passing a CDC:

```
void view::highlight(CDC *pDC)
    // Flip highlight of selection rectangle
{
    if( !m_selectRect.IsRectEmpty() ) {
        // Scale rect, offset is handled by OnPrepareDC
        CRect rect = CRect(
            m_selectRect.left*m_cellSize.cx,
            m_selectRect.top*m_cellSize.cy,
            m_selectRect.right*m_cellSize.cx,
            m_selectRect.bottom*m_cellSize.cy);
        if( pDC==NULL ) { // Need a dc
            CClientDC dc(this);
            OnPrepareDC(&dc);
            dc.InvertRect(&rect);
        } else pDC->InvertRect(&rect);
    }
}
```

As usual, the presence of scrolling requires careful coding. After adjusting the
display context using OnPrepareDC, I use document coordinates.

16.5   The Text in Memory

The view calls the document function getLine to retrieve a line of text. In addition to the characters, a line contains the information about the segments. Each
line is represented by an object of class line:

```
class line : public CObject {
public:
    line(CString &s);

    CUIntArray &getBreaks() { return m_breaks; }
    int getSegCount() { return m_breaks.GetSize(); }
    CString &getText() { return m_text; }
    CString getUrl(LONG col, LONG *startCol);
    void parse();

    CString m_text;        // Contents of line
    CUIntArray m_breaks;   // Indexes of url/non-url breaks
    BOOL m_isFirstUrl;     // True if first break is an URL
};
```

A document consists of a CArray of lines:

```
class doc : public CDocument
{
.. .
    CArray <line *,line *> m_lines;
```

16.5.1 Serializing the Text

Ibrows reads and writes raw text files, so it must serialize character data rather than the line objects. (See Chapter 10 for a discussion of serialization.) The CArchive functions ReadString and WriteString make serializing raw strings relatively easy:

```
void doc::Serialize(CArchive& ar)
    // Read and write raw text
{
    if( ar.IsLoading() ) {
        CString s;
        m_longestLineWidth = 1;
        m_docState = Reading;
        while( ar.ReadString(s) ) {
        // CArchive class picks up EOF exception
        // Could handle other exceptions here
            m_lines.Add( new line(s) );
            if( s.GetLength() > m_longestLineWidth )
                m_longestLineWidth = s.GetLength();
        }
        m_docState = Read;

    } else {
        int count = m_lines.GetSize();
        for( int i=0; i<count; ++i ) {
            ar.WriteString( m_lines[i]->getText() );
            ar.WriteString( _T("\n")); // ReadString strips \n
        }
    }
}
```

During loading, when the CArchive reaches the end-of-file, it throws an exception. ReadString catches that exception but rethrows others that could be picked up here.

While it is reading the file, the document remembers which line is longest so that it can answer the question easily when the view asks. The document also keeps track of its progress in the variable m_docState. The states are defined in a class-local enumeration:

```
class doc : public CDocument
{
. . .
```

```
            // A document is in one of these states
            enum DocStates {
                Empty,
                Connecting,
                Reading,
                Read
            };
            DocStates m_docState;
        };
```

The state is used to help synchronize multiple threads and to control status-bar information (see Section 16.7.3), as well as to control the cursor (see Section 16.8).

16.6   Connecting to the Internet

MFC has classes for creating both clients and servers connected to the Internet. The server classes call upon the Internet Services API (ISAPI). The client classes use the WinInet API extensions and WinSock.[3] The Ibrows program is, of course, an Internet client.

Client communication with the Internet begins with the class `CInternetSession`. A session holds details about how to connect to the network and the class has functions for initiating a connection. The type of the connection dictates what protocol the client can use and what services it can access. Ibrows uses read-only access to files accessible through an URL. The prefix of an URL specifies the protocol that will be used.[4]

Here are the basic steps to read an Internet file using an URL:

1. Create a `CInternetSession` object.
2. Open the URL, get a `CInternetFile` object.
3. Read text from the file.
4. Close and delete the file.
5. Delete the session.

---

[3] Win32 support of the Internet is still evolving. MFC support for Internet clients first appeared with Release 4.2 and will, likewise, evolve. For an in-depth look at WinSock, see *Windows Sockets Network Programming*, by Bob Quinn and David Shute, Addison-Wesley Publishing Co., 1995.

[4] The Internet uses several layers of protocols and some protocols support multiple-access methods. For a cogent introduction, see "Getting Wired Into the Internet: A Crash Course on FTP, Gopher, Web, and More," *Microsoft Systems Journal*, Vol. 8, No. 9, September 1994.

A client can make repeated requests in a single session or have active requests
in different sessions. Without going into the Open Systems Interconnect (OSI)
seven-layer network model, you should know that a session is an abstract concept separate from a physical connection to the network. Multiple sessions can
operate simultaneously over the same physical connection.[5]

In Ibrows, the document class has an embedded CInternetSession object:

```
class doc : public CDocument
{
...
private:
    CInternetSession m_netSession;
```

Constructing the CInternetSession object doesn't generate any network traffic.
Opening an URL does. The function readURL uses the session to open an URL and
trigger reading:

```
void doc::readURL()
{
    try {
        netFile *file = (netFile *)m_netSession.OpenURL(m_urlToRead);

        if( file!=NULL && file->isValid() ) {
            Read the file
        }
    } catch( CException *e ) {
        e->Delete();
    }

    CString buf;
    buf.Format(_T("Cannot open URL \"%s\""),m_urlToRead);
    AfxMessageBox(buf);
    m_docState = Empty;
    ::PostMessage(m_hView,WM_CLOSE,0,0);
}
```

CInternetSession::OpenURL returns a pointer to a CInternetFile. OpenURL
succeeds if the URL is valid syntactically; it doesn't guarantee that the URL actually refers to an existing object. I derived the class netFile from CInternetFile
to add the important functionality described in Section 16.6.2 below.

Before looking at the details of reading the network file, notice that the whole
shebang is inside a try block. There is always a chance of failure when
accessing a local file and even more chance of failure when accessing a file over

---

[5] For a readable description of the OSI model, see *Windows Sockets Network Programming,* by Bob
Quinn and David Shute, Addison-Wesley Publishing Co., 1995.

the network.   Accordingly, operations on files can throw exceptions.   In particular

Operations on	Throw exceptions of type
CFile and CStdioFile	CFileException
CArchive	CArchiveException
CInternetFile	CInternetException

If an exception is thrown during readURL, reading is terminated, the exception is deleted, and a message is posted.

16.6.1 Integrating Internet Access with the Document

In Section 16.5.1 we saw that doc::Serialize reads ordinary text strings from an archive. Recall from Chapter 10 that in response to File Open, the framework opens a file, attaches it to an archive, and then calls Serialize with a reference to the archive. Thus, doc::Serialize reads ordinary text files when the user runs the File Open command in Ibrows.

By creating an archive attached to an Internet file, readURL can also call Serialize. Here are the key statements from readURL:

```
if( file!=NULL && file->isValid() ) {
    CArchive ar(file,CArchive::load);
    Serialize(ar);
    ar.Close();
    file->Close();
    delete file;
    ::PostMessage(m_hView,WMU_UpdateView,0,0);
    return;
}
```

After the file is read, the archive and the file need to be closed and deleted. The need for the call to ::PostMessage will be explained in Section 16.7.4.

16.6.2 Testing an URL for validity

Before the Internet file returned by CInternetSession::OpenURL can be attached to the archive, it must be tested for validity. readURL uses the test

```
if( file!=NULL && file->isValid() ) {
```

The power of an URL is that it puts a uniform face on a variety of objects. For example

```
http://www.awl.com
ftp://ftp.microsoft.com
file://c:\internet\ibrows.cpp
```

refer, respectively, to a Web page, a file transfer protocol (FTP) server, and a file on the local C drive. One consequence of the generality is that there is no easy way to tell if an URL is valid. Many operations on CArchives assert that the associated file is valid. For Internet files, MFC performs a rather ad hoc test. To avoid the assertion failure if the test fails, readURL calls netFile::isValid to perform a similar test:

```
BOOL netFile::isValid()
    // CInternetSession::OpenURL returns success even
    // if the URL doesn't exist.  This test for validity
    // is based on CInternetFile::AssertValid.  We
    // perform it here to avoid ASSERT failures.
{
    if( GetRuntimeClass()==RUNTIME_CLASS(CStdioFile) )
        // A local file
        return TRUE;

    else {  // it must be an Internet file
        switch( AfxGetInternetHandleType(m_hFile) ) {
        case INTERNET_HANDLE_TYPE_HTTP_REQUEST:
        case INTERNET_HANDLE_TYPE_GOPHER_FILE:
        case INTERNET_HANDLE_TYPE_FTP_FILE:
            return TRUE;
        default:
            return FALSE;
        }
    }
}
```

You can see that the test only succeeds for four types of files:

- A local file, file://
- An HTML file, http://
- A gopher request, gopher://
- A FTP request, ftp://

As a result, isValid is fragile. It would be better if this function were provided by the CInternetFile class.

16.6.3 Selecting an URL

In Ibrows, single clicking on an URL highlights it; double clicking opens it:

```
void view::OnLButtonDown(UINT nFlags, CPoint point)
{
    // Clear highlight, if any
    highlight();
    m_selectRect.SetRectEmpty();

    pixelToCell(point);
    line *lp = GetDocument()->getLine(point.y);
    if( lp!=NULL ) {
        LONG startCol;
        m_currentURL = lp->getUrl(point.x,&startCol);
        if( !m_currentURL.IsEmpty() ) {
            m_selectRect = CRect(startCol,point.y,
              startCol+m_currentURL.GetLength(),point.y+1);
            highlight();
        }
    }
}

void view::OnLButtonDblClk(UINT nFlags, CPoint point)
{
    if( !m_currentURL.IsEmpty() )
        theApp.openURL(m_currentURL);
    else ::MessageBeep(MB_ICONSTOP);
}
```

I don't want to bore you with the details of highlighting the text, but you can see that on a single click, the URL is stored in the member variable m_currentURL. On a double click, the view calls Ibrows::openURL which must perform the equivalent of File Open:

```
void ibrows::openURL(CString &url)
{
    CWaitCursor cursor;
    mainFrame *main = (mainFrame *)m_pMainWnd;
    OnFileNew();
    CMDIChildWnd *child = main->MDIGetActive();
    doc *dp = (doc *)child->GetActiveDocument();
    dp->SetTitle(url);
    dp->readURL(url);
}
```

openURL creates a new document window, puts the URL in the title bar, then calls on the newly created document object to grab the file from the network by calling doc::readURL described above. Here is a summary of the procedure, thus far, from mouse click to file read:

```
Single click selects URL
Double click calls Ibrows::openURL
    OpenURL creates a new document window
        Constructor for doc creates CInternetSession
        Call doc::readURL
            readURL calls CInternetSession::OpenURL
            If successful, create CArchive using CInternetFile
                returned by OpenURL
            Call Serialize to read file
```

Unfortunately, this procedure has a significant problem.

16.7 Worker Threads

Going to the network to read a file can take a long time. During the file read, we don't want the program to stop responding to its user interface. This was the same problem encountered in the Wizard installer of Chapter 14 and I'll use the same solution here: a worker thread.

16.7.1 Processes and Threads in Win32

As an experienced user of computers, you probably have an intuitive feel for what a process is. A GUI *process* has, among other things, a main window and an address space. Unless you've delved into concurrent programming, you probably have less feel for a thread. A *thread* is a path of execution through the code of a process. Threads have a stack, an execution context, and a scheduling priority. The operating system schedules threads rather than processes.

Every running process has at least one thread, its *primary* thread. A multi-threaded process has more than one thread. The most interesting feature of multi-threading is that each thread sees the same global address space. The trickiest part of programming multiple threads is that each thread sees the same global address space. A robust multi-threaded application must guarantee that it is safe for other threads to run between every statement in the program. If there are statements that must be executed without interruption, they need to be surrounded by synchronization primitives.[6]

---

[6] When I refer to *statement* in this context, I mean a machine statement. To synchronize a multi-threaded application, read about CCriticalSection in the reference manual. For a more in depth discussion, see *Win32 Systems Programming*, by Johnson Hart, Addison Wesley Longman, 1997.

An object is said to be *thread safe* if more than one thread can manipulate the object at the same time without problems arising. Problems arise when the threads duel over state information in the object. Consider a CString. If two threads attempt to write the string at the same time, the result will be indeterminate. For better performance, neither MFC objects, like CStrings and CWnds, nor Win32 objects, such as list boxes and edit controls, are thread safe.

Concurrent programs are always more difficult to debug than single-threaded programs because they add the potential for time-related bugs. Given the additional flow-control complexity of a GUI application, debugging a multi-threaded GUI application can be a nightmare. Fortunately, the message model used by Win32 removes most needs for multi-threading. Win32 is very capable of processing messages for multiple windows in quick succession, giving the impression that they are being updated simultaneously. The only requirement for the message model to work well is that no message take very long to process. Of course, this is exactly what happens when reading a file from a network.

16.7.2 Background Processing

The MFC reference manual describes two types of threads: those with a user interface and those without. The former are called GUI threads, the latter worker threads. The main distinction between GUI and worker threads is that in order to keep the user interface active, a GUI thread must continue to process messages from its message queue. That is, GUI threads shouldn't perform operations that block. Worker threads have no such limitation and therefore are the right choice for background processing.

I've modified Ibrows to read from the network using a worker thread. ibrows::openURL, shown in Section 16.6.3, now calls doc::openURL:

```
void ibrows::openURL(CString &url)
{
    CWaitCursor cursor;
    mainFrame *main = (mainFrame *)m_pMainWnd;
    OnFileNew();
    CMDIChildWnd *child = main->MDIGetActive();
    doc *dp = (doc *)child->GetActiveDocument();
    dp->SetTitle(url);
    dp->openURL(url);
}
```

doc::openURL spawns the worker thread:

```
void doc::openURL(CString &url)
{
    POSITION pos = GetFirstViewPosition();
    CView *view = GetNextView(pos);
    m_hView = view->m_hWnd;
    m_urlToRead = url;
    m_docState = Connecting;
    m_workerThread = AfxBeginThread(threadProc,this);
}
```

AfxBeginThread takes two parameters, the address of a *thread procedure* and a 32-bit application-defined value. The new thread begins executing at the start of the thread procedure with the 32-bit value as its only parameter (see Figure 16.3). Often, the 32-bit value of choice is a pointer to some object—in this example, the this pointer to the document object. The thread procedure can then use the pointer to access the object:

```
UINT doc::threadProc(void *param) // Worker thread begins here
{
    doc *pDoc = (doc *)param;
    pDoc->readURL();
    return 0;
}
```

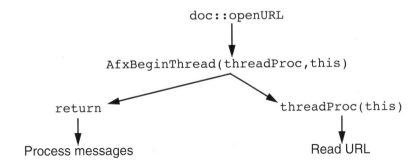

Figure 16.3   The new thread begins executing at the thread procedure. The arrows represent flow of control.

The thread procedure cannot be an ordinary member function because Win32 will not pass the implicit this pointer. It must either be static or global. threadProc is a static member function of doc:

```
class doc : public CDocument
{
. . .
private:
    void readURL();
    static UINT threadProc(void *param);
```

16.7.3 **Synchronizing the Threads**

Once the worker thread has been spawned, what should the primary thread do while it is waiting? The Wizard installer in Chapter 14 posted a dialog that allowed the user to interrupt copying files. Ibrows will return to its message loop, allowing other windows in the program to be active and other URLs to be read. While the worker is reading the URL, the corresponding view is empty; when the worker is done, the view will be updated.

Both Wizard and Ibrows require communication between the threads. Because Wizard didn't have anything else to do except monitor the dialog, it polled the worker for completion:

```
while( ::GetExitCodeThread(bkgnd->m_hThread,&exitCode)
  && exitCode==STILL_ACTIVE ) {
  if( !AfxGetThread()->PumpMessage() )
      m_stop = TRUE;
  if( m_stop ) // Stop a long copy in worker thread
      ::TerminateThread(bkgnd->m_hThread,0);
}
```

In Ibrows, the worker communicates with the GUI thread using shared memory and messages.

In Section 16.5.1 you saw that a document has a m_docState member variable that specifies the state of the document. It takes on one of these values:

Empty	Initially, a document is empty.
Connecting	The worker is attempting to open an URL.
Reading	The worker is reading an URL.
Read	The worker has completed reading the URL.

By examining m_docState, the GUI thread knows how the worker is progressing. The GUI thread displays the state of the worker on the status bar:

```
void doc::onUpdateDocState(CCmdUI *pCmdUI)
{
    switch(m_docState) {
    default:
        pCmdUI->Enable(FALSE);
        return;

    case Connecting:
        pCmdUI->SetText(_T("Connecting to web"));
        break;
```

```
    case Reading:
        pCmdUI->SetText(_T("Reading from site"));
        break;

    case Read:
        pCmdUI->SetText(_T("Site read"));
        break;
    }
    pCmdUI->Enable();
}
```

If the user requests a window to close, the document tests to see if the worker is still active:

```
BOOL doc::CanCloseFrame(CFrameWnd* pFrame)
{
    if( m_docState==Connecting || m_docState==Reading ) {
        if( AfxMessageBox(_T("Internet conversation in progress,"
          " okay to terminate?"),
          MB_YESNO|MB_ICONQUESTION)!=IDYES ) {
            // Keep waiting
            return FALSE;
        }
        ::TerminateThread(m_workerThread->m_hThread,-1);
        m_docState = Empty;
    }
    return TRUE;
}
```

The framework calls the virtual function CanCloseFrame before it closes a document window. doc::CanCloseFrame looks at m_docState to see if the worker is still working. If so, it posts a message box giving the user an opportunity to terminate the network connection. Returning false from CanCloseFrame keeps the window open.

When the worker has finished reading the Internet file, it must tell the view to update the window. If this were a single-threaded application, the document would simply call UpdateAllViews. With a worker thread, we can't take such a direct course.

16.7.4 Sharing Objects Across Threads

Recall that neither Win32 nor MFC objects are thread safe. As a consequence, a program must be very careful about sharing objects across threads. On the other hand, sharing an object, as in the previous section, is the primary way two threads can communicate. There is nothing inherent in C++ that makes it dangerous for two threads to access the same object. Knowing what can and cannot be shared requires a deeper understanding of how MFC wrapper objects work.

Each wrapper object contains a data member that holds the handle of the Win32 object. For example, the CWnd member m_hWnd has the handle of the associated window. To operate on the Win32 object, member functions in the wrapper class refer to the handle. To go in the other direction, from the Win32 object to the wrapper, MFC maintains a handle map. For instance, when a message comes in for a window, MFC's window procedure uses the handle map to find the associated CWnd wrapper (see Figure 16.4). The maps are allocated per thread; a thread's map contains handles for only those objects it created.

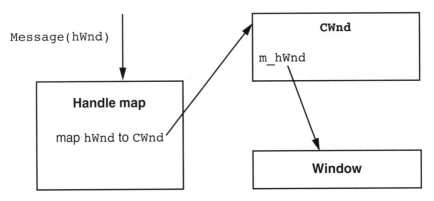

Figure 16.4   MFC uses a per-thread table to map window handles to CWnd objects. When a window message arrives, the corresponding CWnd is found by looking up the window handle in the handle map.

It is possible to add an entry to the handle map for a thread using the Attach function, but doing so invites the potential for one thread to step on the work of another. The safest rule to follow is not to share wrapper objects.

Non-wrapper objects, such as documents and applications, are not present in the handle map. Still, they do have state variables and so contention among threads is possible. To share non-wrapper objects between threads, you need to guarantee that only one thread will modify the object at a time. This can be done by always having the same thread modify the object, as in Ibrows where the worker thread sets and the GUI thread reads m_docState. Alternatively, modifications to a shared variable can be surrounded by a critical section by using the class CCriticalSection.

Back to the problem at hand. Calling `UpdateAllViews` from the worker thread will fail because the `CView` object will not be in the worker's handle map. MFC tests this condition to prevent multiple threads operating on the same view. Instead, when the worker finishes reading, it sends a message to the GUI thread. Before spawning the new thread, the document saves the window handle of the view window:

```
void doc::openURL(CString &url)
{
    POSITION pos = GetFirstViewPosition();
    CView *view = GetNextView(pos);
    m_hView = view->m_hWnd;
    m_urlToRead = url;
    m_docState = Connecting;
    m_workerThread = AfxBeginThread(threadProc,this);
}
```

After reading the file, the worker posts a private message using the handle of the view:

```
void doc::readURL()
{
. . .
        if( file!=NULL && file->isValid() ) {
            CArchive ar(file,CArchive::load);
            Serialize(ar);
            ar.Close();
            file->Close();
            delete file;
            ::PostMessage(m_hView,WMU_UpdateView,0,0);
```

`WMU_UpdateView` is just an integer, although it is important that it not be the same number as a standard Win32 message. Basing `WMU_UpdateView` on the Win32 constant `WM_USER` guarantees that there will not be a conflict. `WMU_UpdateView` is defined in `ibrows.h`:

```
// User-defined message numbers
#define WMU_UpdateView (WM_USER+1)
```

Messages for a window are picked up by the thread that created the window. Thus the GUI thread will find `WM_UpdateView` and call the corresponding handler:

```
BEGIN_MESSAGE_MAP(view, CScrollView)
. . .
    ON_MESSAGE(WMU_UpdateView,onUpdateView)
. . .
```

```
LONG view::onUpdateView(UINT,LONG)
{
    OnUpdate(NULL,0,NULL);
    return 0;
}
```

16.8   Controlling the Cursor

For one final flourish, the view takes over control of the mouse cursor. When the
document is loading, the cursor is displayed as the hourglass. Once loaded, the
cursor is either an arrow or a hand, depending on whether the mouse is over an
URL.

You might recall that the default behavior in Win32 is for the cursor to be set
based on the class of the underlying window. In addition, MFC keeps track of a
temporary cursor per thread. Neither of these mechanisms is flexible enough to
handle the three cursors used by Ibrows. The view class will need to take total
responsibility for the cursor.

As the mouse is moved, Win32 sends the WM_SETCURSOR message to the window
under the mouse. OnSetCursor sets the cursor shape based on the state of the
document and the location of the mouse:

```
BOOL view::OnSetCursor(CWnd* pWnd, UINT nHitTest, UINT message)
{
    if( !GetDocument()->isRead() ) {
        ::SetCursor( theApp.LoadStandardCursor(IDC_WAIT) );
        return TRUE;

    } else {
        CPoint pos;
        ::GetCursorPos(&pos);
        ScreenToClient(&pos);
        pixelToCell(pos);
        line *lp = GetDocument()->getLine(pos.y);

        if( lp!=NULL ) {
            LONG startCol;
            if( !lp->getUrl(pos.x,&startCol).IsEmpty() ) {
                ::SetCursor( theApp.LoadCursor(IDC_Hand) );
                return TRUE;
            }
        }
    }

    return CScrollView::OnSetCursor(pWnd, nHitTest, message);
}
```

If the worker thread isn't done reading, `doc::isRead` returns false and the cursor is set to the wait cursor. If the read has completed, the view looks to see if the mouse is pointing to an URL. If so, the cursor is set to the hand. Otherwise, the view displays an arrow by inheriting the default behavior from `CScrollView`.

Appendix

The companion disk for this text contains the source code, auxiliary build files, and executables for the example programs. You can browse the disk or use the installation program to move files to another disk. The installation program is `install.exe` in the root directory.

There are executables for each of the sample programs in the directory `bin`. The executables were generated with Microsoft's Visual C++ Release 5.0. Each program directory contains the Developer's Studio project files as well as makefiles.

In the root directory of the disk you'll also find an HTML file, `hello.htm`, with links to other HTML on the disk and to the Addison-Wesley Advanced Windows Series Web site. Updates to this text will be posted on the Web site.

Index